Courteous Capitalism

Hagley Library Studies in Business, Technology, and Politics
Richard R. John, *Series Editor*

COURTEOUS CAPITALISM

Public Relations and the
Monopoly Problem, 1900–1930

Daniel Robert

Johns Hopkins University Press
Baltimore

© 2023 Johns Hopkins University Press
All rights reserved. Published 2023
Printed in the United States of America on acid-free paper
2 4 6 8 9 7 5 3 1

Johns Hopkins University Press
2715 North Charles Street
Baltimore, Maryland 21218
www.press.jhu.edu

Library of Congress Cataloging-in-Publication Data

Names: Robert, Daniel, 1978– author.
Title: Courteous capitalism : public relations and the
monopoly problem, 1900–1930 / Daniel Robert.
Description: Baltimore : Johns Hopkins University Press, 2023. |
Series: Hagley Library studies in business, technology, and politics |
Includes bibliographical references and index. |
Identifiers: LCCN 2023003587 | ISBN 9781421447346 (hardcover) |
ISBN 9781421447353 (ebook)
Subjects: LCSH: Monopolies—Public opinion—History—20th century. |
Corporations—Public opinion—History—20th century. |
Public relations—History—20th century.
Classification: LCC HD2757.2 .R63 2023 |
DDC 338.8/2—dc23/eng/20230207
LC record available at https://lccn.loc.gov/2023003587

A catalog record for this book is available from the British Library.

*Special discounts are available for bulk purchases of this book. For more
information, please contact Special Sales at specialsales@jh.edu.*

CONTENTS

Acknowledgments   *vii*

INTRODUCTION   1

1
Courteous Capitalism Begins   18

2
Courteous Capitalism Intensifies   54

3
The Architecture of Consent   87

4
Customer Stock Ownership as Corporate Political Strategy   125

5
Making the News   156

6
Subverting Civics   195

CONCLUSION   237

Notes   *247*
Index   *317*

ACKNOWLEDGMENTS

I would first like to thank Richard R. John for helping me transform this work from a dissertation into a book. Richard has been a pattern to me in both teaching and scholarship since before I started graduate school. He generously read the entire manuscript and provided extensive and valuable comments, even before signing up the work to his book series. My dissertation adviser, Robin Einhorn, also deserves a great deal of credit. She has been a source of enthusiasm, encouragement, and guidance since the first day I set foot on the campus of the University of California, Berkeley, until now. Her feedback buoyed my spirits, improved my arguments, and saved me from many errors. Caitlin Rosenthal contributed her vast historiographical knowledge, offered key insights, and generally boosted this project. David Henkin contributed his own valuable insights, sharp editorial eye, and demand for argumentative precision. Cathryn Carson let me follow my muse. Many others at Berkeley also deserve thanks, including Mark Brilliant, Mabel Lee, Jack Lesch, Massimo Mazzotti, Louise A. Mozingo, Mark Peterson, and Dick Walker. Despite all this wise counsel, mistakes surely remain, some perhaps at my insistence.

My fellow graduate students provided camaraderie throughout the journey. James Anderson's patient ear and mordent humor made for wide-ranging conversations over innumerable cups of coffee. Christopher W. Shaw offered his characteristic keen insight on many subjects, including banking, the post office, and this book. Both are great historians. Josh Benjamins and Sebock Jeon provided welcome lunch breaks from writing. Many others extended a great deal of encouragement and support to me during my years in Berkeley. You are too numerous to list, though I think you know who you are. Thank you all. I also learned a great deal from my former students. I care about each of you.

Outside of Berkeley, Richard F. Hirsch, Richard K. Popp, and other still-anonymous reviewers gave me excellent and thorough feedback on the manuscript. Adriahna Conway, Hilary Jacqmin, Kristina Lykke, Christine Marra, Matthew McAdam, Juliana McCarthy, Angela Piliouras, and Paul Vincent brought the manuscript to life for Johns Hopkins University Press. Ken Lipartito provided valuable comments on telephone history. Josh Lauer, Andrew Popp, and anonymous reviewers for *Enterprise & Society* contributed their own useful feedback on portions of the work. William Caughlin at the AT&T History Center and Archives in San Antonio shared his unparalleled knowledge of AT&T sources and generously made these sources available to me. Scott Combs at AT&T also provided expertise. Nanette Gibbs at the Library of Congress contributed her vast institutional knowledge and many stories besides. Thomas McAnear at the National Archives in College Park located hard-to-find sources. Kathy Young at the Loyola University Archives provided manuscripts and images. Thanks to Sig Bagga, who sorted mountains of photos, and Andy Lin, who recovered those photos on my computer! Thanks to David P. Jordan and Richard Fried for collegial conversation. The Huntington Library's Dibner Fellowship allowed me to find my first evidence of courteous capitalism. Thanks to all those who work at that library, especially those in the reading room. Fred J. Martin Jr. and his eponymous Political History Award further supported this research. Jeff Fearn, Nick Martin, and Ryder Okumura provided valued friendship along the way.

Whether on research trips or taking a break, members of my immediate and extended family let me crash at their homes, eat at their tables, and borrow—or have!—their cars. The Ahns, Bauschlingers, Bellamys, Berniers, Dennys, Drummonds, Feldts, Higashis, Iveys, Kellers, Kellys, Koenigsbergs, LeVons, McNutts, Remmetters, Roberts, Snows, Spraus, Tashiros, Tenbarges, Tsengs, Whelchels, and many others under various names provided warm and welcoming hospitality. My sisters Katie and Kelly and their families are awesome. My parents, Marty and Debbie, deserve some of the greatest thanks of all. Their constant support in every way shaped who I am. Long before graduate school they taught me letters and instilled in me a love for stories. Thanks, Mom and Dad! My wife, Patty, deserves the most credit of all. She has lived with my musing, traveling, and typing for too long. This book would not have been possible without her. Our two boys, Martin and Benjamin, were both born during the writing of this book. They're our real story in two volumes, and are writing their own episodes now. Thank you, Patty, for your love and support. I dedicate this book to you.

D.M.R.

Courteous Capitalism

Introduction

In October of 1921, the vice president of public relations for the Southern California Edison Company, Samuel Kennedy, rose to deliver a speech before the executives of the Stone & Webster Company of Boston. Stone & Webster's streetcar and electric utilities had been targeted by advocates of strict government regulation and outright government ownership, and the company had called on Kennedy to advise it how best to fend off these reform-minded rivals.[1] The stakes were high in this battle over the nation's political economy. Advocates of municipal ownership had recently scored some major victories, as Kennedy knew all too well from the municipalization of his own company's Los Angeles properties in 1917. Since that time, Kennedy had given serious thought to the emerging field of public relations, implemented a comprehensive makeover of his company's public relations, and written a book on the subject, which utility executives considered "the bible of the industry."[2] Kennedy was now regarded as an expert in "transforming public opinion," the title of the speech he was now prepared to deliver.[3]

"The day has long since passed when the management of any industrial or utility organization can ignore public opinion," Kennedy declared. Corporations could no longer ride roughshod over the expectations of customers, as they once had. What mattered now was public opinion, and to transform it corporations needed "the right article in the way of a piece of humanity" at all "points of contact" between the corporation and the customer. "You need to have nice girls answer the phone," Kennedy instructed, "so their voice will make the customer say, 'this is something I am looking for.'" "The elevator operator meets more people than the general manager. Does he do it in the right way? . . . The collector greets more consumers than the treasurer. Does he perform the difficult task of taking people's money and leaving them pleased?" Obtaining the desired behavior would require "careful instruction and continued education," Kennedy cautioned, but "the human machinery must be toned up."[4]

The discussion that followed the speech revealed unanimous agreement among the executives in attendance. Rude clerks had been what cost the Southern California Edison Company (SCE) its Los Angeles business, according to one Stone & Webster executive. Rudeness was also the insult added to injury that made the Southern Pacific Railroad the most hated corporation in America, in this same executive's appraisal. He offered an example to prove his point. He had once been standing in line behind a "refined elderly lady" who asked a Southern Pacific ticket agent, "in a very pleasant tone," for a Pullman car from Los Angeles to San Francisco for that night.

> "Haven't got any," the ticket agent replied.
> "Then I'll have to get one for tomorrow night," she said.
> "Haven't got any for that night either."
> "Then I'll probably have to take one for the next night."
> "Haven't got any for the rest of the week."
> "What can I do then? Is there any other way I can get to San Francisco?"
> In a gruff voice he replied, "Yes, you can walk."

"That was the attitude of the Southern Pacific at that time," the executive recalled, "that is why it became so thoroughly disliked."[5]

The idea that employee behavior represented both a cause and a possible solution to the political problems facing utilities was not confined to this room of executives. In the early twentieth century, thousands of similar meetings took place in which utility executives strategized how to use courtesy to improve public opinion toward their companies. Their logic was simple, though at the time it was revolutionary. Public opinion now ruled the political economy of the nation, these executives maintained. No franchise permit, rate hike, or regulatory structure could survive if it violated the court of public opinion. "The world today is ruled by public opinion," declared Nathan Kingsbury, vice president of AT&T, in 1912.[6] "Public sentiment controls the ultimate destiny of every utility company," echoed Samuel Kennedy in 1922.[7] And since it was axiomatic among executives that public opinion was simply the aggregate of individual customer opinions, executives set out to improve public opinion, one courteous interaction at a time.[8]

I call this strategy *courteous capitalism*, and it profoundly influenced the managerial strategy of executives, the work experience of clerks, and the antimonopoly sentiments of customers. As chapter 1 reveals, managers at streetcar, electricity, and telephone companies throughout the United States compelled their clerks to exude "courtesy," "friendliness," and "sympathy" toward customers. Managers wanted "a smile and a pleasant word," a "friendly feeling," and "the *human* quality" from workers.[9] Clerks had to display "a smiling courteous demeanor," exhibit "a world of patience," and emit a "ray of sunshine during the entire day."[10] Only then would customers warm up to the corporate monopolization of crucial utility services.

To obtain these beneficial emotions, executives developed intensive training programs that affected hundreds of thousands of workers at some of America's largest and most economically important companies. At weekly "demonstration classes," managers enacted both the right and the wrong way to treat customers, and clerks learned to play their part. Executive speeches, employee magazine articles, and some of the earliest corporate training movies reinforced these lessons. As the strategy of courteous capitalism matured, managers prescribed nearly everything about their clerks' job "performances," including their phrases, body language, voice inflection, eye-contact, clothing, and even their combed hair, trimmed nails, and fresh breath, all in an effort to improve public opinion. By the late 1920s, public opinion had improved, but the cost to low-level employees was high. Their plastered smiles and scripted pleasantries represented a great loss of emotional freedom and a new level of managerial control.

In implementing courteous capitalism, utility executives laid claim to their employees' emotional expressions, excavating and filtering their workers' souls as a resource for their company's political and economic goals. Executives not only wanted their employees' brains and brawn, they wanted their employees' emotions too. As one manager put it, the "value" of clerks no longer lay in their fine penmanship, but "in ladling out great quantities of the right kind of courtesy." It "costs nothing," the manager mused, but brings "splendid returns."[11]

This commodification of human emotions bore similarities to what sociologist Arlie Hochschild called "emotional labor" in her insightful study on the work of flight attendants in the 1970s.[12] Hochschild's pioneering work focused on emotional labor in a more recent context. The present volume, in contrast, traces one stream of emotional labor back to the early twentieth century.

This book also argues that courtesy within monopolies was not a commonsense business strategy to beat the competition. Monopolies had no competition. Rather, courteous capitalism was a political strategy designed to fend off government ownership and keep those monopolies private. Utility executives therefore not only commodified their workers' emotions, they politicized them as well. This inserted a political dimension into interactions between clerks and customers that was absent from traditional market settings such as stores and restaurants.[13] Ultimately, the goal of courteous capitalism was not to sell more products in the market, but to change public opinion regarding the market structure itself.

Courteous capitalism can therefore help answer an important question of American political economy: Why did antimonopoly sentiment in the 1920s decline? The sentiment can be traced at least as far back as Andrew Jackson's famous Bank Veto of 1832 in which he emphatically declared that "every monopoly and all exclusive privileges are granted at the expense of the public."[14] The rise of giant railroad and telegraph monopolies in the late nineteenth century only exacerbated this antimonopoly sentiment, as evidenced by the antimonopoly politics of the Grangers, the Knights of Labor, and the Populists.[15] In the decades surrounding the turn of the twentieth century, urban Americans caught the antimonopoly fever as utility companies corrupted city governments and treated customers in a high-handed and contemptuous manner, even while ultimately depending on citizens for franchise permits and rate hikes. Yet on the eve of the stock market crash of 1929, hundreds of streetcar, electricity, and telephone companies enjoyed the same monopoly privileges that Jackson and his successors vilified, but popular protest at the time was muted.

What explains this political-economic change of heart? Did "the people" rein in "the interests" with the harness of regulation, as some historians have argued? Or did the interests fit themselves with the harness and take the people for a ride, as others have written? Or, as still others have maintained, did the people and the interests solve the problem of monopoly through a consensual process? The problem with these narratives is that, while they contain a grain of truth, they linger in the political-economic stratosphere of corporate presidents, politicians, and regulators. A few progressive politicians stand in for "the people" while the actual formation of political sentiments among millions of Americans remains vague and unexplained.[16]

Other historians have simply ignored the politics of utility networks and focused instead on the social history of interacting with such technology.[17] But how did this social history relate to the political history? How did the everyday contact between customers and clerks shape the political sentiments of citizens and voters? Why did the contemptuous corporate culture of the late nineteenth century yield to the courteous corporate culture of the 1920s? Where did this new courteous culture come from, why did it spread, and what difference did it make to workers, consumers, and the regulatory state?[18]

This book answers these questions. But rather than offering a top-down business history that gives executives all the agency or a bottom-up social history that ignores the "visible hand" of management, I follow executives as they conceptualize a causal link between customer service at the lowest levels of the corporation and political regulation at the highest levels of government.[19] In doing so, this book joins social history to political history to offer a new explanation for why Americans accepted the corporate monopolization of utility services.

By dissipating antimonopoly sentiment, courteous capitalism represented an important turning point in one of the central political-economic dramas in the United States between the Civil War and the Great Depression—the rise of corporate monopolies. Like ink spilled on a map, these new corporate entities spread quickly across the United States, extending their reach between cities and deep into the countryside, disrupting former patterns of social and economic life and replacing them with new realities of technology and bureaucratic management. As monopolies, these new organizations generated a considerable amount of public animosity, but as utilities, these institutions provided the crucial infrastructural backbone that facilitated the explosive economic growth of the early twentieth century. America could hardly do without transportation, communication, and energy.

Many of the most important debates of the Progressive Era revolved around what to do about these utility monopolies.[20] Were some monopolies beneficial and even "natural," meaning their high cost of infrastructure prevented duplication and competition? Could monopolies be regulated, or should they be broken up or taken over? The debate raged across the United States at the turn of the century. As jurist Louis Brandeis wrote in 1907, "Shall the public utilities be owned by the public?—[this] is a question pressing for decision in nearly every American city."[21]

Many people believed that corporate streetcar, electricity, and telephone monopolies could improve their physical and customer service but were disinclined to do so because of the lack of competition. These companies often had monopoly franchise permits valid for a half century or more. As public anger began to boil, muckraking journalists, such as Lincoln Steffens, added fuel to the fire by relating numerous examples of how corporate utilities bribed city councils to obtain these "eternal monopoly" operating permits. Soon, bringing these monopolies to heel became a major goal of reformers in an age defined by reform.

As voters erupted in righteous indignation, progressive politicians such as Robert La Follette Sr., Peter Altgeld, and Tom Johnson began battling monopolies at the local and state levels. National politicians also excoriated the monopolies in no uncertain terms. Theodore Roosevelt, in a major speech in 1910, denounced "public service corporations" as "one of the principal sources of corruption in our political affairs."[22] President Woodrow Wilson proved an even fiercer critic. In 1913, he declared that the only thing "natural" about "natural monopolies" was greed. "Private monopoly is indefensible and intolerable," he thundered, "and there I will fight my battle."[23]

Utility executives grew alarmed. "Today," fretted one utility executive in 1911, "there is much comment, nearly always unfavorable, regarding the conditions under which franchises for electric light, trolley roads and power transmission companies have been issued."[24] In 1916, AT&T president Theodore Vail acknowledged that his company was frequently viewed as a "a foreign, greedy, selfish monopoly."[25]

To change these negative views, utility executives began focusing on their lowest-level employees. These ticket agents, conductors, platform men, switchboard operators, meter readers, linemen, telephone installers, cashiers, and clerks represented the public face of what were otherwise considered faceless institutions. Executives believed that if they could control the behavior of these workers and force them to be courteous, they could mollify an angry public, undercut support for government ownership, and apply the brakes to unwanted progressive reform.

The strategy would not work overnight, executives knew, but they firmly believed that a consistent application of implacable courtesy and obsequious deference toward customers would eventually ingratiate monopolies with a skeptical public. Once positive public opinion had been obtained, executives could once again secure the coveted franchise permits, rate hikes, and high profits that the Gilded Age tactics of legislative bribery, stock-watering, and rate-gouging no longer afforded.

The success of courteous capitalism can also help answer the question of how the Progressive movement ended. This question has loomed large in

Introduction 7

the historiography. As one historian asked, "What killed progressivism?" Or as another phrased it, "What happened to the Progressive movement in the 1920s?" Some historians have argued that progressives succeeded so well at solving the problems that concerned them that they lost focus and disbanded. Others have argued that divisions over World War I killed the movement, or that after the war the middle class became more alarmed by the power of labor than the power of business. Still other scholars believe that the cross-party nature of the Progressive movement became a weakness, and its members lacked leadership following President Wilson's stroke in 1919.[26] The present volume focuses on what ended the Progressive movement in relation to one of its central goals, control of corporate monopolies. While corruption and poor service ignited the movement to control utilities, courteous capitalism helped defuse the movement and avoid a government takeover.[27]

Of course, major decisions regarding government intervention in the economy had already been made. The Populists, for example, wanted government ownership of corporate railroad and telegraph monopolies. But the Populists were thwarted, largely through the election of President William McKinley in 1896.[28] Yet in the early twentieth century, the reform spirit began to ferment once again, with many calling for government ownership or strict regulation of utilities. This time, however, the defeat came not through a single pivotal election, but through a longer-term shift in public opinion brought about by corporate public relations.

A fundamental insight of executives that brought about this change was that consumption involved much more than just exchanges of goods and services for money. Consumption involved exchanges of words and looks, smiles or scowls. Economic transactions were emotional, visual, and interpersonal transactions. Utility executives came to view these aspects of exchange as at least as important as the exchange of fees for service, if not more.

According to these executives, their big business predecessors in the late nineteenth century, especially in the railroad industry, had entirely missed the personal aspects of business, and suffered the regulatory consequences. Outside observers similarly connected the dots between customer service and regulation. One railroad industry journalist, Ray Morris, declared in 1910 that "there cannot be the smallest doubt that a persistent condition which may be described as corporate bad manner was in large measure responsible for the exceedingly bitter attacks upon railroads which characterized the so-called Granger period, in the seventies, and, more recently, in the Roosevelt administration." One of the main causes of this animosity, Morris argued, was rude station agents who were "the only representative of the road with whom most travelers and many small shippers ever come in contact." A rude agent, Morris observed, "never fails to make enemies for his company, and not infrequently is the source of an accumulation of petty grievances that find their expression at election time."[29]

In 1913, a railroad executive echoed Morris's observations. "It is, no doubt, true," he wrote, "that little things—the abruptness of an agent or a trainman, a lack of proper courtesy, inattention to the complaints of the public, dilatoriness—often cause quite as much criticism from the public as things of greater importance."[30] In 1909, Hamilton Mabie, the editor of the popular weekly magazine *Outlook*, wrote to streetcar executive William G. McAdoo that "bad manners are at the bottom of a great deal of the irritation against transportation in all its forms." Mabie added that "good manners will go a long way toward bringing railroads and their patrons together."[31] This was precisely the idea behind courteous capitalism.

Executives recognized that customers wanted to feel like they were in charge of corporations.[32] To generate that feeling, managers compelled their clerks to treat customers with deference and courtesy. That way, customers could at least imagine that they were in control, and, for many of them, that proved good enough.

The strategy of courteous capitalism seemed promising to executives, but as chapter 2 reveals, managers encountered a major problem when trying to implement the strategy. They could not supervise all of their clerks all of the time to make sure workers were minding their manners, even in the absence of supervisors. To solve this problem, executives developed new surveillance techniques, including soliciting customer feedback. Customers were invited to complain about poor customer service to management, and then thanked for sharing. Employees now had customer-supervisors and corporate-supervisors.

Managers also hired mystery shoppers to secretly grade clerks on their customer service. Armed with a concealed service sampling checklist, mystery shoppers visited utility offices, recorded lapses in service, and reported the results to management. When service was found wanting, the offending employee was pulled aside for correction or fired. Since employees knew that mystery shoppers lurked, workers improved their service. Sole proprietors had once been able to choose between their profits and their self-respect in the face of a rude customer, but clerks at large corporate monopolies enjoyed no such luxury.

Surveillance helped improve service, but it would be much easier for management if clerks internalized the demands of courteous capitalism and controlled themselves. To develop such self-monitoring employees, executives fashioned a new corporate ideology that downplayed traditional American values, such as independence and individualism, and stressed instead values beneficial to the large corporation, such as subservience and loyalty. Women had already been taught to behave this way since gender roles at the time celebrated women who acted as willing helpmates. Racial minorities had also been required to behave as obsequious attendants in various settings. Courteous capitalism extended this behavioral role to all service workers, including male white-collar clerks.

In addition to ideology, executives quoted the Bible to justify the demands of courteous capitalism. Managers also promoted a secular yet metaphysical "spirit of service" to inspire employees to ideal behavior. These methods encouraged workers to internalize the demands of courteous capitalism and become self-monitoring.

Some workers resisted these methods, but others, in a strange yet understandable way, converted to the role their employers had cast for them. Rather than merely acting, or even trying to feel how they were told they should feel, these workers fully identified themselves internally and externally with the persona of the chipper and solicitous clerk. As a result, customers began to notice a strange artificiality about clerks at utilities, and contrasted this behavior with the genuine interactions they recalled at smalltown mom and pop shops.

※

The courtesy offered at utilities inherited a great deal from the longer history of manners that preceded it. As historians have shown, courtesy originated in royal courts, as the root of courtesy suggests. Within these courts, complex rules developed that prescribed how subjects should behave in the presence of kings and queens. Over time these courtly rituals migrated out of the courts and began to govern norms in the absence of royalty. The "civilizing process" had begun.[33]

In pre-Revolutionary America, the upper class adopted these courtly rules, and purchased large homes and fine clothing to complement them. But after the Revolution, ideals of democracy and equality made it difficult to reconcile pretensions to aristocracy with espousals of republican ideology. To resolve this conflict, the upper-class succeeded in getting the middling classes to adopt courtly behavior, at least to the extent their upbringings and pocketbooks allowed. This permitted the elites to keep their genteel manners and possessions without suffering public opprobrium. In that way, polite manners became de rigueur for anyone aspiring to respectability. Courtesy trickled down once more.[34]

Later, in the nineteenth century as the market expanded, courtesy also proved important for business reasons. Sole proprietors and small business owners had to develop a reputation for good character, hard work, and courtesy to persuade potential customers and prospective business partners that they were trustworthy people with whom to do business. Even starting a business could depend on one's social standing since individuals needed a good reputation to secure credit, or "get trusted." So while American society became more egalitarian for some in the nineteenth century, courtesy survived and thrived.

The emergence of large cities in the mid-nineteenth century could have weakened this tradition of courtesy, but instead, the opposite occurred. Rather than undermining courtesy codes, urban anonymity demanded it. The lack of personal knowledge about strangers made following prescribed rules of interaction all the more important, since without them urban exchanges would lose predictability, and life in the metropolis would become utterly chaotic.[35]

The crush of immigration and urbanization during this time raised the question of whose conduct codes would prevail. The answer became the codes of Victorians, who maintained cultural hegemony in the United States from roughly the 1830s through the 1890s. These middle- and upper-class inheritors of courtly etiquette defined appropriate behavior for the rest of the nation, disseminated their views through print and interpersonal communication, and replicated their culture through child-rearing, social pressure, and the control of influential institutions such as colleges, publishing houses, and government.[36]

What happened to courtesy during the late nineteenth century? What happened to interpersonal market relations as industrial capitalism wrought sweeping changes to the nation? According to one narrative, the rise of big business ended the long-running "refinement of America" by creating a class of misbehaving rich. The nouveaux riches of the late nineteenth century consumed conspicuously, which violated genteel prohibitions against the os-

Introduction   11

tentatious display of wealth. And the "public be damned" attitude of some of these Gilded Age industrialists further alienated business tycoons from the rest of society. To make matters worse, their low-level service employees mirrored their employers' contemptuous attitude toward customers.[37]

Yet this story needs to be brought forward through the first three decades of the twentieth century. During this time, progressives launched a reform movement aimed at controlling utilities. In response, utility executives launched a counter-reform in which they resuscitated the waning courtly behavioral codes and put them to work in defense of their corporations. In this refinement of corporate America, clerks were made to follow specific behavioral codes to placate a public scorned. Courtesy trickled down to the lower classes once again, this time at the prompting of the corporations that had threatened courtesy's existence.

This counter-reform of courteous capitalism relates to key concerns of historians of emotions. These historians have long been interested in the relationship between economic change and emotional control. They have studied how emotional regulations are approved, disseminated, and enforced. Historians of emotions have examined institutions and practices such as romantic marriage, family, and child-rearing. In many studies, market structure has been shown to shape emotional experience, though the reverse has also been detected.[38]

This book continues this line of inquiry by identifying big business as exerting a growing influence on emotional regulation at a time when big business began dominating key sectors of the economy and employing large numbers of workers. This book also connects emotional regulation to political regulation. In the case of utility monopolies, the market structure influenced the emotional labor of clerks, which influenced the emotional experiences of customers. This, in turn, improved public opinion, which increased the durability of corporate monopolies and the regulatory state.

Historians of Victorian culture have also studied emotional regulation, especially in relation to Victorian concerns about character and sincerity of self-expression. One important question for these historians is: When and why did Victorian culture decline? While seeing both continuity and change, scholars have often identified the 1920s as the key decade in which Victorian culture gave way to a less conservative culture. The strict moral codes of Victorians yielded to a freer mingling of the sexes, while the Victorian emphasis on self-control and delayed gratification yielded to a consumer ethos of "buy now and pay later." The ethic of hard work continued, yet people increasingly identified with what they owned, rather than who they were, internally and occupationally.[39]

This book finds that courteous capitalism reinforced certain aspects of Victorian culture into the 1920s, while at the same time weakening some of its vital underpinnings. Clerks at utilities learned to behave in what were largely Victorian conduct codes, and this perpetuated and even expanded Victorian culture. Indeed, entire training departments emerged that essentially functioned as giant finishing schools for employees from working-class and immigrant backgrounds. Executives also insisted on "sincere" and "genuine" emotional expressions from clerks, which continued Victorian anxiety about whether one's external actions matched their internal emotional states. Customers, for their part, enjoyed the social deference they received from clerks, and some imagined themselves as enforcers of Victorian character by giving feedback to managers or directly to clerks.

Yet utilities also changed how courtesy codes were learned and how they were enforced. Rather than courtesy being learned in the home, through small social groups, or from advice books, corporations now taught large groups of employees how to behave through formalized courses. Enforcement also became codified. Whereas gossip, social cues, and social ostracism functioned to enforce conduct codes in the nineteenth century, by the early twentieth century gossip had been proceduralized into a corporate feedback system. And after receiving feedback, managers, not friends or family, dispensed discipline, including not-so-subtle cues such as dismissal from one's job.

Courteous capitalism also changed the behavioral norms themselves. Displays of anger, which had once been under severe restriction in the nineteenth century, were by 1930 at least occasionally permitted, though only for customers.[40] Customers were allowed to lose their temper, and even invited to, while clerks were instructed to simply sit there and take it.[41] This permitted a wider expression of human feelings from customers, while demanding a more restricted emotional performance from clerks. These emotional privileges and responsibilities shaped the growing consumer culture by creating a more polite society on one side of the counter, though not always on the other.

Importantly, the motivation to adhere to courtesy norms also changed. Whereas Americans in the nineteenth century often sought to regulate their emotions as part of an internal aspiration to virtue, good character, and self-

Introduction 13

mastery, the motivations of utility employees understandably hinged more on monetary interests and the need to keep their job.[42] So just as consumer culture shifted people's focus from who they were to what they owned, courteous capitalism shifted clerks' motivations for courtesy from internal and personal to external and material.

❧

Courtesy proved effective at reducing animosity toward utilities, but utility executives did not rely on courtesy alone. Rather, courteous capitalism formed just one part in a fourfold public relations campaign that also included office architecture, customer stock ownership, and publicity. As chapter 3 reveals, executives sought to improve public opinion by remodeling their customer service offices where courteous interactions took place. To do this, workers tore down the iron bars, high counters, and wooden partitions that divided clerks from customers and replaced these "closed offices" with new "open offices," as managers called them. By removing obstructions to bodies, sights, and sounds, executives sought to architecturally communicate to customers the supposedly open and aboveboard operating practices for which utilities wanted to be known.[43]

Architectural historians have largely focused on the importance and symbolism of the downtown skyscraper, yet branch offices—monopoly capitalism's architectural ambassadors to America—were far more numerous than skyscrapers, architecturally distinctive in their own right, and heavily patronized by the public.[44] As electricity and telephone use skyrocketed in the early twentieth century, customers streamed into these local offices to sign up for service, pay their bills, or dispute a charge. By the late 1920s, thousands of branch offices appeared in towns and cities throughout the country, making these meek open offices, rather than the defiant downtown skyscraper, the physical symbol of monopoly utilities for many, if not most, Americans.

The interiors of open offices featured upholstered chairs, rich carpets, and fresh flowers, while their exteriors resembled the single-family homes in the surrounding residential neighborhood. This corporate domesticity, as it may be called, overlaid managerial capitalism with a veneer of middle-class family values in a bid to diminish consumer anxiety over the rise of giant monopolies.

Utility executives explicitly intended corporate domesticity to make customers "feel" a certain way. In particular, utilities wanted customers to feel comfortable, relaxed, and at home with monopolies. After remodeling their offices, utility employees observed what environmental psychologists would later prove, that pleasant interiors do indeed generate feelings of relaxation and comfort within occupants. These feelings, executives predicted, would pacify customers into accepting corporate monopolies.[45]

The design of offices not only encouraged customer trust, it also facilitated managerial surveillance. Utility managers intentionally laid out customer service offices and telephone operating rooms to extract courtesy through design. In the new open offices, low-level clerks sat in the front of the office, facing forward and performing the most emotional labor. Behind these workers sat their supervisor, and behind them sat an even higher-level supervisor who oversaw the entire office without easily being seen. At utility offices the title *Supervisor* meant all that the term implied. Each higher rung on the corporate ladder offered not only more money, but also greater visual knowledge and disciplinary power. Similarly, telephone operating rooms were intentionally designed so that operators sat with their backs toward the "monitor," who literally oversaw the operators while not being easily seen herself. The panopticon idea of philosopher Jeremy Bentham obtained physical realization at hundreds of telephone operating rooms and open offices.

Executives also paid a great deal of attention to the design of the exterior of their offices. They wanted each office to seamlessly blend in with the local neighborhood in which the office was located. If utilities could fit in architecturally, perhaps they could fit in politically, executives reasoned. With that in mind, architects designed each branch office in the local architectural vernacular, such as the Spanish Mission style in California or the Cape Cod style in Massachusetts.

As chapter 4 demonstrates, utility executives also sought to undercut agitation for public ownership by supplanting it with "customer ownership." Managers required their clerks to sell utility stock directly to customers. Since these customers were also voters, the dividends customers received were bound to pay dividends of their own, back to the company, whenever municipal ownership referendums came up at the ballot box.

To identify potential customer-owners, utilities bypassed traditional brokerage firms, which mainly catered to the rich, and instead required their employees to visit customers, family, and friends in order to sell them small amounts of stock, often on an installment plan. Since utilities employed clerks, conductors, and operators, as well as engineers, accountants, and lawyers, employees were able to reach tens of thousands of Americans who would not normally have opened a brokerage account or been solicited by a securities salesman. By farming these interstitial regions of America's financial landscape, utilities harvested millions in capital, but, more importantly, they harvested a great deal of customer goodwill.

Courteous capitalism, open offices, and customer stock ownership represented important public relations strategies, but utilities did not overlook the strategy of advertising. Yet advertising by utilities was often aimed not at newspaper readers, but at newspaper editors. As chapter 5 reveals, the advertising purchases of utilities routinely functioned as a bribe to persuade editors to publish "news" articles and editorials written by utility publicists. These articles extolled the virtues of corporate monopolies. Utility managers believed that these articles, not the ads, would do the real work of generating support for corporate monopolies.

This ads-for-articles scheme was especially prevalent among small-town editors who thirsted for the advertising revenue that large utilities could provide, and who were conveniently located where many of the municipal ownership fights of the 1920s took place. In thousands of documented cases, newspaper editors published whole articles and editorials authored by utility publicists in exchange for advertising dollars. In nearly all cases, no attribution of the articles' original source appeared. By misleading readers about the true authorship of their news articles, utility managers sought to convince Americans that corporate monopolies operated in the customers' best interest.

This was not the first time newspaper content had been influenced by business leaders.[46] Yet the utilities' practice of space grabbing represented one of the most pervasive and best-documented instances of this in the history of American journalism. According to careful surveys conducted by utilities, hundreds of thousands of column inches of print matter authored by utilities—the equivalent of thousands of full newspaper pages—were published "verbatim" by newspapers.[47] Furthermore, 75 to 95 percent of newspapers in several multistate regions of the country participated in publishing utility content. What ended up in front of readers, and what did not, mattered when it came to forming knowledgeable opinions regarding corporate monopolies, and the extent to which the issue could even be discussed.

Utility executives also sought to control the public sphere in ways that went far beyond ads and articles, as chapter 6 explains. In what became the largest nongovernmental publicity campaign in America till that time, utility managers attempted to capture or control nearly every conceivable outlet of information on utilities, including textbooks, movies, radio programs, civic lecturers, and college courses. Managers lobbied publishers to rewrite textbooks that criticized corporate utilities. Managers also flooded schools with free books authored by utility publicists. Some managers personally visited local teachers and principals to place these books in classrooms. Yet in many cases, visits proved unnecessary because teachers eagerly requested copies. In several states, well over 70 percent of students received lessons from utility-authored textbooks in the 1920's. By inundating public schools with free corporate literature, utilities sought to produce not just good future employees but good corporate citizens. In doing so, utilities exercised one of the most extensive degrees of corporate influence in the history of American public education.

Utility publicists also produced propaganda films that were screened before tens of millions of school children and public audiences across the country. Many viewers of these films had no idea they were watching movies produced by corporations since utilities usually kept their production role a secret. Utility managers, advertising executives, and even movie critics lauded the power of these films. AT&T managers called them "propaganda," while theater audiences applauded after viewing the films.[48]

In addition, rank-and-file utility employees delivered tens of thousands of speeches at schools, colleges, and civic clubs throughout the country. These speeches may have personally reached well over 10 percent of the American population—an extraordinary amount of Americans to reach face-to-face. Although a few well-known public relations consultants, such as Ivy Lee and Edward Bernays, have received the majority of the scholarly attention, utility workers, both male and female, communicated their pro-corporate, anti-government-ownership message in a far more personal, widespread, and effective way then a few well-paid publicists ever could.

The personal influence these face-to-face methods exerted may bring to mind for some readers the famous "two-step flow of communication" theory proposed by Elihu Katz and Paul F. Lazarsfeld in 1955. The theory posited that most people do not form their opinions directly from mass media, but from personal contact with "opinion leaders." These opinion leaders consume media, then share the information they receive, along with their opinions regarding it, with their friends and neighbors face-to-face. "Ideas," Katz and Lazarsfeld summarized, "flow *from* radio and print *to* opinion leaders and *from them* to the less active sections of the population." These opinion leaders were not high and mighty political leaders, and not necessarily even local elites, but friends and acquaintances who transmitted their views "at the person-to-person level of ordinary, intimate, informal, everyday contact."[49]

Yet what Katz and Lazarsfeld did not contemplate was that the very corporations that produced the media could co-opt opinion leaders to such an extent that media producers and opinion leaders became indistinct. Many opinion leaders of utility issues were paid employees of the corporations that produced the media they disseminated, including articles, textbooks, speeches, and plays. These employees/opinion leaders acted at the instructions of their employers to distribute utility-produced anti-government-ownership opinions, usually at a personal level. Although the influence of utility employees was "horizontal," it was not as "unwitting" as Katz and Lazarsfeld supposed. In the case of utilities, the media had been surreptitiously meddled with on such a grand scale that the distinction between media producers and opinion leaders became blurred.[50]

The four strategies of courteous capitalism, open offices, customer stock ownership, and publicity help explain how corporate utilities survived the first third of the twentieth century. As shown in the "Did ____ Work?" sections of this book, each strategy proved effective to some degree in improving public opinion. The conclusion of this book then argues that while executives believed in all four strategies, they especially emphasized the strong effectiveness of courtesy in improving public opinion.

Each of the four strategies analyzed in this book matter as histories in themselves, but together they tell a larger story. These strategies shaped public opinion regarding the role of the state in a capitalist economy. In doing so, these strategies help explain why antimonopoly sentiment dissipated, progressive reform faded, and why Americans changed their mind regarding corporate monopolies—or had it changed for them.

CHAPTER ONE

Courteous Capitalism Begins

In February of 1908, just days before William Gibbs McAdoo opened the first subway line connecting New Jersey to Manhattan, he gathered his employees together to tell them exactly how his new line would operate. "Safety and efficiency of the service are, of course, the first consideration," McAdoo began, "but, among the things of the highest importance, are civility and courtesy in your dealings with the public." Conductors must not yell at passengers to "step lively"—a common practice used at the time to hustle passengers onto waiting trains. Customers found it "irritating and objectionable," McAdoo explained. Employees would undoubtedly encounter "rude and offensive" passengers, McAdoo admitted, "but," he cautioned, "you must learn to take such things in good temper, it is a part of your job."[1]

McAdoo's courtesy policy had one major problem, however. Neither McAdoo nor his managers could observe all their employees all the time. They needed a way to control clerks even when not under direct supervision of managers. This was a problem recognized by executives to exist at all large corporations. Unlike proprietors of early nineteenth workshops who lived and worked with their charges, managers of large firms could not continuously oversee all their employees. As a result, executive pronouncements from on high did not necessarily translate into employee obedience down low. Discussions of the problem occupied a great deal of the management literature of the time, with some executives advising being "friendly"—thought not "chummy"—with employees, while others sought solidarity by adopting an open-door policy with respect to their offices.[2]

McAdoo devised his own solution. He enlisted his customers directly into the surveillance of their own corporate servants by posting signs throughout his stations soliciting customer feedback. McAdoo and his managers could not observe every interaction, but customers could, and now customers could provide feedback about those interactions, and without pay. "One has only to report the number on the cap of the offending employee to assure redress if offense has been given," McAdoo assured an audience at Harvard Business School in 1910. McAdoo promised his workers that all complaints would be "fairly investigated," yet he also told his audience that "we . . . discipline our employees for rudeness."[3] McAdoo now had his enforcement solution. Employees now had supervisors on both ends of the commercial spectrum, from managers above and customers below.

McAdoo's new courtesy policy had nothing to do with beating the competition. He had none. His line possessed a monopoly on subway traffic between Manhattan and New Jersey, slashed commute times compared to taking the ferry, and was undoubtedly going to see immense ridership.[4] Indeed, McAdoo's line received so much traffic that it helped transform the Garden State into a streetcar suburb. But McAdoo opened his line directly on the heels of the Panic of 1907 and just as antimonopoly sentiment among New Yorkers was reaching a crescendo. For McAdoo, the timing could not have been worse.

On the New Jersey side of McAdoo's line, Woodrow Wilson would soon be elected governor. This occurred in large part because suburban residents who traditionally voted Republican liked Wilson's promise to regulate commuter rates, which he did soon after entering office in 1910.[5] On the New York side of McAdoo's line, residents had recently elected Charles Evans Hughes as governor. Hughes had risen to popularity by prosecuting gas company monopolies for high rates. In his first message to the legislature as governor, Hughes proposed abolishing the existing utility boards, which had become political spoils for whatever party was in office, and replacing these boards with a single Public Service Commission with real power to regulate rates and securities. The utilities fought the idea but lost. "The sentiment of the people was with the bill," explained a reporter, "[New Yorkers] were tired of being herded in foul-smelling cars . . . [and] excessive gas and electricity bills."[6]

One of the first targets of the new Public Service Commission was the Metropolitan Railway Company, which monopolized streetcar traffic in most of New York City. Passengers ridiculed the company for providing "rattled transit" and having too few cars and poor facilities.[7] The Public Service Commission sent its own investigators, who agreed. But when the commission asked the company to fix its infrastructure, the Metropolitan argued that it could not afford to do so without raising rates. This led to an investigation into the company's finances, which revealed a sordid history of overcapitalization, political donations, and a $50,000 bribe to a rival financier to keep him from building a competing line. Even Wall Street, "accustomed to bad smells, sat up dazed," the *Saturday Evening Post* reported.[8]

The full truth did not come out until the Panic of 1907 bankrupted the Metropolitan. That was when the public learned that William C. Whitney, who organized the company, never had any intention of actually running a profitable line. Instead, in a scheme similar to the Crédit Mobilier scandal a few decades earlier, Whitney and his partners made their money by controlling a construction firm. The firm always won the streetcar company's contracts, despite quoting vastly inflated prices. The money to pay for these contracts came from shareholders of Metropolitan, who bought into the company even as Whitney and his partners unloaded their own shares and diverted shareholder money into the construction company. After the Panic, it was discovered that when Whitney died in 1904, his estate was worth millions but did not contain any shares of the Metropolitan.[9] In 1910, just two years after McAdoo opened his line, a journalist observed that the scandal was still "ever present with the citizen[s] of New York."[10]

Whitney was not the only streetcar organizer heavily involved in financial and political corruption in the early twentieth century. There were many, as Americans were increasingly becoming aware of thanks to muckraking journalists like Lincoln Steffens. In his 1902 "Shame of the Cities" series for *McClure's* magazine, Steffens never had to look further than the local streetcar company to find the prime culprit for all that ailed American municipal politics.[11] Soon, the names of William Whitney in New York, "Dollar" Mark Hanna in Cleveland, and Charles Yerkes in Chicago were well known and much hated by Americans.

The dismissive attitude of Charles Yerkes in Chicago was representative of the group. In 1896, when a shareholder asked Yerkes if he would add more cars so passengers could sit down rather than stand up and hold the straps, he replied: "Why should I? It's the people who hang to the straps who pay you your big dividends."[12] After that, "public sentiment" became "thoroughly aroused," noted one reporter, and Chicagoans voted 142,000 to 28,000 for municipal ownership of its streetcars.[13]

The streetcar systems in other cities mirrored those of New York and Chicago. In Los Angeles, the streetcars were so overcrowded that "refined young women" were forced up against "sport men" "so tight that every portion of their bodies touched," according to one journalist. Sick passengers coughed in others' faces and passengers spit into the breeze only to have the spray come back on fellow passengers. Meanwhile, the conductor elbowed his way through the packed cars yelling: "Move up, please; there's *plenty* of room inside."[14] These were the rude, overcrowded, and overcapitalized streetcars that one historian hailed as an "unheralded triumph."[15] To the passengers who rode on them, they were unheralded indeed.

"The Public Be Pleased"

It was in this political-economic climate that McAdoo annunciated his famous phrase "the public be pleased." The phrase was an obvious reference to railroad tycoon William H. Vanderbilt's infamous outburst of 1882, "the public be damned." "The day of 'the public be damned' policy is forever gone," McAdoo declared in 1908. "It always was an objectionable and indefensible policy, and it will not be tolerated on this road under any conditions."[16]

Vanderbilt uttered his "public be damned" comment after two Chicago reporters asked him if he ran his railroads for "the public benefit." "The public be——," Vanderbilt retorted. "I don't take any stock in this silly non-sense about working for anybody's good, but our own." He then characterized "anti-Monopolists" as "frauds and blackmailers." The next day, editors from New York to San Francisco splashed the statements across their papers. It did not go over well with the public. Looking back from the vantage point of 1922, one railroad industry insider noted that Vanderbilt's "public be damned" comment wreaked "incalculable damage" on the entire industry.[17]

Yet it was not just the attitude of top executives like Vanderbilt that angered the public. Nor was it even the rate discrimination and sudden rate changes, which favored large customers over small shippers. These were important issues, but the public also hated the rude treatment they received from railroad workers. The author of a book on business etiquette observed this in 1922. "In the beginning," she noted, "'big business' assumed an arrogant, high-handed attitude toward the public and rode rough-shod over its feelings and rights whenever possible. This was especially the case among the big monopolies and public service corporations, much of the antagonism against the railroads today is the result of the methods they used when they first began to lay tracks and carry passengers."[18] This discourteous capitalism did not win friends, but it did influence people.

McAdoo understood this and eventually so did many other executives. The idea preoccupied McAdoo as the opening of his subway line approached.

For weeks he had been searching for a way to differentiate himself from Vanderbilt and other monopolists, and wanted a slogan that would be, in McAdoo's words, "the antithesis of that famous saying of William H. Vanderbilt, 'the public be damned.'" Then one night, as McAdoo lay in bed, "the public be pleased" came to him. He scrolled the phrase into the notebook on his nightstand, and even as he wrote, McAdoo recalled, he knew he had his motto.[19]

"The McAdoo Policy," published in the *Jersey City Evening Journal*, July 21, 1909, and reprinted in William G. McAdoo, *Crowded Years: The Reminiscences of William G. McAdoo* (New York: Houghton Mifflin, 1931).

McAdoo's "public be pleased" policy proved immensely popular with New Yorkers. Passengers and editors alike lauded the policy. Hamilton W. Mabie, an editor of the popular weekly magazine *Outlook*, wrote to McAdoo "to say what a great many men who use the tunnel would like to say, that everybody appreciates the many ways in which you are quietly endeavoring to serve the public, not only efficiently, but courteously."[20] In 1910, New York's Joint Subway Committee acknowledged that not all monopolies were bad: "The McAdoo system, for example, enjoys as complete a monopoly in its field, yet the operation of Mr. McAdoo's system is satisfactory to the public." This contrasted with the Interborough Rapid Transit Company monopoly, whose service was "largely unsatisfactory." It was not monopolies so much as the people who ran them that made the difference, people began to think. "Does anyone doubt," the *New York Times* inquired, "that if Mr. McAdoo were placed in charge of the Interborough system that the attitude of the Interborough toward the public would be radically changed?"[21] McAdoo's "public be pleased" policy had worked a major public relations coup. It had transformed a monopoly from a target of reform into a rallying point of reformers.

McAdoo was not the first business owner ever to compel his employees to treat customers courteously. Shopkeepers, department stores managers, and even a few utility executives had thought of the idea before. But McAdoo annunciated the strategy more clearly than anyone before him, stressed the political and not just commercial benefits of courtesy, and zealously combined courtesy with customer surveillance of workers. McAdoo also publicized his courtesy policy among the public, rather than just quietly implementing it among his employees. These were major innovations, and they spread rapidly.

The success of McAdoo's "public be pleased" policy soon brought him national attention. In 1913, President Woodrow Wilson selected McAdoo to serve as secretary of the treasury. McAdoo went on to become Wilson's son-in-law, secretary general of the railroads during World War I, and a strong contender for the Democratic nomination for president in 1920 and 1924.[22]

McAdoo's business policies spread in direct proportion to his fame. As soon as the "public be pleased" idea began making headlines, utility executives around the country began adopting and refining it. This occurred not only in the streetcar industry, but also in the gas, electricity, and telephone industries. McAdoo's influence in these industries was direct and unmistakable. In 1912, the employee magazine of the Southern California Edison Company (SCE) urged every employee down to the "office boy" to adopt "'the Public Be Pleased Idea.'"[23] In 1914, a Pacific Telephone & Telegraph Company

"Adopt a 'Public Be Pleased' Policy," published in the NELA newsletter *Service Suggestions* 1, no. 5 (December 1921), republished in "Report on Commercial Service and Relations with Customers Committee," *NELA Proceedings* (1922), 1:360.

(PT&T) manager noted that the first corporate slogan among utilities was "'the public be damned,'" but now it was "'the public be pleased.'"[24] In 1913 an engineering professor observed that utilities in the past "assumed too much of what has been called the 'public be damned' policy. Complaints were met with silence." But now, "the 'public be pleased' policy is the cry of the hour, and the importance of it cannot be overemphasized."[25] McAdoo's ideas were not always perfectly implemented in these early years, but executives now had a plan to buttress the tottering political framework of corporate monopolies.

Utility History

The reason other streetcar, electricity, and telephone executives quickly adopted McAdoo's policies was that all three industries shared common challenges and similar histories. Many streetcar companies in the United States originated in the consolidation of omnibus lines, which were horse-drawn streetcars that rode on metal rails. Before the advent of steam-powered streetcars in the 1860s and electricity-powered streetcar lines beginning in 1888, many cities had numerous privately owned omnibus lines. The teamsters who plied these lines were famously "cranky and perverse" toward customers, and their culture of service—and perhaps even the teamsters themselves—migrated over when their lines were consolidated and mechanized.[26]

Consolidation and mechanization did not improve passenger experience. The capital-intensive nature of these projects brought financial speculators into the field, many of whom had no interest in operating their line in the interest of the public.[27] Instead, speculators such as William Whitney and others sought fifty- to ninety-nine-year "eternal monopoly" franchise permits, which they often obtained through bribery of city council members. Once they had their franchise, financiers made money through stock-watering, construction firms, and rate-gouging, while spending as little as possible on actual service and infrastructure.[28] This angered the public and stoked antimonopoly sentiment. As a result of the public outcry, many executives adopted McAdoo's ideas.

Like streetcar companies, electricity firms emerged in the lightly regulated environment of the late nineteenth century, which similarly led to some unpopular practices and eventual public backlash. When electricity first emerged for lighting purposes, individual buildings, such as theaters and city halls, generated their own electricity on-site. Then, in the 1870s and 1890s, direct current, and then alternating current, became commercially available from "central" generating stations. These distributed current from one central location to multiple surrounding buildings. Initially, several companies competed to provide electricity, but this led to multiple sets of unsightly wires and price wars that prevented companies from obtaining the capital they needed to expand their networks to serve outlying customers. In San Francisco, for example, this economic free-for-all, born out of the state's anti-railroad antimonopoly constitution of 1879, led to the unintended consequence of generating an electricity monopoly, as companies combined to survive. Then came calls for monopoly regulation or ownership.[29]

Many city councils at the time wanted to illuminate downtown to promote civic pride and evening dining, shopping, and strolling. When towns first introduced outdoor lighting, it caused a sensation among the public. Night itself had been overthrown! But in their rush to light up Main Street—and sometimes in their rush to collect the boodle—city council members sometimes signed away valuable long-term monopoly permits. Initially, many small towns felt lucky just to secure a service provider and accepted almost any deal.[30] But when these contracts yielded less-than-anticipated infrastructure and service, discord between companies and customers emerged.

The smallest towns could not attract a corporate electricity supplier. Yet in their anxiety to join the twentieth century a few years ahead of schedule, they floated bonds and constructed their own power plants. A decade or two later, however, technological improvements in generation made these small municipal plants less efficient than the newer corporate plants. And the development of high voltage power lines allowed these central stations to distribute electricity to towns miles away.[31] Soon, small towns began to look like appealing markets to large outside corporations, if those corporations could win the approval of local residents. Hundreds of municipal ownership fights followed as residents divided over whether to support the outside power company or stick with the local municipal plant. During these fights, corporations employed all manner of public relations methods to persuade citizens to accept corporate power.

Townspeople were not the only ones who desired electricity. When electric motors were first demonstrated for factory use in the 1880s, factory owners practically salivated over the prospect of a near-infinite supply of cheap modular power. Their hopes were not disappointed. In the first two decades of the twentieth century, the amount of power consumed by factories increased by over 2,000 percent.[32] The Second Industrial Revolution was on its way.

Farmers too, when they could, connected to the grid and powered their irrigation pumps, grain millers, egg heaters, and milk refrigerators.[33] Yet these business owners could break ranks with electricity executives if progressive proposals to municipalize corporate networks appeared to provide a cheaper and more reliable source of energy. This is what happened in 1917 to SCE; it discovered that while utilities enjoyed eminent domain to build their networks, it worked both ways. Municipalities could—and did—condemn corporate utility properties by claiming that they were not adequately maintained, and then operate the networks themselves. This provided a strong motivation for electricity executives to court the support of all Americans, rural and urban alike.

After electricity came to Main Street and the factory, it entered the home where it created new comforts and conveniences.[34] Electricity powered many of the most popular consumer products of the early twentieth century. These included soft reading lights, hot water heaters, coffee makers, toasters, vacuum cleaners, fans, electric ranges, and the ubiquitous electric iron, which replaced the "sad iron" (actually made of iron) and allowed "ironing day" to revert back to Tuesday. If these devices eventually made "more work for mother" by raising housekeeping standards, as one scholar has argued, consumers in the early twentieth century exercised little caution.[35] In 1910, these "electrical servants" were a luxury for the rich. By the 1930s, they had become a necessity for the many.[36] Yet the more customers came to depend on electricity, the more they paid attention to its regulation, and the more utilities had to justify their monopolization of such an important service.

Telephony displayed a similar pattern of invention, popularization, and controversy. Just one year after Alexander Graham Bell uttered the first words over a telephone in 1876, commercial telephone exchanges began to open. Initially these exchanges only connected subscribers within a single city and mostly served businessmen. The Bell Telephone Company, which became the American Telephone & Telegraph Company (AT&T), controlled these networks through a monopoly on several key patents. But in the mid-1890s, Bell's patents expired, fierce competition ensued, and Bell's market share plummeted.

Independent companies rapidly gained subscribers by offering a potent mix of local connectivity and local pride. In many places, subscribers had a choice between two networks: the local independent and the Bell affiliate. A few people—such as doctors who needed to connect to large numbers of people—had two phones on their desks, each connected to a different network and a different set of subscribers.

By 1905, the independent telephone companies controlled nearly half of the telephone market, and maintained an especially strong position in the Midwest. Over the following decade, however, Bell interconnected its networks from one city to another, bought out rivals, and offered one interconnected system. Regional "Baby Bells" came under the umbrella of the parent company, AT&T, which, along with the Westinghouse telephone manufacturing company, collectively became known as the Bell System. The independents lost ground, but Bell's emerging monopoly generated antagonism as well as convenience and required the company to defend its monopoly through public relations.[37]

By the early twentieth century, it was possible for many Americans to call their friends on the telephone, make evening plans to take the streetcar into downtown, walk around under the lights, enjoy a gas- or electrically cooked meal, watch a movie (perhaps an AT&T propaganda film), then return home again via the streetcar. It was also possible for all of these services to be monopolized by corporations, a fact that many customers did not embrace with open arms. The skepticism and even disgust with which some customers viewed corporate utility monopolies and their service provision drove executives to adopt courteous capitalism.

Public Opinion and Clerks

At the heart of courteous capitalism was the logic that public opinion controlled the political economy of the nation. "In all times, in all lands, public opinion has had control at the last word," AT&T president Theodore Vail proclaimed in his company's 1910 *Annual Report*.[38] If executives failed to generate positive public opinion, they believed their companies would be doomed, politically and financially. Without positive public opinion, utilities would fail to obtain the basic franchise permits they needed to operate.

Rates, too, depended on public opinion. As the influential Chicago utilities magnate Samuel Insull told gas company executives in 1921, "Our income, our earning capacity, is dependent, primarily in my judgment, upon public good will."[39] The following year, AT&T vice president E. K. Hall told Southern Bell employees: "I want to emphasize this point—whether we get adequate rates and so can be assured of a safe margin depends almost absolutely in the last analysis on public opinion."[40] In 1929, a streetcar lawyer told his colleagues at an industry conference that "immediately, and always eventually, councilmanic and legislative acts follow public opinion."[41] In the mind of utility executives, public opinion reigned supreme.

But what exactly was public opinion and who was the public? According to Theodore Vail in AT&T's 1910 *Annual Report*, "public opinion" was "but the concert of individual opinion."[42] The definition was widely shared throughout the utilities industries. In 1912, AT&T executive Nathan Kingsbury stated that "the aggregate of private opinion gives us public opinion."[43]

Executives defined "the public" in various ways. Some included employees, shareholders, and bankers in their definition, but all included customers. And since over 95 percent of urban American consumed utility services by the late 1920s, and more than half of Americans lived in cities by that time, utility customers and the American public were nearly synonymous.[44] "Go to a big ball game, and you'll see your public, or rather the masculine half of it," stated AT&T vice president William Banning at a company conference in 1921.[45] Samuel Kennedy offered a similarly wide-ranging and gendered definition. "The public is made up of individuals," he said. "It is the man in the street and the woman in the home who mold Public Opinion."[46]

The most effective way to improve public opinion toward monopolies, according to utility managers by the 1920s, was to provide courteous service. Executives made a habit of stating this in the strongest of terms. In 1924, a Michigan Bell supervisor declared that "courtesy to our patrons is the greatest factor in successful public relations."[47] In 1925, the *Pacific Telephone Magazine* stated that "courtesy should be the foundation of all our work" since "the progress of our company depends upon the good will of the public alone."[48]

This was more than just rhetoric for the consumption of employees. Executives made similar statements behind closed doors. As early as 1911, Samuel Insull told executives of the large Byllesby utility company that: "I know of no qualification so necessary in our business—I will put it before engineering ability, or technical skill, selling ability, or any other line of business ability—as the ability to deal in a satisfactory manner with the people with whom you come in contact from day to day."[49] In 1930, after years interviewing utility customers, psychologist and business consultant J. David Houser concluded that "the customer attitude toward public ownership or private ownership is determined to very large extent by the way the public feels about service. And the way they feel about service," Houser added, "is determined almost entirely by the way they feel about the way they are treated by employees."[50] Findings like these propelled executives to adopt courteous capitalism.

The strategy of courteous capitalism made especially good sense since negative public opinion regarding utilities could not be blamed on high rates. In the nineteenth century, railroad monopolies had charged exorbitant rates to small shippers, and that had sparked a great deal of the Populists' discontent. Yet the rates charged by streetcar, electricity, and telephone companies in the early twentieth century were reasonably low. Electricity was one of the smallest items in the monthly budget for most urban consumers, and streetcar and telephone costs were not much greater.[51]

Proponents of public ownership still argued that government-owned utilities could reduce rates even further, yet this was a complex argument to make to busy Americans.[52] The argument ran that government-owned utilities could offer lower rates because they did not mulct the public for large profits and send them away to distant holding companies and financiers. There were examples to prove it, proponents maintained. Defenders of corporate utilities replied that government-owned utilities only appeared to be cheaper because the municipal plants received massive government subsidies, such as not paying property taxes. When these were properly accounted for, government operation was actually more expensive than corporate service, not less, and there were examples to prove it. Besides, utility executives argued, government could never operate a complex enterprise such as a utility as efficiently as a private business; the government's job was to oversee, not operate. To sort out the truth of all this required customers to delve into account books and municipal finance records, and most Americans did not bother. Courtesy, not rates or rationality, executives believed, offered the best chance to improve public opinion toward corporate monopolies while maintaining the overall monopoly structure and profits of the industry.

The idea that courteous service would improve public opinion was clearly conceptualized in the gas and electricity industries as early as 1910. In that year, the Pacific Gas & Electric Company (PG&E) published an employee magazine article about how employees should treat their customers when answering the phone. "The promptness of response, the tone of the voice, the courtesy displayed or lacking are all little things that count," the article noted, "and, in the aggregate, with tens of thousands of customers, they make for popularity or public resentment." This public perception was then directly tied to politics. The article prophesied that if all employees provided courteous service "the public effect will gradually become evident, and every local condition applying to the company will be made a little pleasanter."[53] No doubt, securing a more pleasant political environment was precisely what PG&E longed for in 1910, three years after the Southern Pacific Railroad's political machine in California broke down and right before progressive Republican Hiram Johnson was swept into the governorship on a platform that included utilities regulation.[54]

Tying the deportment of clerks to the actions of politicians became increasingly common throughout the utilities industries during the 1910s. "Convert the people, and they will take care of the legislators," *Public Service* magazine succinctly stated in 1911.[55] "The public utilities problem involves something more than statutes, court decisions, [and] orders from commissions," the former chairman of the Illinois Public Utility Commission told utility managers in 1921. "Laws and decisions have no permanency unless back of them is the sentiment of the people."[56] Executives believed this. They believed in the power of public opinion. They believed in democracy—feared it even—so they sought to convert the people to their point of view.

Since individual customer opinions were linked to political regulation, every customer interaction became political, not merely commercial. When clerks received payment for bills, spoke to customers on the phone, or signed up customers for service, these clerks simultaneously shaped the political opinions of customers. The aggregate of those customers' opinions shaped legislation and therefore the political economy. The sphere of utility politics, once primarily confined to politicians and businessmen, now expanded to include every utility user in the country.[57] These customers were not generally organized into interest groups, but their opinions translated into legislative action. In the case of utility politics, the Progressive Era—a term I use as shorthand for the first two decades of the twentieth century—was not characterized by the decline of mass participatory politics and the rise of organized interest groups, as scholars have seen in other political areas at the time. Instead, it was the reverse. In the important arena of utility politics, the Progressive Era and 1920s saw a diffusion of politics from the few to the many, and from the explicitly political to the implicitly political. While voting declined in the Progressive Era, other acts, such as interacting with companies, became politicized, whether or not customers, or even clerks, knew it.[58] Through these crevices of capitalism, politics seeped into everyday life.

Clerks Matter

One conclusion executives came to by connecting clerical courtesy to political regulation was that, in a very real sense, clerks mattered more than executives. As one National Electric Light Association (NELA) pamphlet stated in 1925, "No matter what the executives may do . . . it's the man at the counter—the man who comes in contact with the public who determines our success in serving our fellow man."[59] Samuel Insull expressed the idea in 1921 when he told his employees that "the opinion of the public with relation to a utility such as ourselves, is molded, not by the people who direct the undertaking, but by the people who are typified by the girl, say, who sits behind the cashier's desk, and who may have a grouch on in the morning because she had a row with her best fellow the night before."[60]

The stenographer recording the speech noted laughter from the audience after the comment, but Insull's speech contained more than just humor. By acknowledging that the company's success depended in large part on clerks, Insull was admitting that the success of the firm did not entirely depend on his own ability. In doing so, Insull expressed a new managerial mindset that executives in the Gilded Age would have found troubling. In the Gilded Age, as shown in the writings of William Graham Sumner and Andrew Carnegie, executives believed that their dominance in the market was the result of their own superiority. In this Social Darwinist view, corporate officers were manifestly superior to their employees and competitors since the corporate titans had successfully triumphed over others in the treacherous terrain of the market.[61] During the Progressive Era, this self-conception shifted as executives began to realize the importance of their lower-level employees. Company presidents began to view the contributions of these employees as at least as important as their own. The "visible hand" of management was invisible to customers. What customers saw was the behavior of clerks.[62] "Good relations with the public," stated a utility firm's policy manual, "cannot be gained or maintained without the cooperation of all employees, for it is by their attitude and knowledge that the company is judged."[63]

This statement could be read as an attempt to inflate employees' sense of self-importance in an effort to get them to do their jobs better. Yet executives expressed the same ideas when talking among themselves. Insull told executives that, in terms of "influencing public opinion . . . those of us who direct the policy of large enterprises can do but little unless we have the assistance of the men who are operating the plants and coming in contact with the public from day to day."[64] A 1929 NELA report written by and for executives emphatically stated that "most people judge companies with which they deal, more largely through the employees with whom they come in contact than through any other single factor." The report added that "neither advertising nor the general policies of the company, nor the physical service of the companies has any effect as that of the direct personal contact either in face-to-face interview, through correspondence, or over the telephone."[65] A stronger endorsement of courteous capitalism could hardly be made.

The Ideal Clerk and the Work Experience of Clerks

With the fate of monopoly utilities hanging on the behavior of employees, executives developed a detailed vision of exactly what they imagined in an ideal clerk. Executive speeches, industry conference papers, and employee magazines became filled with such descriptions. "A pleasing manner and a pleasing personality. That is what I have in mind," mused Samuel Kennedy in 1921.[66] "A courteous, pleasant manner," envisioned another manager.[67] "A sympathetic understanding" and "a continual friendliness to the customer," offered a manager in a prize-winning essay on how to solve the problems in the electricity industry.[68] A manager in Boston wanted clerks to exude a "friendly glow,"[69] a manager in California wanted "service with a smile,"[70] a manager in Denver wanted "attentive and obliging" clerks who "cheerfully" attended to customers.[71]

This behavior was required of clerks no matter how customers treated them. Even in the face of the rudest customers, clerks were expected to

Courteous Capitalism Begins   33

reject any emotional reactions within themselves that did not conform to the overarching logic of improving public opinion. "You must treat people courteously, no matter how they treat you," William G. McAdoo bluntly told his workers.[72] "Let the other fellow lose his temper—you stand pat," instructed an employee customer service manual.[73]

If contrary emotions did arise, employees were expected to filter them and express only those emotions that fell within the narrow spectrum acceptable to management. Customers "will fly into a rage, use the worst language, and fling all sorts of abuse," acknowledged the chief clerk at a utility, but clerks still needed to provide the "utmost courtesy."[74] In another glimpse into the work experience of clerks, a streetcar manager admitted to *Business Magazine* that "there are selfish and greedy passengers whom it would be a compliment to call cattle." But, the manager added, "We instruct our conductors to overcome evil with good, and to return a surly question with a courteous answer."[75] Some mystery shoppers, following company instructions, treated clerks "gruffly and sometimes savagely," and then rated the clerks' response. Clerks had specific instructions to simply endure such treatment.[76]

Employees were also instructed to abjectly conform to whatever customers wanted. Samuel Insull of Chicago's Commonwealth Edison Company taught his employees in 1915 to "conform, as far as we can, not only to the good judgment of the public and to their proper desires, but also to their peculiarities and idiosyncrasies, that is what is involved in the question of courtesy to the public."[77] Doing that would require clerks to reject their own individual identities, even their own souls, but managers explicitly argued that this was a cost worth paying. "Withhold nothing of work and soul and patience," enjoined the SCE employee magazine in an article entitled "From Every Man."[78] Playing on the Progressive idea of self-sacrifice for the greater good, an employee magazine article from 1913 urged employees to lay aside "all personalities" in order to "advance the legitimate interests of our employer."[79] In 1923, the president of PG&E went as far as saying that good customer service was worth "devoting one's life to."[80]

Yet these emotional demands took a toll on workers. One former operator wrote in gendered terms that the operator "must assume that the subscriber is always right, and even when she knows he is not her only comeback must be: 'Excuse it, please,' in the same smiling voice." The operator "was a person," the former operator observed in 1930, "where now she is a machine."[81] Another operator told a journalist that "you always have to be pleasant—no matter how bad you feel." If a customer was rude, she noted, "you just take it with a grain of salt and just keep on working. Inside you and in your head you get mad but you still have to be nice when the next call comes in. There's no way to let it out."[82]

The struggle centered on the soul of workers, as clerks clearly recognized. One Bell employee declared: "I . . . longed to get into some open competitive field . . . a *man's* competition, where I could call my soul my own, and tell people to go to my competitors or to the devil if my ways did not suit."[83] Another utility employee lamented that the operator was "once . . . a free, untrammeled soul" but "gradually her own identity has been lost."[84] Courteous capitalism, with its incursion into the soul of clerks, clearly hurt their work experience.

"Sincerity Must Be Genuine"

Despite the deindividualizing and self-alienating nature of courteous capitalism, clerks were admonished to make their performances genuine. Executives wanted "a real smile."[85] Cashiers at bill-payment windows were expected to say "'thank you' . . . politely, and as if he or she meant it."[86] Clerks were supposed to display a "genuine desire to serve"[87] and be "personally enthusiastic."[88]

Executives did not want mere acting, they wanted the real emotions from inside of clerks. "Real civility and courtesy must come from within a man and not from without," observed the Southern California Edison employee magazine in 1917.[89] "There is the formal courtesy of the lip and manner and there is the courtesy that flows from the heart," Kennedy noted in 1921.[90] According to executives, only when clerks genuinely felt the emotions they expressed would their customer service be perceived as genuine. "A genuine spirit of accommodation," an Illinois Bell manager told colleagues in 1922, "requires a real desire and will to serve. . . . When a man is doing something because he *wants* to do it, he is necessarily expressing himself, his own identity and his own ideals, rather than merely acting."[91] "Sincerity must be genuine," streetcar president William G. McAdoo attempted to clarify in 1910, "it cannot be feigned. The people are quick to discover a counterfeit."[92] This shows how utility managers perpetuated Victorian concerns about sincerity of self-expression.

But how could the outward expressions of clerks be genuine when those very expressions had been so thoroughly prescribed by others? Victorians, a few decades earlier, had worried about a similar problem. They had fretted over whether their outward displays reflected their true inner feelings, or

Courteous Capitalism Begins   35

just conformance to rigid social codes of behavior. If Victorians dissembled about their true emotions in any way, they considered themselves hypocrites, a horrific state akin to a confidence man or painted woman. Could one always remain sincere and transparent with respect to one's feelings and yet consistently adhere to social norms? By the turn of the century, Victorians had exhausted themselves with introspection, loosened their demands for emotional transparency, and relinquished their disdain for small bits of dissembling.[93] Yet shortly after this transition took place in Victorian parlors, executives began insisting on sincerity in customer service centers, which were modeled on parlors.

This story could be read as supporting the argument that managerial capitalism, with its rewards for putting on appearances and dressing for success, welcomed confidence men and painted women into mainstream American life in the early twentieth century. In the nineteenth century, confidence men and painted women were criminals whose external appearances did not match their internal intentions. They appeared respectable and trustworthy to unsuspecting visitors to America's growing cities before stealing their victims' money, luggage, and sometimes much more.[94]

Yet if confidence men and painted women were anything, they were autonomous, shifting their identities and behavior to advance their own goals. Within monopoly corporations, however, clerks were far from autonomous. They did not choose how they conducted themselves before others. They were controlled by both managers and customers.

It is true that some clerks at utilities moved up the corporate ladder by adopting a friendly persona, but upward mobility at large corporations was becoming more challenging as college degrees became increasingly required for accounting, engineering, and management positions.[95] In 1926, one utility manager looked back on the bygone era when "anybody who could read [and] write" could obtain a professional position at utilities. "That situation has passed," the manager observed.[96] "Oftentimes," another manager noted in 1928, "I hear men say, and particularly young men, that a fellow doesn't have the same chances that he did twenty-five or fifty years ago." Employee dissatisfaction was high due to declining prospects and the demands of emotional labor.[97] No wonder F. Scott Fitzgerald had Amory Blaine in *This Side of Paradise* (1920) declare that he did not want to get "lost in a clerkship, for the next and best ten years of my life." The job "would have the intellectual content of an industrial movie." Perhaps he had seen utility training movies. Blaine went on to defend government ownership.[98]

Alternatives to service work, such as blue-collar labor, also entailed great difficulties. Yet blue-collar workers knew they were better off than white-collar clerks in at least one area: they did not have to engage in emotional labor.[99] When journalist Ida Tarbell asked a group of coalminers why they stayed in the mines, their replies included, "Nobody bothers you when you are working with a pick" and "[It's] nice and quiet in the mines." "In the end," Tarbell concluded, "there was probably no larger percentage of those who did not like the work they were doing than there is in the white-collar occupations." While blue-collar work was immensely difficult, white-collar service work also proved very trying, partly because of courteous capitalism.[100]

In demanding emotional displays, utility executives explicitly acknowledged that they were commodifying the emotions of their employees. In 1913, investment banker Frank Rollins, who invested in utilities, penned an employee magazine article entitled "The Value of a Smile Transmuted into Dollars." "Did you ever take time to figure the money value of a smile?" Rollins asked. "Did you ever estimate what a gleam of white teeth from between happily parted lips with laughing eyes was worth when transmuted into dollars?" As the former governor of New Hampshire, Rollins had surely thought about the value of a smile in other political contexts. "A smile has as real a money value as a gold watch or a cord of wood," he proclaimed. "Great corporations have to suffer for the incivility of their employees, but courtesy covers up a multitude of defects in service."[101]

What made courtesy so appealing to Rollins and others was that it was not only necessary for industry survival, it was cheap too. Rollins emphasized this fact when he described what happened to him one day when he boarded a Pullman railroad car but forgot his ticket back at the office. The conductor refused to give him a seat so Rollins complained about the discourteous worker to the railroad's superintendent. After that, "there was a shaking up of dry bones," Rollins recounted. "I bet that conductor smiles now. It costs nothing but is worth millions."[102]

Many others confirmed Rollins's low-cost yet high-yield valuation of workers' emotions. "Courtesy means much and costs so very little," a Southern Bell employee rejoiced in 1922.[103] Samuel Kennedy urged employees to "give back a smile for a frown" since it represented "no expenditure, yet never fails to yield handsome returns."[104] In implementing courteous capitalism, clerks and executives were both made to smile, but for different reasons.

Courtesy Training

By the early twentieth century, executives knew they wanted courteous service, but they did not always know how to obtain it. Extracting courtesy was "baffling," one manager lamented in 1909.[105] Initially, executives simply told clerks what to do through speeches, memos, and instructional pamphlets. One of the earliest of these efforts was *Tactful Relations with Customers*, published in 1903 by the National Electric Light Association (NELA). NELA was the most important industry association for the electricity business, and everyone who was anyone in the industry attended its annual conference. There, executives shared technical information, commercial strategies, and presented committee work such as *Tactful Relations*. The pamphlet instructed clerks to "be courteous," "be polite," and follow the department store magnate John Wanamaker's adage, "the customer is always right."[106]

The president of SCE, John B. Miller, penned another early attempt at extracting courtesy in the form of a company memo published in 1905. "The Public gains its impression of the Company through contact with its representatives," Miller wrote, so employees "will, therefore, be held responsible in every instance for carrying out the well-established policy of the Company—'GOOD SERVICE, SQUARE DEALING, COURTEOUS TREATMENT.'" Miller's three-sentence memo became the guiding policy of the company, and in 1931 it was cast in bronze and enshrined in the lobby of the company's new headquarters.[107]

Executives soon found, however, that simply telling employees how to behave did not quite work. Looking back from the vantage point of 1928, one executive observed that the "bromidic mottoes" of the early twentieth century did little to "secure that distinguished performance in the service of customers which is essential to the best public attitude."[108] Samuel Kennedy expressed his frustration with extracting courtesy as late as 1921 when he told fellow executives that "officers think they have adopted progressive methods," but have not "promulgated" the methods among "the employees down the line." "Orders issued from leather-lined swivel chairs" and "across mahogany tables," Kennedy declared, "will be entirely ineffective if the crux of the subject is overlooked." And for Kennedy, the "crux of the subject" was actual contact with customers, because it was "in the contact that good will is made or ill will engendered."[109]

Despite these early difficulties, executives remained determined to secure courteous conduct from clerks. Since directives failed, executives developed an array of training courses to make sure employees knew exactly how to behave in nearly every situation. Employees still attended company-wide meetings with speeches from senior executives, but now these meetings also included outside speakers and some of the earliest corporate training movies.[110] One movie, entitled *Good and Bad Customer Relations Practices*, starred actual electricity employees acting out true stories gathered from experiences with customers.[111]

The most common training method, however, was the demonstration class in which managers and employees acted out various customer service scenarios and employees learned how to act.[112] Consultant J. David Houser endorsed this method, which he called "the conference scheme," because it allowed employees to "do the preaching."[113] Some employees, however, appear to have mocked these proceedings by exaggerating the very courtesy that managers were trying to teach. "The surrounding group of fellow employees inspires statements sometimes very distinctly in the 'company manner' rather than the characteristic style of the individual," complained an exasperated manager in 1929.[114]

Some training classes included employee chants, such as "I am the company," which SCE employees were instructed to say "again and again, and believe deep down."[115] Bell employees sang the "Blue Bell Song" to the tune of "My Country 'Tis of Thee," which included admonitions to customer courtesy.[116] Boston Edison employees learned to cheer: "E-d-i-s-o-n! / I Will, You Will, We Will, Good Will! / Want to see—Loyalty-Courtesy!"[117] These chants bureaucratic were augmented in some organizations by a pledge of allegiance to the company. The pledge at PG&E read: "I am at all times the individual personal representative of and for this company, and it is for me to see that the policy of this company—that of rendering service in its broadest sense—is carried on."[118]

Managers and aspiring managers were also trained how to reach customers through college courses in psychology from top schools, including Northwestern University and the University of Southern California.[119] Although some classes met on Friday nights and employees sometimes had to pay half the tuition, the courses were well attended.[120]

Courtesy training occurred frequently. Utilities held bimonthly or monthly meetings for managers to train them how to instruct subordinates, and monthly, weekly, and even daily training meetings for frontline clerks. The meetings for clerks often included lectures, handouts, and written and oral tests.[121] Some companies put their employees through multiple courses with different topics and texts for each course. One streetcar company developed separate courses on "politeness," "attentiveness," "speech," "appearance," and "loyalty."[122] Since transforming public opinion was not a onetime act like passing a law, and since utilities had a significant amount of turnover, employee training occurred continually.[123] "Training has to keep on practically forever," declared one public relations consultant.[124]

Nearly every utility employee received training. As AT&T vice president E. K. Hall stated, "We are seeking especially to make each member, whether he be a cable splicer, operator, trouble man, installer, clerk, engineer, general manager, or office boy, realize that he is the official representative and spokesman of the company." Even tree trimmers and telephone pole installers received training on how to do their job without angering customers.[125]

Managers eventually developed specific instructions for nearly every type of job. Repairmen were taught to take off their shoes before tracking mud into a customer's house, and how to respond if asked to do additional repairs or even to watch a baby while the mother ran an errand. "If he is obliging [and] courteous, he has gained a friend for his company," an employee magazine wrote, apparently implying that babysitting was allowed. "But if he is gruff, curt, tracks up a clean floor with mud and is not accommodating, he has made an enemy."[126]

Streetcar conductors also received specialized training. They learned how to be "polite yet firm" when passengers spat on the floor, put their feet up on seats, smoked in the nonsmoking car, or shouted obscenities at other passengers or the conductor. A survey of streetcar companies found that all thirty respondents taught conductors to use a "courteous, pleasant manner" when explaining why a transfer was invalid. And nearly every company told instructors to accept invalid transfers rather than make an enemy.[127] Several companies worried about loquacious or flirtatious conductors trying to chat up passengers. Use a "courteous manner," instructed a Philadelphia streetcar company, then "on receiving proper fare, thank passenger and shut up."[128]

Instructions eventually became so detailed that by the late 1920s managers instructed employees in everything from posture to hygiene, and from pronunciation to letter writing. One NELA committee suggested that managers ban chewing gum, tobacco, and "any annoying habits, such as humming or whistling." Not even bad breath escaped managerial scrutiny. It made the list of "typical" items checked for when grading service clerks.[129]

To reinforce these lessons, companies plastered bulletin boards and company hallways with corporate posters summarizing the main points of courtesy.[130] Companies also produced volumes of employee magazines filled with articles that focused on behaving and grooming oneself properly. One gathers how much employees enjoyed these rags by that fact that when SCE introduced its new employee magazine in 1928, the first issue promised it would be less "preachy" and "long-winded" than the old version.[131]

If all these methods failed to reach employees, there was always personal reproof.[132] "Any day," warned the patronizing editor of the *Pacific Telephone Magazine*, an operator "whose manners are falling short of the standard . . . may be summoned as her shift goes off: 'When West 230 repeated her number for you, you forgot to say 'Thank you!' You want to keep up the standard of this room, don't you? You will remember next time; I know you will.'"[133] One electricity manager in Salem, Oregon, advised other managers to hold "heart to heart talks with individual employees, in private" in order to cause the employees "to heed and follow the suggestions offered." The practice "will be productive of excellent results," he promised.[134] Other managers were less sanguine. "We've got some fresh youths down there who need taking down," one utility manager reported to another in 1912. After that, the manager recounted, "a few brisk remarks are made in a certain office an hour later, and one or two young men are made to realize that mere perfunctory, ordinary . . . not-interested-particularly courtesy doesn't fill the bill, . . . that they have given their business careers quite a little of a setback and that it will take some effort on their part to remove an unfortunate impression."[135] Employees did not always find these reprimands fair. When a streetcar conductor was "called up" for a talk after a customer complained about him, he protested: "I have been polite all the time. I am always polite. I don't know why they called me up."[136]

For Bell telephone operators, courtesy education was institutionalized in the form of operator training schools. Here, young women learned courtesy, enunciation, and inflection, as well as geography, vocabulary, and psychology, "which sounded 'highbrow' to the girls," according to an employee magazine editor.[137] "A good deal has to be done," stated a Bell magazine editor, "to turn each voice which used to rasp, and send curt answers over the wire, into the cheery tones of a Pollyanna."[138] Yet the company was willing to undertake the project in the interest of improving public opinion.

Even after Bell closed its last operating school in 1930 after nearly three decades, the company still continued to concern itself with its employees' deportment "both on and off the job."[139] Although the Depression and the increased use of automatic dialing forced the schools to close, in their place Bell introduced a "self-development course" that employees could take on their own time. The course, which was clearly aimed at women, discussed work etiquette, but also covered table manners, dating, reading, conversation, and home-planning. One worksheet entitled "A 'Checker-Upper' on Reading Habits" asked employees if they spent time reading every day, if they occasionally purchased a "good book," and if their literature consumption contributed to their "conversational abilities." Answering "No" to any of these questions resulted in ten points off the test taker's quiz score.

Another worksheet called "My Manner of Acting" covered dating and work, as well as "every-day affairs." The dating section asked women employees if they "refuse to dance with one man and then immediately dance with another? Refuse to change dancing partners when another cuts in? Suggest what to do for the evening, though my escort has not asked me?" or "explain my inability to accept an invitation simply by saying I have another?" The section on "work" asked each quiz-taker whether she would "show a spirit of cooperation and loyalty" or "go into a tantrum or otherwise display my nerves?" The "home" and "every-day affairs" sections inquired whether employees assisted with the housework, behaved "cheerfully" toward family members, or placed their "purse and gloves on a restaurant table" when going out.[140]

To further promote favorable public opinion, executives scrutinized their employees' dress, making sure that the physical appearance of clerks matched their behavior. Male clerks were required to shave their faces, keep their hair cut and combed, and keep their hands clean and nails trimmed. Shirts had to be clean, pressed, and of a "conservative in color." Collars also had to be clean, and ties had to be conservative and neatly knotted. Wearing a blazer was required at all times, even during the summer. Only black or brown shoes were allowed, and they had to be polished.[141] McAdoo admonished his employees to keep "clean in body and habit and dress" as well as to provide courtesy.[142] As the editor of the *Pacific Telephone Magazine* observed, "Unshaven faces, spotted clothes, and mourning finger nails add not attractiveness to the scenery of a transaction."[143]

Metermen and repairmen had even stricter dress and cleanliness requirements, partly because they traversed customers' properties. One account of a repairman's visit to a customer's home explains why. The repairman barged into the house, then spoke abruptly to the woman who lived there. According to her account, "His hat was torn, his trousers were greasy, his shoes were muddy, and his face looked as though he hadn't shaved for a week" After entering the house in this disheveled state, the repairman said, "'Hello, honey,' to my [the woman's] baby, poking a finger at her."[144] Such negative presentations had to end if utilities wanted to improve public opinion.

With that in mind, executives started requiring nonoffice employees to wear uniforms. A picture from 1929 shows the metermen of the Public Service Company of Northern Illinois, an Insull company, all dressed in identical double-breasted coats, flat-topped caps, and identification badges. The caption reads, "The uniform neatness and courtesy of the company's meter readers is a valuable asset in good public relations."[145] Samuel Kennedy instructed SCE employees to look in the mirror and "see how you measure up, by asking the reflection in the glass a few questions," such as "What sort of person is this? What is the physical appearance? Is he tired looking? Are the clothes well pressed? Are the shoes polished? Are the hands and nails tidy? . . . Does he make a good impression? Does he reel or attract?"[146]

The Los Angeles Railway Company made it even easier for employees to engage in reflected appraisal. They provided conductors with a mirror with labels indicating what constituted proper attire. A note at the top of the mirror reminded conductors to keep their "cap clean," then slightly lower, to have a "clean shave," a "white collar," and, at the bottom, their "shoes shined." For these "white collar" employees, their dress was controlled from head to toe.

Women, who were entering the office in greater numbers in the early twentieth century, presented a special problem of dress. The subject came up in a discussion among executives in Boston when one executive observed that some women within his organization showed up for work "in the kind of gowns they wear to a theatre party or to an evening's entertainment." The executive added that "this is very undesirable in the office." His solution was to have the "chief" lady tell the younger ladies not to wear clothing with a "peek-a-boo waist" or in "colors that are not in conformity with the surroundings and with business conditions." He noted that "the hint is usually accepted."[147]

The dress codes implemented by executives were not empty requirements. By the late 1920s, executives had discussed them at length and were acutely aware of how much power managers had and where their limits were. A NELA committee on attire reminded executives that they could not "run entirely counter to the community or current fads or fashions" and cautioned managers against adding a new requirement simply because it "'sounds well' but which experience has shown will not be adhered to."[148] Although small,

A Los Angeles Railway Company mirror. Photograph: "Employee at Div 3 mirror '30s"; Photo Album: "LARY [Los Angeles Railway] People," Los Angeles County Metropolitan Transportation Authority Library and Archive, https://www.flickr.com/photos/metrolibraryarchive/2950275659/in/set-72157617530992247.

there was employee resistance, and items such as "riotous socks" continued to defy executive prescriptions.[149]

The extensive courtesy, dress, and grooming classes at utilities functioned as giant finishing schools for poorer Americans and the children of European immigrants. This demographic increasingly staffed the customer service positions at large corporations in the early twentieth century.[150] These clerks could communicate well enough in English but needed additional training to smooth out their rough edges. As William G. McAdoo patronizingly empathized to a Harvard audience, "many" of his employees "had little or no advantages and, while they may want to do the right thing, they don't always know how." Yet McAdoo assured his audience that "by patient and kindly admonition we have succeeded in educating them to the required standard."[151] In 1922, the author of a book on business etiquette, Nella Henney, made a similar observation, sighing that "many of the poor girls in business have never known anything but poverty. . . . They have had no home training in the art of behavior (for the people at home did not know how to give it to them)." Yet Henney found that the easiest girls to train were the ones from "moderate circumstances" who represented the majority of new employees. In contrast, "the wealthy girls who, through a turn of fortune have been forced into work and have gone unwillingly, are another matter." According to customers, they were "the rudest girls" at corporations.[152]

Thankfully, a clerk's "breeding and refinement," as one Bell manager put it, could be improved through education.[153] Character was malleable, in the mind of executives, and proper training could augment what a poor upbringing had neglected. In a remark that would have pleased historian Norbert Elias, one executive summarized that "courtesy may have been born in the court of a prince; but it can dwell and thrive in the court-yard of a peasant."[154] "Through training," a Bell film affirmed, the operator "gains those gentler qualities of unfailing courtesy so essential everywhere."[155]

Training clerks to transcend their backgrounds was no altruistic crusade, however. One Bell executive told his colleagues that this personnel work had to pass the "economic test." "Does what is proposed make for ultimate economical operation?" he inquired. "Is the effort worth what it costs?" The purpose of personnel work, he reminded his colleagues, was "to create, by education and training, the affirmative, favorable Public Opinion."[156]

Although executives viewed all these training methods as paths to improving their poorer employees' character, training still had limits in terms of what it could do for workers. In the 1920s, virtually no women, no matter

Courteous Capitalism Begins   45

how well trained, worked in managerial positions in electric company commercial offices, or above the position of chief operator at telephone companies. Even as late as the mid-1950s, SCE only had a few female managers, and they worked in the stenography and punch card departments.

Furthermore, African Americans could only obtain jobs at utilities as janitors throughout the 1920s and 1930s.[157] Only the labor shortages of World War II and the extensive civil rights pressure of the 1950s and 1960s forced managers to hire the first black customer service employees.[158] And it was not until the mid-1960s that Bell companies in the South hired their first black operators. Yet by that point, most customers no longer spoke with an operator when placing a call.[159]

For white job applicants, certain minimum standards still had to be met before receiving training. To make sure applicants qualified, managers thoroughly scrutinized their prospective hires. As a Bell employee magazine from 1916 revealed, if an applicant for a telephone operator position passed all the mental and physical tests, then a manager would visit the woman's house to see if she was "comfortably situated," or if the house was "too far from a carline to make a trip at 10 o'clock at night safe for the unescorted girl."[160]

Male employees also received home visits. In 1920, one electricity executive justified such visits by inquiring of his colleagues: "How many times do you suppose an employee is unfriendly with the public because he has troubles at home of which we have no conception? . . . How can we know when such help is needed by the employees, unless we make a business of keeping in touch with the personal problems?"[161] Such "personal, kindly investigating work" represented a "good investment," one manager stated. The Ford Motor Company, he proudly noted, was not the only corporation involved in "welfare work."[162]

This investigative work was not limited to the moralistic Progressive Era. It continued into the later business efficiency movement. In 1930, the American Gas Association published a form that allowed personnel managers to learn about their job applicants' "present personal history." The form included questions about the applicants' alcohol, tobacco, tea, and coffee use, as well as their "constipation, exercise, [and] menses." The form also included space for notes on hemorrhoids, fistulas, "hyp sphincter," and the applicant's "genitalia."[163]

The "Committee on Office Personnel," which published the form, wanted to make sure that employees were interested in their jobs, "efficient" at their jobs, and physically capable to do their jobs. If not, managers would make "adjustments." And since there were "many cases in which adjustments for physical reasons can be made to great advantage," clerks were physically examined. These physical exams were given to new employees at "many companies," according to the committee, and some companies further required periodic medical examination after getting hired. Some companies asked on their job application: "Will you submit to physical examination?" The humiliation and lack of privacy that some applicants endured just to apply for a job at a utility was almost without limit.[164]

To organize and facilitate all this training and personnel work, executives established new positions and departments. By 1922, one utility had a "director of education,"[165] while another had a "superintendent of complaints."[166] The Bell System began hiring "public relations engineers" and "business office coaches," while some companies employed a "public relations engineer" or a "commercial engineer."[167] By the end of the 1920s, Samuel Insull's Peoples Gas Light & Coke Company, known as People's Gas, had an entire "training and education division."[168]

The names of existing positions and the organizational structure of companies also changed to reflect a more customer-centered orientation. SCE modified the job title of "general agent," which had existed in 1913, to "manager, consumers' department" by 1924.[169] The manager of the "consumers' department" now reported to a new position, the "vice-president for public relations and business development."[170] By 1924, the Pacific Gas & Electric Company also had a vice president in charge of public relations and sales.[171]

Contact by the Numbers

Utilities needed these new positions and departments because of the immensity of their courtesy training. Utilities employed a large number of people and most trained their low-level workers in courtesy.[172] In 1929, the Bell System was the largest employer in the United States outside the federal government and employed over 450,000 people, many of whom were service workers.[173] In the same year, the electricity industry represented the thirteenth-largest industry by employment in the country, employing 230,000 people.[174] In 1929, the Peoples Gas Company of Chicago alone employed one thousand workers with "direct contact with customers" and trained them on a "day-to-day" basis.[175]

These workers had an extraordinary amount of direct personal contact with the public. Between 1910 and 1930, tens of millions of Americans signed up for telephone and electricity service, many of them in person.[176] In 1928 alone, Bell's twenty thousand commercial clerks engaged in over one hundred million face-to-face interactions with customers.[177] In 1926, Peoples Gas counted 2.8 million personal contacts of all kinds, not including the more than two million telephone conversations they had with customers and the ten million bills sent out and collected through the mail.[178]

Employees outside of commercial offices also regularly interacted with millions of customers a year.[179] According to one estimate, telephone installers spent three-fourths of their time in subscribers' homes.[180] In 1923, Insull noted that Peoples Gas responded to over a half million turn-on and turn-off requests per year, since nearly half of the city's population moved annually.[181] The company's clerks also personally replied to numerous letters of complaint.[182] In 1922, streetcar conductors served twelve million passengers.[183] In 1916, one Bell maintenance supervisor observed that, although his workers were "not supposed to have any direct dealings with the public," in fact, "the plant men come in close personal contact with a great many thousand telephone customers each day under conditions that are often trying, and where the personal attitude of the employees . . . can go a long way toward molding popular opinion." Altogether, Bell workers trained in political courtesy may have contacted more people face-to-face than any other organization in the United States, with the possible exception of the Post Office.[184]

"Smile"

In addition to developing internal training, executives also organized courtesy campaigns across companies. These campaigns sought to advance the public relations goals of the entire utility industry within a region. By the mid-1920s, the electricity industry had become so well organized that it could launch massive public relations campaigns involving tens of thousands of people in a short amount of time. In February of 1924, the entire electricity industry in California launched its "Smile" campaign, which organized thirty-one thousand electricity employees into a "Courteous Service Club" in just one month. The employees included utility workers, equipment manufacturers, appliance wholesalers, and salesmen.

Membership in the club was not entirely optional since, as the club's brochure explained, the "personal advancement" and the "happiness and health" of employees depended on whether or not they chose to "be courteous." To join the club, workers signed a card that read: "I believe the Courteous

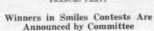

Winners of the "Smile Contest" held by the Courteous Service Club. "Winners in Smiles Contest Are Announced by Committee," *Journal of Electricity* 54, no. 2 (January 15, 1925): 67.

Service Club will be of great value to me and every fellow worker in the Electric Industry—and hereby enroll myself as a member and pledge myself to secure other members to this Club." Recruiting others to join the club was necessary, according to organizers, because the club needed "a great many people to solicit members and spread the gospel." In return for joining, members received a lifetime membership card, a little red "Smiles" button, and a subscription to the quarterly newsletter called *Smiles*, containing bits of news, encouraging stories, and a "suggestive cartoon."[185]

There is no reliable record of how the employees received the program, but if one organizing executive is to be believed, an employee wrote to him stating: "I am strong for the smile—at work and at play." Although the employee admitted that she did not deal with the public much, "being a switchboard operator in my Company's steam plant," she still declared that "I find it pays big to give courteous service." If this letter is authentic, the organizers achieved their goal "to instill in each man and woman's mind the value to the individual of courtesy, backed up by a real smile."[186]

In addition to treating customers courteously, executives also wanted employees to treat each other courteously. In 1924, a Bell employee magazine from Chicago tried to promote internal cooperation by charging workers to "be pleasant and have a kindly feeling toward all."[187] In the same year, a Michigan Bell employee magazine inquired, "How many times have you, as a toll operator, received a surly answer from the distant office of the phrase 'What'd you want?'" This offered a peak into the working conditions of operators, though the article quickly added: "Of course you pass your order in a pleasing tone of voice because you are refined and are the possessor of courtesy. You are a good operator. . . . I am certain that you surely do appreciate courtesy from your fellow-employees."[188]

The ideal of internal courtesy also extended to managers and executives. A PG&E magazine article entitled "How to Get the Best Results from Workmen" advised managers to show their appreciation to employees by cheerfully saying "good morning."[189] "We don't shout at people nowadays and hammer the desk," noted AT&T executive Walter Gifford on his company's personnel policies, "we really hardly give orders."[190] Courteous capitalism not only increased the apparent friendliness of clerks toward customers, but it also encouraged courteous behavior within the firm.

What about Regulation?

Some readers of this book might object that all this talk of emotions and courtesy would be better left for the parlor, not the serious talk of political economy. In fact, utility executives designed their customer service offices to look like parlors, as we shall see in chapter 3. But the main point of the criticism might be that political regulation, not courtesy, was the real reason why corporate monopolies survived the reform period of the turn of the century. It is true that a great deal of regulation occurred in response to the rise of utility monopolies, yet this regulation was by no means the end of the story.

As soon as streetcar, electricity, and telephone utilities emerged in the 1870s through 1890s, towns and cities began regulating them. Shortly thereafter, state legislators created regulatory boards, beginning with Wisconsin and New York in 1907.[191] By 1917, forty states had established state regulatory boards, and the rest would soon follow.[192] These boards could approve or reject franchise permits, set rates, and regulate utility securities. In short, they had real power.[193]

Federal legislation also occurred at this time. In 1910, the Mann-Elkins Act designated telephone lines as common carriers, which allowed the Interstate Commerce Commission to regulate rates. The act also regulated utility securities and created the Federal Communications Commission. Following that, the McReynolds settlement of 1913 forced the Bell System to limit its takeover of independent telephone companies. The Clayton Antitrust Act and Federal Trade Commission Act of 1914 further increased federal utility regulation, and the Water and Power Act of 1920 created federal oversight of hydroelectric power.

This regulation dampened some criticism, but it did not represent the final solution to the problem of monopoly. This was partly because the effectiveness of regulation was often limited. Antitrust regulation broke up a few monopolies, though largely in the oil and tobacco industries and in a symbolic manner. In the utilities industry, the McReynolds settlement between AT&T and the Justice Department temporarily prevented Bell from buying out rivals.[194] Yet the agreement also approved Bell's existing monopoly, which required Bell to court public opinion all the more.

State regulation also produced mixed results. While the boards appeared to bring utilities under government control, they simultaneously bottled-up local reform by concentrating regulatory power in a small number of typically governor-appointed regulators. The small state boards were much easier to manage for utility executives than a bevy of wily city council members or an entire state legislature.[195] This was precisely why utility executives favored regulation by state boards.

But because they stifled efforts at local control, many citizens viewed state regulatory boards with skepticism. Not only were board members often nondemocratically selected, but regulators were often industry insiders, which made the boards even more suspect. Furthermore, regulators were often located in distant state capitals, far from the people and issues they oversaw. The skepticism toward boards became so great that some states saw movements in the early 1920s to abolish the boards.[196] Far from eliminating dissatisfaction with monopolies, regulation increased it in some cases. In 1922—well after the establishment of regulatory boards—a journalist for *World's Work* magazine observed: "If there is one thing the average American citizen dislikes more than anything else, it is privately operated monopoly."[197] As late as 1928, the chairman of the New York state regulatory commission observed that "the regulatory idea in government has not met with general popular acceptance."[198] Overall, regulation worked no miracles with public opinion.

The group that most strongly believed that regulation did not solve the problem of monopoly was monopoly executives themselves. They believed that public opinion shaped regulation, not the other way around. Without public support, regulations would not stand, these executives maintained. "It is the public that has created the commissions, courts, and legislative bodies," reminded a 1927 PT&T handbook under the heading "Public Opinion Affects Regulation."[199] "The company's right to exist comes from the public and what the public can confer it can also withdraw," warned Samuel Kennedy in his

1921 book *Winning the Public.*[200] This was precisely why winning the public was so important.

Rather than shaping public opinion, regulatory boards often followed it. As young institutions, utility boards could not risk their own legitimacy by flagrantly violating public opinion. "When the customers of a public utility company fight [a rate increase]," a utility publicist observed in 1922, even "a most just public service commission will find it difficult to secure as satisfactory rates as the company which has good public relations."[201] An AT&T vice president agreed, stating that, in the early 1920s, "universal hostility" against AT&T was "reflected in the attitude . . . of some of the commissions." Some regulators even advised executives that they needed to drum up support for a rate increase, or the commission would not be able to issue it.[202]

There was nothing inevitable about the eventual longevity of regulatory boards. If executives had never embraced courteous capitalism, utilities in America might well have become state-owned, as often happened in Europe in the early twentieth century. To support a favorable regulatory state yet limit government intrusion, executives in America courted the customer. By buttering-up customers with the emotions of clerks, executives sought to convince Americans that government should regulate, not operate, utilities.

Weber and Emotional Bureaucracies

The finding that executives infused their firms with human emotion is the opposite of what sociologist Max Weber was currently theorizing about bureaucracies. In *The Theory of Social and Economic Organization*, published in 1920, Weber argued that the most significant aspect of the modern Western world was the relentless rationalization of society, which was primarily driven by bureaucracies, including corporations. According to Weber, these corporations were dominated by "a spirit of formalistic impersonality" and were therefore "without affection or enthusiasm." Here *affection* has also been translated *emotion.*

In Weber's account, as these impersonal yet efficient companies expanded across time and space, they swallowed up small shops and shopkeepers, and annihilated the personal and familial modes of organization that went with them. By the early twentieth century, these corporations had grown mammoth and impacted the lives of nearly everyone, except the leaders of these firms who alone were immune to their organization's domination of the market and the soul. But far from purging emotions from their companies in the name of efficiency, utility executives infused emotion into their companies in the name of survival.[203]

Weber's view of steadily organizing yet soul-crushing bureaucracies had a strong influence on historical interpretations of the Progressive Era. One classic interpretation argued that the Progressive Era was primarily characterized by a shift from a decentralized and personal society to a centralized and impersonal one. Technical experts took control from local laypeople as bureaucratic order marched steadily along. According to another influential monograph, a new "bureaucratic orientation" emerged around 1900 that "obliterated the inner man." Workers mindlessly hammered away on the assembly line, while students uncritically memorized facts. For these scholars, as for Weber, modernization and bureaucratization entailed the erasure of the soul.[204]

Yet executives at America's largest corporations saw a much different change taking place. In their view, the political challenges of the Progressive movement brought a shift away from the contemptuous corporate culture of the late nineteenth century and ushered in a new corporate culture of personalized and courteous service. Utility executives and outside observers clearly identified the change as it was taking place. "There was a time when public utilities didn't pay much attention to an unfriendly attitude. That time has gone," declared the president of the Brooklyn Edison Company, M. S. Sloan, in 1925. "The pendulum has swung. It had to. Abandonment of the old attitude was inevitable."[205] "Until recently," confirmed a senior executive at a NELA conference in 1924, "the public utility men of this country. . . . exalted mechanical efficiency and, just as we emphasized it, we minimized the human element in our business." Yet this myopic focus on technical problems created a problem of public opinion, he argued. And solving it required something "from the heart, not the head."[206] At the very time when Weber published his theory of emotionless bureaucracies, it quit holding true at American utilities. Yet the use of emotions did not hurt these corporate monopolies; it promoted their expansion and durability.

Conclusion

As this chapter has shown, William G. McAdoo largely initiated courteous capitalism at utilities through his "public be pleased" policy in 1908. After the success of the policy in New York City, utility managers everywhere adopted and refined McAdoo's ideas. These managers believed that clerks were more important than executives in the sense that clerical behavior shaped public opinion, which in turn shaped the political economy. As a result of this line of thinking, courtesy training became widespread across the United States, and the job of customer service became more difficult.

Yet as the next chapter will show, executives faced several problems in implementing courteous capitalism, and had to develop new surveillance techniques and psychological methods to produce employee conformance. Eventually, however, these strategies worked in changing public opinion in many cases, as specific examples show.

CHAPTER TWO

Courteous Capitalism Intensifies

In 1929, William Durgin of the Commonwealth Edison Company complained to colleagues about a frustrating problem. He had been trying to observe his clerks' customer service habits, but the very fact that he was watching changed their behavior. It had "a most distorting influence" that made "unbiased measurement" impossible, huffed Durgin. "We must have some technique which will get the measurement through the eyes of the public rather than those of anyone associated with the company."[1]

To measure customer service "through the eyes of the public," Durgin began hiring mystery shoppers to visit utility offices and secretly grade clerks on their customer service.[2] He hired these customer-critics by placing ads in newspapers soliciting "Housewives for interesting, part time work." After each transaction, mystery shoppers completed a "Service Sampling Check List" to rate utility employees in four categories: appearance, information, speech, and politeness. "Politeness" had originally been termed "courtesy" and defined as "bearing and charm," but the description proved too open to interpretation, so it was changed to "politeness," defined as "good manners."[3]

Initially, mystery shoppers rated their clerk's politeness on a fifty-point scale, with five increments labeled "very gracious," "rather gracious," "ordinary attitude," "somewhat brusque," and, finally, "discourteous, tactless." But by 1929 Durgin had simplified the form to ask simple "yes/no" questions. Under "Speech," shoppers were asked if their clerk's voice had a "disagreeable or patronizing inflection." Under "Politeness," shoppers were asked if their clerks "Give you a pleasant greeting? Look at you while he talked? Remain seated while you were standing," "Address you by your name," and said "'Thank you,' 'you are welcome,' 'good-bye'" For "Appearance," shoppers judged if employees needed "a hair cut or shave," had "soiled" hands or nails,

Courteous Capitalism Intensifies   55

and if the clerk's desk was "orderly." Shoppers also rated the employee's "appearance" as either "excellent-good-fair-poor" or "very poor." A separate form rated telephone operators. Did the operator "speak distinctly and clearly? . . . use words you could not understand? . . . interrupt you or argue with you?" Did they say "'please,' 'I am sorry,' or 'excuse me?'" Finally, did the operator utter the forbidden explanation "It's the company's rule"?[4]

The Bell Telephone System went even further with their surveillance. They embedded microphones into their customer service counters in the late 1920s. This allowed Bell managers to listen in on customer-clerk interactions from a hidden room behind the commercial office.[5] This technique was a logical extension of Bell's long-held practice of listening in on operators for quality-assurance purposes. Yet as direct dial phones became more popular, clerks at branch offices became the face of the company, so Bell began focusing

SERVICE SAMPLING CHECK LIST FOR DESK MEN		
APPEARANCE Per cent....................	**POLITENESS** Per cent....................	
1. Pleasant expression on his face? Yes No	1. Give you a pleasant greeting? Yes No	
2. Need a hair cut or shave? Yes No	2. Look at you while he talked? Yes No	
3. Clothing pressed, neat and clean? Yes No	3. Remain seated while you were standing? Yes No	
4. Hands and nails soiled? Yes No	4. Address you by your name? Yes No	
5. Desk orderly? Yes No	5. ''Thank you,'' ''you are welcome,'' ''good-bye?'' Yes No	
6. Appearance excellent – good – fair – poor – very poor	6. Politeness excellent – good – fair – poor – very poor	
WHY?	WHY?	
INFORMATION Per cent....................	**SPEECH** Per cent....................	
1. Answer all your questions? Yes No	1. Disagreeable or patronizing inflection? Yes No	
2. Volunteer necessary information? Yes No	2. Voice especially pleasing? Yes No	
3. Did you understand the explanation? Yes No	3. Tone too loud or too low? Yes No	
4. Inspire confidence that what he said was correct? Yes No	4. Words distinct and clear cut? Yes No	
5.	5. Words you could not understand? Yes No	
6. Information excellent – good – fair – poor – very poor	6. Language and voice excellent – good – fair – poor – very poor	
WHY?	WHY?	

A checklist used by mystery shoppers. Byron F. Field, "Appendix C: Public-Contact Training," in *Public-Contact-Training Methods and Principles: Experiences of Member Companies Presented and Discussed at the Chicago Conference, September, 1929: A Report of the Industrial Relations Committee, Public Relations National Section* (New York: National Electric Light Association, 1929), 15.

more on the courtesy of their customer service clerks. By 1930, 70 percent of Bell's face-to-face customer service interactions at large Bell offices were under surveillance in some way, up from just 45 percent the year before.[6]

As this chapter explains, executives used mystery shoppers, hidden microphones, and other surveillance methods to enforce courtesy. This chapter also analyzes additional methods managers developed to generate courtesy, such as corporate ideology and the "spirit of service." The psychological toll these techniques had on employees will also be analyzed, as well as the changes to consumer culture that resulted from courteous capitalism. In its conclusion, this chapter will answer the question: Did courteous capitalism work? As specific cases studies will show, courtesy helped to defend corporate monopolies. Significantly, Bell's discourteous service during the period of telephone nationalization in World War I alienated Americans from government control. This was probably intentional on the part of Bell employees and further promoted the corporate monopoly structure of the utilities industry.

Surveillance Expands

The origin of surveillance programs among utilities went back to William G. McAdoo's customer-feedback program. In 1908, McAdoo invited streetcar passengers to write to him directly about offensive employees, as chapter 1 showed. McAdoo claimed that he did not receive many letters, but other streetcar executives who adopted the policy received up to five hundred complaints a month. Managers tried to channel these complaints to the company rather than to politicians or regulators, so that the managers could address any recurring problems before they reached the attention of regulators. Otherwise, as one manager warned, a "wave of hostility" could result.[7]

Executives also feared that if too many complaints about rudeness reached regulators, regulators might permanently expand their purview to include courtesy control. This extension happened in a few cases, such as in Oklahoma, where the state utility board ordered a gas company to fire all of its clerks who had been charged with "impoliteness and discourtesy to customers." In a similar case in Missouri, the Utility Commission forced a utility to fire one of its managers.[8] Rather than risk this kind of control, executives steered complaints away from regulators and directly to the utilities.

To obtain customer feedback, many executives simply asked for it. In 1912, the president of the Boston Edison company sent letters to each of his forty-five thousand customers asking if they had "any fault to find with the Edison

Courteous Capitalism Intensifies   57

service."[9] Early on, some utility executives also called their own companies and impersonated a customer to determine the quality of their clerks' service.[10] The attitude of the employee who answered the phone, the amount of time the "customer" was put on hold, and the number of times the caller was transferred gave executives some idea about how actual customers were treated. Executives also sent individuals to district offices to see how face-to-face service appeared from the other side of the counter. Yet these informal practices only provided impressionistic results.[11]

In an attempt to obtain more accurate measurements, executives in the 1920s began formalizing these earlier methods. Samuel Kennedy, the vice president of public relations for the Southern California Edison Company (SCE), took one of the first steps in this direction in 1921 by creating a "Department of Greater Service" within his company. Kennedy handpicked forty men, "patiently schooled" them in all aspects of the company, and gave them a good salary. No "young fellows" or "fly-by-nights" were admitted. After the training, Kennedy assigned each employee to one of his company's district offices where they functioned as Kennedy's eyes and ears in the field. Each month, these workers called on six hundred customers at their homes and interviewed them to "obtain the mental attitude of each customer." After each interview, the employee filled out a card that categorized the customer's views as "in accordance with the company," "indifferent," or "antagonistic."

Kennedy's employees also observed service at their assigned district office, and occasionally helped customers, some of whom came in and asked for them by name. Although these workers had a desk at their assigned district office,[12] they bypassed the normal chain of command and reported directly to Kennedy instead of the office manager.[13] This way, Kennedy could carry out surveillance, even on his managers.

After listening to Kennedy talk about the Department of Greater Service, one outside executive noted that "the knowledge that men are travelling over the territory, talking with customers and checking service, must put the employee on his mettle." It did indeed, Kennedy assured the executive: employees were now "much more alert" and "tuned up to a higher point" since they knew they were being observed and talked about by customers.[14]

Other companies established similar surveying programs. In 1925, the Boston Edison Company, which had no formal relationship with SCE, initiated a Visiting Representative Division, which interviewed customers about service.[15] In 1920, the Bell company in Wisconsin also visited customers to solicit their opinions. Doing so "appeals to his egotism," one Bell executive explained to another. "The subscribers, after having been consulted, seem to feel that they are really part of the deal themselves, and it removes any feeling of combativeness."[16]

During the 1920s, many other Bell companies established similar programs under what they called the "Office of Service Representatives." The office studied customers' phone habits and then sent former operators to the homes of customers to talk to them. Since representatives were supposed to "gain the good will of the customer," the job qualifications included possessing "personality, cleanliness, wholesomeness, versatility, appearance, voice, kindness, understanding, sympathy, gentleness, [and] intelligence."[17] Upon arriving, the representative was taught to "size up the character, disposition and temperament of the person with whom she is engaged in conversation." After that, service representative provided explanations regarding company policy in a "tactful, pleasant, yet businesslike manner."[18]

The Office of Service Representatives program worked, at least in some cases. In one instance, a customer in Southern California denounced the Bell representative and her company: "'Robbers! Cheaters! Humbugs! That's what you are. . . . In Denver they don't charge no such rates 'cause the government owns 'em—no dirty robbers there. . . . It's the corporation. If only the government owned 'em like it does in Denver.'" But the representative patiently explained that Bell's rates were overseen by the California Railroad Commission, which ensured the rates were "reasonable and fair," and after that the customer was satisfied, according to the report of the visit.[19]

Companies also created programs that followed up on feedback from customers. In 1926, Samuel Insull's Peoples Gas Company established an "Error Bureau" that measured complaints and then "traced errors to their source." According to a company article entitled "Errors Checked, Manners Improved," the Error Bureau reduced employee mistakes, which resulted in customer complaints going down and customer satisfaction going up.[20] Peoples Gas also sent out reply cards and called customers after they visited a branch office or received a visit from a repairman.[21]

These programs provided executives with some idea about the quality of customer service at utilities. Yet executives still felt that their methods did not fully capture public opinion. Corporate officials realized that letters from customers usually involved extreme cases that did not reflect the average level of customer service. Company representatives also found that customers were frequently reticent to share the details of their last customer service experience, perhaps because they did not want clerks to lose their jobs. In other cases, interviewers found that too much time had passed since the customers' last visit, which made their recollections vague and unuseful.[22] By the late 1920s, executives were frustrated with their inability to accurately measure public opinion.

To solve this problem, the Bell System dramatically expanded the scale of its interviewing programs. Bell employees eventually conducted an exceptionally large number of personal interviews. In 1928 alone, Southwest Bell completed 117,000 face-to-face interviews with customers, and nearly three times that many over the phone.[23] In the same year, Northwest Bell completed almost ninety thousand interviews. At the same time, the company's sales discussions barely exceeded 4,500.[24] This shows that while companies used face-to-face interviews to increase business, they mainly used them to measure and improve public opinion.

Utilities also turned to outside consultants to obtain public opinion data. This included hiring one of the nation's leading business consultants, psychologist J. David Houser. Houser's namesake firm boasted the capability of carrying out consumer-attitude surveys across a company's entire service territory, as well as conducting employee-attitude surveys within the company.[25] To measure customer service, Houser employed a large number of mystery shoppers to systematically rate utility employees on their job performances.

In 1930, Houser excitedly announced the conclusions from his mystery shopper surveys involving seventy-five utility firms from across the United States. "[The data] is the most fascinating single set of generalizations on public relations that I have ever laid my eyes on," Houser enthused at a utility industry conference in 1930. The study included interviews with "probably a hundred thousand customers, actual customers, bona fide customers, interviewed in regard to what they thought about public utilities," declared Houser, hardly able to contain himself.[26]

Executives initially received the data with less excitement. Houser's survey of "public attitude" indicated "a degree of favor toward private ownership of about 26" out of a 50-point scale. According to this result, barely a majority of Americans favored private ownership of utilities in 1930, though the rest were not necessarily antagonistic. Houser also measured "customer attitude toward service," which focused on "the way employees treat the public as they come into the various utility companies." In that category, utilities performed even worse, earning only 26 points on a 100-point scale.[27]

Customer service scores varied by the customer's age and looks, Houser found. Eight female mystery shoppers who completed nearly one hundred samples found that "an elderly, pleasant-faced and unpretentious woman who fits in with the prevalent conception of 'mother' will secure notably better service in the long run than the younger, prettier and more stylishly dressed sampler." No explanation was offered for this, though it may have been easier for younger clerks to respect their elders than to grovel before their peers.[28]

The surveys of the telephone industry produced only slightly better results. In 1929, Bell observers found that 43 percent of customer service interactions at branch offices were free of defects. In 1930, that number had increased only slightly to 53 percent. Though the numbers were not great, executives believed they were accurate since the Bell System had just standardized their observation methods.[29]

The results of these studies only confirmed to executives that more courtesy and surveillance were needed. But what else could they have concluded? Could they admit that public distaste for corporate utilities partly stemmed from the fact that utilities monopolized key markets and resources, sent profits to distant headquarters, and were often weakly overseen by compliant and usually nondemocratically selected regulators? These were precisely the criticisms leveled by critics of corporate monopolies, but for executives to admit them would have been heresy. It would have called into question the very framework in which corporate utilities operated. Instead, executives renewed their commitment to courteous capitalism and intensified their surveillance of clerks.[30]

Ideology and Christianity

Surveillance helped executives control clerks, but it would be much easier if clerks internalized the demands of courteous capitalism and controlled themselves. If clerks did this, surveillance itself might become unnecessary. To create such self-monitoring employees, executives developed a number of techniques, including promoting a corporate ideology. The ideology sought to convince employees to exchange traditional American values, such as independence and individualism, for values that would benefit the corporation, such as subservience and loyalty. Executives also emphasized cooperation, obedience, and enthusiasm. These words were loaded with ideological meaning as they were used in employee magazines, executive speeches, and company mission statements.

The most important value in this new corporate ideology was loyalty. Loyalty was built up in importance by associating loyalty with sacrifice and sacrifice with patriotism. "The greatest faculty of qualification that a man can have is that of loyalty," declared one executive in an employee magazine article entitled "Judgment, Enthusiasm, Obedience and Loyalty."[31] Another executive defined loyalty as "a willingness to sacrifice your time."[32]

Yet time was not the only possession that employees were called on to sacrifice. Each employee's own personality was also a legitimate item of sacrifice, and not only for the company's benefit, but also for God and country. "Only the craven are deaf to the voice that bids the valiant sacrifice personality to patriotism," declared an employee magazine article entitled "Duty" written as the United States entered World War I. An employee, the article claimed, "may serve his country as faithfully and valuably by sticking to his post in the operation of some utility as by going on a battleship or fighting in the trenches."[33]

During the war, utility managers implied that the entire fate of the republic rested on clerks providing more emotions. The more "cheerfulness, energy and enthusiasm that we throw into the war work," declared one employee magazine article, "the sooner the restoration of civilization will be achieved." The article also argued that those not fighting on the front must still be "good soldiers and not slackers," who "will be ready to respond quickly and cheerfully whenever the call comes." It was not clear, perhaps deliberately, whether "the call" referred to the nation's call or the customer's call. This article, published at the end of 1917, concluded by telling employees that "only when we have done all the things which conscience bids us to do, will we greet the New Year with the assurance of conscience that we are sincerely in the business of winning the war."[34] In other words, the company taught employees that if they were parsimonious with their emotions they should experience dissonance in their conscience. Using articles such as these, managers tried to develop an ideology within their employees' psyches that would cause them to behave as the company wanted them to and reject any reservations against doing so.

The new ideology that highlighted loyalty contrasted loyalty with disloyalty and associated disloyalty with independence, a formerly positive American value but now made negative. Disloyal employees, known as "knockers," criticized their employers, whereas loyal employees cooperated. In one case, a manager saw a knocker angrily slam the door on the way out of his boss's office. Upon seeing this, the manager disdainfully remarked, "I think they call that being independent."[35] Such a declaration of independence reflected poorly on the knocker since, in an economy dominated by large corporations, independence had to give way to cooperation.

The behavioral dictates of subordination, cooperation, and courtesy were not easy for any worker. But courtesy put a particular strain on the gender conceptions of male employees, such as conductors and "counter men." This was because gender roles at the time celebrated female "helpmates" who behaved in a hospitable and subservient manner, but such behavior was less celebrated in men. Men could behave as "gentlemen," and upper-class men were occasionally known to greet their social inferiors in a courteous and humble manner, but this was viewed as optional, not universally practiced, and came from a position of power, which male service workers lacked.[36]

Women sometimes used their supposedly natural tendency toward helpfulness to obtain corporate jobs for themselves, often as "administrative assistants."[37] Some female utility workers subscribed to the idea that they were naturally helpful. One telephone operator wrote that "courtesy comes easily and naturally" to women operators due to their "anxiety to please" male customers.[38] Another woman employee stated that each woman "puts love into her work" due to a "women's ardent, devoted nature."[39] The only female manager in the utility industry in the 1920s told her male colleagues at a National Electric Light Association (NELA) conference that the "distinguishing qualities of women are social, practical, and utilitarian. Let us use these qualities of our women employees to better advantage in our Public Relations work."[40]

Men, in contrast, found obsequiously serving customers as not only emotionally difficult, but also emasculating. Asking men to play the role of a helpful and subservient clerk while in the socially inferior position of clerk was akin to asking them to behave in the gender role of a women, some thought. Male clerks viewed genuflecting to customers as so unmasculine that one of the most popular etiquette books of the time spent an entire chapter trying to convince men that using good manners in business was neither "'effeminate'" nor "'soft.'"[41]

Behaving in a subservient manner also had a racial dimension. During slavery, African Americans ultimately had to express deference to their masters and whites in general. After the Civil War, black men and other racial minorities frequently had to labor in customer service positions, such as in the job of Pullman porters. White men, however, had often been able to avoid these jobs. But by the 1920s white men found themselves in regimented customer service positions that forced them to behave in ways previously associated with women and minorities.[42]

Another barrier to men behaving courteously was that not talking back to rude customers and restraining one's emotions indicated that the worker was

Courteous Capitalism Intensifies   63

neither emotionally nor economically free. In the nineteenth century, the ideal of "free men" as a function of "free labor" held tremendous ideological importance. But the rise of giant monopolies weakened that equation, which demanded a new ideology.[43] Male customer service clerks, though not "wage slaves," were certainly the customers' servant, and they felt emasculated for that reason.[44] Executives realized this, so they crafted an ideology that portrayed emotional labor as masculine.

Executives did this by first defining the ideal man as a strong courteous gentleman. "Genuine courtesy is a characteristic of strong men," an employee magazine told readers in 1915. When Oliver Cromwell and George Fox "stood face to face," read the article, "one observes and feels a veritable exchange of manly courtesy."[45] Another article assured its male readers specifically that "dignified service is honorable and in no way degrades, unless the servant, himself, degrades it."[46]

Some employee magazines even recited poetry to convey how masculine it could be to provide courtesy. One such poem, written by Walt Mason and entitled "The Big Men," circulated widely in utility publications. Mason wrote that: "The big men dare, and the big men do;/they dream great dreams, which they make come true,/And the cheap men yelp at their carriage wheels, /as the small dog barks at the big dog's heels." The poem went on to criticize "small men" who seek to tax the big men, and the "four-eyed dreamers" with their "theories fine."[47]

By publishing this poem in numerous employee magazines and utility-industry magazines, managers implied that utility employees could be big men themselves, as long as they worked together with the executives and not against them. This encapsulated the corporate ideology of utilities in the early twentieth century. A harmony of interest existed between capital and labor, including service labor. Only the small-minded—who were also characterized as small-statured—could fail to recognize the big picture. To dissent from the big men was not only immoral, it obstructed progress. Collective uplift could occur, but not through government taxation and increased intervention. Only the mostly unregulated, lightly taxed, and at least somewhat masculine corporation could produce progress. This was the corporate ideology that executives promoted among their employees.

Executives suggested that employees who loyally cooperated to make the corporation a success might personally realize some its rewards. One article from 1913 declared that "no employee who has been loyal, industrious and honest, and has made the best use of his talents in his employer's service, can fail to be appreciated by him because, as is said in the Scripture, 'A man that is diligent in business shall stand before kings.'"[48]

Quoting Scripture to justify the demands of courteous capitalism was not an uncommon practice for utility executives. If clerks could be convinced that a higher power beyond the executive required polite behavior, then surveillance itself might become unnecessary. To develop such self-monitoring employees, executives associated the demands of courteous capitalism with God's will and used the Bible to justify the connection. It was "a sin" not to provide good customer service, the editor of a Southern Bell employee magazine preached in 1921.[49] Samuel Kennedy quoted Solomon's proverb that "a soft answer turneth away wrath, but grievous words stir up anger." Kennedy was fond of quoting the wisest man ever, and was not the only executive to do so.[50]

Many executives explicitly connected their courtesy ideas with Christianity. In a speech to other executives about courtesy, John Britton, the president of the Pacific Gas & Electric Company (PG&E), repeated a long passage he had memorized from Sunday school about duty, honor, reverence, temperance, chastity, and diligence in labor. Britton then declared that "corporation policy should consist in so training subordinates that they will learn, teach and apply the foregoing precepts."[51]

Some lower-level employees also used the Bible to legitimate the demands of courteous capitalism. In 1929, a chief operator quoted the biblical passage of Martha serving Jesus, then exhorted her fellow operators to "take heart and be assured, for the Great Executive has approved your course."[52] Chief executives could not have said it better themselves.

The explicit use of Christianity in the 1920s may seem surprising since evangelical Christianity was losing resonance among some Americans at this time. Yet the emergence of social Christianity, which took the place of evangelical Christianity in some quarters, helps explain this apparent contradiction. Social Christianity preached practical service to all humankind. And this gospel of service closely matched the gospel of customer service, which utility executives preached to their employees.[53]

In the social gospel, "service corporations," as utilities were called, found a valuable partner. "Remember the words and teachings of the Savior as our greatest example," exhorted the editor of a utility employee magazine in 1915. "His was a life of service—'Servant of ye all.'" The editor went on to declare that customers had a right to courteous service, and that utility workers should "render unto Caesar the things that be Caesar's." To clarify the point,

Courteous Capitalism Intensifies 65

the editor expounded "things" to mean "courtesy" and "Caesar" to mean "consumers." In other words, the editor argued that Jesus taught that clerks should be courteous.[54]

The Spirit of Service

Closely allied with the religious admonitions to courtesy was the existence of something commonly called the "spirit of service." Employees also called it the "spirit of courtesy" and the "spirit of cooperation." Utility employees employed these terms so frequently that "the spirit" was clearly more than just a common turn of phrase, although it was also used that way on some occasions. Depending on who was speaking and the context, the spirit was something between a real, metaphysical presence, and Émile Durkheim's "social fact," which he defined as a feeling that can only be experienced as part of the group.[55] Some executives imagined the spirit of service as an uncreated ethereal presence that provided hope and dispensed rewards, while others likened it to school spirit or an *"esprit de corps."*[56]

Whatever its exact nature, the spirit was real, according to the testimonies of executives and employees. In 1922, a Southern Bell employee magazine editor declared that "the 'spirit of service' . . . is a thing we believe in strongly."[57] A 1928 Pacific Bell training manual confirmed that "'The Spirit of Service' . . . has a real existence."[58] In his book *Winning the Public*, Samuel Kennedy testified that "the spirit of cooperation" formed an "intangible and yet a real force."[59] Perhaps this was why Kennedy's book was canonized as "the bible of the industry."[60]

Like the Holy Spirit, the spirit of service could come upon anyone, even lowly clerks. William McAdoo hoped—perhaps prayed—that his employees would "catch the spirit," since once this happened, it "animates them," he observed.[61] A Pacific Bell employee made a similar observation in 1928, finding that "the Spirit of Service . . . animates the men and women of the Bell System."[62] Others said that the spirit was a "potent force" that "inspires." The "spirit is responsive to human needs" and "prompted telephone men and women to respond to those needs," according to a Bell editor.[63]

Once employees caught the spirit, they could express it to customers, who could then "feel" the spirit, or be "affected by it" themselves.[64] According to one employee, "translating . . . the Bell 'Spirit of Service' so the public could know its existence" was the main job of customer service clerks.[65] For utility employees, there really was a Protestant work ethic and a spirit of capitalism, and it provided a windbreak against government ownership.[66]

Cultivating the spirit was a primary responsibility of utility executives. They carried this out through motivational speeches, welfare capitalism techniques, and, yes, pay raises.[67] "You leaders of this industry are the ones responsible for the spirit," one executive exhorted his peers at a utility conference. "The spirit must permeate the organization like a religion and the top boss must be the evangelist, the Billy Sunday."[68] Failure to carry out this task could lead to destruction of a company, executives warned.[69]

When corporate success came, executives did not forget to thank the spirit. In AT&T's *Annual Report* for 1923, President H. B. Thayer credited the "spirit of cooperation" for providing "an important part of the company's success" in surviving the trials of World War I.[70] In 1935, after decades of work for a local Bell company, one operator recalled the intense "devotion" of her co-workers to service. "Under the most trying circumstances, it steadfastly stands," she marveled, "just why, I do not know. An elusive element—'the Spirit of Service'—grips each one of us.'"[71] In the late 1920s, after nearly a decade of company prosperity, a Pacific Bell employee declared that "the Spirit of Service" was "largely responsible."[72] The "spirit of service . . . makes it possible for the Company to carry on," intoned another operator.[73] It was indeed a "wonderful spirit," smiled E. K. Hall in 1922, the AT&T executive responsible for corporate morale.[74]

Although William McAdoo and Theodore Vail had touched the spirit earlier, the spirit came upon most companies in the 1920s. In that decade, utility workers around the country began talking about the spirit with much greater frequency and more detail. The American Gas Association produced a movie called *The Spirit of Service* in 1921 and screened it around the country. The next year, Hall proclaimed that "the greatest *esprit de corps* in the history of the System has been started."[75] Throughout the decade, the spirit of service continued to serve as a potent force in legitimating courteous capitalism. Together with the corporate ideology and the Bible, the spirit encouraged workers to internalize the demands of customer courtesy and become self-monitoring.

Self-Conversion

The idea that companies wanted clerks to internalize the demands of courteous capitalism and become self-monitoring is no mere repetition of French critical theory; it was the explicit statement of executives.[76] At a Bell Personnel Conference in 1922, a manager noted the limits of "the eye of the man-

Courteous Capitalism Intensifies   67

agement" and stressed instead the "self-supervision by [the] employee" as its necessary replacement.[77]

At the same conference, another Bell manager, Verne Ray, observed that "an employee, under close supervision, may be made to conform to proscribed mechanical processes . . . of courtesy," but that that was not "a genuine spirit of accommodation" and a "full measure of ungrudging and whole-hearted service." To obtain that, Ray stressed, the employee must be led to "self-convert" to the company's way of being. Once "self-converted," the employee would carry "the idea into his daily work as his own, with an enthusiasm which he would not have if the conclusion were forced on him." Managers should not order an employee to convert, Ray insisted, since that would not obtain genuine conversion. Instead, employees should be "unobtrusively guided toward and allowed to reach a conclusion by their own thought." Once employees absorbed the company's doctrines, Ray promised, they would not only perform their jobs more enthusiastically, they would "take an interest in propagating it further" by proselytizing their co-workers.[78]

The self-conversion of utility employees was deeper than what sociologist Arlie Hochschild called "deep acting." Hochschild defined deep acting as individuals trying to make themselves feel how they believed they should feel in a given situation. She contrasted this with "surface acting" in which individuals merely put on an outward show without attempting to bring their inward emotions into conformity with their outward expressions.[79]

In contrast even to deep actors, self-converts at utilities did not try feel how they thought they should feel, they actually felt the way they behaved, without the need for conscious internal mediation. The souls of self-converted clerks adopted their employer's emotional repertoire and then bounded their emotional experience to within the limits set by their employer. Theorists and historical examples both show that this self-conversion happens in certain cases, especially when a group has a monopoly and where there are seemingly no alternatives. In these cases, individuals sometimes participate in their own domination and adopt the ideology of their captors.[80]

The sources indicate that many utility employees experienced this self-conversion. In 1921, Bell operators in Holyoke, Massachusetts, held a service improvement meeting behind their supervisor's back in which they adopted the slogan "Nothing but Perfection," and set a goal of reaching a perfect service rating. The operators only told their boss about the meeting after it had occurred, and eventually earned the perfect service rating. Considering that New England operators had once organized one of the most powerful unions in the country during World War I, this new variety of behind-the-scenes organizing must have been a welcome change for management. At other Bell offices in New England, operators decided to see how many times they could get customers to say "thank you," though this was partially at the instigation of the supervisor. At other Bell offices, employees used their own time to visit unhappy customers to convince them that the operators genuinely wanted to provide good service. Other employees stayed late or came in on their day off to escort the mayor or other local notables on tours of Bell facilities.[81] One operator all but bowed down and worshipped the idea of providing courteous service. In a speech to her colleagues at a Bell chief operators conference in 1929, she mawkishly confessed, "I do believe, and I fervently desire to continue to believe, that sentiment is a very potent element in all of our activities and relations with our people!"[82] The spirit of service had come upon her.

Managers noted this self-conversion in employees. In 1922, AT&T vice president E. K. Hall observed that "under the influence of morale the individual comes to want to do the things which it is in the interest of the group that he should do."[83] In the same year, an Illinois Bell manager boasted that his clerks were "clamoring for inclusion" in a service improvement program, which employees wrongly thought had been started by other "minor employees," but which had actually only been made to appear that way by managers.[84]

It is difficult to square these accounts of eager participation in the work of emotional labor with the difficulties such work entailed. How could some workers have participated so willingly in their own domination, while others quit with great frequency or occasionally went on strike? These reactions may not have been as opposite as they might appear. For utility workers, going along with their managers' constant demands for courtesy was probably the path of least resistance, as long as the employees intended to stay on the job. When the work became too difficult, employees might quit or organize, but, until then, performing emotional labor was probably easier than trying to resist the combined power of bosses and customers, which would only led to reprimands from both.

Furthermore, after World War I, the option of organizing for better working conditions became much more difficult because executives broke the power of the unions. This was especially important to telephone operators, whose organizing had been the most prominent out of all utility positions. At

Courteous Capitalism Intensifies   69

one point, operators maintained one of the strongest women's unions outside of the sewing trades. But by the early 1920s, operators had lost a significant amount of strength, partly because their unions had been co-opted by company unions, or employee representations committees, as they were called. These company unions mostly expressed the will of management through self-converted employees, as indicated by the fact that in the 1920s, these committees became forums through which employees expressed their desire to perform their work more courteously.[85]

Quitting was still possible, but the skills of utility workers, such as telephone operating and streetcar conducting, were not easily transferable to other industries. Most utilities monopolized these occupations within their service territory, which often covered multiple states, so employees could not easily find work at another utility without moving long distances. Many employees also simply had to work to make ends meet, even if that meant emotional labor. "You can't afford to get angry," an employee magazine rudely, yet accurately, reminded employees. The observation must have rung especially true for many female clerks, who also faced occupational sex discrimination and therefore had even fewer employment options than their male counterparts.[86] With the avenues of organizing and quitting foreclosed for many employees, and under immense pressure to conform from managers and customers, some employees convinced themselves about the rightness—perhaps even righteousness—of courteous capitalism, and self-converted.

This self-conversion becomes even more comprehensible when one considers evidence from social psychologists. Although this type of evidence is often not admitted by historians, clerks may not have been able to dismiss it so easily. Psychologists have found that individuals paid small amounts of money to make statements contrary to how they actually feel about a tedious task often later report agreeing with their own lies. Psychologists explain this by arguing that individuals try to resolve the cognitive dissonance they feel after lying by bringing their emotions into conformance with their statements. Since the paltry reward these subjects received does not seem to justify their lying, they eventually convince themselves that they must have actually enjoyed the task. Psychologists identified this phenomenon experimentally in the 1960s, though Samuel Kennedy and others observed it in practice much earlier. In 1922, Kennedy explained to colleagues that, with respect to clerks required to be courteous, "those men who go into it against their will, [but] who put into effect the rules and regulations you make, a little later become enthusiastic."[87]

Whether clerks, conductors, and operators could justify their emotional labor with their wages, and therefore would not have been subject to this psychological phenomenon, depended on each worker's financial circumstance and the time period in which they worked. Before the 1920s, operators made more than women manufacturing workers and urban saleswomen, though less than schoolteachers. After 1920, however, the wages of both men and women in service sector jobs declined relative to other positions.[88]

Social psychologists have also found that individuals told to assume facial expressions and body postures begin to feel how they are acting. Since both facial expressions and postures of low-paid customer service clerks were all under strict control, it is not surprising that some of these low-paid emotional laborers began to feel how they were acting.[89]

Whether self-converted or not, customers noticed that utility clerks exhibited odd interpersonal behavior. "The voice [of the operator] seems strangely impersonal; little more than the sound of an automaton, wound up always to say the same things over and over again," one telephone user observed.[90] "The thing about the utility industry that interests, almost fascinates me, is the tremendously personal service which it renders," wrote John Colton, a closet critic of the streetcar industry while working as editor of the American Electric Railway Association's magazine, *AERA*. Colton wrote this passage to his friend, John Sheridan of Missouri, who also worked as a publicist in the utilities industry. Sheridan replied that utilities were drilling too many "yes-men" who did not have "much mind of [their] own."[91]

The strange behavior of utility clerks was also noticed by an executive assistant named Richard Smith. In the mid-1930s, Smith wrote an article describing the changes in the utility industry over the last generation. He also described how his father, who had owned a general store, had provided genuinely friendly service to customers. Smith then asked an important question: "In the interval between Dad's day and mine what has happened to change the relation between a merchant and his customers?" Smith provided his own answer in a section entitled "Putting on a Front." "I have a feeling that there is something artificial about all of us who have come into positions even of minor authority," he observed, intending to include utility clerks. "It would be difficult for me to return to Dad's store and pick up the work where he left it. It would be hard to be natural," Smith said, "I know that I have acquired traits and mannerisms which would be misunderstood. That is why a professional actor is out of place in a group of ordinary men and women; he has lived so long in an artificial environment, so much of his life has been devoted to pretense and make-believe, that he cannot be natural."[92] According to Smith, the interactions between clerks and customers at utilities had changed dramatically since the days when the economy was dominated by mom-and-pop shops. In an attempt to "humanize" and "personalize" interactions with enormous organizations, utility executives created a strange unnaturalness to human interactions.[93]

Welfare Capitalism for Courteous Capitalism

Although utility companies used ideology and self-conversion to extract emotional labor, they also used more down-to-earth methods. The most straightforward of these was welfare capitalism. Scholars have understood welfare capitalism as the strategy of providing benefits to employees in an effort to undermine union agitation and increase production, which it certainly was.[94] Yet at utilities, welfare capitalism operated in the service of courteous capitalism.[95] In a speech on the connection between welfare work and public relations, an AT&T manager declared that "these two policies, while they can be given two separate names, are either linked together like the Siamese twins, or perhaps better, they are different aspects of the same thing."[96] As AT&T vice president E. K. Hall declared at a personnel conference in 1922, "Public Relations is a double-header, accomplishing two purposes at once, building up the internal morale and building up good will outside."[97]

Utility executives believed that welfare benefits would produce happy employees who would then pass on that happiness to customers.[98] As an AT&T manager declared, "Personnel work is for the sake of building up morale, which will, in turn, is one of the main factors in developing the desired public relations." In providing welfare benefits, he noted, "really our ultimate objective is the development of public relations."[99]

To obtain this improvement in public relations, utilities offered their employees all kinds of benefits, including company picnics, trips to amusement parks, summer camps, paid vacations, stock ownership plans, pensions, and life insurance. Companies also offered sports leagues, service awards, flowers for sick employees, and classes in fitness, sewing, singing, and dancing. One company even offered courses from Yale's Department of History![100] PG&E and SCE built health clubs for their employees throughout their territories, the latter to boost the "Edison spirit," as one executive put it.[101] SCE also sponsored its own chapter of Masons, sixty-strong, and lent the "Edison Masons" company cars to allow them to visit other Masons in California.[102]

Many utilities also built well-appointed break rooms where employees could relax or recuperate before another shift at the customer service counter, switchboard, or streetcar.[103] Some utilities even built entire club houses where workers could hang out after work.[104] Samuel Kennedy noted the public relations intent of these facilities when he told executives the club houses were "valuable in connection with the general question of relations with employees, which means also relations with the public."[105] A Michigan Bell employee expressed the purpose and success of his company's club houses when he declared that the parties held there were "rousing, cheering, fret-destroying. Therefore, they build for good service."[106]

Many other executives also noted the success of welfare capitalism in producing courteous service. The vice president of the San Joaquin Light and Power Company enthused that, due to his company's employee stock ownership program, which attracted 98 percent participation, each employee-owner "has a different point of view" and now "seeks to make friends for the company, and . . . [is] an earnest promoter of good will."[107] In AT&T's 1916 *Annual Report*, President Theodore Vail observed that the pension, employee stock ownership, and insurance programs offered in 1913 had succeeded in producing "the beneficial effects then hoped for" since employees were now performing their jobs "cheerfully."[108] These same welfare benefits were also offered at Bell System's Western Electric manufacturing plants in an attempt to increase production. But perhaps more importantly to Vail, the benefits improved Bell customer service at operating companies, which promised to thwart government ownership.[109]

Vail noted this government-ownership context in the 1916 *Annual Report* when he stated that there had recently been "movements to nationalize or municipalize the telephone service." He then reminded shareholders that "the attitude of the public is determined by the quality of the service and by the attitude of those giving the service and coming in direct contact with the public."[110] So while AT&T's manufacturing company, Western Electric, used welfare benefits to produce products, AT&T's operating companies used welfare benefits to produce courtesy. Manufacturing companies employed welfare capitalism to solve internal labor problems, while utility companies employed welfare capitalism to solve external political problems.[111]

Utility executives understood other early twentieth-century management strategies such as system and efficiency, but they realized that the customer service line was not the assembly line. Customers could not be rushed or treated curtly, even if that improved through-put. "Zeal for departmental

Courteous Capitalism Intensifies   73

efficiency should never be permitted to . . . disadvantage of the composite service rendered to our customers," taught a Pacific Telephone & Telegraph Company (PT&T) training manual.[112] "Life is not so short but that there is always enough time for courtesy," stated the company's magazine, quoting Ralph Waldo Emerson.[113]

Rather, executives taught clerks to take their time, individualizing each customer. In 1921, Samuel Insull advised his employees to chat up customers about the weather, since that might make the customer "feel more agreeable, and take her mind off her desire for a discussion as to the amount of that particular electric light or gas bill."[114] A Bell manager wrote that every employee had to "do his or her part in providing for the customer, as an individual."[115] "The duty of the counter clerk is to . . . render personal service, not mere company service," noted a Michigan Bell employee magazine. This would help in "winning the public."[116] While some historians have argued that "customers" became mere "consumers" in the Progressive Era, courteous capitalism reveals an important exception. Utilities put the *custom* back into *customer* and did so on a massive scale.[117]

"Friends"

In a sense, what executives were doing was trying to make friends with customers. Executives sought to befriend customers, not irritate them. Industrialists in the Gilded Age had also tried to make friends, but their friends were financial and political elites, not everyday Americans. One famous historian has observed that Gilded Age railroad tycoons specifically referred to certain individuals as their "friends," either in correspondence with them, or in discussion about them when writing to close business associates. These "political friends," as this historian dubbed them, were usually politicians, financiers, or political power brokers, whose influence had been brought into line with the railroads through campaign donations, securities discounts, construction contracts, free traveling passes, or other considerations.[118]

Political friends had also once existed at the municipal level between utility executives and city council members. But when these friendships were glaringly exposed by muckrakers, utility executives found themselves in want of new friends. Executives then sought regular everyday customers as friends, instead of political bigwigs. In the Progressive Era and 1920s, having friends still mattered, but who they were, how they were made, and how many one needed changed dramatically.

Although utility executives now sought a new group of friends, the purpose of having them was still political. A 1913 employee magazine article observed that "in this day of universal unrest there seems to be slowly but surely developing a strong prejudice against the larger business concerns, and more especially toward those that are classed as public utilities." The solution, the article maintained, was for every employee to "develop a spirit of friendship that will counteract this prejudice." The article concluded that "the standing and reputation of the company" depended on employees "pleasing the public, and thereby developing friends." The editors of *Public Service Management* dispensed with all subtlety when they published "Using Your Friend." "Most public utilities have a *few* friends at least," a May 1921 editorial allowed. "The friend is anxious to defend the company under unjust attack but he has no information with which to refute the false statements of the demagogue." The solution, the magazine suggested, was for managers to buy their friends a subscription to *Public Service Magazine*, a similar publication to the one for managers, but especially designed for friends. The editors promised that copies "placed in the hands of your friends every month will prove a great power for good, because it will give these same friends a supply of ammunition to be used against the enemy. . . . By winning his neighbors he will be helping you."[119]

Executives now wanted to make friends with customers, or rather, they wanted their clerks to do it for them. Giving a magazine subscription was good, but the most effective method was to give courteous service. As a PG&E employee magazine article taught employees, "telephone-talk is often the means of making or losing a friend."[120] The New England Telephone and Telegraph Company published a similar article entitled "Friendly Service" in its employee bulletin. "Everybody has Friends," the article observed, "our friends are our friends because first they know us, and second they like us. We know they are friends because they always speak well of us."[121] In the Progressive Era and 1920s, executives still spoke the language of friends, but who they were and how they were made had changed.

Loyal Complainers

By US entry into World War I, customers began internalizing their role as friends. This proved especially true in the aspect of giving feedback to companies. Ever since McAdoo invited passengers to complain to him, customers had been told that complaining was not annoying, but rather a favor. "Help us take pains to please you by cooperative criticism," a Boston Edison ad-

Courteous Capitalism Intensifies 75

vertisement subserviently implored.[122] AT&T vice president E. K. Hall instructed his employees not to "bristle at the man who makes a complaint" but to "make him feel that he is doing you a favor."[123] One gets some insight into how this complaining impacted clerks from an employee magazine article that stated: "Every week day the counter-men of the San Francisco Gas and Electric Company stand patiently and take the public's kicks."[124]

To make complaining easier for customers, managers trained clerks to receive complaints with seriousness and concern. Rather than being scoffed at, displeased customers were now thanked. Some utilities even built separate "complaint booths" so that customers could complain in private and not infect other customers. When customers came in to complain, they were triaged to a separate area where they were attended to by a specialized "complaint clerk." One company, which installed several of these rooms, reported that they produced "satisfactory results."[125]

The invitation to complain sharply contrasted with the time period before courteous capitalism. A Stone & Webster vice president recalled that in the late nineteenth century when customers complained at his Tampa Bay streetcar company, employees just thought, "Oh well don't pay any attention to that. He's always kicking against the company." The executive mused that, back then, he "didn't know anything about public relations; in fact, public relations wasn't a subject that was discussed at that time by anybody."[126] In the late 1920s, AT&T president Walter Gifford recalled that before about 1910, if customers came in to complain, employees said to themselves, "For Heaven's sake, don't come in here and bother us!"[127] In 1906, the employee magazine of the Pacific Electric streetcar line blamed passengers for their own dissatisfaction and referred to them as "impatient people, ignorant people, stupid and obstinate people . . . cross people, drunken people, unreasonable people." Ten years later, the company declared that passengers deserved "gentlemanly and courteous attention," and managers sought to eliminate "cross" conductors.[128]

Many customers reciprocated the courtesy they received. "Verily courtesy breeds courtesy," McAdoo observed.[129] "Courtesy is contagious," noted a telephone operator, "the subscriber involuntarily responds to her [the operator's] cheerful phrases in the same pleasant tone of voice."[130] Yet even this operator noted that telephone subscribers sometimes behaved rudely and that operators could not do anything about it.

Other customers appear to have delighted in their newfound power over service workers. Contemporary accounts show that some customers sauntered

A customer and "complaint clerk" in a "complaint booth" at the Consolidated Gas, Electric Light, and Power Company of Baltimore, Maryland. "Conducting a Public Utility Complaint Department," *Public Service*, April 1913, 130.

around the commercial office scrutinizing products and people, and rejecting both without deigning to give an explanation. Some customers also disparaged clerks, operators, and conductors. By the 1920s, this had become an acceptable, and even admired, form of behavior in the mind of some consumers. Executives approved of this abrupt behavior, and even invited it. "Talk back to us," encouraged a Boston Edison advertisement that solicited customer complaints.[131] A PG&E publication instructed customers: "Go down to the Gas Company's Office with visage determined and grim, You'll see a

Courteous Capitalism Intensifies   77

young fellow there smiling, then go tell your troubles to him, Tell him your meter is leaking—your Gas Bill was never so high . . . just go down and unload them on him."[132] The text was written somewhat in jest but the emotional roles and power relations were still clear. In the roles defined by courteous capitalism, the customer was the honored guest, the clerk the obsequious servant. The customer was entitled to feel like a king, and the job of maintaining that feeling fell to the clerk.

Occasionally, however, clerks ruined this role-playing by failing to stay in character. In some cases, this occurred when clerks realized they were not going to make a sale and figured there was no point in treating the customer nicely anymore since no commission would be forthcoming. Yet when this happened, customers faulted the clerk's character, and specifically the clerk's lack of self-control and delayed gratification. The clerk should have remained solicitous, the critique went, since doing so might lead to a sale in the future, and perhaps a loyal customer. The clerk was just out to make a quick buck and lacked the long-term outlook that resulted in eventual success. As one business consultant advised, sales clerks should focus on "making a customer" not "making a sale."[133]

Accusing a clerk of lacking the traits of self-control and delayed gratification was no casual critique, it cut to the heart of Victorian personhood. Victorians defined each other by their character, the two central pillars of which were self-control and delayed gratification. To critique an individual regarding these traits amounted to a serious attack. Yet by playing the role of the reproving customer, ever ready to correct the failings of clerks, customers could imagine themselves as upholders of Victorian character, even while relinquishing their own delayed gratification by buying appliances on credit, which Victorian economic morality frowned upon.. By pretending to accept these reproofs, clerks negotiated a way for customers to engage in the growing consumer culture of the early twentieth century.[134] Commercial utility offices were therefore a central theater in the tug-of-war between Victorian culture of the nineteenth century and the consumer culture of the twentieth century.

As customers began expecting courtesy, and complaining when it was not forthcoming, they also began developing a consumer class consciousness. In this class system, consumers held power by virtue of their potential to spend money. Yet what was unique about this class system was that, unlike racial or aristocratic classes, the clerks themselves could quickly jump out of their roles as service workers and transform themselves into shoppers by punching

A clerk waits on customers as they inspect an electric coffee percolator at the Southern California Edison commercial office in Santa Monica. Santa Monica office of SCE, June 17, 1916. G. Haven Bishop, photographer, Call No. 02 03681, SCEPN.

the clock and stuffing a fistful of dollars from their pay envelopes into their pockets. As the *Saturday Evening Post* suggested in a cartoon that was reprinted by PG&E, workers could easily adopt the identity of a consumer or even the capitalist.[135] In 1914, *System* magazine asked clerks to imagine themselves in the customer's shoes so that the clerks could provide "the right kind of service."[136] This task was not difficult for clerks. Anyone who had money, or even the willingness to use credit, including off-duty clerks, could play the role of shopper. This included exercising the uncivil prerogatives that went with it. This may help explain the longevity of courteous capitalism.

One exception to this was race. African American customers may not have been able to exercise the same power over utility clerks as white customers. The sources are mostly silent about this, but a Southern Bell employee magazine recounted an instance in which a white clerk treated a black customer in a discourteous manner. The customer made a joke, but rather than accepting the humor, the clerk replied in an officious and condescending manner that included a recitation of company policy. The article gave no indication

The *Saturday Evening Post* recognized that workers could easily change roles, as shown in this cartoon. "P. G. and E. Progress," January 1928, cartoon reprinted from a 1927 *Saturday Evening Post*, Box 440, Folder 8, SCE Records.

that this treatment was not allowed, rather, the opposite was implied. Yet such rude and inflexible treatment of white customers was already strictly forbidden.[137] Although courtesy toward customers meant courtesy irrespective of class, this did not necessarily mean courtesy irrespective of race, and race seems to have trumped class when it came to who received courteous service.

Did Courteous Capitalism Work?

Did courteous capitalism work? In addition to William McAdoo's rousing success, other cases show that the strategy worked. One successful practitioner of courteous capitalism was Samuel Kahn, who ran the Market Street Railway in San Francisco. Kahn became the trolley company's vice president in 1925, when the line was purchased by the Byllesby Company, one of the largest utility operators in the United States.

At the time of the purchase, the Market Street Railway had a major public relations problem. It had formerly been headed by a protégé of J. P. Morgan named Patrick Calhoun, who sullied the company's reputation by being indicted for municipal corruption in the Overhead Graft Scandal in the first decade of the twentieth century. Yet Calhoun was cleared thanks to a hung jury and continued to oversee the railway until he retired in 1913.

In that year, the Market Street Railway's plight worsened when San Francisco voters approved a referendum extending the city's publicly owned streetcar system into the service territory of the Market Street Railway. Several strikes by employees of the line followed, further weakening the company. By 1917, investors demanded the refinancing of the company's debt, and the bank that analyzed the company's bonds found that one of the line's main problems was "adverse public opinion." By 1924, when the Byllesby Company purchased the line, the Market Street Railway had just five years remaining on its original fifty-year franchise, after which time it would face a referendum on its future. Samuel Kahn had to turn around public opinion, or the company would lose its license.

To do this, Kahn embraced courteous capitalism.[138] He told his employees that he wanted "every person who rides on our cars to have a friendly feeling towards us," and that he wanted his employees to "make friends as well as money."[139] To train his workers to do this, the company began featuring a "Better Public Relations" column in its employee magazine. The March 1926 column entitled "Avoid Antagonism" taught that "a conductor should handle each passenger in such a manner that he will feel that special interest is being taken in his case." If this was done, the column promised, passengers would have "greater respect for the employee and the Company he represents." "People are not all bad," the column allowed, instead, "those who are inclined to be hostile we can make our friends by showing an interest in them rather than arousing their antagonism." Another "Better Public Relations" column covered "Collecting Fares for Children," which instructed employees to avoid giving offense to parents while still collecting the money.[140] "The passenger may be taking the child along, not because she wants to," explained the columnist, "but because she has no place to leave it. And she imagines that the Company is taking an unjust advantage of her inconvenience." Conductors were therefore instructed to insist on full fares for children over five, but to do so courteously. Perhaps to offset this policy, Kahn offered free travel for school children during field trips to the zoo and other destinations, and teachers and honor roll students received free rulers and other giveaways.[141]

The Market Street Railway Company spent so much money on public relations that city officials began complaining that the money could be better spent actually running the line.[142] Yet people loved the newly refashioned company, and when the referendum came up in 1929, over 55 percent of San Francisco voters chose to extend the company's franchise for another twenty-five years.[143] This vote was not the result of Americans in the 1920s becoming disinterested in reform and eager to reduce taxes and the size of government. The previous year, the same voters in San Francisco approved a $41-million bond issue to buy out the city's hated private water monopoly and create a city-owned water utility in its place.[144] Kahn won the referendum for the Market Street Railway by implementing courteous capitalism.

Testimonies of utility executives and regulators also indicate that courteous capitalism worked. The policy worked so well that by the late 1920s executives were practically gleeful about the public attitude toward utilities and the current state of regulation, and believed that courteous capitalism had been the secret to achieving this state of affairs. In 1927, Martin Insull, Samuel's brother, boasted before a NELA audience that he had taken over utilities in Indiana and "changed the public opinion of those communities from one of unfriendliness to one of friendliness." Martin Insull credited "giving service in the broadest sense to those communities," which caused "a very great change" in the local opinion "toward those various operating companies."[145] In a 1925 speech to utility managers, the president of a Brooklyn power company recalled a time "when our industry was universally viewed with suspicion and antagonism." There were still some people who felt that way, he admitted, but he did not think "they are general, or representative of the basic views of the majority of our American people. We have reason to believe they are not."[146] Samuel Kennedy also noted that, after focusing on customer service, "the public is satisfied," and his company did not "have many of the difficulties now which we hear exist in other places and which we used to have. The attitude of our people is satisfactory." Kennedy credited this improved customer satisfaction with creating friendlier political oversight. "If we want a right of way in some particular location, we don't have any trouble getting it," he noted. "If we want a permit or a franchise or something like that, we don't have any difficulty in getting it. We find that the [California] Railroad Commission, individually and collectively, is friendly all the way down the line, and, with all modesty I say it, that our Company is held up as an example in public relations."[147]

Personnel at the California Railroad Commission, which oversaw utilities in the state, also noticed the change. The commission's chief engineer recalled that, before the improvement in public relations, one company had asked for a rate increase, yet when its representatives showed up for the rate hearing, the room was "packed with protestants." The commission granted the rate hike anyway, arguing that it was financially justified, but both the commission and the utility received an enormous amount of "scorn." Then the company appointed a new manager who "believed in fair treatment and confidence and honesty with his consumer." A year later, when the company asked for another rate increase, they received it without public backlash.[148] Kennedy also noticed the change at commission hearings. Before one rate hearing, the commission notified every customer, but when the company's representatives showed up, they found a small room that "wasn't half full." There were lawyers from a few municipalities, but even they were not opposed to the rate increase. "Although I do not say it is the entire reason," Kennedy summarized, "I believe that the attitude of the public toward the company had a great deal to do with the favorable manner in which the increased rate was received."[149]

These observations were confirmed by customers. Many wrote in to thank utility workers for their kind treatment. One customer wrote to thank SCE for "the courtesy shown me" by those installing "gas at my place." The customer also thanked "all others in your office with whom occasion brought me in contact during the past" and whose service "leaves a pleasant memory instead of a sting." Another customer of the same company wrote to thank everyone, including "the man who climbs the pole," who had "been more than courteous, and have shown [every] consideration possible."[150] One Commonwealth Edison customer in Chicago penned a handwritten letter begging the company to "please"—underlined three times—come out and fix his lights and adjust his bill, or else uninstall his meter. A short time later, the same customer wrote again with an illustration of two men shaking hands and one saying, "Thank you for prompt attention and courteous treatment, also the satisfactory adjustment of my little 'tale of woe.'" The company had made another friend.[151]

Discourteous Government Control

The opposite of courteous capitalism also strengthened corporate utilities by helping to thwart government ownership. During World War I, the US government nationalized the telephone network and placed it under the control of the postmaster general. Bell employees still operated the lines but beginning in July 1918, they took orders from Postmaster General Albert Burleson. Burleson and many others within President Wilson's administration wanted to permanently nationalize the telephone lines. But in what can be called "discourteous government control," Bell employees succeeded in destroying the reputation of government control through rude treatment to customers.

When the government took control of the nation's telephone lines the worst nightmare of Bell executives became a reality, despite the fact that AT&T president Theodore Vail personally got along with Postmaster Burleson. Since they both hated unions, Vail tried to use the opportunity of nationalization to weaken the operators' unions. But Burleson sought to make nationalization permanent, which Vail of course opposed.[152]

To prevent permanent nationalization, Bell employees began providing poor service. When the government took over the lines, courtesy and customer service at Bell plummeted. Many customers suspected that this was an intentional attempt by Bell employees to undermine government ownership. And since Burleson had adopted McAdoo's idea of inviting customers to complain directly to him, many telephone users did not hesitate to inform Burleson of their suspicions. One customer from Sacramento wrote that PT&T employees were "insolent" and "very impudent over the phone without reason," and that this all began "since the Co's have been taken over by you." The customer added, "In my opinion—and others give me their views same as mine—the Company thru their employees are seeking to discredit

Government management."[153] The district manager of the Sacramento office who was named in the letter denied the accusation when his boss wrote to him to find out the details. Yet the boss did not seem to care very much.[154] Ironically, in making this complaint, the customer mistakenly did not write to Burleson but to McAdoo, who by this time had become director general of the railroads. Like Burleson, McAdoo also favored permanent nationalization, but now McAdoo's own strategy of courteous capitalism was working against him. Corporate monopolies had learned the destructive power of rude clerks and the benefits of courtesy and were now seeking to destroy government ownership through poor customer service.

Other customers also suspected the Bell System of purposely providing poor service to sink government ownership. One lawyer from Portland wrote Burleson that "since the Government has taken over the telephone lines here the service has been something fierce." The customer recounted that it took him nearly a half hour to reach "central," and when he finally got through and inquired if the switchboard had enough workers, the chief operator told him that the office was not understaffed at all. The customer then informed Burleson that he would not complain if the war effort had caused the delay, "but I know certain interests are greatly alarmed lest government control be a success."[155]

Eventually Burleson got fed up with the rude behavior of Bell employees. He wrote a letter to Bell companies fuming that he was receiving "a number of letters . . . stating that patrons of the telegraph and telephone service are not always accorded courteous treatment by the employees, also that when [a] complaint is made the employees frequently state that the delay or other trouble is due to instructions issued by the Post Office Department when such is not the case." Burleson dictated that "indifference or non-concern in relations with the public or the service rendered will not be tolerated and must give way to a spirit of interest." Borrowing a page from utility managers, he claimed that "close attention to duty and courteous treatment involve no hardships and cost nothing, but mean much to the public." Burleson ended his edict threatening that "those in charge will be held strictly accountable for the service, also for the conduct of the employees under their supervision, toward the public."[156]

Yet simply making demands of employees was not how to elicit courteous service, as executives at privately owned utilities had already learned. Yet Burleson did not know this because he directed a government-owned mono-

Courteous Capitalism Intensifies 85

poly. The Post Office had never had to provide courteous service, since it had always been government owned.[157]

Burleson's blustering did not change the attitude of Bell managers and employees. In addition to tolerating discourteous clerks, when government control began Bell managers started rigidly enforcing policies in ways they never would have before. Customers' objections to these policies were rudely dismissed. When Burleson increased the installation charge for new telephones from $3.50 to $10 on September 1, 1918, employees at PT&T informed all its customers who had already signed up for new service but who had not yet received installation that they too owed more money thanks to the government-mandated fee increase. PT&T managers strictly interpreted Burleson's installation charge "to be on the safe side," the president of the company said. If customers did not want to pay the extra money, PT&T made no objection and simply did not install the phone. The president of PT&T admitted that customers had a point when they argued that they had already entered into a contract with his company before the higher rate was announced, but that did not stop the company from enforcing the new charge.[158]

Predictably, the strict reading of Burleson's order angered customers. One customer in Spokane wrote the government to express his displeasure and noted that he knew "others who are greatly dissatisfied."[159] Another customer contacted a lawyer.[160] One woman complained in writing to the Post Office and received a letter back from the assistant postmaster in Washington, DC, stating that she should not have to pay the charges. But when she showed the letter to her local telephone manager, the manager said he was under different instructions from PT&T and that if she wanted the phone installed, she would have to pay the higher fee. "This is a matter affecting scores of others besides myself," she wrote to the government, "and I feel that it is not the desire of your Department to have the public unjustly dealt with."[161]

After several letters of complaint reached AT&T, a company vice president, Nathan Kingsbury, wrote a letter to the vice president of PT&T clarifying that the Post Office did not want the higher charges applied to customers who had already signed up for service. But even Kingsbury, a Bell executive who had built his career on public relations, was not that bothered by the behavior of PT&T employees.

It is nearly impossible to imagine that any Bell manager by this time would have treated customers this way had nationalization not been in effect. Before nationalization, Bell executives frequently told managers that they should let small charges to customers slide and not enforce policies too rigidly in the interest of public relations. But during the period of nationalization, PT&T disregarded all these past policies.

Eventually, Bell's sabotage of government ownership through discourtesy, coupled with Burleson's poor labor relations and his raising of telephone charges, destroyed any chance of permanent nationalization. By June 1919, the American Federation of Labor ceased calling for permanent nationalization. Before World War I and the experience with Burleson's management and Bell's discourtesy, many people supported the idea of nationalization of the wires. But that support eroded by the end of the war.[162] After the war, Bell had to reinstill courtesy throughout its organization, but at least it had its monopoly back.

Conclusion

In the Progressive Era and 1920s, customers focused their political anger on utilities and demanded an end to political corruption and financial mismanagement. These aspects of utility operation changed, but at a cost. Customers became the subject of numerous interviews and surveys, while utility clerks endured a steady stream of complaining customers. Managers used this customer feedback to regulate the emotional conduct of clerks. Executives also sought to make clerks self-regulating through ideology, Christianity, and the spirit of service.

Customer service improved, yet sincerity during interpersonal interactions declined. As the emotional freedom of clerks declined, the artificiality of interactions increased. Yet this did not undermine the success of courteous capitalism. As specific cases have demonstrated, courtesy reduced animosity toward corporate utilities, while discourtesy during World War I increased opposition toward government control. Encouraged by the deference of clerks, Americans relinquished their antimonopoly sentiments, lost faith in municipal ownership, and accepted the corporate monopolization of important utility services.

CHAPTER THREE

The Architecture of Consent

At the beginning of the twentieth century, a typical utility office where customers went to sign up for service, pay their bill, or dispute a charge looked like the one in the photograph on page 88, which shows the Edison Electric Company in 1906. The door on the left reads "Accounting Dept." Here a busy hive of bureaucrats took in information, processed it, and stored it for later use. By rationalizing the enormous amount of information inherent in the large corporation, these clerks made the corporation legible to itself, making the late nineteenth century accounting office "arguably the most important production site in the industrializing economy," according to one historian.[1]

In the early twentieth century, however, utility executives shifted their focus from the account clerks in the foreground of this photograph to the customer service clerks, their customers, and the physical barriers that stood between them, in the background of this photograph. A few of these customers are barely visible here through the bars, frosted glass, and partitions at the back of the office. Executives began to realize that these clerks, and the offices they worked in, not only made the corporation legible to itself, but also made the corporation legible to customers; and increasingly executives did not like the message customers received there.

This negative impression not only resulted from poor customer service, executives believed, but also from the office design itself. The bars, partitions, and counters at utility offices barricaded employees from outsiders and architecturally expressed to customers the secretive and embattled mentality of monopolies. This impression of secrecy bred suspicion among customers that utilities had something to hide. During the era of "zealous muckrakers," a *Southern Bell Telephone* magazine editor noted, "most public utilities enveloped their actions in a veil of secrecy."[2] In turn, customers viewed utilities

The accounting office of the Edison Electric Company in Los Angeles, a predecessor to SCE, 1906. Call No. 01 00592, SCEPN, http://cdm16003.contentdm.oclc.org/cdm/singleitem/collection/p16003coll2/id/287/rec/10. Thanks to Jennifer A. Watts, Curator of Photographs at the Huntington Library, for helping to date this photograph.

as "very secretive" and "suspected" them of having "lots of political pull," observed B. C. Forbes, a financial journalist and utilities consultant.[3]

Utility managers directly linked this negative view of utilities to their opaque office architecture. "For years," a utility manager wrote in 1922, "executives have been pictured by demagogues as corpulent tyrants possessed of hoofs and horns who sit behind closed doors and frosted glass and figure only on how they can mulct the public out of a few more pennies."[4] If one goes to "buy some current, some gas, some transportation," a utility publicist complained in 1922, "you must approach, amid a long line of applicants, a small window in a heavy grille, behind which sits an austere person." Poor architecture and sour clerks, the publicist argued, were "an unfortunate hangover from the good old days of monopoly" when utilities held all the power and consumers had none.[5]

To fix this negative image, executives ordered the wholescale remodeling of their customer service offices. Workers removed the barred windows, frosted glass, and high counters that separated clerks from customers, and replaced these "closed offices" with new "open offices," as managers called them.[6] Executives reasoned that if customers could see and hear what was going on in the customer service office, and physically move around within these spaces, the widespread suspicion of utilities would be replaced with confidence that private monopolies had nothing to hide. By the late 1920s, utility executives had remodeled not only the behavior of their clerks, but also the interiors of the offices in which they labored, all in an effort to improve public opinion.

Branch offices have mostly lived in the shadow of their bigger siblings, the massive downtown skyscraper. Yet branch offices were far more numerous than skyscrapers, symbolic in their own right, and much more familiar to the public.[7] As utility use rapidly expanded in the 1910s and 1920s, customers streamed into these offices to sign up for service. One telephone office in Alameda, California, averaged 10,300 visitors a month in 1914 and recorded a single-day high of 802 customers.[8] And this was but a fraction of the ten million Bell subscribers who signed up for service nationwide between 1910 and 1930, many of whom had to do so in person.[9] Electricity connectivity surged even more over the same time period, going from less than 10 percent of urban residents to well over 90 percent, with a third of customers in the late 1920s still having to register for service in person.[10] Customers also visited commercial offices to pay their monthly bill, "kick" against the company, or buy streetcar tokens, light bulbs, stock certificates, or electrical appliances.[11] Visiting the local office was so common that one executive stated in 1923 that 95 percent of electricity customers knew "the front office and persons in charge there."[12]

Utilities maintained scores of branch offices to handle the large number of customers. In 1921, the Southern California Edison Company (SCE) maintained sixty branch offices, many of which featured the new open office design. In 1928, Public Service Company of Illinois provided thirty-eight branch offices, which also frequently featured the open office.[13] The Bell System built even more commercial offices. By 1930, the Bell System possessed nearly 6,000 buildings total, including 749 branch offices, 400 of which had open layouts. These offices served small towns and residential neighborhoods throughout the United States. By the late 1920s, hundreds of open offices existed in towns and cities throughout America, making these meek branch offices the physical symbol of corporate utility monopolies for most Americans.[14]

Utility executives were keenly aware of the importance of these branch offices, and made sure their employees understood it as well. One "reading assignment" in a Bell System training manual stated that branch offices were "very important" since "nearly all the business negotiations involving . . .

A "closed office" at a predecessor to the Southern California Edison Company called the Edison Electric Company, Los Angeles, 1907. The office features high counters, iron bars, and frosted glass. The sign at the top left reads "Payments"; the sign on the top right reads "Applications and Adjustments." This is the same office shown in the photograph on page 88, but from the customers' point of view. G. Haven Bishop, photographer, "Teller Payment Windows at the Los Angeles Business Office," 1907, Call No. 02 00595, SCEPN, https://hdl.huntington.org/digital/collection/p16003coll2/id/12455.

A new "open office" at SCE in 1919, featuring low counters, no bars, and no glass partitions. Smiling women also replaced scowling men in many customer service positions by this time. G. Haven Bishop, photographer, "Edison Building (3rd & Broadway)," "Typical Edison Business Office," Call No. 02 05170, SCEPN, http://cdm16003.contentdm.oclc.org/cdm/singleitem/collection/p16003coll2/id/16740/rec/3.

serving the customers" were conducted in the offices. "The commercial department thus represents the entire company," the manual taught.[15] Another reading assignment noted that "when our customers come into a commercial office to transact their business . . . it is of vital importance that they carry away with them the impression that our offices are well arranged, well handled, and attractive."[16]

Department stores, dime stores, and chain grocery stores had already spearheaded the mass reproduction of commercial storefronts, and in the post–World War II era a great deal of America would be covered with these structures. Utilities were early participants in this trend, yet also unique since the goal of utility offices was not merely to sell products but to improve public opinion in order to maintain their monopolies. Unlike shoppers at traditional retail outlets, customers at utilities had no choice of where to purchase their service. Many utility offices, especially telephone ones, did not even have any tangible products to sell.[17] Like the strategy of courteous capitalism, utility offices were not mainly designed to sell products but to sell the idea of good corporate monopolies.

The Open Office and Surveillance

The first attempt to bring about a positive impression of utilities through architecture occurred in the electricity industry around 1910. At that time, executives began removing partitions and lowering counters to make clerks more visible and accessible to customers.[18] Executives believed that if they removed the physical barriers between clerks and customers, they could remove the political barriers between them as well. By eliminating the obstructions in the closed office, the new open office invited customers to inspect the utility's operations and linger within a shared architectural space like members of a family.[19]

This transition from the closed office to the open office was no accident. It was not simply a haphazard change as companies grew and styles changed. Rather, each feature of the open office was meticulously selected with the goal of pleasing customers. "Every detail of the arrangement and management" of the new open offices was specifically designed to provide "good service with courteous attention," reported an SCE magazine in 1914.[20] "Give your office a clean, open appearance, and you are going to please your customers," declared Samuel Kennedy, a vice president at the same company, in 1921. Grating and glass, Kennedy taught, "make the consumer feel that he is something on the outside of the organization, that he must come in on his hands and knees to do business, and that while he is waited on, he is at the mercy of this terrible man who looks out at him through a little cubby hole." But, "if you look a consumer squarely in the face and he looks you squarely in the face, you are going to feel different toward each other, than if you are dodging back and forth, looking through a pigeon hole."[21]

Visibility of employees to customers was therefore a key design goal of the new open office. The open office was "so arranged that the district agent and his assistants are at all times visible and accessible to the company's customers and the public," boasted an SCE employee magazine article in 1914. The design allowed customers to see both managers and employees as soon as customers entered the office.

After the advent of the open office, however, Kennedy noted that some managers were hiding, "probably in a back room." The problem was visual. "You can't see him. A customer can't see him," Kennedy complained. The manager was "not visible." "Now then," Kennedy declared, "in business hours, he should be visible; he should be accessible to take care of customers who want to see him."[22]

A closed office of the Edison Electric Company in Long Beach, California, 1905. A customer, wearing a hat, is barely visible in the back of the photograph. "Edison Electric Company Office Staff, Long Beach," 1905, Call No. 01 00784, SCEPN.

The Architecture of Consent 93

An open office of SCE in Pomona, California, 1923. The corporate hierarchy within the office was reflected spatially. "Local Offices A–Z," 1923, Call No. 02 08845, SCEPN.

The open office not only made employees more visible to customers, it also made lower level employees more visible to supervisors. Typical open offices included a few rows of desks with the lowest-level clerks, usually women, occupying the front row. This row was closest to customers and the clerks who sat there performed the most emotional labor. Behind these clerks sat their supervisor, known as the chief clerk, as well as a bookkeeper or two. Behind them sat their own supervisor, the assistant manager. Finally, at the very back of the office sat the manager, always a man, literally overseeing the office. The disciplinary hierarchy at utility offices was therefore finely graded and spatially embedded within the office layout.[23]

When customers entered an open office, they could see all the faces of the employees, though the district manager's face was farthest away. The manager could see the faces of customers, as well as the backs of his employees, though his employees could not see him without turning around.[24] Clerks in the front row therefore occupied a kind of valley of vision, in which they could only see customers but were visible to both customers in front and managers behind, and scrutinized by both.[25]

In a similar way to electricity offices, managers at telephone offices sat in the back, or in the corner, where they also enjoyed a visually privileged location.[26] From the back corner, workers were even more visible to managers because the manager's desk was located at the side of the office, rather than at the back. Managers therefore had a profile view of clerks, and could also see customers as they entered the office and conducted their business.[27]

Supervision within Bell commercial offices was extremely high. In smaller offices, a manager might oversee just one cashier and one or two other employees, but if the numbers increased more than that, Bell executives required that oversight be delegated to several people. Often, the ratio of clerks to assistant managers was just four to one.[28] This close supervision directly related to Bell's monopoly. The public thought that Bell's monopoly made it "greedy," a Bell training manual for commercial office employees noted. "What can be done?" the manual asked. Its first solution was "the development of supervisory control."[29]

Since the open office design facilitated supervision of low-level clerks, executives believed that it would improve customer service. "By all means, let the manager be in a position to see everything that is going on in the office," Kennedy told executives in a talk about how to improve public opinion. "The first and most important factor in business office management is 'viewpoint,'" a Bell manager told colleagues at a conference: "direct, on the job, personal supervision is the most effective form of supervision and control."[30]

The new open offices contrasted sharply with the earlier closed offices. At closed offices, workers crammed desks into every available space with little thought about orientation save immediate necessity. Clerks sat facing each other, a wall, or a window. Some desks were the once-popular rolltop variety that featured a looming cabinet in front of the user.[31] Customers would have had difficulty making eye contact with clerks in this layout and could barely see into these closed offices in the first place. In the closed office no one's view was privileged over anyone else's. But in the open offices, employees faced forward, ready to be seen by customers. As a Bell employee magazine declared, open offices had "each associate's desk facing the entrance."[32] Like iron filings toward a magnet, open offices pulled the gaze of employees toward customers.

The supervision at business offices in general has led historians of white-collar culture to ask why workers tolerated such conditions. One reason is obviously that clerks needed a job, and corporate jobs sometimes came with paid vacations, a pension, and even prestige. Yet another reason is that the difficulty of working under surveillance motivated employees to comply with it. Doing so could lead to promotion, and a promotion provided not only an increase in pay and prestige, but also a decrease in supervision and a reduction in the amount of emotional labor one had to perform.[33] In other words, employees tolerated supervision, and participated in it, because doing so held the promise of reducing that supervision. Unlike blue-collar jobs, where historians have found emotional bonds among work crews, in white-collar positions, at least at utilities, employees appear more willing to correct each other to obtain a promotion.[34]

Getting promoted reduced supervision, yet promotions partly depended on internalizing the discipline given by one's superior, or at least appearing to do so. When employees received a promotion, they immediately began disciplining those in their former position. Employees did this because it was better than doing the job themselves, and if they did it well enough, they might get promoted again, until someday they could sit in the back of the office, where they did not have to engage in much emotional labor at all and could not easily be seen. "The new employee who holds the lesser position is required to 'service his time' in the disagreeable job of waiting on the public or at the 'complaint window,'" a New England gas executive told colleagues. Therefore, "the ambition of the recruit is to hurry up and get promoted, so he, too, can go to the rear, have a nice, quiet, private office where he will not be bothered by customers with grievances and requests for information." Each rung in the corporate ladder came with a new desk location, less emotional labor, and more privacy.[35]

Utility open offices appear to have originated in the electricity industry in California, yet the design soon caught on in many other places. Electricity companies as far east as Boston also reported removing the bars and cages from their offices. A significant number of Bell System offices also adopted the open office, though they did so about five years later than electricity companies. The adoption at Bell was somewhat uneven. In 1914 the Pacific Telephone & Telegraph Company still had not adopted the open office as evidenced by the company's description of its Alameda, California office as featuring "counter and gratings . . . of a design usually seen in banks."[36]

The connection to banking architecture was not coincidental. In the early nineteenth century, as one historian has shown, bankers practiced something called "insider lending." This involved lending to relatives, friends, and even the bank's own directors. Bank architecture at the time reflected this close relationship through an open office layout. But when insider lending declined, the separation between insiders and outsiders was architecturally symbolized through the erection of high-counters and iron cages for clerks. Max Weber's "iron cage" of capitalism was no mere metaphor for many late-nineteenth century bank tellers.[37] Borrowers on the outside no longer had easy access to the bank's reserves, physically or socially.[38]

Samuel Kennedy was aware of the architectural genealogy of the closed office because he had once served as the director of a bank before moving to the electricity industry. While working at the bank, Kennedy chafed against the closed office and tried to implement his open office ideas. He did not believe that bars and cages would prevent robberies, as many argued, and instead maintained that the real result of such obstructions was poor customer relations.[39] Kennedy failed to change his bank's architecture, but he maintained his crusade when he moved to the electricity industry. "There is . . . some hereditary feeling that public utility offices should be hemmed in with all kinds of obstructions," he complained to electricity executives, but "what do banks need them for?"[40] Eventually, however, banks came around to Kennedy's viewpoint and readopted the open office.[41] Yet this occurred after utility managers successfully reinvented the open office.

Did Open Offices Work?

After developing open offices, utility managers discovered the customers responded favorably to the new design. A Bell manager from California reported that his new open office was "enthusiastically received" and that customers told him that "they greatly appreciate the efforts being made by the telephone company to give them the best of service in every respect."[42] A manager from a small town in Massachusetts reported that he removed his clerk from the "cage" and now "customers come in, put down their bundles, lean over the desk and talk to him while they are going through the process of paying their bills. They like it lots better than they did to push their bills in a little window along with their money." Then the manager remarked to colleagues that "if you can get a man to lie down across the counter while you take away his money, you have got him right by the neck." The stenographer recording the meeting noted "laughter" after this last comment.[43] Perhaps the managers laughed all the way to the bank to deposit their customers' money.

Customers were not the only ones seduced by the new design. The same Massachusetts manager noted that his cage-free clerk also liked the new open design. "The cashier says he didn't like looking through those bars all day," the manager reported, and added that the cashier now brought flowers to put on his desk. "Well, they have taken you out of the cage, have they?" a customer chided a cashier after the renovations. "Guess they aren't afraid you are going to run away any more."[44] Another manager said that the lack of bars permitted "a most friendly attitude on our part."[45]

The Unit Plan

After electricity executives developed the architectural strategy of the open office, Bell executives developed an organizational strategy called the "unit plan." Like the open office, the unit plan was intended to enhance customer service. Under the unit plan a specific set of employees was assigned to a specific set of subscribers based on where the customers lived. When customers entered the telephone office, rather than being waited on by the next available clerk, they were greeted by a "floor director" who asked customers where they lived and directed them to the appropriate set of clerks. Telephone operators did the same when customers called with service questions. Special wiring inside Bell commercial offices allowed customers to be transferred directly to their set of clerks based on geography. Each unit of clerks was assigned approximately nine thousand subscribers and was overseen by a designated manager.[46]

To allow clerks to handle all their customers' service needs, clerks working under the unit plan were trained as "generalists" rather than "specialists," as the company called them.[47] At exactly the same time as Bell employees on the assembly line were being deskilled and shifting from generalists to specialists, the reverse was occurring to Bell employees on the customer service line.[48]

Executives adopted the unit plan in the early 1920s in response to customers who did not like the anonymity and impersonal service at large urban telephone offices. One customer, who preferred small-town life but found himself living in Atlanta, complained before the advent of the unit plant that: "you go to this big office and stand in line like you were buying tickets at a baseball game, and some young fellow waits on you that you never saw before, and most of the subscribers never see the manager and wouldn't know him if they saw him." The man added: "I reckon they do the best they can, having so many people to serve, but I like to know the man I'm dealing with."[49]

Managers believed the unit plan would solve this problem. According to one Southern Bell employee, the unit plan would "permit that same close

98   Chapter 3

relationship between the company's representatives and the patron as exists in the small exchange." Since subscribers would have repeated contact with the same clerks, the unit plan would generate "a more intimate acquaintanceship," according to one Bell manager.[50] By employing the unit plan, the multistate Southern Bell Telephone company sought to reverse the anonymity of the large corporation in the big city and emulate the general store in smalltown U.S.A.

The adoption of the unit plan was not uniform across the Bell System. Due to Bell's decentralized structure, organizational and architectural innovations at one operating company did not necessarily transfer to other operating companies, at least not immediately. Bell's Atlanta office adopted the unit plan of customer service in addition to the architectural strategy of the open office. Yet other Bell companies adopted neither, or just one or the other. The Bell office in Seattle, for example, implemented the unit plan in 1922, but not the open office layout. In fact, Seattle employees boasted of their "collection tellers' counter . . . with a bronze grille of pleasing design."[51] In San Francisco, commercial office managers also employed the unit plan, yet as late as 1925 they approvingly described their "tellers' cages" and the "parapets on the counters . . . of bronze, with chipped glass panels."[52] These architectural features no longer impressed many electricity executives, nor some Bell managers. Yet, the Seattle and San Francisco offices at least used the unit plan, and therefore employed courteous floor greeters. In Seattle, the floor greeter was described as being used "not only for the purpose of directing people and answering any question, but for the purpose of greeting every one cheerfully and seeing that all those entering the office are promptly and courteously waited up."[53] These closed, yet courteous, offices show how courteous capitalism preceded the open office in many locations.

One especially behind-the-times office in the Bell System was that of Pasadena. It built a new customer service center in 1927 featuring high counters and wood partitions, though no grillwork, and the office did not use the unit plan, despite having thirty-two thousand subscribers. In the same year, however, the Spokane branch built a new office with the open layout and employed the unit plan.[54] Spokane therefore adopted the unit plan, pioneered five years earlier in Atlanta, and the open office, originally developed by SCE in 1910.[55] Customer service innovations therefore traveled across companies, across industries, and across the country.

Counterless Offices

After electricity executives developed the open office, telephone executives took the revolution in corporate architecture one step further by removing counters altogether. Beginning in the mid-1920s, Bell managers introduced what they appropriately called the "counterless office." As the name implied, the counterless office had no counters running across the office that separated the clerks' from the customers' spaces. Instead, clerks sat at individual desks with one or two chairs facing them. Each furniture constellation was comfortably spaced apart from others so that customers could easily walk around and even behind these desks to reach a free clerk.

A counterless office in Oakland, California sometime between 1927 and 1930. The clerks' desks face the front of the office. The office manager and his secretary sit in the background of this photograph facing both entering customers and clerks. Bouquets of flowers adorn the office. Photograph 13706, July 1930, Folder: Pacific Bell—California Prints—by Exchange—Oakland-Buildings and Facilities—3545 E. 14th St. Business Office, 1927–1930, Box 19, RG 8, Collection 3, AT&T-TX. Courtesy of AT&T-TX.

This provided an unprecedented level of physical and visual access in the utility office.[56]

When customers entered a counterless office they were greeted by a "first contact clerk," whose job was similar to that of a greeter under the unit plan, but more closely resembled a host at a restaurant. Rather than just point customers to the correct line at the counter, the first contact clerk ushered customers to a chair at the desk of a free clerk. If no clerks were available, the host invited customers to sit in the waiting area, which featured comfortably upholstered chairs.[57] The *Pacific Telephone Magazine* described what happened once a customer was introduced to an available clerk: "'Good morning, Madam! Will you be seated?' This is the gracious manner in which subscribers are being introduced to the satisfactory personal service in Alhambra's new counterless business office."[58]

Bell executives were never fully satisfied with the open office, as indicated by the fact that they only adopted it in some locations. But when the counterless office was introduced, Bell managers around the country adopted it in earnest. The earliest mention of the counterless office dates to 1927, and by 1929 there were nearly three hundred such offices in the Bell System.[59] A year later, that number had risen to 444.[60]

The development of the counterless office came at a time when top Bell officials began focusing even more attention on office architecture as a possible way to improve customer service. In 1927, Bancroft Gherardi, vice president of the American Telephone & Telegraph Company (AT&T), summarized a set of recent executive meetings, informing an absent colleague that "the matter of business office service came in for considerable discussion." A partner at one of Bell's favorite architecture firms had been invited to the meetings and his "talk on the appearance of telephone buildings touched upon a matter in which we are all much interested." The goal in redesigning commercial offices, Gherardi stated, was to make "every subscriber to feel that he would like to have contact with our commercial office again."[61]

Clerks' Performances in the Front Region

The development of open and counterless offices created a "front region" where customer service "performances" took place, while the location of bookkeeping was removed to the "back region," to use the terminology of both executives and sociologist Erving Goffman.[62] "The manager cannot give too much attention to what goes on in the front of his office," Samuel Kennedy stressed in *Winning the Public* (1921).[63] "There are no records in the public office, they are kept in the interior office," observed a *Southern Telephone News* editor about a counterless office in New Orleans.[64]

If employees did not display "that distinguished performance in the service of customers," as a National Electric Light Association (NELA) committee termed it, managers were not afraid to fire the clerk.[65] "Get your employees to do what you want in their contacts with the public," advised Kennedy. "If they don't, take them away. There are some men who can never be toned up. Shove such men away back where they can do the company no harm." Executives were also known to handpick certain clerks for important customer service roles in the front region.[66]

This division of space therefore included a division of labor. In the early twentieth century, utility clerks who labored on account books often shared an office with clerks who labored on utility customers. In many cases, the same clerks did both. But that was when clerks worked in the closed office.[67] With the advent of open and counterless offices, those who kept the books were written out of the script and relegated to the back region.

Public relations, not just organizational efficiency, provided a major motivation for this change. Both the division of space and the division of labor may have been less efficient. In 1929, the *Southern Telephone News* explained why: "When the commercial representatives in the public office need records while dealing with customers, they call employees in the interior office who give the information desired." In other cases, a messenger went to collect the desired information. The interior office contained "69 employees who do the clerical work," the article noted, none of whom the customer could see, and vice versa.[68]

The new isolation of account clerks affected their work experience. The treasurer of an electricity company lamented in 1927 that "it has been said, and it is more or less true, that the work of the accountant being cloister work, so to speak, is narrowing and confining and gets one out of touch with the rest of human beings and sort of de-humanizes one." It had not always been that way, the treasurer noted, but "with the expansion and growth of the business, that [old] situation has passed."[69]

Although open and counterless offices appeared to show customers the entire office, at many offices the unseen back region made this transparency an illusion.[70] This back region included not just an accounting office, but also a surveillance room. A Bell open office in New Orleans, for example, featured a "public office" where the manager dutifully stationed himself so that "those wishing to see him" could "do so conveniently." Yet behind this public office existed an "interior office" where various workers labored, including a "service observer." This observer listened in on customer-clerk interactions occurring in the public office via microphones embedded in the desks of clerks.[71] Service observers also listened in on customers when they placed phone calls to company clerks.[72]

Courtesy by Design

The idea of improving visibility in the front region also influenced the design of the back region. Engineers designed operating rooms to maximize operator supervision. Designers did this because they believed that greater surveillance of operators would improve customer service and therefore public opinion. Scholars have shown that factory layouts and machines in some industries were designed not only to increase production but to individualize employees and sow discord among workers. The design of telephone operating designs presents a contrasting case. Rather than trying to shape the sentiments of workers, the telephone industry sought to shape the sentiments of customers through design. To do this, telephone engineers designed operating rooms and switchboards to increase supervision of workers, improve customer service, and thereby shape the political views of customers. Of course, improving supervision was not the only design goal. Cost of ownership, user connectivity, call-connection speed, and reliability were also important design considerations. But switchboard engineers also considered how to increase supervision of operators and thereby mold public opinion by design.[73]

By the turn of the century, the goal of high operator supervision resulted in a switchboard and telephone operating room that maximized operator surveillance. Unlike previous designs, operating room layouts by 1900 featured switchboards located against three walls of a room, forming a U shape. Operators sat on the inside of the U facing outward toward the walls, and supervisors stood directly behind the operators, as seen in the photograph on the following page. The operators were overseen by "supervisors" who stood directly behind them, literally breathing down their necks. Supervisors oversaw just six to twelve women and could plug their headphones in to any switchboard and listen in while the operator took calls. Next came the "monitor" who sat at a special desk that allowed her to listen in on any operator without the operator's knowledge. The monitor reported errors to the "chief operator," who had worked her way up from being a regular operator, but whose job represented the highest position a woman could hold within Bell operating departments. The chief operator

A U-shaped Bell System operating room, 1914. This design commonly existed since at least 1906. A Bell employee described this as "a typical exchange." The chief operator, sitting in the middle, oversees the standing assistant supervisors who oversee the operators facing the walls. "The Reality—A Typical Exchange," *Pacific Telephone Magazine*, October 1914, 14, Courtesy of AT&T-TX.

sat at the top of the U and could see all her employees without easily being seen, and could also listen in on calls anonymously.[74] Enlightenment thinker Jeremy Bentham never built any of his panopticons, but utility executives built hundreds of operating rooms and open offices.[75]

This U-shaped layout commonly existed since at least 1906, but was not inevitable.[76] Many alternatives existed. "There were almost as many kinds of switchboards as there were central offices," recalled one operator about the early days of telephony. In one early design, known as a "lamp-shade" layout, four operators sat facing the four sides of a central column mounted with switchboards. This design limited the number of lines that could be connected, but also made supervision difficult because seeing the operators required walking in a circle around the column. In another early design, operators faced each other across switchboards mounted parallel to the floor, as if playing chess. This resembled the layout at large telegraph offices, but in terms of supervision, the operators on one side could plainly easily see supervisors on the other. Another design from the 1890s placed all switchboards on a single wall, which turned the operators' vision away from

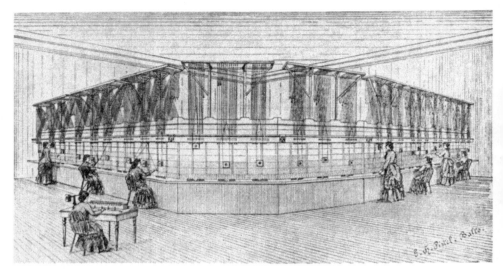

This design was common in major exchanges across the United States in the 1880s but limited the visibility of supervisors. John E. Kingsbury, *The Telephone and Telephone Exchanges: Their Invention and Development* (London: Longmans, Green, 1915), 232–233.

supervisors, but the switchboards were located on two floors, which also made supervision difficult. Yet another design resembled the U-shaped pattern that would eventually dominate, except that the operators sat on the outside of the U, rather than on the inside. There was a still a monitor observing the workers, but the operators could see her more easily, and the monitor's view of some of the operators farthest away was obstructed by nearer operators.[77]

None of these early designs persisted. At a switchboard design conference in 1889, an AT&T engineer explained one reason why—surveillance. "It is better to have the operators work from the inside of a circle [rather] than around the outside," he explained. That way "all operators are at once within view of the chief operator." The monitor's desk should also be located so that "all [switchboard] sections may be easily seen." Not only could the monitor easily see the backs of all the operators, but the operators could not see her. Finally, the engineer offered, the operating room "should be free from elevator shafts or other obstructions," such as additional lampshade switchboards that had sometimes been installed in the middle of the U. Engineers wanted enough space for supervisors to do their "patrolling," which previous designs lacked. The desire for improved supervision of operators even provided one motivation for engineers to consolidate the small exchanges, which had once been scattered throughout cities, and combine them into one large exchange in each city.[78]

In addition to the telephone operating room layout, the design of the switchboards themselves also enhanced surveillance. In 1895, engineers added a small light on the front of each switchboard tellingly called a "supervisory signal." These lights helped supervisors know when an operator was not on a call so there could be no pretending to work. Engineers also designed switchboards so that monitors could listen in on any operator without her knowledge.[79] The designed may have improved customer service, but it hurt the work experience of operators, by helping make telephone operating one of the most intensely supervised jobs in the industrialized economy.[80] By the early twentieth century, the U-shaped switchboard layout, with operators sitting on the inside, became the standard.[81]

Exterior Architecture

In attempting to create offices that improved customer service, executives did not overlook the exterior of their offices. Rather, the exterior of utility buildings formed an integral part of the overall goal of improving public opinion. Executives believed the exterior of their commercial offices should exhibit the company's values. Sometimes these values were expressed through a bold and majestic skyscraper, but more often they were expressed through a subdued and accommodating branch office.

Executives wanted their neighborhood commercial offices to fit in with the surrounding residences, so they hired architects to design each office in the local style. An editor for the *Bell System Quarterly* wrote that "especially careful thought has been given to the exterior appearance of the little buildings to the end that they, too, may blend into their surroundings."[82] One of AT&T's favorite office architects wrote that "suburban telephone buildings have a deliberately disguised look" since each neighborhood's "homogeneous architectural flavor must not be destroyed by a building noticeably out of character."[83]

Since housing styles varied by region, each office received a distinctive design. In Casa Grande, Arizona, the local Bell company built an adobe and log office, while in Ojai, California, the company adopted a Spanish Mission style, with whitewashed adobe walls, arched doorways, and a terra cotta–tiled roof.[84] In Dallas, Bell constructed a telephone building in what employees called "the Aztec architecture of the Southwest." In San Francisco's Chinatown, the Bell company built a "China Office" in 1909, complete with curved eaves, multiple tiers, and vertically mounted signs in Chinese. The structure was actually designed in a Mandarin style, despite being located in a predominately Cantonese-speaking neighborhood, but Bell architects and executives do not seem to have noticed.[85]

One Bell architect was so intent on fitting in with the local surroundings that he quarried stone from the building site and used it for the exterior of the office.[86] Architect Frank Lloyd Wright did the same thing at his Fallingwater house, but Bell's motivation was political—not natural—harmony. So in Scituate, Massachusetts, Bell built a branch office that looked "every inch a comfortable modern New England rural home," according to a Bell description. "Its picket fence and weathered shingles fit into the Massachusetts landscape as naturally as the wind-swept wild roses by the New England roadside," the observer added.[87] If utilities lived here, perhaps corporations really were people.

In many cases, these home-like structures did not even have anyone working in them. Instead, they served as electrical substations or telephone switching stations. Nonetheless, these structures resided in residential neighborhoods and were therefore masked as single-family homes. One unoccupied Commonwealth Edison structure located in the Windsor Park neighborhood of Chicago imitated the style of a French cottage with white plaster walls, exposed brick quoins, decorative mounting hardware for the gutters, and lattices for roses.[88] Another Commonwealth Edison substation adopted the look of a stately English manor with two doors leading into the building and a bench outside placed among the trees and bushes, even though no one worked there to sit on it.[89] The Bell System also built unoccupied structures in residential neighborhoods such as a brick Cape Cod building in Armonk, New York, which featured a flagstone path leading up to an arched doorway, windows bordered with white shutters, and shades on the inside pulled halfway down. Another unoccupied Bell switching station in Bedford Village, New York, also adopted the Cape Cod style, this one featuring a small iron-railed balcony above the doorway.[90]

Beyond simply trying to fit in, utility architects in the 1920s also sought to visually reference a quaint preindustrial past. If the smoke-belching factories of industrial capitalism could be erased from suburbanites' minds and replaced with scenes of bucolic tranquility, perhaps the recent growing pains that attended the rise of big business could be forgotten. Commenting

A PT&T telephone office. The caption under the photo, published in PT&T's annual report of 1929, reads "Treatment is such as to blend architecturally with the community served." Central office in Del Mar, California, 1929, Folder: Pacific Bell—California Prints—by Exchange—Del Mar—Buildings and Facilities—Box 6, RG 8, Collection 3, AT&T-TX. Also published in PT&T, *Report of the Board Directors to the Stockholders for the Year 1929*, 9, Box 1, Record Group 5, Collection 3, AT&T-TX. Courtesy of AT&T-TX.

on this, a writer in *Architecture and Building* magazine wrote that a colonial brick telephone office in Mamaroneck, New York, was "reminiscent of the day when stage coaches lumbered along the Boston Post Road." Another Bell structure in Westhampton, Long Island, according to the same writer, was designed to be "reminiscent of the manor of an English squire," while the Bell office in Katonah, New York, resembled "an Early American cottage." If one looked closely through the "shuttered, mullioned windows," the journalist offered, "one with imaginative eyes might see the dull gleam of firelight on polished pewter or the whirring of a busy spinning wheel."[91] Nothing, apparently, resembled preindustrial virtue like the offices of America's largest corporation.

Executives not only designed their buildings to resonate with the local architecture and history, they also carefully maintained the grounds on which

An adobe Bell commercial office in Casa Grande, Arizona, 1928. *Telephone Buildings: Bell System* (New York: AT&T [1930]). Courtesy of AT&T-TX.

these houses resided. In 1914, a substation manager for Samuel Insull's Commonwealth Edison Company wrote that "in recent years some considerable attention has been devoted to beautifying the grounds surrounding the various substations by landscape gardening, flower beds, window boxes." To maintain its properties, the company hired several groundskeepers. Keeping up the properties, one manager noted, "tends to remove much of the usual prejudice against the location of such industries in residential districts."[92] In 1921, Samuel Kennedy told a group of utility executives that "you should not have a steam plant that is decrepit looking, that is dirty on the outside, that has a broken down fence around it that has broken windows in it, or anything about it that does not look well kept."[93]

Yet this broken windows theory was not motivated by crime reduction but by public relations. The "average man" and the "ordinary individual" have pride in their community, Kennedy explained, and they do not like poorly kept properties. Even unoccupied buildings still needed to be freshly painted, with the weeds pulled and the litter picked up, Kennedy instructed his col-

The "China Office" of the Pacific Telephone & Telegraph Company, located in San Francisco's Chinatown, 1909. Folder: Pacific Bell—California Prints—by Exchange—San Francisco (Chinatown)—Buildings and Facilities—Exchange Office, Box 34, RG 8, Collection 3, AT&T-TX. Courtesy of AT&T-TX.

leagues.[94] The Bell System also paid considerable attention to the landscaping. One office boasted "evergreens and flower beds" and photos at many Bell offices reveal planted hedges and freshly mowed lawns.[95] The company also left as many trees as possible on their lots when building residential customer service centers.[96]

Bell commercial offices: one in Scituate, Massachusetts (top right), and another in Scarsdale, New York, both designed to match their specific local surroundings. Richard Storrs Coe, "Bell System Buildings—an Interpretation," *Bell Telephone Quarterly*, July 1929, photo insert between pages 214 and 215.

Did Exterior Architecture Work?

Customers appreciated the landscaping and exterior design of branch offices, according to newspaper reports. The *Chicago Tribune* reported in 1929 that the exterior architecture of one of Commonwealth Edison's residential properties was so pleasing that it raised property values in the surrounding neighborhood. Identifying the company's goal with suspicious accuracy, the journalist noted that "the beautiful building excites favorable comment which in turn increases the good will of the public toward the company."[97] Writing in *Pacific Coast Architect* magazine in 1929, architect Harris Allen praised both the inside and outside of San Francisco's New Montgomery Street Telephone Building, calling it "a thing of beauty" that provided a "reason for praising its creators." Utility sources also noted customer approval. A *Bell System Quarterly* article from 1929 declared that residents proudly pointed out their local Bell telephone office, which they viewed with civic pride.[98] The Public Service Company of Northern Illinois noted in 1931 that the company's architecture "has been the source of much favorable comment throughout the territory served for a number of years."[99]

A telephone switching station in Armonk, New York, 1931. Despite the fact that a mother and child are seen approaching this building, no one worked there. Nonetheless, the building still featured the appearance of a single family home and attentive landscaping. "Telephone Central Office Buildings in the Small Communities," *Architecture and Building* 67, no. 2 (February 1930): 59.

Corporate Domesticity

Utility branch offices not only masqueraded as residential homes on their exterior, but also on their interior. Like any homeowner with genteel aspirations, the interior of utility offices featured fine furniture, rugs, potted plants, flowers, and framed pictures on the wall. One employee magazine noted with pride that "deep upholstered davenports and comfortable chairs are provided for customers."[100] These home-like customer service offices also featured electric lamps and other electrical appliances, and displayed them as if to certify the utilities' membership in the middle class.

Electric and telephone utilities also referred to their offices as a "home" or "house," and spoke of customers as members of "our family."[101] As such, family members were free to move about the home, use the appliances, or sit in the subdivided "waiting area," which included arm chairs, space heaters for cold feet, and a telephone, free for members of the family.[102] Utility offices sought to emulate the suburban home in this way.

Yet if the suburban home came into the world by going out of the world, far from the sullying influence of commerce, the new utility offices fused the two back together, combining the bureaucratic and technical capabilities of the big corporation with the order and relaxation of the home.[103] This corporate domesticity, as it can be called, gave corporate monopolies the decorative aesthetic of the middle class in the hopes of winning middle-class goodwill.

Corporate domesticity differed from the later warehouse aesthetic of Wal-Marts, which promoted consumption by expressing frugality. Corporate domesticity also differed from the grandiose department stores of the late nineteenth and early twentieth centuries, which enticed shoppers with tantalizing baubles for every taste and budget.[104] Instead, utilities emulated their customers' middle-class sensibilities of refinement with restraint, and elegance without ostentation.[105] Utility service provided by corporate monopolies was often more expensive than government-owned service or service from independents, yet some customers were willing to pay a bit more for quality physical service and good customer service. Utilities therefore did not need to portray themselves like a thrifty Wal-Mart. Yet utility service was fast becoming a necessity, so utilities did not want to appear like a luxurious department store either.[106] Therefore, utility architecture in the 1920s aimed for a respectable yet approachable appearance with corporate domesticity.

Utility employees explicitly acknowledged the public relations intent of corporate domesticity. One worker declared that "attractive retail sales and service stores are valuable assets in public relations."[107] Another stated "function" of the display kitchens at commercial offices was not only to encourage the use of gas appliances "but to obtain complete public confidence."[108] Some companies posted educational literature next to appliances, and one executive noted that the displays appeared "merely educational" but were really "masking a most desirable purpose . . . to eliminate dissatisfaction and inspire confidence in the company's methods."[109]

To fully convey this middle-class persona, many utilities installed entire domestic rooms in their local offices. Here corporate domesticity attained its highest expression. One office in the Chicago suburb of Libertyville featured a "customers' lounge," which was nearly indistinguishable from a well-furnished living room. Two stuffed armchairs sat on either side of the lounge's fireplace, while a couch sat opposite the fireplace. A clock and a can-

The Architecture of Consent 113

delabra sat on top of the mantel. A floor lamp and end-table were arranged on either side of the couch, with a coffee table in front of the couch, illuminated by an overhead lamp. Light also streamed through the windows featuring proper window treatment. The only features of the lounge that failed to match a middle-class living room were the walls, which did not extend all the way up to the ceiling, and the abundance of table lamps displayed on the built-in bookshelves.[110]

Insull's customers' lounge was not unique. Other utilities installed rooms that resembled a den, parlor, bedroom, dining room, or library. A NELA committee recommended that display rooms be located "such that customers coming in to pay their bills, or upon any business, will pass entirely through the room, thus enabling the attendant salesman to meet and, if possible, become better acquainted with them." One of the most popular rooms for utilities to build into their commercial offices was the kitchen, which utilities installed "complete in the most minute detail," including "running water and sewage connections."[111]

Several companies went as far as building entire homes for displaying appliances, hosting receptions, and exuding corporate domesticity. In 1929, the Public Service Company of Northern Illinois built a "model bungalow, completely furnished" within the company's new store. The firm also owned another bungalow-store in Oak Park, the Chicago suburb where Frank Lloyd Wright maintained his home and studio.[112] Other monopolies from San Francisco to Boston also built bungalows or other styles of homes in the 1920s. These home offices came complete with living areas, as well as a laundry room, kitchen, bathroom, office, bedroom, and nursery.[113]

Utility employees frequently invited "guests" to come over to these home offices for a visit. One company sent out calling cards to invite customers to a "refrigeration tea." Utilities also let civic clubs, high school groups, and women's societies borrow these facilities for their own uses. Surrounded by the aesthetic of corporate domesticity, customers could inspect the latest appliances, learn how to use them, and agree, perhaps unconsciously, that corporate monopolies shared their interests and values.

To further convey corporate domesticity, utility executives also built employee break rooms, or "rest rooms," as they were called. These rooms served the dual purpose of providing employees with a place to relax and providing companies with elegant rooms to show off to customers and the media. To accomplish these tasks, rest rooms featured interior furnishings that were nearly indistinguishable from a typical middle-class family room.[114]

The "customers' lounge" at the Libertyville district office of the Public Service Company of Northern Illinois. The collection of lamps on the right wall, and the fact that neither the left or right walls reach the ceiling, hint that this room is actually part of a customer service and retail office. "New Stores Opened," *Public Service Company of Northern Illinois Year Book 1929*, 18, Box 55, Folder 8, Insull Papers. Courtesy of Loyola University Chicago Archives and Special Collections.

Descriptions and photographic evidence of these rooms reveal upholstered couches, rocking chairs, tables, flowers, books, magazines, drapes, wallpaper, and a piano, radio, or phonograph. One rest room in Nashville had actually been a private residence before the Southern Bell Telephone Company purchased it. The space featured "beautiful woodwork," "handsome mirrors," and "lovely light fixtures," as well as a piano, an overstuffed couch, and additional furniture made of mahogany and wicker.[115] The rest room at the San Francisco headquarters of PT&T included a piano, a glass-doored bookcase, rocking chairs, a chaise lounge, framed art, potted plants, and vases with flowers. A Bell rest room in Homewood, Illinois, and built in 1927 provided the town's operators with "a place of relaxation," and included wicker armchairs, a floor lamp, tables, a double bed, carpeting, drapes, a fan, flowers, and reading material.[116] Even the selection of reading material signaled an improving mindset. The most commonly subscribed to magazines for operators were *Good Housekeeping*, *American*, and *Hygeia*, published by the

A living room featuring "proper illumination" in a model electrical home owned by Vancouver Electric. Norman S. Gallison, "The Electrical Home for the Electrical Man," *Journal of Electricity and Western Industry*, December 15, 1922, 446.

American Medical Association. Some managers departed from this a bit by also ordering the movie magazine *Photoplay* as well as *Cosmopolitan*, though the latter was not quite what it is today.[117]

Tours

Although rest rooms were not mainly intended for customers to use, thousands of customers streamed through these rooms during behind-the-scenes tours. The goal of these tours was to dispel the negative image of the working conditions at utilities, and to educate customers on the difficulties of providing utility service. Some customers wrongly imagined telephone operating rooms as poorly supervised places where operators sat around talking to friends while customers tried futilely to place calls. A cartoon entitled "The Average Subscriber's Idea of a Telephone Exchange," published in *Life* magazine in 1914, depicted operators lounging around, listening to music, and flirting with men, while customers angrily shouted through the switchboard, "Say! I've been waiting two hours!!" "Is everybody dead up there?!!!" "Blanketty blank!"[118] The cartoon exaggerated the point, but many customers suspected that operators had lots of spare time, listened in on telephone calls,

A "pretty rest room in New Bessemer, LA," stated the *Southern Telephone News*. The operators on both the left and right are still wearing their headsets and mouthpieces. The framed triangle above the lamp is the logo of the Southern Bell Telephone Company with its three sides of efficiency, service, and cooperation. "Pretty Rest Room in New Bessemer, LA., Exchange," *Southern Telephone News*, December 1921, 32, AT&T-TX. Courtesy of AT&T-TX.

and sometimes told customers that the person they were trying to reach did not answer when the operator had not even bothered to place the call.

Other commentators, in contrast, more accurately viewed the working conditions of telephone operators as exceptionally difficult. Beginning in the Progressive Era, these observers, which included health officials, started to critique Bell's employment practices. They witnessed how operators' fingers flew over the switchboards inserting plugs, answering calls, and connecting subscribers at a rate of one connection every 3.5 seconds in 1910.[119] By 1930, that number had fallen to just 1.4 seconds due to relentless Taylorizing of operating procedures.[120] When answering a call, operators had to use a rigid set of phrases and speak with exaggerated intonation. Customers sometimes lost their temper and verbally abused operators, but operators simply had to repeat "I am *sorry*"—with an emphasis on "sorry"—and then: "Number please." If the customer remained uncooperative, operators had to transfer the caller to a supervisor.

These strict procedures took a physical and emotional toll on operators. Doctors reported that the job frayed the nerves, and stories from operators

The Architecture of Consent   117

revealed the high emotional price of bottling up their emotions.[121] "There's no way to let out your emotions," agonized one operator.[122] Operators could not talk to neighboring operators, eat at their stations, or use the bathroom without permission. When on duty, operators sat on a hard chair in front of a hot switchboard while wearing long dresses with long sleeves and a heavy headset with a microphone.[123] During shift changes, a bell would sound, and a new set of operators would literally march in single file and stand beside the operator whom they were going to replace. When a second bell rang, the operators switched places and the off-duty women marched out to the rest room.[124]

The Bell System wanted to counteract the negative images of operating rooms being both too lax and too demanding. To do this, Bell began inviting customers to see operating room conditions for themselves. "Many of our subscribers have but a hazy idea of what goes on in a central office," a Southern Bell employee explained, yet the "the irritation sometimes felt because of a slight delay . . . would probably vanish if the subscriber could see just what was going on at the switchboard."[125] Customers would "accept with patience any contingencies or conditions" after a tour, one Pacific Bell employee foretold.[126] With that hope in mind, hundreds of thousands of bill inserts, posters, and press releases went out inviting the public to visit.[127]

On a typical Bell tour, customers visited a live switchboard operating room where they learned just how much went in to placing each individual call and could observe the order and supervision of the rooms. Then customers were led to the rest room where they took in a scene of corporate domesticity and received an introduction to the matron. The matron kept a benevolent watch over her charges, while they relaxed in tranquility and comfort of the rest room. For operators with a "sudden case of 'grippe,'" there was an adjoining "silence room," where the "girl" could lie down and the matron would attend to her. This information must have been especially reassuring to mothers during the periodic bring-your-mother-to-work days.[128] According to one visitor's report, the matron could also be consulted on "matters of health . . . athletics and amusements, and the thousand and one little problems which may confront any modern girl." With such well-appointed and well-staffed facilities, what more morally beneficent place could there be, except the Victorian home itself? At the end of these tours, guests received a pamphlet and subscription form for stock ownership in case visitors now wanted to invest in this culturally wholesome and economically promising institution.[129]

These tours were not infrequent affairs occasionally arranged. Utilities consistently offered tours as a matter of policy, and thousands of customers availed themselves of the offer.[130] In 1929 alone, over 116,000 people toured Southwestern Bell facilities.[131] Between 1926 and 1935, over 240,000 visitors toured Illinois Bell facilities, including many students. In 1930, the number of people who toured Ohio Bell facilities approached 5 percent of the company's subscribers.[132]

Electricity companies also invited the public to tour of their rest rooms, interior offices, switching stations, and even generating plants.[133] The Pacific Gas & Electric Company (PG&E) hung "Visitors Welcome" signs at the entrances to their hydroelectric plants, and offered guided tours to civic groups and school children.[134] During the tours, guests received a twenty-eight-page booklet with full-color pictures of the plant, a map of the company's network, public relations copy, and statistics showing how many people the company employed in California, how much capital the company invested in the state, and how much state and federal taxes the company contributed.[135] The Boston Edison company offered similar tours.[136]

Judging from newspaper accounts, AT&T succeeded in its goal of convincing visitors that the company's employment of women and service to customers were all anyone could ask for. In 1927, one journalist for the Portland *Telegram* found his or her tour of Bell's local facilities impressive, noting how the rest room featured "comfortable wicker furniture and restful drapes" and was equipped with an "orthophonic talking machine and a piano." There were also "magazines and inviting davenports." Next door there was the "'quiet room,' a well-insulated dormitory where complete rest and relaxation may be had." A Portland *News* reporter was particularly impressed with the matron of the operators, Mrs. Wightman, who greeted all the visitors, and "who has come to be called 'The Mother of a Thousand Girls.'" Her job was to be available to the "girls" when "they need the advice and aid of an experienced counselor." AT&T was also eager to point out that the matron also managed the company's sickness and disability benefits.[137] Through newspaper accounts like these, many customers who did not attend tours themselves could still receive the good report.

Other visitors also indicated that tours had been successful. In an article entitled "Seeing Is Believing," a Southern Bell employee stated that, after tours, "not once, but hundreds of times, is the comment made, 'Well, if that's the sort of girl "Central" is, I'll be more considerate in the future.'"[138] An employee from Detroit in 1924 concluded that "it may be justly said that our relations with the public are better than they have ever been," and credited the tours and switchboard demonstrations with contributing to this outcome.[139]

Open Houses

In addition to tours, utilities held evening open houses and house warming parties. These events were nearly indistinguishable from traditional polite entertaining, with female employees playing the role of hostesses. In the case of utilities, however, the "house" where the entertainment took place was actually a local branch office. At one Bell open house in Tifton, Georgia, the office's female employees greeted guests at the receiving line at the head of the stairway, which was decorated with streamers in the company's colors of blue and white. Other female employees served punch and slices of cake that had been frosted in the company's colors and marked with an "S.B.T.," for Southern Bell Telephone. In another room, other women employees dispensed party favors—cigars for the men, flowers for the women—while yet another group of female employees attended guests on their tour through the operating room and rest room. To highlight the domesticity of the operators' rest room, two operators played its piano. According to the company's employee magazine, all the female employees attending the event dressed in "lovely summer frocks," and descriptions of similar gatherings frequently made mention how pretty the operators looked. In Tifton, the evening ended with dancing and was counted as a great success by those involved based on the many expressions of pleasure from the guests and the fact that many departed on the late train home.[140]

In other cases, office receptions could be followed by dinner elsewhere. At a Bell reception in Kokomo, Indiana, visitors received an extensive tour of the company's commercial and plant departments, the operators' rest room, a look at the cafeteria, and an explanation of the switchboards. Then the guests repaired to another bulwark of middle-class morality, the local YMCA, where a banquet was served to all 785 guests. During the event, "bank presidents mingled with school boys; [and] teachers and superintendents of manufacturing plants rubbed elbows with their workmen, all seeking for knowledge," wrote *Bell Telephone News*. After this love feast, attendees heard speeches from local notables such as the secretary of the town's chamber of commerce, and the "employees renewed their pledge to help their city in its growth and to make the citizens more satisfied with living here by giving the best telephone service possible." The evening was capped by a few numbers from the Lions' Club quartet.[141] The gathering in Kokomo was no idle affair. Municipal politics mattered, especially in Indiana, which had been a hotbed of anti-Bell sentiment in the nineteenth century.[142] Yet the forces of political economy extended beyond city council races and political platforms. The opinions of local civic organizations and business leaders mattered too, so in Kokomo, as in many other places, Bell managers allied themselves with the town's local power structure and thought leaders.[143] After doing so, it is hard to see that how much harmful sentiment or legislation could emerged against the company.

These gatherings proved quite popular among customers. At one Bell party in Seattle in 1922, so many customers accepted an invitation to a party that the fire marshal had to turn away people at the door. Still, an estimated two thousand couples squeezed onto the floor of the company's office, where they danced the night away, along with their antimonopoly sentiments, or so Bell officials hoped.[144] Not every tour was as extensive as the ones in Seattle, Kokomo, and Tifton, but nearly all events gave guests a tour of the switchboard and rest rooms.[145]

As dial telephones began to replace manually switched phones for some Bell customers around 1920, plant tours became even more important because Bell no longer personally interacted with customers on as frequent a basis.[146] In 1927, when the Bell office in Pasadena "cutover" from manual to automatic switching, they also built two new commercial offices. To show them off, the company hosted an open house in which three thousand customers, about 10 percent of the company's local subscribers, visited the new buildings and observed the new switching equipment in operation.[147]

Whether touring an office, paying a bill, or signing up for service, utility customers by the 1920s entered corporate spaces whose every detail had been calculated to please. The unobstructed view of the clerks, the ability to walk around the office, the domesticity of the interiors, and the design of the single-family home exteriors had all been specifically chosen to make corporate monopolies acceptable to Americans.

The Environmental Psychology of the Office

In creating pleasant office interiors, executives acted on instinct, yet they anticipated what psychologists would later prove: that beautiful interiors create positive feelings in the room's occupants. One of the first psychologists to show this was Abraham Maslow. Maslow was already famous for his "hierarchy of needs" concept when, in the 1950s, he turned his attention to architectural psychology. During his research he ran an experiment in which he placed subjects in three different rooms: a "beautiful" room, an "average" room, and an "ugly" room. Maslow then asked his subjects to rate the

The Architecture of Consent   121

"fatigue/energy" and "displeasure/well-being" in the photographs of faces he showed his subjects as they sat in each room. Maslow found that subjects in the beautiful room "gave significantly higher ratings (more 'energy' and 'well-being') than subjects in either the 'average' or 'ugly' rooms."[148] Maslow concluded that in pleasant rooms, people perceive others as pleasant; while in unpleasant rooms, people perceive others as unpleasant.

What is most striking about this finding for the history of commercial architecture is how closely Maslow's beautiful room matched the interiors of open and counterless offices. Maslow's beautiful room featured "two large windows, beige-colored walls, an indirect overhead light, and furnishings to give the impression of an attractive, comfortable study. Furnishings included a soft armchair, a mahogany desk and chair combination, two straight-backed chairs, a small table, a wooden bookcase, a large Navajo rug, drapes for the windows, painting on the walls, and some sculpture and art objects on the desk and table. These were all chosen to harmonize as pleasantly as possible with the beige walls." Maslow's subjects described this room as "'attractive,' 'pretty,' 'comfortable,' 'pleasant.'"

Maslow's beautiful room was nearly identical to descriptions of utility offices, all the way down to the lighting, colors, and furnishings. A counterless office in New Orleans, which opened in 1929, included "five large windows" that "flood the room with natural light, augmented at dusk by graceful hanging chandeliers of paneled opaque glass and dull bronze." The office also featured "comfortable furniture" including "desks in walnut to match the paneling." The walls were decorated with "rich brown walnut paneling" and "antique glazed ornamental plaster decorated in golden-brown tones for the high lights, with warm sepias for the shadows; [and] subdued bronzes where necessary." The floors had "rich rugs over warm colored terrazzo floors."[149] An open office of the Southern California Edison Company, built in 1917, featured interior lighting that was "indirect and . . . so designed that a uniform intensity of light, practically without shadows," was "obtained at all points."[150] A "beautiful" commercial office of the PT&T company in Los Angeles featured "deep upholstered davenports" in green leather with matching drapes.[151] Utility offices also featured framed pictures and potted plants or fresh flowers. These offices matched Maslow's beautiful room to an exceptionally close degree.

The "average" room included gray walls, a wooden desk and chairs, a metal filing cabinet, metal book case, shaded overhead lighting, and was "in no way outstanding enough to elicit any comments."[152] Maslow's "ugly" room, in contrast, looked similar to the closed offices of utilities in the late-nineteenth century. Maslow's ugly room included: "two half-windows, battleship-gray walls, an overhead bulb with a dirty, torn, ill-fitting lampshade, and 'furnishings' to give the impression of a janitor's storeroom in disheveled condition. There were two straight-backed chairs, a small table, tin cans for ashtrays, and dirty, torn window shades. Near the bare walls on three sides were such things as pails, brooms, mops, cardboards boxes, dirty-looking trash cans, a bedspring and uncovered mattress, and assorted refuse. The room was neither swept nor dusted and the ashtrays were not emptied." Occupants found these rooms "'horrible,' 'disgusting,' 'ugly,' 'repulsive'."

These ugly rooms resembled utility offices before the open office revolution. Photographs and descriptions of the older closed offices reveal that they had dirty windows, dim lighting, and dusty cluttered counters piled with loose papers, empty inkwells, and broken lamps and machines. Spittoons and overflowing garbage cans littered the floor, wires stretched across the walls and ceilings, and cobwebs clung to the corners.

Since Maslow's study, environmental psychologists have confirmed and extended his findings. These scholars have found that store design not only unconsciously affects customers' impressions of clerks, but also how customers feel themselves. Some interiors cause customers to feel relaxed and in control, as utility executives wanted, while other designs elicit a feeling of being dominated and subdued. Psychologists have found that feeling in control "is enhanced by a feeling that you can look anywhere, rummage around, and handle everything," exactly what open and counterless offices sought to convey.[153]

It might seem conspiratorial to argue that utilities designed their offices to elicit feelings in customers, yet this was explicitly what utility employees stated. In 1929, a Bell employee noted that all "the architectural design and character of furnishings" of the counterless office in New Orleans had been "chosen with a view to placing the visitor wholly at ease."[154] One employee stated that a telephone office in Southern California had been designed to make customers feel "restful" and "comfortable." "The interior of the business office," the employee noted, "reflects a cool and restful atmosphere" using temperature controlled rooms, walls painted "in an adobe brown, with pastel shades of green and sunset skillfully blended together," and an "abundance of light and air . . . admitted by a large front window."[155] When PT&T opened a new counterless office in the Bay Area 1930, an employee noted that the "color, woodwork, floors, and furnishing" of the office, made it not only "comfortable," but also "friendly."[156] In 1925, John Bakewell Jr. of Bakewell & Brown, observed regarding an office he designed for PG&E that "new problems... and new materials, and new ideas" changed the "architectural forms and motives," and the "entire spirit and effect of architecture."[157]

Samuel Kennedy confirmed there was an "effect of architecture" in his 1921 book *Winning the Public*. The book included sections entitled "The Psychology of Environment" and "The Hospitable Office." In the latter section, Kennedy taught executives to ask themselves: "What is the effect [of offices] upon the company's customers?"[158] He offered his own answer based on a decade of experimentation. Ugly closed offices, Kennedy explained, "obstruct the view and to make the consumer feel that he is something on the outside of the organization." Instead, utilities should make customers "feel at home" using beautiful open offices as well as courteous clerks.[159] Maslow could hardly have said it better himself.

Environmental psychologists have further found that the two crucial design factors that produce feelings of restfulness and comfort in occupants are pleasant interiors, such as beautiful rooms, and low stimulation, such as low noise and soft lighting. Combining beautiful interiors with high stimulation induces in occupants feelings of excitement and spending, a combination that more closely matched the department stores of the late nineteenth century.[160] But since utility executives wanted to make customers feel comfortable and in control of monopolies, they created office interiors featuring beautiful rooms with low stimuli.

To create a low-noise environment one Bell commercial engineer specified "sound absorbing materials" in his commercial office designs. He explained that these materials would "gain the advantages of quiet offices both for public contracts and for telephone contacts with customers."[161] A counterless office in Spokane featured a "ceiling of sound-proof composition" and floors made of sound-damping "attractive rubber tile."[162] The walls and ceiling at a counterless office in New Orleans "received acoustical treatment by the application of a special plaster composition," boasted an employee magazine article. "Noise is reduced to a minimum. Echo and reverberation are absent."[163] This muting of sound but enhancing of vision ushered indoors a nineteenth-century project of segregating the senses. Other office buildings at the time used sound-suppressing technology to increase employee efficiency, but utilities used it to make customers comfortable and relaxed.[164]

Conclusion: Did Courtesy by Design Work?

Many employees noted that these designs worked in generating the desired feelings in customers. A manager in Brooklyn, New York, said that community groups frequently met at the commercial office of the utility because they "feel at home."[165] A Bell employee observed that the interior decorations in New Orleans "tend to bring about a feeling of comfort and understanding between the company and the public."[166] At a new counterless office in El Centro, California, a Bell employee noted that the office "produces an atmosphere of friendliness and cordiality." In 1929, in an extensive Bell article on the company's architecture, an employee noted the "formative influence which such buildings exert" and referred to Bell offices as "indispensable instrumentalities used in the work of rendering service."[167] Executives had succeeded in shaping customers' sentiments through architecture.

When New York utility managers invited customers to their offices by saying, "Your visit, we are sure, will prove pleasurable," were they just reciting a common turn of phrase? Or did the managers have good reasons for such confidence?[168] The experience of executives and the later research of environmental psychologists demonstrate that these managers had good reasons for their statement. In the 1920s, executives deliberately sought to shape the sentiments of customers toward monopoly utilities through the design of corporate spaces. These offices made customers feel relaxed and in control. Yet the more in control customers felt, the more they were actually being controlled.

This chapter has shown that utility executives not only focused on courtesy, but also on the customer service offices in which courteous interactions took place. To dispel suspicion and negative impressions, utilities developed open offices, which were designed in the style of corporate domesticity. Subsequently, the Bell System developed the unit plan and counterless offices. These also sought to improve customer impressions and generate goodwill. Executives further sought to make the exterior of their offices blend in with their surroundings. For that reason, utilities built branch offices in the local architectural style and meticulously maintained these properties for the sake of producing positive public opinion. Customers felt comfortable in these offices, a reaction that executives intentionally brought about through design.

CHAPTER FOUR

Customer Stock Ownership as Corporate Political Strategy

In July 1914, the treasurer of the Pacific Gas & Electric Company (PG&E), A. F. Hockenbeamer, had a very good idea, at least from his perspective. California progressives had been calling for public ownership of utilities, so Hockenbeamer introduced "customer ownership," a slight variation in terms intended to bring about very different results in practice. To launch customer ownership, Hockenbeamer began selling shares directly to his northern California customers. Since these customers were also likely voters in California's new referendum process, the quarterly dividends customers received would likely pay dividends of their own, back to the company, whenever measures regarding public utilities came up at the ballot box.

To inform customers about the new stock offer, PG&E "opened up with a veritable barrage of a quarter of a million circulars directed to the company's consumers," as the firm's employee magazine later recounted. Newspaper advertisements reiterated the message. In addition—and in what became a hallmark of future customer-ownership campaigns—PG&E began selling stock directly to customers from the company's branch offices.[1] The company also offered $100 shares at par value for $82.50, either in cash or on an installment plan for as little as $5 down, and with none of the minimum purchase requirements or commission fees that typically attended stock purchases made at brokerage firms.[2]

Scholars have identified customer stock-ownership programs as beginning with American Telephone & Telegraph (AT&T) after World War I, but that was not where corporate executives and *Wall Street Journal* editors located the strategy's origin.[3] They unanimously credited PG&E with inventing customer ownership during the 1910s and praised the company for its organizational ingenuity in the face of the threat of public ownership. The

Wall Street Journal called PG&E and another smaller company "pioneers," while the president of the Southern California Edison Company (SCE) told executives at an industry conference that customer stock ownership began with PG&E.[4]

Identifying the origins of customer stock ownership with PG&E in 1914 is the first of three main arguments made in this chapter, and the one that most touches a historiographic nerve. In contrast to previous work that viewed customer stock ownership as arising out of Liberty Bond sales during World War I and the work of Harvard political economy professor Thomas Nixon Carver, this chapter traces the origins of customer stock ownership to utilities before World War I. Utility executives did not learn the strategy of customer stock ownership from Liberty Bond campaigns or Carver. Rather, utility executives invented customer stock ownership themselves and did so in response to the political threat of municipal ownership facing their monopoly utilities. Carver himself even acknowledged that electric utilities invented customer stock ownership in 1914, which was long before he began advocating the strategy.[5] Customer stock ownership emerged, not from the bureaucratic offices of Washington or the ivy-covered halls of academia, but from the oak-coffered boardrooms of corporations.

The second main argument this chapter makes is that millions of Americans became corporate shareholders in the 1920s not only because of customer demand, but also because of corporate supply. Utility companies did not merely offer stock to Americans; utility employees actively pressured their customers, friends, and neighbors to buy stock by knocking on their doors, calling them on the phone, and pitching them stock at electricity, telephone, and streetcar offices. Historians often recount how Americans clamored to buy stock on margin in the 1920s, yet this conception of customer demand must be augmented by an understanding of corporate supply.[6] The supply-side social history presented here reveals how utility clerks personally sold stock to 20 percent of the total number of shareholding Americans by the Crash of 1929, and did so in a determined effort to undermine municipal ownership.

Did customer stock ownership work? Did utility executives accomplish their goals of reducing antimonopoly sentiment and improving public opinion toward corporate monopolies in the 1920s? The answer to these questions is a qualified yes. In elaborating on this last main argument, this chapter concludes that the result of customers owning stock was the decline of antimonopoly sentiment toward corporate utilities.

The Origins of Customer Stock Ownership

Hockenbeamer and his Pacific Gas & Electric Company, based in Northern California, launched its customer stock-ownership program in direct response to events taking place in Southern California. In 1907, Los Angeles voters approved bonds for an ambitious infrastructure project that would bring in fresh water from the Owens Valley. Three years later, Los Angeles residents added a small municipally owned power plant to their plans. Over the next several years, plans for the small power plant evolved into proposals for a much larger plant. In May 1914, Los Angeles residents voted to construct a large municipally owned power plant and buy out the city's privately owned electricity distribution network controlled by SCE. The vote delivered a crushing blow to the company, which lost nearly 75 percent of its business. It also sent a wake-up call to the company's largest neighbor to the north, PG&E headquartered in San Francisco. PG&E.[7] In 1913, the San Francisco city council approved a new rate schedule that PG&E deemed "confiscatory."[8] San Francisco residents had also been toying with municipal ownership, and in 1910 they approved a water project in the Hetch Hetchy Valley to free themselves from their hated privately owned water utility.[9] Like an earlier version of the Owens Valley plan, San Francisco's Hetch Hetchy project called for a small municipally owned power plant. But with LA's 1914 vote to enlarge the city's power plant, San Francisco's plans began to look like creeping socialism to executives at PG&E. Not willing to sit back and watch San Francisco residents follow in the footsteps of Los Angeles, PG&E executives quickly launched their customer stock-ownership program. Just three months after residents voted for municipal ownership in Los Angeles, PG&E began selling stock to customers in San Francisco.[10]

If the threat of low rates and public ownership provided PG&E with an initial motivation to sell stock to customers, state utilities regulation provided a convenient justification. In 1914, after several years of record growth, PG&E wanted to build a new power plant and petitioned the California Railroad Commission for permission to issue additional bonds to pay for the project.[11] But the Railroad Commission, which oversaw utility financing in the state, rejected PG&E's financing plan.[12] The commission limited the total amount of bonded debt a utility could carry to a certain percentage of the firm's annual profits, and PG&E had reached that limit. The only financing plan the commission would accept was for PG&E to issue additional stock.[13] And as the president of the Railroad Commission noted that year, if public utilities could not attract investment capital, then "the tendency will be to substitute public ownership for private ownership"; an outcome to which the president of the commission was not opposed.[14] It was in this context of a drift toward municipalization and strict regulation that PG&E began selling stock to customers.

The Railroad Commission essentially forced PG&E to sell stock, but the decision to sell this stock directly to customers rather than to large investors was the company's own choice, and an overwhelmingly political one. As the company's magazine declared in 1915, "One of the surest ways of solving the so-called corporation problem and enlisting the good-will and support of the public, is to appeal to its self-interest by giving it the opportunity of becoming a partner in the corporation enterprise and sharing in its profits."[15] Less than a month after the company initiated its customer-ownership plan, the *San Francisco Chronicle* observed that the program was "generally regarded as a master stroke of diplomacy."[16] Four months later the *Chronicle* declared that "the distribution of this stock is the worst blow ever delivered municipal ownership on this Coast."[17] It was still too early to tell, but PG&E certainly hoped it would be.

Although PG&E only offered "preferred stock," which did not include corporate voting rights, customer appetite proved stronger than outside observers, and even the company, expected.[18] Each month hundreds of customers handed over $82.50 for one share of PG&E stock yielding a 6 percent dividend on its $100 par value, or an actual return on investment of 7.27 percent; much better than the average savings account.[19]

Since each individual customer did not typically subscribe to large quantities of the stock, the number of subscribers soon became large. By December 1916, PG&E had vaulted itself into the ranks of the top twenty industrial corporations in terms of the number of stockholders.[20] Other electric companies began to take note. By US entry into World War I and the first Liberty Bond Campaign, thirteen electricity companies had developed customer-ownership plans. During the war, fifteen more electric companies launched customer stock ownership plans.[21]

After the war, customer stock ownership spread quickly throughout the electricity, gas, streetcar, and telephone industries. In 1919 and 1920, a total of forty-six electricity companies launched customer-ownership plans. In 1921 alone, no less than thirty-seven electric utilities in all parts of the country initiated customer-ownership plans, a number only exceeded by the next year's totals.[22] Also in 1921, AT&T introduced its own customer stock-ownership program.[23] In other words, AT&T only adopted the strategy of customer stock ownership when the movement to initiate plans in the electricity industry was already nearing its peak.

The main goal of all these stock-ownership programs was not to raise capital but to raise political support, as utility executives explicitly stated. The president of SCE flatly told an audience of electricity executives that "our activity has been wholly along the line of securing partners, not of raising money." David F. Houston, the president of the Bell Telephone Securities Company, made an almost identical statement, telling Bell managers that "the central thought in this [customer-ownership] plan is not that of raising large sums of money and of raising them quickly. It is rather that of establishing better public relations." Samuel Insull, the president of the Commonwealth Edison Company of Chicago, told his securities salesmen in 1923 that customer stock ownership was "the solution, the answer to the demand for municipal ownership."[24]

These comments were not made for public consumption, but utility firms made no secret of their political designs. If a potential customer-owner asked, "Why do you not go to Wall Street for funds?" a National Electric Light Association (NELA) manual instructed electricity employees to answer, "The company is now offering the citizens of the communities it serves an opportunity to invest . . . first, to increase public friendship and good-will."[25] Insull told an audience at Princeton University in 1923 that he believed "community ownership leads to community good will" and that it was "natural for the man, or the woman, or the boy or girl to think that his electric light and power company is all right if he owns stock in that company."[26] It was therefore no accident that the Customer Stock Ownership Committee of NELA met under the public relations section of the organization, and not under accounting.[27] Customer ownership was overwhelmingly about politics.

As customer stock ownership became common throughout the utilities industries, credit to PG&E for inventing the strategy began pouring in. Members of the National Electric Light Association (NELA), the major electricity industry group, routinely credited PG&E with inventing customer ownership.[28] An executive at the Oklahoma Gas & Electric Company told a NELA gathering in 1922 that "the industry as a whole owes a debt of gratitude to the Pacific Gas & Electric Company for having inaugurated this scheme which is now being pushed so generally."[29] An SCE vice president traced his company's use of customer ownership to PG&E, telling a group of utility executives that "from San Francisco the scheme came down to Los Angeles."[30]

This was the same SCE that had lost nearly three-quarters of its business in 1914 when Los Angeles residents voted for municipal ownership. At the time, the president of SCE thought the company might go bankrupt, but it survived due to the growth of Los Angeles' suburbs, where the company still operated. The company's properties outside the city limits were untouched by the city's municipalization. After that experience, however, the company took no chances with public opinion in its remaining markets and became a major practitioner of customer stock ownership.[31]

The idea of selling stock to utility users was not entirely new in 1914 when PG&E began selling stock to customers. But previously, the idea had been employed by fledgling utility organizations that sought to provide service in rural areas where utility service would not otherwise be available. Often, these small telephone and electricity organizations were boosted by farmers, merchants, or doctors who constructed rudimentary networks and offered service to nearby residents in exchange for the residents paying for a share of the equipment. These small organizations can best be thought of in the same way they thought of themselves, as cooperative associations, or "mutuals." In contrast, PG&E, when it first introduced customer stock ownership, was a multimillion-dollar company with tens of thousands of customers, and shares of its stock traded on the San Francisco Board of Stocks and Bonds. In terms of organizational size, technological sophistication, and a clear division between customers and the corporations, PG&E was a different kind of organization offering a different kind of ownership program. The customer stock-ownership program introduced by PG&E in 1914 can therefore rightfully be considered the first program of its type in American business history.[32]

The Utilities' Situation after World War I

After World War I, customer stock ownership spread rapidly because the strategy was now used to fight municipal ownership and another common enemy of utilities—low utility rates as set by regulators. In the inflationary period during and directly after the war, many Americans began to scrutinize their utility bills, as did the utilities. Prices on labor and materials were going up, but the rates utilities could charge were fixed by state utility boards. After a long period of price declines due to technological efficiency gains, utilities now wanted customers to accept higher rates, which many did not want to do.[33] The result was a struggle over rates. But it was more than just a contest over who would get the most out of a jealous commercial relation-

Stock Ownership as Corporate Strategy   *131*

ship. For utility companies, the struggle over rates was every bit as serious as the threat of public ownership. If a vote for public ownership meant death by democratic guillotine, consistently low-rate rulings meant death by financial starvation. In both cases, the survival of the firm was at stake. If utilities failed to secure rate increases, their existing infrastructure would crumble, their ability to meet growing demand would decline, and customer satisfaction would evaporate. Calls for public ownership might easily reappear, and the next national emergency—a prolonged depression, say—might make the next experiment in government ownership the last. The experience of the railroads during World War I provided a sobering reminder to utility executives that strict rate regulation combined with terrible public relations could lead to poor infrastructure, an angry public, and ultimately, nationalization.[34] Although the railroads received their property back after the war, the industry had much more government interference than either the telephone, gas, or electricity industries cared to deal with.[35]

The issue of low rates was particularly pressing for AT&T after World War I. Before the war, going back to the nineteenth century, AT&T had carefully cultivated its public image by advertising extensively, reducing call-placement times and training operators in customer courtesy.[36] But the period of telephone nationalization during World War I destroyed much of what AT&T had built up in terms of its public image and customer service. Unionism was on the rise, employee morale was low, and training was insufficient due to high turnover during the war. Workers were also upset over low wages and passed their frustration on to customers. In addition to these internal problems, AT&T faced a large number of rates cases directly after the war and its share price was slipping.[37] Some historians have seen the McReynolds settlement of 1913, in which AT&T accepted certain restrictions in exchange for government recognition of its monopoly, as a key turning point in the history of the firm, which it was.[38] Yet the years immediately after the war represented another critical moment for the company. It was the "greatest crisis in the history of the Bell System," AT&T vice president E. K. Hall stated in 1922.[39] It was a period of "critical emergency," recalled AT&T president Walter Gifford.[40]

It was in this political-economic context that AT&T initiated its first customer stock-ownership program in 1921. The strategy provided AT&T with a solution to the difficult riddle of how to secure rate increases while at the same time improving public opinion. By selling stock to thousands of Americans and returning a portion of the company's profits back to customer-shareholders,

AT&T hoped that any lingering antimonopoly sentiment would decline each time customers opened their dividend checks, as shown in this AT&T advertisement for stock ownership. AT&T, "Owned by Those It Serves," *Southern Telephone News*, October 1922, back cover, AT&T-TX. Courtesy of AT&T-TX.

AT&T could cast itself not as a greedy monopoly but as the responsible steward of the nation's small investors. To oppose AT&T rate increases would be to oppose the many small investors themselves.[41] AT&T executives also calculated that stock ownership would additionally make customers more willing to trade special privileges, such as a nationwide monopoly, for user benefits, such as quality service, when that deal came with the ultimate user benefit—a healthy $9 dividend.[42]

Before launching their own customer-ownership plan, AT&T executives had been observing the strategy in the electricity industry and, after adopting the idea, the company received advice on its customer-ownership program from electricity executives. In 1920, before AT&T initiated its customer ownership plan, a manager for the Pacific Telephone and Telegraph (PT&T) noted that "a large public utility in the light and power field in our own territory advertises the issue of notes at a rate which will net the purchaser 7.70 per cent."[43] He was probably referring to either PG&E or SCE. When PT&T began offering stock directly to customers, none other than A. F. Hockenbeamer, the man who pioneered customer ownership at PG&E, wrote to the president of PT&T and advised him that if PT&T wanted to sell any of its new preferred stock, the company needed to declare immediate dividends.

Hockenbeamer's letter eventually reached AT&T president Walter Gifford, the dividends were declared, and stock sales followed.[44] Far from inventing customer stock ownership, AT&T learned the strategy from the electricity industry.

The Social History of Employee Stock Selling

In order to sell as much stock as possible to customers, utility executives in all utility industries used advertising, of course, but they were not content to wait for customer demand. Instead, executives developed innovative methods to supply stock directly to customers. The most important of these was forcing utility employees to peddle stock to their family, friends, and neighbors.[45]

Since the Bell System alone employed over 400,000 workers in 1929—the largest employer in America at the time—and the electricity and gas industries employed another 230,000 workers, the relationship networks executives tapped into was immense.[46] And since these employees were not only managers, lawyers, and engineers, but also clerks, conductors, cashiers, linemen, metermen, operators, and ticket agents, these workers were able to reach thousands of Americans who would not normally have been solicited by securities salesmen or gone into a brokerage firm.[47] By tapping into this individually limited but numerically large market, executives raised capital, but, more importantly, they tied their customers' financial future to their utility's political future.

Utility employees received almost no training in their new job of stock selling. Typically, executives introduced their company's customer-ownership program in a large meeting where managers stressed that anyone could sell stock and then offered a few pointers, such as suggestions for opening sales lines. When knocking on a customer's door, employees should say: "I have come to see you at the company's request. They want me to tell you of an opportunity the company is offering to its customers." People in a rush were not receptive to sales offers, managers advised, but "after a rest and a supper a man is likely to be in a buying mood." Employees should therefore visit customers at night. Above all, employees should try to gain access to the customer's house rather than make their pitch from the doorstep.[48]

Also during introductory sales meetings, managers asked employees to subscribe to the company's stock themselves since no employee could be a good salesman "unless he takes a dose of his own medicine," as Samuel Insull explained. Sometimes, managers planted an employee in the audience to be the first to volunteer to buy stock in order to get the other employees to do the same. Regarding these shills, executives cautioned managers to "tell them to say nothing about it."[49]

Managers also sought to develop a list of sales contacts at these introductory meetings. A manual written by executives experienced in customer-ownership drives advised managers to require each employee to provide the names and addresses of ten acquaintances "on whom he agrees to call. THEN LOCK THE DOOR AND LET NOBODY OUT UNTIL THEY TURN IN THE TEN CARDS EACH. Don't be put off by those who say they will think it over and turn in a list later—experience has shown that it then becomes a tremendous task to get in the names."[50] According to a 1925 American Electric Railway Association (AERA) report, this practice was "often found useful."[51]

Once managers obtained the information of their employees' friends, managers sent personalized mail to the prospects' houses, after which managers were instructed to "insist that the employee carry out his agreement and see the ten people." Each employee's efforts were tracked, and those who failed to sell were pulled aside at work and individually admonished about the need to sell stock.[52]

While employees received little sales training, they received even less financial education. "No effort was made to acquaint the rank and file with the details of the financial statement of the Company," a Bell executive admitted during a presentation about employee stock selling in 1929. If a potential investor asked a Bell employee whether the company's stock had any value, the employee was simply instructed to reply that "it had or the company would not be selling it."[53] Electricity employees were taught that if a potential shareholder asked what the likelihood of their company failing was, employees should answer: "None. Based upon the history of utility companies in the United States, there is much less chance of failure than in other sound enterprises."[54] As long as workers owned some company stock themselves and knew "a few other 'talking points' about the security," they were "equipped to take orders," an AERA Customer Ownership Committee declared.[55]

Yet according to stories traded by executives and employee magazine editors, no real knowledge of stocks was necessary. One *Pacific Telephone Magazine* editor reported that an employee sold 936 shares in nine days, proving that workers should just "place your story before your man, then hand him your fountain pen with the little pink slip for signature and see how quickly he reaches for his check book."[56] One Bell manager told colleagues that a telephone repairman pitched stock to a major newspaper publisher while in his office working on his phone. After having a few simple questions answered, the publisher decided to take one hundred shares. The repairman pulled out a "soiled application blank and told him to, 'sign on the dotted line and yours truly will do the rest.'"[57] Stories like these told managers that not much training was needed.

To enforce selling, utilities established sales quotas that ranged from two shares a month to one share a year per employee to get employees to sell stock.[58] This selling had to be done strictly off the clock, on the employees' own evenings, weekends, or lunch hours. "No employee must slight his own work," declared one executive told others in 1924, "we hold them very strictly to account as regards their own job and their own line of work."[59]

Utilities offered small commissions to motivate employees. These commissions varied from 50¢ to $2 per share sold at a par value of $100, or 0.5 to 2 percent of the selling price. Employees who sold shares on the installment plan received a lower commission, usually 25¢. Supervisors also received commissions based on how many shares their employees sold.[60] Since selling small amounts to large numbers of people produced more goodwill than selling large amounts to a few people, employees often received lower commissions the more stock they sold.[61] Clearly, executives cared more about establishing friendly customer relations than raising capital.

To further motivate employees, companies divided their departments into rival sales teams, which NELA recommended to create "a natural basis for the inter-team rivalry."[62] Some companies referred to these teams as "armies or divisions," with the managers known as "commanders, captains, [and] lieutenants."[63] Managers at SCE went as far as dividing each office into a red team and a blue team, and setting them against each other.[64] "Everything was done to arouse competition," the company's president told his peers at an industry conference.[65] It was no surprise that employees at his company soon fell to bickering over who would get credit for stock sales made to customers who spoke with more than one employee before buying stock.[66]

For teams who won monthly sales competitions, companies offered trophies or company pennants, while particularly enthusiastic individual employees received flowers, a letter of commendation, or a write-up in the company's employee magazine.[67] Despite these inducements, most employees appear not to have been very enthusiastic about selling stock. One manager observed that his employees were overjoyed when news arrived that their company would not be assigning quotas that year.[68] But some managers

Employees at the central information office of PT&T display the banner they received for selling the most stock in their region. "Customer Ownership Helps," *Pacific Telephone Magazine*, November 1925, 22, AT&T-TX. Courtesy of AT&T-TX.

reported that employee morale increased as workers delivered sales pitches to neighbors.[69] One Bell employee even sold more dollars' worth of stock than the value of the office building in which he worked.[70]

Stock Sales at Branch Offices and Elsewhere

In addition to selling stock to friends and acquaintances, utilities sold stock directly to customers at local utility offices. As customers streamed into offices of utilities in the 1920s, customer service clerks had numerous oppor-

Stock Ownership as Corporate Strategy   137

tunities to sell stock. These clerks were exempt from the prohibition against selling stock while on the clock. Rather, they were required to peddle stock to every customer who walked in the door. To do this, one enterprising employee at SCE stationed himself between the clerk who took the customers' bill and the clerk who took the customers' money. In that position, he would glance down at the name on the bill and then launch into a sales pitch before customers could complete their transaction. When that held up the line too much, clerks began intercepting customers as they walked in the front door toward counter in order to strike up a conversation with them about buying stock.[71]

Streetcar companies installed stock purchasing booths inside stations, stations agents and platform men distributed pamphlets about stock to passengers, and conductors harangued passengers about buying stock when they traveled in the cars. Streetcar companies also plastered their waiting rooms, platforms, and cars—inside and out—with posters and banners advertising stock and provided stock purchasing booths at stops. "This is 'hand-feeding' the public with a vengeance," exalted a streetcar manager. "You almost literally take the passenger's nose between your thumb and finger, make him open his mouth, and then you pour your great truths, a spoonful at a time, into his system. . . . A man doesn't have to buy a newspaper . . . but, how different it is on the street car! . . . He is in your custody."[72]

Eventually, this constant pressure to buy stock got on customers' nerves. Managers reported that customers were demanding "peace" on the subject of stock ownership. "I don't want to talk Edison stock," fumed one customer at an SCE office in 1921, "I want to pay my bill."[73]

Besides selling stock at local offices and to friends, utilities used other methods to reach potential customer-owners. AT&T set up displays at county fairs that included technology demonstrations along with the opportunity to buy stock.[74] The particularly eager Southern California Edison Company sent salesmen to local factories to ask the owner if he would mind "having his employees encouraged in thrifty ways."[75] Many owners assented, called their employees back ten minutes early from lunch, and let the salesmen talk ten minutes into the afternoon shift. After the sales pitch, salesmen were allowed to walk through the company and sign workers up for stock. One SCE employee reported that out of six hundred factories, "less than 1 per cent did not cooperate to the limit." Using this method, the company enlisted eleven thousand new shareholders in one week, many of whom must have been blue-collar workers and, importantly, local customers and voters.[76]

Like many utilities, SCE maintained a staff of full-time securities salesmen who augmented the sales efforts of the company's regular employees. These handpicked salesmen went door-to-door, even in rural areas, interviewing customers about service quality and inquiring whether the customer owned stock. "I understand your neighbor next door is a stockholder in the Southern California Edison Company," salesmen were instructed to say. "Have you given the matter any thought?"[77]

SCE executives also utilized their welfare capitalism programs to sell stock. The company provided club houses to employees, which employees paid dues to use and which managers were not allowed to enter. But the company wanted the clubs to sell stock, so the vice president of finance told his full-time stock salesmen to "make friends" with the club presidents and "get in under their skin" in order to get them to pressure club members to invite their friends to club meetings at which stock would be pitched.[78]

Electricity, gas, and telephone managers also gave speeches about customer ownership at local civic clubs, high schools, and colleges. School speeches were "particularly effective," noted one manager who reported that parents were coming to local utility offices to buy stock after hearing about it from their kids.[79]

Of course, utilities also used advertising to promote their customer-ownership plans. One advertisement featured a picture of an old woman with a caption that read, "I'm a widow and I can't afford to lose a cent of my money, so I have it safely invested in Preferred Stock of Pennsylvania Power & Light." Another ad read: "I'm a working man, I can't afford get-rich-quick schemes."[80] Other ads featured depictions of George Washington, Abraham Lincoln, and Santa Claus. AT&T, in particular, employed ubiquitous and folksy ads to sell stock. One featured a grandmotherly looking AT&T shareholder snapping peas, which was intended to make the company seem familiar and approachable, rather than shadowy and suspect.[81]

Utilities advertised their stock in a wide range of publications and locations. SCE advertised its stock in all three hundred papers within its operating territories as well as on the region's once-plentiful streetcars.[82] The company's advertising strategy, as its president described it, was to "bear down heavily" for a few weeks, and then "let up for a little while and allow the public to catch its breath." Then another "surge" would follow.[83] Some utilities also advertised in American newspapers published in foreign languages.[84]

Yet, utility stock advertising went beyond just newspapers and magazines. The Bell System distributed more than a million copies of the stock promotion pamphlet "Some Financial Facts" in the 1920s.[85] The Bell Telephone Securities Company also sent fifty-two thousand copies of the *Bell Telephone Securities Manual* to bankers and brokers, printed sample stock certificates for use in window displays at telephone offices, and hung "Orders Received Here" signs over counters at local offices.[86] Many electric and gas companies sent a "friendly letter" regarding stock purchasing to all of their customers, inserted pamphlets into bills, placed stock brochures on counters at commercial offices, and also advertised in company windows.[87] Yet all this print represented only one component of the utility's massive customer ownership program that relied more heavily on face-to-face contact than print to induce stock sales and change political sentiments.

The Regional Aspect of Customer Stock Ownership

Like most of American politics, the politics of customer ownership had a regional dimension. This was especially true for AT&T's customer-ownership program. One of main goals of the company's stock-ownership program was to reduce the concentration of AT&T stock in the Northeast and increase it in the South, West, and Midwest, a project AT&T officers called their "redistribution campaigns."[88] By redistributing stock, AT&T executives hoped to "develop a . . . better understanding" of the company among area residents, as AT&T's 1922 *Annual Report* stated.[89] To see if this redistribution was possible, AT&T launched its first customer ownership campaign in 1921 in an impoverished area of West Texas where the local cattle and lumber industries were hurting. Texas was also teeming with independent telephone companies, and had been for some time.[90] If shares of a monopoly could be sold there, they could be sold anywhere. Despite the poor local economy and tradition of independent telephony, Southwestern Bell employees succeeded in selling twenty-five thousand shares of the company's preferred stock with an average sale of just four shares per customer. AT&T then tried a customer-ownership campaign in Wisconsin, another hotbed of independent telephony and home to Senator Robert La Follette, one of the nation's strongest advocates of government utility ownership. In just four days, the Bell-affiliated Wisconsin Telephone Company sold $5 million worth of preferred stock, with an average sale of just five shares per customer. Following this, customer-ownership drives took place in West Virginia, Maryland, and Washington, DC.[91]

It was only after the success of these initial tests that AT&T executives decided to launch their customer stock-ownership program nationwide. To do this, AT&T officers formed the Bell Telephone Securities Company in

1922. The Securities Company served as AT&T's own underwriting and brokerage firm and allowed AT&T to sell stock wherever and to whomever the company found most politically advantageous. Regarding this locally placed stock, the president of the Bell Telephone Securities Company, David F. Houston, stated that it was "not necessary or desirable to have it leave the territory.... This would not be consistent with the underlying purpose."[92] Referring to the distribution of stock, AT&T president H. B. Thayer stated in the company's 1921 *Annual Report* that "we believe that a wide distribution of the securities of the System geographically and among individuals, is advantageous... with a wide financial foundation, better understandings and relationships result."[93] Ironically, Bell Telephone Company founder Gardiner G. Hubbard hated the telegraph monopoly of Western Union and promoted decentralized ownership of the Bell company in order to prevent a similar monopoly in the telephone industry. Yet in the early 1920s, the Bell System again promoted nationally dispersed ownership, but this time in a defense of its own monopoly.[94]

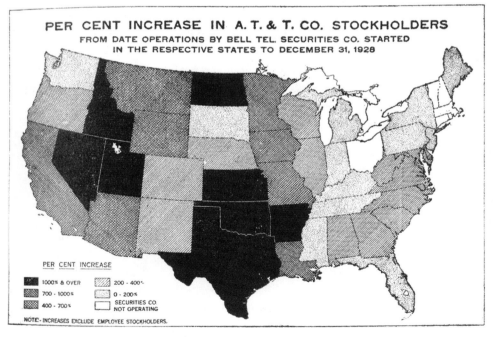

The increase in AT&T shareholders between 1921 and 1929 exceeded 1,000 percent in many western states. Bell Securities, *Annual Report, 1928*, 7. Courtesy of AT&T-TX.

Gas and electric utilities also sold stock in nearly all parts of the country. As early as 1924, they were offering customer ownership in every state in the continental United States except the Dakotas, Mississippi, Nevada, New Mexico, and Wyoming. By 1927, every state but Nevada, North Dakota, and Wyoming had customer-ownership plans on offer.[95]

As utilities began selling stock to customers, shareholders began to appear in places far from the traditional centers of banking and finance. Gas and electric companies had sold stock to nearly ten thousand customers in West Virginia, twenty thousand customers in Kentucky, and thirty thousand customers in Alabama by 1927.[96] Between 1921 and 1924, AT&T increased the number of its shareholders by over 200 percent in California, Iowa, and Wisconsin; by 300 to 600 percent in Minnesota, Montana, Nevada, Wyoming, Idaho; and by no less than 926 percent in North Dakota.[97] Considering that Robert La Follette came in first or second in each of these nine states in the

Map showing towns and cities where electric utilities operated customer stock ownership campaigns in 1925. "Customer Ownership Committee," *NELA Proceedings* (1926), 324.

presidential election of 1924, and that the first plank in his platform was a demand for public ownership of utilities, AT&T's stock redistribution campaign was not an unwise decision in the eyes of management.[98] This is not to argue that customer ownership was the only or even main reason La Follette lost the election. But the conservative nature of politics in the 1920s was not inevitable. It depended on specific changes in voter sentiment, some of which executives intentionally tried to bring about. By redistributing stock into the traditional heartland of populism and public ownership, AT&T almost certainly contributed to dispelling the antimonopoly sentiment in those regions.

Mechanics of Placing Stock

AT&T's impressive sales feats in the 1920s demonstrated the Bell System's extraordinary organizational capability to place stock directly into the hands of customers across the country. To do this, AT&T extended its organizational tentacles deeper into the affairs of its regional operating companies. Whenever AT&T directors approved a new stock issue—which occurred almost every other year in the 1920s—local Bell employees fanned out across the country, soliciting their friends to buy stock and taking subscriptions at local commercial offices. Simultaneously, thousands of circulars and subscription warrants were mailed to existing stockholders and announcements sent out to all the largest newspapers in the United States, as well as overseas. At the end of each day, the orders from each region were tallied and communicated to the Bell Telephone Securities Company, which would fill the orders, either by buying the shares off the New York Stock Exchange or taking the stock directly out of the company's vaults and then mailing them to the customer.[99]

To handle the spikes in volume that attended new stock issues, the Securities Company augmented their full-time staff of two hundred with up to seven hundred temporary workers and a small army of college interns. Together these clerks filled orders, worked the phones, and staffed the company's New York sales counter. They also replied to over a hundred thousand letters, many of which required personalized responses. During one sales campaign, just sealing envelopes required fifty gallons of "mucilage." On the closing day of the 1926 stock drive, the Securities Company handled more than fifty thousand subscriptions at the local offices and through the mail. By 1928, customers were lining up three and four deep at the Securities Company sales counter in New York to purchase shares directly from the company.[100] Americans were getting used to buying stock, and many were doing so directly from utilities.

Stock Ownership as Corporate Strategy 143

Customers buying stock directly from AT&T at the company's headquarters in New York. H. Blair-Smith, "The 1928 Stock Offer of the American Telephone and Telegraph Company," *Bell Telephone Quarterly*, October 1928, photo opposite p. 264, AT&T-TX. Courtesy of AT&T-TX.

By turning every local office into a brokerage firm and every employee into a stockbroker, AT&T and other utilities supplied vast amounts of stock directly to Americans in all parts of the country. Considering that the Bell System maintained over seven hundred branch offices across the United States, even in very small towns, the Bell System almost certainly became the largest brokerage in the country during the 1920s in terms of geographic reach and possibly also in terms of volume.[101] Bell's properties were so numerous that an editor for the *Bell Telephone Quarterly* suggested that they were "probably the largest group of buildings belonging to any one organization in the United States."[102] With the possible exception of the US government, this may have been correct.

At local Bell offices, customers could buy stock for cash or on the installment plan and sell their shares, or warrant rights in the case of AT&T, for cash.[103] Beginning in 1925, over 50 percent of AT&T customer-buyers purchased their shares on a payment plan. In 1923, around one-third of electricity customer-shareholders also purchased their stock on the installment plan.[104] At many electric and streetcar utility offices, customer-shareholders

Processing stock at the Bell Telephone Securities Company. A security guard stands watch in the back right corner while managers hover over each row of clerks. H. Blair-Smith, "The 1930 Stock Offer of the American Telephone and Telegraph Company," *Bell Telephone Quarterly*, October 1930, photo opposite p. 253, AT&T-TX. Courtesy of AT&T-TX.

could also sell shares for cash. Offering this buy-back service was one of NELA's "Ten Cardinal Rules of Customer Ownership" and was designed to reassure customers that their shares could easily be sold at any time.[105] By bypassing the stock exchanges and acting as their own brokers, utilities could also sell shares to customers without the high transaction fees that formerly made small purchases uneconomical. And in terms of creating political allies, the vote of a small shareholder was just as good as the vote of a large one.[106]

The 20 Percent

The result of these personalized selling techniques in numerical terms proved dramatic. Counting only those stock sales specifically attributed to customer stock-ownership campaigns, and not counting sales made to institutional investors or through traditional brokerages via the stock exchange, the total number of shareholders obtained through customer-ownership plans in the gas, electricity, and telephone industries exceeded two million by the Crash of 1929.[107] If the number of stockholders in the United States by that time was ten million people—a commonly cited number—then customer-ownership programs sold stock to no less than 20 percent of the total number of stockholders in America by the late 1920s.[108]

Who were the 20 percent? Many of them were first-time shareholders with moderate incomes. This was because utility executives specifically used

Stock Ownership as Corporate Strategy   145

their clerks to reach people of modest incomes. The Bell Telephone Securities Company's *Annual Report* for 1923 noted that their shareholders were often people of "small means, many of whom apparently are relatively unacquainted with investments."[109] Customer-owners also came from a wide range of occupations. According to utility company lists, shareholders included bakers, barbers, beauticians, bell hops, boilermakers, bootblacks, brick layers, butchers, carpenters, chauffeurs, clerks, coal dealers, cobblers, contractors, cooks, coroners, druggists, farmers, fruit packers, housewives, janitors, mail men, mechanics, movers, nurses, pawn brokers, porters, preachers, priests, sailors, salesladies, soda dispensers, teachers, telephone operators, stenographers, taxi drivers, and waiters. By far, the largest categories of shareholders were housewives and clerks.[110] Since the beginning of customer ownership, utilities reported that over half of their shareholders were women.[111]

Utilities also boasted that their shareholders came from a wide variety of ethnic backgrounds. One executive, whose company promoted customer ownership in a coal mining region in Pennsylvania, stated that his company's shareholder list looked "like the immigration roster at Ellis Island." There were "all the Z's and Y's and W's imaginable, Czechoslovaks, Jugoslavaks, Poles, Creeks, Italians, Finns, and Huns, and in fact practically every known nationality."[112]

Shareholders also came from a wide range of ages. Executives were particularly surprised that many young people bought stock.[113] One employee magazine featured a story and photo of a fifteen-year-old, Thomas L. Taylor of Portland, Oregon, who plunked down $500 at a local telephone office to buy four shares of AT&T in cash and one more share on the installment plan. Taylor had saved his money by selling newspapers and working at his high school print shop.[114]

Cultivating the Political Sentiments of Shareholders

Once executives obtained customer-shareholders, they carefully endeavored to mold their new investors' political sentiments. Executives mailed shareholders the latest issue of the company's magazine and stuffed dividend envelopes with political tracts about upcoming ballot measures.[115] One gas and electric company sent the anti–government ownership pamphlet "Bureaucracy in Fine Flower" along with a dividend check to its forty-five thousand shareholders.[116] In Michigan, a power company sent twenty thousand road maps to shareholders, which showed the location of the company's power lines and dams "so that as the owner passed a line in his travels he knew it belonged to 'his company.'"[117] The Byllesby Corporation sent its shareholders a calendar featuring a specially commissioned painting depicting "Dividend Day," with this new four-times-a-year holiday highlighted for each quarter.[118] Another company changed its dividend payment schedule from quarterly to monthly so it could have "12 favorable impressions in a year, instead of four."[119] This repeated favorable contact between utilities and shareholders was one reason why executives preferred stocks to bonds. Bonds created partners only until the bonds matured, but stocks kept paying dividends year after year.[120]

Even small shareholders were made to feel like part of the corporate community. Companies hosted unofficial shareholders' meetings in locations throughout their territories so as many shareholders as possible could attend. PG&E held dozens of these each year, which included speeches, musical performances, and a short movie.[121] Not all shareholders could make shareholder meetings, admitted executives in New Jersey, but they still felt it was "most desirable" to meet as many shareholders as possible "face to face."[122] Shareholders were also invited as special guests at entertainments held at Edison Clubs operated by the employees of the Southern California Edison Company. "They have darned good times. It all helps," observed the company president.[123]

Did Customer Stock Ownership Work?

Did customer stock ownership work in its stated goals of thwarting public ownership, obtaining goodwill, and securing rate increases? Executives, regulators, and outside observers—even critical ones—agreed that it did. Herbert Pell Jr., a former congressman from New York, considered utility executives "utterly irresponsible" but acknowledged in 1925 that "so long as dividends are paid no complaints will come." Henry L. Stimson, the once and future secretary of war, stated at an academic conference in 1925 that "some critics tend to belittle the new [customer-ownership] movement. . . . I think that they underestimate the immense change which is being effected in public opinion and the power of that public opinion. . . . Upon that public opinion the new proprietorship is producing a most potent change."[124] Many other observers confirmed Stimson's view. A 1929 NELA report on customer ownership concluded that its "effect upon public relations has been profound and far reaching—in fact, it has entirely changed the character of electric light and power companies in the public mind."[125] The vice president of the

Stock Ownership as Corporate Strategy 147

San Joaquin Light and Power Corporation observed in 1925 that when a customer buys stock, "almost invariably, and usually unconsciously, he takes a new interest in the utility and its affairs. His dividend checks come as symbols of his ownership.... he learns something of the doctrine of self-interest... 'you scratch my back and I'll scratch yours.'"[126]

Only in the streetcar industry did executives find customer stock ownership less successful, though it was not for lack of trying. Streetcar companies had trouble convincing customers to invest in an industry facing the daunting challenge of jitneys and automobiles. Furthermore, streetcar companies served fewer people. For these reasons, streetcar utilities had difficulty selling stock to customers and the strategy of customer stock ownership was not as widespread in the streetcar industry as it was in other monopoly utility industries.[127]

Yet in the gas, electricity, and telephone industries, observers noted that resistance to rate increases declined as a result of customer ownership. A staffer for the California Railroad Commission observed in 1926 that "the sale of stock to customers has had a most beneficial effect.... As a result of the practice the tears of despair that formerly were shed at rate cases was changed into the radiant smile." A Byllesby executive confirmed the observation, telling the *Wall Street Journal* that, thanks to customer ownership, his company had enjoyed "a remarkable history of rate increases, the majority of which were obtained without controversy by simply showing facts. We hear little or nothing of municipal ownership any more, at properties where we have home-shareholders."[128] A stronger endorsement could hardly be made.

Customer ownership even helped convert some former socialists to capitalism, including John Spargo, a founding member of the Socialist Party of America and biographer of Karl Marx. In 1924, Spargo penned a "Confession" in *Outlook* magazine, in which he declared that "governmental ownership and operation of railroads, telegraphs, telephones, and similar public utilities now appears to me to be inherently inferior to the new type of enterprise we are so rapidly developing, characterized by popular ownership." To call these companies "monopolies" with a "sinister meaning," wrote Spargo, was "to misuse language."[129] Spargo's antimonopoly sentiment had disappeared due to customer stock ownership. For Spargo, and perhaps many others, the term "monopoly," once mostly a pejorative, now seemed promising. Newspapers reported that some current socialists appeared on the shareholders' rolls of corporate utilities.[130]

148   Chapter 4

Other socialists had no such change of heart, however. In 1923, the socialist Public Ownership League of America passed a resolution calling for state laws against utilities selling stock to customers. Samuel Insull bragged that this just showed "the importance of our [customer-ownership] action in changing public opinion."[131] Another utility executive argued that socialists hated customer ownership because it weakened the socialists' position and popularity and created an "impregnable wall around private business."[132] Even after utility publicist John Sheridan turned critical of corporate utilities, he still believed that customer ownership led to the "destruction of radical thought among the people."[133]

Customer-owners also played a role in defeating specific public-ownership referendums. In Radford, Virginia, shareholders of a corporate utility, among others, campaigned against a bond measure to build a municipally owned hydroelectric plant, and the bill was defeated.[134] In California, electricity executives believed that customer-owners directly contributed to the defeat of the California Water and Power Act. The measure advocated municipal ownership of utilities and appeared on California referendum ballots in 1922, 1924, and 1926. It was defeated each time. In 1922, the referendum was rejected by 70 percent of voters, with the number of shareholders to voters at about 12 percent.[135]

In the United States as a whole, the percentage of Americans who purchased stock directly through customer stock-ownership programs was lower than 12 percent. Utility employees succeeded in selling stock to about two million people through customer ownership plans by the crash of 1929. Since the population of the United States was about 123 million at the time, utility shareholders formed a little over 1.5 percent of Americans. These shareholders were concentrated in regions where utilities practiced customer stock ownership.

Yet many utility executives believed that customer-owners were more influential than their numbers suggested. Executives believed that customer ownership changed the opinions of even those Americans who did not own utilities stock.[136] Due to customer stock ownership, corporate utilities could no longer be viewed as representing large concentrations of individual wealth, executives argued. Instead utilities could now only be seen as owned by millions of small investors.[137] Furthermore, many people purchased utility stock through other means, such as from traditional brokers, and some, probably most, of these shareholders, connected their politics to their pocketbook.

Because of the voting implications of customer ownership, managers kept careful track of how many customer-owners lived within their service territories.[138] A reliable study by NELA in 1928 found that 11.8 percent of electricity customers were shareholders, or about 2 percent of the total population within the territories served.[139]

Some executives even kept track of exactly where each of their shareholders lived. Insull's Commonwealth Edison Company maintained a giant map

"Map Showing Stockholders, Commonwealth Edison Company," reads the text at the top of the map. The text at the bottom left reads "Every Dot a Stockholder." This map of Chicago is orientated with the north at the right and Lake Michigan at the bottom. "Sales Manual for Public Utility Employees: Subcommittee for Use in Customer Ownership Campaigns," *NELA Proceedings* (1922) 1:71.

of the city of Chicago with the residence of each shareholder literally pinpointed on the map.

Utility executives and the press also reported anecdotal evidence that customer ownership had created corporate allies at the grass-roots level. Insull told a gathering of managers about how one customer-owner tipped off utility employees about his neighbor's current theft when the employees came to drop off the customer's stock certificate.[140] Insull also told a story of a state legislator in Minneapolis who told his neighbor about his plans to introduce a bill that would hurt the local utility. "Well Jim," the neighbor told him, "you had better be careful. Everybody around here except you is an owner in that utility property."[141] The *Wall Street Journal* reported that an electric company received a call from a stockholder when the company's construction workers accidently left a large spool of wire near her house.[142] "If it belongs to the Edison Company, I am a stockholder and I want it looked after," the woman told the company. Stories like these circulated throughout the business community during the 1920s and indicated to executives that what Samuel Kennedy said about customer stock ownership was true: "If you sell a share of stock to an individual, he becomes your partner, and it's partners you want. That man is not only putting his money in, but he is working with you."[143] When customers became shareholders, they also became supporters of their company.

Upping the Ante

Although observers declared that customer ownership worked wonders on public opinion, it was not the case that the more stock utilities sold, the safer they became. This was because utility executives gambled with every bit of public goodwill they received from customer stock ownership. As soon as consumers signaled their acceptance of one type of corporate behavior, executives raised the stakes by pushing the boundaries one step further. By continually testing the limits of public acceptance, utilities never fully insulated their industries from political risk.

This was especially true in the electricity industry. The industry took two great risks in the 1920s: creating financially dubious holding companies, and expanding their monopolies to the point of creating "superpower" networks, which were giant interconnected grids that covered multiple states and were controlled by a single top-level company. The two developments were interrelated. Holding companies sold stock in order to generate the large amount of capital necessary to purchase operating companies. These individual op-

Stock Ownership as Corporate Strategy   151

erating companies were then stitched together by holding companies to form superpower monopolies. In many cases, holding companies not only purchased operating companies but also other holding companies in order to expand their network even faster.

Corporate law and corporate voting rules combined to make these purchases profitable, as long as the overall economy remained strong. Because owning 51 percent of a company's shares gave investors 100 percent control over a company's board, holding companies could purchase an operating company and siphon off all its profits for just over 50 percent of the company's value, essentially half-off. If another holding company purchased the first holding company, the deal got even sweeter. For 51 percent of the first holding company, organizers of the second holding company could control the first company and divert the profits of the base-level operating company into the new holding company for just a quarter of the operating company's value. In this way holding companies magnified money and for this reason they became very popular among financiers in the 1920s. As consolidation of the electricity industry accelerated during the 1920s, holding companies piled themselves one atop another, sometimes six and seven companies high.[144]

To afford to purchase operating companies, holding company officers issued reams of stock to consumers while keeping a controlling portion of the shares for themselves. Only when a lucrative deal came along would organizers agree sell their shares, with minority shareholders given no choice in the matter. This was no shareholders' democracy—it was a financial food chain in which the most recent owners made a great deal of money.[145]

Proponents of holding companies defended these institutions by arguing that holding companies provided centralized, and therefore cost-saving, legal and technical expertise to the operating companies they controlled. But the more consequential function of holding companies was to separate the volume of corporate shares in circulation from the volume of corporate assets in existence. In the speculative fever of the late 1920s, holding companies could scarcely issue stock fast enough to satisfy consumer demand, even though these companies did not directly own any tangible assets or manufacture a product. The lack of blue-sky laws, stories of rags-to-riches investors, and the New York Stock Exchange allowing holding companies to offer their shares starting in 1929 further stoked the speculative fires. In 1921 almost no holding companies existed; by 1927 there were 160 of them. The very next year there were three hundred, and in the first half of 1929, a new holding company was established nearly every single day.[146]

AT&T, although a holding company in part, operated in a more conservative manner in the 1920s, partly because of its conservative corporate structure. When AT&T's predecessor company was founded in 1876, it lacked the capital necessary to develop Alexander Graham Bell's telephone patents. To solve this problem the company licensed the patents to others with the money to develop local telephone networks.[147] This was how the regional "Baby Bells" were born, operating under patent-license from AT&T. As telephone usage grew and AT&T succeeded in attracting more investors, the parent company began to reel its children back in by selling shares of AT&T stock and using the money to buy shares of the regional operating companies. In 1905, AT&T lacked a controlling share in nine of its thirty regional operating companies; by 1926 that number had shrunk to just two of the twenty reorganized companies.[148]

This financial integration of the Bell System facilitated its technological integration as AT&T began stringing long-distance lines between its various operating company hubs. Even before the McReynolds settlement in 1913 when AT&T pledged not to buy out noncompeting rivals, AT&T president Theodore Vail realized that the one area in which independent telephone companies could never compete with AT&T was in providing long-distance service. Vail therefore pursued a policy of physically interconnecting Bell's numerous urban telephone networks, and by the 1920s he had created a truly nationwide network. Because AT&T directly owned and operated most of these long-distance lines, the company became not just a holding company, but now also an operating company.

This dual function of AT&T, and its single-tier holding company structure, was much more conservative than much of what was going on in the electricity industry. Yet the firm's integrated structure also produced risks. The company's near-nationwide monopoly on long-distance service, and the huge profits this service produced beginning in 1925, demanded that the company cultivate goodwill in proportion to profits. In the first half of the 1920s, the company had successfully resolved many of its rate cases, but in the second half, it continued to sell stock to customers in order to increase consumer goodwill.

The Crash and the Aftermath

Electricity holding companies had many more tiers than AT&T, and it was only a matter of time before this precarious financial structure fell apart. When the Depression set in, the reduced profits of electricity operating com-

Stock Ownership as Corporate Strategy   153

panies could no longer pay dividends to so many shareholders and the system collapsed. That was when investors learned the hard truth about holding companies—they could magnify losses as well as profits. Like a farm riddled by drought, the reduced yield of operating companies could only feed so many, and those last in line were left holding a worthless meal ticket. When the stock market crash of October 1929 hit, the high-stakes gambling of electricity holding company organizers came to an end.

Only a few analysts predicted the crash, but those who did were close observers of the electricity industry.[149] One of those observers was B. C. Forbes, the magazine publisher and loyal critic of the electricity industry. In a speech at the annual meetings of the National Electric Light Association (NELA) in 1926, Forbes warned that, due to holding companies, the "common people" might "bring about something which it isn't polite to mention in these days, namely, government ownership. . . . Think that over." The speech did not go over well with the electricity executives in the audience. The president of NELA, who hosted the session, reminded Forbes that most of the industries' stocks were regulated, then quickly moved on to other business. Forbes's warning went unheeded.[150]

Another critic of the electricity industry in the 1920s was the Harvard economist William Z. Ripley. Ripley's 1927 book *Wall Street to Main Street* exposed the problems of holding companies, corporate voting rights, and the exploitable patchwork of state business laws. Most of the book's examples came from the electricity industry. But the main problem in the economy, Ripley argued, was that stock ownership had dissolved the traditional relationship between private property and personal responsibility. Shareholders owned companies but did not control them. The corporate officers who did control the companies were not making decisions about their own property and therefore lacked a sense of stewardship. A man would never let his ox gore a neighbor, Ripley summarized, but he would let his company gouge a customer.

At least one utility employee agreed with Forbes and Ripley. In a letter marked "<u>PERSONAL AND CONFIDENTIAL</u>," utility publicist John Sheridan asked another publicist what could be done when financiers "sell securities based on blue sky or hot air, and rates must be kept up to pay returns." Utilities are "not loaded dice to be employed in a craps game in which investors and the public are injured," Sheridan complained.[151] But in the Roaring '20s, Sheridan's concerns, and those of others, went unheard.[152]

When the stock market crashed in October of 1929 all the utilities' rhetoric about safe and secure utility stock was put to the test. Shareholders in AT&T

continued to receive their $9 dividends throughout the Depression, even though the company had to dip into its savings for the first time to pay for them. The company's decision to pay dividends while simultaneously laying off workers met with strong criticism from some quarters, but AT&T executives argued that dividend payments represented the only source of income for many shareholders, so the company had a "moral obligation" to pay them.[153] Customer-owners of SCE, PG&E, and many other electric utilities also continued to receive their dividends.[154]

Things ended differently for the customer-owners in some of Samuel Insull's companies. In Insull's case, the temptation to create holding companies proved too great, and in 1928 and he formed the Insull Utility Investments, Inc., and then the Corporation Securities Company the following year. Shares of these holding companies were sold directly to customers at Insull's commercial offices.[155] In 1930, with the stock market crumbling, one large investor offered Insull a large block of shares in an operating company that Insull already partly owned. Not wanting the shares to fall into anyone else's hands, Insull bought them with the cash reserves from one of his holding companies. In other words, Insull dipped into the money given to him by shareholders in one holding company to buy shares in an operating company. Insull planned to pay back the money and continue paying dividends to the holding company's shareholders using the profits from the operating company, which he now controlled more firmly than ever. But as the Depression deepened, Insull could neither pay dividends nor pay down the principal he owed. As a result, several of Insull's holding companies collapsed and several of his operating companies went with them.[156]

Many of Insull's shareholders lost everything. One woman wrote to Insull in 1936 telling him that she had invested "all my life savings" in an Insull holding company in 1926 and 1928 and that now she was "just about penniless."[157] Another formerly wealthy investor told Insull that she had invested in one hundred shares of one of Insull's holding companies, which had "made a beggar out of me," and that now "being a widow find it necessary to do housework for a living."[158] One customer-owner accused Insull Jr. of engaging in "unfair tactics" and having "peculiar" ethics after the customer was repeatedly assured by clerks at an Insull utility office in 1930 that Insull's holding company stock would end up fine.[159]

The replies to these letters from Insull and his son were always the same: the companies were bankrupt, "there is nothing left for its stockholders."[160] When Insull's companies collapsed, he fled to Paris, then Greece since it did

Stock Ownership as Corporate Strategy   155

not have an extradition agreement with the United States. But Greece expelled him and Insull was arrested in Turkey and returned to the United States to stand trial.[161] His bail was set at four times the gangster Al Capone's.[162] Insull was tried and acquitted three times on various financial charges and lived the rest of his life in disgrace in Paris, where he died in 1938.[163]

Conclusion

There used to be a painting of Insull that hung in his office; a space that doubled as the Commonwealth Edison Company's board room. After the Crash and Insull's humiliation, the painting was taken down and given to his family. In an unguarded moment while writing his memoirs, Insull mused on the incident: "How the mighty hath fallen," he wrote, then struck the line from the final draft.[164]

As for A. J. Hockenbeamer, the inventor of customer stock ownership back in 1914, he was promoted to president of the Pacific Gas & Electric Company in 1927 and continued in that position until he died in 1935 "of a weakened heart and a condition of general exhaustion," according to the company.[165]

The history of customer stock ownership helps answer some important questions about American political economy. How did corporate monopoly utilities, which sat so uncomfortably on the line between government ownership and private enterprise during the Progressive Era, secure a less precarious seat for themselves in the economy by the late 1920s? How did Americans in the 1920s relinquish their traditional antimonopoly sentiment and come to accept corporate monopolies? How did corporate utilities in the United States, unlike in most of Europe, manage to survive the first three decades of the twentieth century? One answer to these questions is that utility employees offered stock to customers and customers literally bought into it.

CHAPTER FIVE

Making the News

On December 12, 1922, residents of Poplar Bluff, Missouri, opened their afternoon newspaper to find a front-page article extolling the virtues of corporate utilities. Two days later, John Sheridan, the secretary of the Missouri Committee on Public Utility Information, informed his boss that the entire article had been copied from the *News Bulletin*, which Sheridan edited and largely authored himself. This was not the first time the paper's editor, Dwight Brown, had copied an article from the *News Bulletin*. And, Brown was president of the Missouri State Press Association. Such plagiarism should be rewarded, Sheridan declared to his boss, who operated the local power plant in Poplar Bluff. "If there is anything you can do for Mr. Brown, I am sure you will do it."[1]

It would have been impossible for Sheridan's boss to have missed the hint. Less than a year earlier, Sheridan and utility executives had come to a clear agreement with the editors of the Missouri Press Association: the utilities would increase their newspaper advertising by $1 million a year, and, in return, the editors would express more goodwill toward utilities in their newspaper columns. As a condition for accepting the deal, Sheridan insisted that utility managers had to purchase advertising directly from their local editors, rather than the utilities as a whole purchasing a large block of advertising from the state's press association, which would then divvy up the advertising amongst itself. This way, Sheridan reasoned, each local utility manager could "form the closest possible relations" with editors and "inform them that they may inform the people."[2]

After brokering this latter-day Missouri Compromise, Sheridan reported the deal to utility executives throughout the state. "The time is ripe for forming an enduring and profitable relation with the press in Missouri," Sheridan announced. "I found the editors to be very fine men and really anxious to do the right thing, but they naturally are looking for all the business they can get." True to the terms of the agreement, Sheridan reminded executives not to forget the small-town editors. "If we can develop a little advertising for the small country newspapers," Sheridan predicted, "there is no doubt that the utilities will have the country press working hand in hand with them."[3]

Foreseeing a partnership of lasting importance, Sheridan pretended to have come up with this ads-for-articles scheme himself. In a letter to his boss in 1922, Sheridan boasted: "It struck me that if we got the companies working on appliance advertising, that the newspapers will be friendly, and print a good deal of educational matter free of charge." "Educational matter," as his boss would have understood, included material informing readers of the benefits of corporate utility monopolies. "I have not the least doubt of its good effect," Sheridan mused in satisfaction, "you have always got to grease the rails in these publicity campaigns."[4]

As the agreement between editors and utility agents took hold, Sheridan could virtually dictate the content of some newspapers. In 1923, he wanted an article he had written published, so he mailed it to a manager at the North Missouri Power Company and instructed him to take it to his local editor to have it published, but without Sheridan's name on it. "I desire to get this editorial printed as coming from the newspaper itself," Sheridan explained to the manager. That way, Sheridan could "reprint it as a special bulletin, credit

Front and center, "The Real Value of Public Utilities" appeared on page 1 in the *Excelsior Springs Daily Standard* of Missouri on June 15, 1923. Microfilm, State Historical Society of Missouri, Columbia.

the newspaper in which it appeared . . . and distribute it to all newspapers in Missouri." Two days later, "The Real Value of Public Utilities" appeared on the front page, center column, of the *Excelsior Springs Daily Standard*. No author was cited. The utilities were good advertisers in the *Daily Standard*.[5]

Sheridan's cultivation of the press proved extremely productive. His article in the *Excelsior Springs Daily Standard* represented just one of thousands that he and others planted in Missouri papers. For the year ending May 1, 1927—the first year Sheridan kept track—he found 77,903 column inches of articles printed in Missouri newspapers that had been copied from Sheridan's *News Bulletin*. That equated to thirty-eight full newspaper pages. The next year, the number increased to fifty-six full pages.[6] Readers might have interpreted these articles differently had they known who wrote them. But nearly all of the articles appeared without any attribution as to their original source, and in many cases the articles appeared below the name of the paper's editor.[7]

In bribing editors with ads, Sheridan was not alone. By 1925, there were twenty-seven other state utility information bureaus, all practicing the same strategy and with similar results. Together, they planted thousands of newspaper pages' worth of articles and editorials in exchange for advertising purchases. Utility publicity directors called the practice "space grabbing" and it was especially prevalent among small-town editors who needed advertising and were located where most of the municipal ownership battles of the 1920s took place.[8] By disguising their advertisements as articles, utility publicists sought to convince customers that corporate utilities operated in the customers' best interest.

Scholars have skillfully analyzed the content of these advertisements, but the relationship between these ads and the articles that surrounded them has received less attention.[9] Yet an intimate relationship existed between the two. In the case of utilities, ads and articles often shared the same corporate creator; articles were simply ads in a different form. The difference between the ads and articles was not that ads were created by corporations while articles were created by editors. The difference was that utility ads acknowledged their true authorship, while articles did not. Furthermore, the articles appeared due to the ads. Ads and articles were two sides of the same coin, and their simultaneous appearance in newspapers was no accident.

Utility representatives also sought to control information in ways that went far beyond articles and advertising. As demonstrated in the chapter 6, utility managers pressured publishers to rewrite their high school and college textbooks that criticized utilities, lobbied teachers and principals about their textbook choices, wrote their own textbooks, and distributed them free of charge. Utility publicists also paid professors to influence utility teaching on campuses, forced socialists off the Chautauqua speaking circuit, spoke on the circuit themselves, and produced "educational" and popular movies, which were screened before millions of school children and movie audiences. In addition, utility workers delivered pro-corporate utility speeches to a large number of Americans at schools, civic clubs, and chambers of commerce. Long before Paul Lazarsfeld and Robert Merton theorized that effective propaganda required monopolizing the message and supplementing it with face-to-face contact, utility employees were doing just that.[10]

A few historians today, as well as some politically motivated observers in the 1930s, have noted some aspects of this story. But these authors mainly relied on secondary sources or focused on a single utility or public relations strategy. Yet even when doing so, these observers have still concluded that the utilities' publicity efforts in the 1920s represented nothing less than the largest nongovernmental public relations campaign in America till that time.[11] Yet the publicity campaign of utilities was even larger than these authors realized. By limiting their focus to one industry or strategy, these writers overlooked the organizational interconnections that joined the streetcar, gas, electricity, and telephone industries together. The public relations campaign of these four industries was not separate but collectively planned, funded, and executed. And the campaign was not focused on just one source of media but on virtually every channel through which Americans received information about corporate utilities.

This is not to argue that the public relations campaign of the utilities represented a centralized conspiracy. Rather, it was deliberately decentralized. This made the campaign both less obvious and more effective. Unlike the nationally organized public relations campaigns of other large businesses such as Swift, Standard Oil, and International Harvester, the public relations efforts of utilities were organized at the state, county, and even school-district level, which ensured that local knowledge could be leveraged in ways that centralized campaigns could never achieve.[12] Rather than a top-down campaign, utility publicity directors ran a national yet decentralized and locally customizable campaign to improve public opinion toward corporate monopolies.[13] In doing so, utility managers exerted influence on nearly every conceivable outlet of information on utilities, including advertisements, newspaper and magazine articles, textbooks, public lectures, movies, and radio programs.

160   Chapter 5

Wherever people obtained their information, utility representatives were there trying to manipulate it in a pervasive and detailed campaign to mold public opinion regarding monopolies.

The evidence for this history largely comes from Federal Trade Commission (FTC) investigation into the gas and electricity industry, and the Federal Communications Commission (FCC) investigation into the Bell Telephone System. The FTC investigation began in 1928, when Senator Thomas J. Walsh, a progressive Democrat from Montana, entered a Senate resolution to investigate gas and electricity companies. Walsh had opposed corporate monopolies before he entered the Senate in 1913, though he was not an opponent of big business in general, nor of utilities in particular. As a western politician, Walsh favored the leasing of federal lands to business interests, which other progressives such as Robert La Follette and Gifford Pinchot opposed. Yet Walsh opposed corporate corruption and had helped uncover the Teapot Dome scandal in the early 1920s.

After leading the Teapot Dome investigation, Walsh became increasingly suspicious that all might not be right in the gas and electricity industries. The idea was planted in his mind by Pinchot, who had been writing Walsh letters on the subject. Walsh had also been reading the work of Harvard economist William Z. Ripley, whose research identified growing monopolization and propaganda in the utilities sector. Walsh soon wanted an investigation into the power companies.

In 1926, Walsh's desire received a boost when progressive legislators renewed their push to pass the Swing-Johnson Bill to construct Boulder Dam. Throughout the 1920s, several congressmen had battled the utilities over Boulder Dam, Muscle Shoals, and other public works projects, all of which centered around the question of who would control the means of electricity production. The Swing-Johnson Bill, in particular, had already been introduced in Congress several times in the 1920s but had never passed, partly due to an immense publicity campaign waged by electric utilities. As Walsh no doubt calculated, exposing the underhanded propaganda methods of utilities would weaken their political hand and help Congress pass the Swing-Johnson Bill.[14]

In February of 1927, as another Swing-Johnson Bill neared a vote, Walsh entered a resolution for an investigation. "Not that I don't believe the telephone and telegraph and radio industries should be investigated," Walsh clarified for the *New York Times*, "but I did not want to take in any broader field than the light and power companies."[15] Walsh's opponents tried to stop

Making the News   161

the resolution in committee but that failed, and in 1928, after intense debate, a coalition of progressive Republicans and Democrats voted 46-31 for an FTC investigation.[16]

Unfortunately for the utilities, but fortunately for historians, the FTC pursued its work with an ardor that defied expectations. Immediately after the resolution passed, dozens of FTC investigators rushed—subpoena in hand—to utility companies, utility information bureaus, and utility industry associations, ransacked their files, and carried away thousands of letters, memos, and reports. Many of these texts were "better left unwritten," groaned an attorney for the National Electric Light Association (NELA), the main electricity industry group.[17] To help the FTC better understand these documents, investigators called over forty utility executives and managers to testify before the commission and introduced over 6,200 documents into evidence. Transcripts of the proceedings ran seventy-seven volumes, each numbering hundreds of pages. Only in 1934, after seven years of investigative work, did FTC investigators rest from their labors.[18]

Telephone companies avoided the FTC investigation, but their turn came in 1935 after a joint resolution of Congress directed the FCC to investigate the telephone industry. Congress instructed the FCC to determine "whether or not the companies have sought, through propaganda or the expenditure of money or the control of the channels of publicity, to influence or control public opinion, legislative or administrative action, or elections."[19] The resolution was sponsored by New Deal Democrats Samuel Rayburn and Burton Wheeler, chairs of the House and Senate Commerce Committees, respectively.[20] At the outset of the investigation, the president of the American Telephone & Telegraph Company (AT&T), Walter Gifford, declared that AT&T had "no skeletons in our closet." But the investigation proved otherwise.[21] Over the course of three years, FCC commissioners carefully documented the publicity and propaganda activities of the Bell System, collected seventy-seven archival boxes of material, and summarized their findings in a report, which itself filled eighteen additional boxes, including exhibits.

Post–World War I Publicity

The publicity work that these investigations documented began before World War I. Yet the efforts of utilities to shape public opinion became much more systematic and coordinated as a direct outgrowth of the federal government's information campaign during the war. During that time, George Creel led the government's massive Committee on Public Information, which sought to improve public opinion toward World War I. Many utility executives greatly admired Creel and his methods, and, after the war, they founded state public utility information committees modeled on Creel's committee.

One of these executives was Samuel Insull, the influential president of the large Commonwealth Edison Company of Chicago. Insull established the first state utility information committee in April of 1919 and named the organization the Illinois Committee on Public Utility Information after Creel's Committee on Public Information. Insull also emulated Creel's strategies. As Insull told members of the American Electric Railway Association (AERA) in 1922, "we took the idea [for utility publicity] from some of our activities in Illinois during the war."[22]

During the war, Insull had worked with Creel's public relations organization as chairman of the Council of Defense of Illinois. In that position, Insull oversaw the Four-Minute Men in Illinois and other public relations groups. These groups helped bring about a massive transformation in public opinion in Illinois regarding the war. At the beginning of the war, most residents in isolationist Illinois bitterly opposed American intervention in Europe, but by the end of the war, most residents supported it, a fact some credited to Insull and his tireless publicity council.[23]

This lesson was not lost on Insull. He emerged from the war with new ideas about how to change public opinion and new connections with which to change it.[24] When the war ended, Insull turned his attention from making the world safe for democracy to making Illinois safe for monopoly. To do this, he hired George Mullaney to serve as the director of Insull's Illinois Committee on Public Utility Information. Insull and Mullaney had met during the war when Mullaney worked as a publicity writer for Insull's Council of Defense of Illinois. Like many future utility information directors, Mullaney had once worked as a newspaper reporter and possessed many useful contacts among editors. Mullaney's combative disposition and contempt for government overreach made him the perfect complement to Insull's similar views, ambitious plans, and deep pockets.[25]

Mullaney began his work by developing a free weekly news bulletin containing articles and editorials favorable to corporate utilities. Newspaper editors could copy the articles free of charge and did not have to attribute the articles to their actual authors. To promote the new service, Insull wrote a letter to every newspaper editor in Illinois, laying out a dire picture of the nation's economy and what was at stake if editors failed to do their part.

Seventy-one streetcar companies had already failed nationwide in the few months since the war, Insull cautioned, and, in Illinois alone, utilities represented $850 million in investment capital, employed forty-five thousand workers, and spent $65 million per year on construction. Panics were no longer possible thanks to the establishment of the Federal Reserve, Insull opined, but "a condition as bad as the worst panic can arise from another source," namely, the demise of corporate utilities. If newspaper editors wanted to avoid this catastrophe, they should publish the articles sent to them. "Your good work in the war," Insull solemnly intoned, "suggests that you will be equally alert to the peacetime needs."[26]

To further promote the news service, Mullaney sent copies of the news bulletin to utility managers throughout Illinois, and instructed them to read the bulletin and then go out and "jog each editor's memory on it from time to time." To facilitate this, Mullaney advised managers to buy advertising space in order to establish an acquaintance with editors. Then, after the editor's "interest" had been acquired, managers could broach the subject of printing articles from the bulletin. Mullaney also recommended that managers write to their local editor using phrases such as "please try to have some of the enclosed news articles used."[27]

Yet Insull and Mullaney were not content to space grab in Illinois alone. They exported the strategy nationwide. In 1919, in his typically brash style, Insull stood before a group of utility executives at a NELA convention and ordered them to "get busy and do something." Insull wanted executives to establish of their own state information committees. In Mullaney's fawning analysis, Insull's speech led to the establishment of twenty-eight publicity committees, though other executives also acknowledged Insull's pivotal role.[28] Most of these new information committees were founded between 1920 and 1923.[29] By the mid-1920s, the institutional structure for the large-scale space grabbing by utilities was in place.[30]

State public utility information committees employed only a few people, yet their influence exceeded their size. A typical committee consisted of a director and his secretary, and occasionally, a stenographer or part-time assistant.[31] Yet these committees were not just sideshows that utilities threw a little money at. Rather, they constituted the central base of publicity for utilities in the 1920s. As the American Gas Association (AGA) reported in 1925: information committees represent "the keystone of our publicity" and their operations "cover practically the entire country."[32] Each information committee usually covered one state, but in some regions, such as New England or the sparsely populated West, a single committee oversaw activities in multiple states.

Organizationally, the director of an information committee was not beholden to any single company. Rather, he served as an unofficial vice president of public relations for his entire state or region. Information directors coordinated employees across companies and across territories, and carried out projects that were too sensitive for any one company to associate itself with directly, beneficial to all companies, or, frequently, both. Information directors also authored clipsheets, trained managers to plant articles from them, and encouraged managers to advertise liberally to facilitate this space grabbing. Information directors also organized speakers' bureaus made up of utility employees, wrote speeches for the employees to give, and exchanged strategies and articles with other state directors at industry conferences.[33]

Industry associations, such as the National Electric Light Association (NELA), the American Electric Railway Association (AERA), and the American Gas Association (AGA) facilitated the activity of utility publicists, but they did not control them. Sometimes directors from these national organizations authored pamphlets or made suggestions, but they could not force state directors to use them. Yet the frequent meetings of these associations kept state directors in close contact, and the mail circulated a common flow of ideas, articles, and advertisements. Though organizationally independent, and geographically separated, state information directors remained united in their materials, methods, and goals.[34]

All four utility industries collectively organized and funded these state committees. Streetcar, gas, electricity, and telephone companies all contributed funds.[35] "The big problem of public relations is not being solved by any one company," summarized a utility publicist, rather "every company that amounts to anything . . . is behind the movement."[36] In Pennsylvania, for example, the state information committee received money from executives in all four industries in the state, all of whom collectively rejoiced in 1923 that they could present a "solid front" to the public.[37] This cross-industry funding made sense considering that many companies offered more than one type of utility service, as names such as the Pacific Gas & Electric Company and the New Orleans Railway and Light Company implied. An analysis of utility publicity can therefore not be separated by industry any more than the companies themselves can be separated.

Making the News 165

The telephone industry may appear to be an outlier in this cross-industry cooperation, but, the Bell System provided both personnel and financial support to state utility information committees. Between 1926 and 1935, Bell companies spent at least $200,000 supporting state committees, most of it before 1930.[38] In 1928, Southwestern Bell was the number-one financial supporter of John Sheridan's Missouri Committee on Public Utility Information.[39] Bell managers also worked closely with less formally organized groups on specific projects. AT&T executives knew about these activities, including the underhanded ones, and supported them.[40]

Reaching Readers through Editors

A primary goal of information committee directors was to plant newspaper articles to improve public opinion. Throughout the 1920s, corporate utilities faced municipal ownership fights, proposals for government-owned electricity plants, and, especially in the telephone industry, resistance to rate increases. Utility managers believed that news articles critiquing these proposals and celebrating corporate utilities would counteract these threats. "News stories mold public opinion," an Ohio Bell advertising manager succinctly declared at a publicity conference in 1923. "If publicity is favorable, public opinion will be favorable."[41] This favorable public opinion could then lead to rate increases. As Sheridan told newspapers editors in 1925, utility executives wanted to possess the readers' "good will and confidence to such an extent" that readers would "approve any demand you may make for increase of rates."[42] Goodwill and good profits went hand in hand.

To secure the goodwill of the public, managers first needed the goodwill of editors. That was where advertising came in. Advertising purchases would ingratiate managers with editors, according to utility publicists, and then editors would agree to publish articles written by publicists. During the FTC hearings, an FTC examiner asked the director of the Iowa utility information committee, Joe Carmichael, if he had increased utility newspaper advertising because he knew "it would bring about a more friendly attitude on the part of the newspapers toward the utilities?" Carmichael freely answered "Yes."[43] When Sheridan was asked the identical question he replied, "Surely. That is fundamental all the time."[44] The examiner also asked Sheridan about a speech he made to the Missouri Press Association in 1922: "Is not every intimation from your speech there that one of the considerations for the advertising is the good will of the newspaper?" "Oh, yes; that is clear," Sheridan unabashedly responded. "That is clear?" the examiner asked incredulously. "That is clear," Sheridan blithely confirmed.[45]

The fact that some utility managers placed such a high value on the written word reveals that they did not view the public as wholly irrational. Rather, managers emphasized that the public could be both rational and fair. "The great bulk of the public are honest and will act honestly, according to their lights," observed AT&T president Theodore Vail in a backhanded compliment.[46] In another backhanded compliment, electricity lawyer and future Republican presidential nominee Wendell Willkie told managers in 1929 that "the great mass of the American citizens are both conservative and fair and surprisingly intelligent in the grasping of such public utility problems if the facts are presented to them."[47]

As these statements show, executives did not excessively emphasize the rationality of consumers, yet they did not dismiss it either. In the view of executives, customers were susceptible to both rational and emotional appeals, often in the same person. "Education is getting at people through the brain, [good] treatment is getting at them through the heart," AT&T vice president E. K. Hall told employees in 1923.[48] Hall and others primarily emphasized reaching people through the heart using courteous capitalism, yet they also appealed to the rational side of customers through print.

To prove the wisdom of using print, executives told each other stories that affirmed the existence of a rational reading public. In one widely circulated account, an individual witnessed an argument about the on-time performance of the railroads while traveling in a railroad smoking car. During the discussion, one participant produced a newspaper and read out loud an article stating that the Illinois Central railroad had a good on-time record. "Those present agreed instantly that the Illinois Central was all right," observed one witness to the conversation, though they still maintained that the other lines had poor records. "The press and the use of the mails enabled the Illinois Central railroad to accomplish what looked almost impossible," the line's president rejoiced, modifying "public opinion in favor of an industry."[49]

Yet the rational public and the power of print presented a quandary for managers. On the one hand, managers penned articles to get the facts out, while on the other hand, they secretly planted these same articles. And their right hand knew what their left hand was doing. "Nothing can do you gentleman so much harm as to be caught in an attempt to 'put something over on the public,'" a *Boston Herald* editorialist verbalized to members of NELA. "The error will cost you what it may take years to regain."[50] Utility executives

Making the News   *167*

knew this, and worried about it, but they chose to space grab anyway. The decision would come back to haunt them.

Interacting with Editors

Perhaps utility workers engaged in space grabbing so extensively because it proved so easy in many cases. Editors often readily obliged in publishing articles in exchange for ads. Samuel MacQuarrie, of the New England Bureau of Public Service Information, visited a large number of small-town editors and reported that "a good many of them said frankly, 'If you want to get into our news columns, why don't you advertise?'"[51] In early 1921, the editor of the *Excelsior Springs Daily Standard* reminded Sheridan in Missouri that he had already asked Sheridan to "send me whatever propaganda you were able," adding that "since the *Standard* is on the best of terms with the public utilities concerns of Excelsior Springs . . . we will be glad to publish articles."[52] In these cases and others, editors openly hawked their news columns in exchange for ads.

Yet even when the exact terms of the ads-for-articles agreement were not explicit, the implication of a trade was often there nonetheless. This was especially obvious when editors felt their services were not being fully appreciated. In 1927, the editor of the *Aiken Standard* complained when Southern Bell canceled its advertising. "Right now the Southern Bell is seeking to secure an increase in rates in Aiken, [South Carolina]," the editor wrote to the company. "I have been of assistance in this matter. There has been opposition. I had hoped at the beginning of the year to have had more copy." Upon receiving the letter, Southern Bell managers decided to place some more ads, since, as one of the managers stated, "I think it advisable to do nothing at this time which would affect that situation."[53]

In another case, the editor of the *Missouri Trade Unionist*, Charles Fear, complained to John Sheridan in 1922 that Southwestern Bell had not been forthcoming with advertising. When the company wanted a franchise, "they promised me support and advertising if I helped them," Fear huffed. Sheridan immediately contacted a Southwestern Bell manager, then told Fear that the manager would send Fear an ad "right away." Sheridan could not remember the exact specifics of the deal during his FTC testimony, but noted that "I have not the slightest doubt that in all human probability I tried to get him an ad, because that was my constant practice."[54]

Fear seems to have been persuaded to continue his cooperation because in 1926 Sheridan described Fear's paper to a utility manager as "the most useful and best newspaper friend that the utilities have."[55] At the beginning of the Progressive Era, utility executives bribed city council members to obtain rate hikes and franchise permits, but journalists exposed that practice. So in the 1920s, utility executives simply bribed the journalists.

Utility managers used various methods to make editors friendly. In some cases, managers purchased advertising after editors published favorable articles, rather than before. In 1925, the editor of the *Bourbon Stock Journal* of Louisville, Kentucky, received advertising because "the editor of the journal has been very friendly and helpful to us in many matters," a Bell manager noted. The manager added that "a few dollars spent with this paper will tend to maintain the cordial relations."[56] In 1928, an editor in Birmingham, Alabama, received "a complimentary advertisement" from Southern Bell for the "splendid work being done . . . in connection with his fight against the question of taxes," according to a local Bell manager.[57]

Utility managers also used ads to soften up negative editors. In 1923, Southern Bell managers in Mississippi violated their own rule against advertising in special editions because the editors of the *Clarion Ledger* of Jackson had been "very unfriendly toward the telephone company" and the utility wanted to continue its "efforts to bring this paper into line." Later, a Bell manager clipped a flattering article from the paper about the telephone business and sent it to his boss, with a note scrawled on it stating: "the increased advertising has <u>helped</u>."[58]

In other cases, advertising purchases functioned as a political donation. In 1924, Southern Bell increased its advertising in the *Times-Journal* of Bowling Green because the paper's vice president was Alabama's lieutenant governor and Bell had been contemplating a merger in the state.[59] In another case, the *Milan Exchange* of Milan, South Carolina, received Bell ads because the paper's owner was a state representative, had asked for the advertising, and there was talk of an independent telephone company forming. The representative was "our friend," explained the local Bell manager, and Bell "was going to need all the friends" it could get for the upcoming battle against the independent.[60]

Utility managers also provided free telephone service to editors in order to obtain their goodwill. Some editors rejected the free service, but others accepted it.[61] Southern Bell provided free service to members of the North Carolina Press Association from at least 1927 to 1934. In March of 1927, after receiving the free service, Beatrice Cobb, the secretary-treasurer of the North Carolina Press Association and editor of the *News-Herald* of Morgantown, sent a "Thank You" note to Evelyn Harris, the assistant to the president in charge of public relations at Southern Bell. In Cobb's note, she enclosed an editorial on telephone service that she had written and published in her paper. Bell managers considered Cobb "a very influential person in North Carolina public affairs" and were doubtlessly happy to see the article. Harris wrote back to Cobb stating that he hoped she would continue to use the free service.[62]

A few years later, in December 1932, Cobb again wrote to Harris, this time telling him that she would "always stand up for the telephone company to the utmost of my ability." She hastened to add that she was "not unduly influenced by . . . the favors you have extended me." The letter was proudly circulated among the Southern Bell's top executives, including the president and general counsel.

A short while later, the chairman of the Legislative Committee of the North Carolina Press Association also wrote Harris to thank him for the free service. On *Evening Telegram* letterhead, the chairman stated that he would "reciprocate the courtesy at any future time, you need but to command me."[63] By this point, the relationship between the utilities and the press had gone from "hand in hand," as Sheridan had predicted in 1922, to something more like hand in glove.[64]

Utility publicists also sought to command the goodwill of editors by paying for entertainment. In 1926, Edwin Bemis, a newspaper owner and secretary of the Colorado Editorial Association, wrote to the director of the Rocky Mountain Committee on Public Utility Information to thank him for the party he had thrown for the editors of his association. Bemis told the director that the newspaper editors had enjoyed the party and the "extremely friendly relations which existed between the utility bodies and the newspapers." Bemis, who taught journalism at the University of Colorado, added: "Any time you desire any cooperation from the papers, which we can give, I hope you will feel free to call on us."[65] Apparently, Bemis did not stress the idea of journalistic objectivity, but he did know the business side of the industry.

To further shape public opinion through the press, utilities hired journalists who still worked elsewhere. In Texas, the utilities hired Associated Press (AP) editor William C. Grant to serve as director of the Texas Public Service Information Bureau. Yet Grant never quit the AP. Instead, he used his access to the AP wire to send out a prolific number of articles that served his newest employers' interests. In November 1927, for example, Grant wrote a story about how independent telephone companies were rapidly being bought up. Research for the story came from a member of Grant's own oversight committee at the Texas information bureau, who was also the general manager of the Gulf States Telephone Company. The story may have been intended to boost the stock price of the general manager's company by making the market for telephone companies seem bullish. Grant sent the story out over both the AP and United Press news wires, then informed his utility boss that he had completed the task assigned to him.[66] Such actions lent credence to one editor's contemporary critique that the AP was "the wet-nurse for all other monopolies" whose "news-gatherers . . . only obey orders."[67]

Yet Grant and other utility publicity directors did not generally produce deliberate lies. Some stories may have been embellished, as was the case with a few stories about heroic employees saving customers from calamity. But utility columns mostly presented factual information about recent utility construction projects, community utility happenings, or quotes from executives. While selective in what they covered, and surreptitious in how they appeared in the papers, the articles generally did not misreport stock prices or peddle outright lies, as some financiers, journalists, and politicians had done in the past, not to mention the present.[68]

When utility executives hired reporters who were still employed elsewhere, the utilities went to elaborate lengths to cover their tracks. In 1927, executives hired Mrs. John D. Sherman, whose first name does not appear in the records. Sherman served as president of the General Federation of Women's Clubs. She also wrote columns for *Better Homes and Gardens* and *Woman's Home Companion* about the benefits of gas and electric appliances for women. These magazines paid Sherman $250 for her columns, yet NELA paid Sherman an additional $350 for these articles, and paid her agency $90. In other words, Sherman made more from NELA than she did from the magazines that published her work. And at the same time as her agent, the Lord & Thomas & Logan ad agency, represented Mrs. Sherman, it was also running a nationwide advertising campaign for NELA. Meanwhile, Sherman's General Federation of Women's Clubs received $80,000 from NELA and the AGA to carry out a three-year survey of electrical appliance use among women.[69]

In a few cases, utility managers dispensed with all subtlety and simply handed over the boodle. The editor of the labor paper *Work* received $100 a year from the Ohio Bell Company to publish articles in his paper that Bell publicists authored. No Bell advertising appeared in the paper. The paper was published in Columbus, Ohio, by the former head of the miners' unions in Ohio and Pennsylvania. The president of Ohio Bell, C. P. Cooper, knew about the deal and approved it. It is unclear how long the agreement was in effect, but a letter written in 1925 stated it had been going on "for a number of years." Ohio Bell wrote down these expenses in their account books as "Charity Advertising" or "Space Bought during 1927 But No Copy Run in Publications."[70]

In a similar case, AT&T paid Harry Basset, the owner of the *Union* newspaper $3,500 between 1918 and 1924. In return, Bassett wrote articles and published them in his paper, including a series entitled "How About Conserving the Public Utilities." AT&T also paid the *Union* to reprint articles and distribute them to "all the newspapers." In one article, Basset argued that "there must be a revision upwards of the fixed rates for public utilities." In 1934, AT&T vice president Arthur W. Page sent Bassett data about customer stock ownership and told Bassett that, if he could "make up an article from that data, I should be very glad to pay you $250, as you suggest." Not long after, the check was sent.

In favoring corporate utilities, Bassett walked a fine ideological line. As a labor paper editor, he promoted worker organization, yet he did not support municipal ownership of utilities. Probably referring to the presidential race of 1924, Basset told Page, "We have stood with Mr. Gompers," the president of the American Federation of Labor, "in his strong fight against socialism but we cannot accompany him into the La Follette camp which is simply an advance camouflage of sovietism in America." La Follette supported government ownership of utilities.[71]

In other cases, however, utility managers could not just waltz into newspaper offices and dictate to editors all the news that was fit to print. Many editors maintained pride in their editorial independence and could get offended if utility managers propositioned their news space too directly. In November 1921, Harlin Clark, the editor of the *Cass County Democrat* of Missouri, published an editorial entitled "Just Plain Boobs," which criticized the space-grabbing efforts of utilities.[72] Clark later told John Sheridan that if utilities wanted a good relationship with his paper, they could "come clean by discarding their watered capitalization and padded expense accounts and fictitious valuations—in other words, tell the truth."[73]

In Texas, the editor of a small-town paper mailed back publicity sent to him by a utility manager and included a "Notice to the Free-Publicity Hounds of the Universe," which the editor had previously published in his paper. The notice stated that when newspapers print material for free, "the other fellow gets the money and the newspaper gets the 'Ha, ha.'" Therefore, the editor declared, he would be throwing all "publicity dope" in the garbage.[74]

In other instances, editors took bribes but ruthlessly extracted as much money as they could from utilities. In 1923, Charles Lane, the owner of a newspaper in Huntsville, Alabama, issued what a local Bell manager characterized as "almost a threat." According to a Bell manager, Lane declared that he would "agitate a rate reduction in telephone service," as his readers wanted him to, unless Bell purchased advertising space. Bell's advertising manager for Alabama advised the local Bell manager who dealt with Lane to give him "a small ad each month as I think he will keep down the rate question through his paper." Otherwise, the state manager cautioned, "a great deal more money will be spent in quieting the [negative] write-up."[75] In another case in Alabama, the editor of the *Labor Advocate* of Birmingham used methods that "had all the earmarks of intimidation, reference being made by them to their legislative influence," according to a Bell manager. The manager eventually made a small contribution to a brochure for the Alabama Teachers Association, which the paper was printing, but insisted that Bell's name not appear.[76] Editors also price gouged utilities when editors knew utilities needed to advertise before buying out a rival.[77]

Overall, however, utilities maintained the upper hand in their relationship with the press. In some cases, publicity managers mercilessly reminded editors of their dependence on utility advertising. In 1923, the director of the Nebraska utility committee sent a combative letter to local utility managers, telling them: "I want you to ask the publisher or his representative, when you hand in your copy, how much advertising he has had from the municipal water plant or any other municipally owned utility within the year. Go further," the manager implored, "ask him how much advertising the newspapers in the next town has had from the municipally owned electric or gas plant in that town."[78] Another publicity director instructed managers to remind editors that "small mutual telephone companies, [and] small electric light plants . . . can scarcely afford to make an appropriation for advertising that would be worth the trouble of the newspapers to secure."[79]

As these cases show, utility managers sometimes used strong-arm tactics against editors. In many cases, the same managers who charmed customers also pressured editors; their job covered both duties. This provides some indication of how sincere the courtesy of managers really was. Courtesy could give way to coercion as long as the defense of monopoly remained the

Making the News   173

highest goal. Yet pressuring editors, or influencing them through lucrative advertising purchases, worked. In 1928, John Sheridan in Missouri estimated that "newspapers are 99 percent with the privately owned utilities . . . we showed them very clearly that there was nothing in municipal ownership for them."[80]

News Services

Utility executives also sponsored independent news services that produced newssheets for editors. These news services authored articles, compiled them into clipsheets, and distributed these sheets for free to newspaper editors throughout the country. By far the largest utility news service was E. Hofer & Sons, founded by Ernest Hofer, an Oregon newspaper owner. In 1912, Hofer began sending out his utility newssheet to around two hundred papers in Oregon. The following year, he decided to sell his newspaper and concentrate all his efforts on his utility newssheet.

Like utility executives, Hofer believed in the power of the press. "Editorial work," he told utility executives, helps utilities by "changing public consciousness" from an "uninformed or destructive attitude to constructive tendencies." Hofer warned executives that "when the Nation is flooded with inflammatory press comment . . . or when radical agitators are disturbing the people with unsound doctrines, business conditions become unsettled, industry imperiled . . . and profits fall off."[81] But positive articles from his clipsheets counteracted these radicals, Hofer offered. "A good editorial on utility problems, taxation, or public ownership," he declared, "helps build up a public understanding" and "assures a more open-minded hearing."[82]

By the early 1920s, the "Hofer Service," as it was called, had grown to reach rural newspapers in fifteen western states. Yet Ernst Hofer's son, Robert, was not satisfied with regional distribution. In 1922, Robert requested a meeting with top utility executives on the East Coast in order to tap into the increasing publicity expenditures of utilities there. The meeting took place in January of 1923 at the New York apartment of Charles Coffin, the founder and former chairman of General Electric. Other attendees included AT&T public relations vice president E. K. Hall, A. W. Flor of the Electric Bond and Share Company, Philip H. Gadsden of the United Gas Improvement Company, and two executives from the United Bond & Share Co. In short, the meeting included some of the biggest players in the industry, and in American business in general. Together, they hatched a plan to massively expand Hofer's news service to all forty-eight states and fund the expansion through

174   Chapter 5

the companies controlled by the men in the room. Two years later, Robert Hofer was sending his free weekly and monthly newssheet to fourteen thousand editors in 48 states.[83]

Like the state information committees, the Hofer Service was jointly funded by all four utility industries. In addition to the money from Coffin and his friends, individual utility companies were expected to "subscribe" to the Hofer Service by making regular donations. Between 1915 and 1936, AT&T paid the Hofer Service over $100,000, made up of monthly payments of $1,200 each.[84] Individual Bell Companies also subscribed, as did streetcar, gas, and electric companies.[85] In the late 1920s, when some utility executives tried to cancel their subscriptions, Robert Hofer called on his influential New York patrons to pressure the executives to continue their support.[86]

Sheer Volume

The sheer volume of articles that utility managers planted proved staggering. Corporate utility content flooded into newspapers in the 1920s. In 1922, in its first year of operation, the New England Bureau of Public Service Information identified 9,513 column inches of planted articles in newspapers. "This means more than 453 newspaper columns," boasted the bureau's director, "or 56.5 full pages of solid reading matter the size of the *Boston Herald*." The next year, the bureau increased its space to seventy-two full newspaper pages of planted articles.[87] For the four years ending March 31, 1927, the Connecticut Committee on Public Service Information planted an average of 69.5 newspaper pages per year.[88] From 1919 through 1923, the Illinois Committee on Public Utility Information planted an average of 163 newspaper pages per year—enough to fill a good-sized book.[89] Finally, for the year ending June 30, 1927, the Texas Public Service Information Bureau planted no less than 38,360 column inches of content, equivalent to 227 newspaper pages.[90] No wonder the Texas bureau director praised Texas newspapers as "the unfailing agents of the bureau."[91]

The volume of planted articles proved so high that in 1925 the Illinois committee quit keeping track. "We were afraid they would become public," admitted the associate director of the Illinois committee to the executive secretary of the Connecticut committee.[92] The executive secretary of the New England bureau also feared a leak of space-grabbing numbers, so in 1928 he vowed he "would not publish it under any circumstances."[93] For the same reason, the Texas bureau labeled some of their space-grabbing reports as "CONFIDENTIAL."[94]

Making the News   175

AT&T, which sent out its own publicity bulletin, also tracked its success in getting articles published. Based on a three-month survey of 284 US newspapers in 1932, AT&T employees estimated that newspapers published 103,770 column inches of articles from AT&T clipsheets, equivalent to 616 full newspaper pages. And that was just AT&T.

Individual Bell companies sent out their own clipsheets, purchased their own advertising, and planted their own articles. In 1927, the Northwestern Bell Telephone Company conducted a detailed survey of 534 different newspapers in its operating territory and identified 9,888 articles or images published from the company's clipsheets. Northwestern Bell, which operated in the Dakotas, Iowa, Minnesota, and Nebraska, found that 506 out of 534 newspapers surveyed, or nearly 95 percent of the papers receiving the company's publicity, used Northwestern Bell's material.[95] The New England bureau carried out a similar study and found that 74 percent of the 309 newspapers it surveyed published some articles from its bulletin.[96] In other words, the number of columns printed was not only high, but the number of papers that participated in publishing them was also high. The number of readers utilities contacted through these papers is difficult to quantify, yet it was surely immense.

The Hofer Service also proved successful in getting its articles published. In 1926, according to Ernst Hofer, 233 Massachusetts papers published "verbatim" 33,246 column inches of Hofer's articles, equivalent to 197 full newspaper pages. In the same year, 167 Nevada papers printed 118 pages of Hofer articles, 574 Pennsylvania papers printed 414 pages, and 613 Iowa papers printed 449 pages of Hofer articles. In 1927 alone, Hofer claimed to have placed a total of over three million column inches of articles, or over 18,400 full pages of articles in newspapers throughout the country.[97]

The accuracy of these numbers is difficult to determine. Hofer used his numbers to attract financial support from utility executives, and therefore had an interest in high estimates. Yet Hofer wrote one manager that, while his numbers might "seem exaggerated," they had "borne the closest investigation" from people like "Charles A. Coffin, E. K. Hall . . . Martin Insull, and many others." The total number of readers contacted through Hofer's articles is also difficult to determine, though Hofer told his utility sponsors that the service was "reaching more people continuously . . . than are being reached by any other single agency." Astonished by the growth of the news service he had helped create, utility executive A. W. Flor told colleagues in 1927 that the "results surpass anything I expected."[98]

176   Chapter 5

While Hofer's estimates may have been high, the space-grabbing estimates of state committees and the Bell System may have been low. These organizations thoroughly combed through newspapers to identify planted articles, yet they believed they did not find everything of interest. Both the Texas and New England bureaus estimated that they found just half of the utility articles that were actually printed, but reported only what they found.[99] Internal communications also indicate that the space-grabbing numbers reported by state committee directors were accurate. Some directors also reported declines in space-grabbing numbers, indicating they did not make up numbers just to please their bosses.[100]

The extent of space grabbing in the 1920s makes it nearly impossible for historians to use newspapers as a source for authentic descriptions of positive public opinion toward corporate utilities. Yet the error has occurred. When cliometrics first became popular, one business historian searched periodicals for keywords such as "antitrust" and argued that the word's relative frequency could be correlated to changes in public opinion regarding big business. But some of the same publications this historian searched also contained large amounts of utility advertising. For his survey of 1920s publications, he thought he detected a decline in antimonopoly sentiment, but what he may have actually detected was an increase in space grabbing.[101]

Content of Articles

What did the planted utility articles say? The articles mostly contained arguments against government ownership and material highlighting the contributions of utility companies to the local community. The bulletin of the Rocky Mountain Committee on Public Utility Information, for example, included headlines such as, "There Goes Your Old Argument for Municipal Ownership," "Cost of Indiana's City-Owned Utilities Greater than Private Companies," and "Customer Ownership Will Solve Utility Problems."[102] One of John Sheridan's favorite articles was "The Story of Failure of Radical Theories in North Dakota." He liked it so much he copied it from Mullaney's Illinois bulletin and reprinted it in his own.[103]

The appearance of these articles mattered, yet so did what never appeared in newspapers. Due to the close relationship between utility managers and editors, many negative articles never saw the light of day. An advertising manager for the New York Telephone Company boasted to colleagues that the company had been "able to correct, sometimes around one or two o'clock in the morning, a story which otherwise would have rather disagreeable statements." The manager noted that "a great deal of that is due to the very good relations that we seek to cultivate and maintain."[104] In 1928, the publisher of the *Raleigh Times* told a Bell executive that he had letters from people who were "very violent in their condemnation" of Bell's new dial system. Yet the editor promised that these letters would not be published, adding in a less than subtle hint that "the very attractive advertising that you have been sending to *Raleigh* recently is receiving a hearty welcome. We are hoping there will be many more orders in the near future." A Bell executive replied to the editor that "we are grateful to you for not publishing the letters" and "I am glad you like the advertising copy we are sending you and hope to continue a rather full schedule this year."[105]

In other cases, utility managers succeeded in virtually stopping the press. In 1927 in New York City, a utility manager caught wind of a negative story and called the newspaper publisher who contacted the printer. "We have got that all set up in type," the printer told the publisher, "it is just about to go to press." Yet the utility manager succeeded in stopping the story's publication. He had "very intimate relations with newspaper people," explained AT&T vice president Arthur W. Page, so the manager was "able to keep out of the papers some very misleading and very damaging statements." In almost the same breath, Page added that stories submitted by utilities to newspapers "are run without rewriting."[106]

The Bell System was not the only utility organization that succeeded in filtering negative stories from publication. When socialist Carl D. Thompson was scheduled to speak at several civic events in Missouri, most editors in the area kept silent. Sheridan boasted to a utility executive that he had so many newspapers on his advertising rolls that readers found almost no mention that Thompson was even in town. "It is not very easy for anyone to bite the hand of a good customer," Sheridan shrewdly remarked.[107]

Negative articles still slipped through, however. Employees would come across them during their surveys for planted content. The Southwestern Bell Telephone Company had a specific procedure for what to do in those cases. When the employee who scanned the newspapers came across critical articles, he or she would immediately alert the district manager. The manager would then notify division headquarters "within the hour" about the article's appearance along with his plan for contacting the paper's editor and anyone mentioned in the article.[108] The policy was strictly enforced.[109]

When a negative article appeared, utility managers often visited the editor who published the article and the offended customer, if there was one. In several cases, such visits proved effective. The editor of the *Daily News* of Boonville, Missouri, received a visit from a Bell manager named Crawford after a negative article appeared in the paper. The editor swore he had not read the article before it went to press and "offered to publish anything that Crawford might suggest" to make amends, according to a Bell report of the visit. The editor also promised that, in the future, he would make "every effort to keep such articles from being printed until Mr. Crawford has had the opportunity of looking them over."[110] Another editor had been brought into line.

In another case, managers tried to visit the author of a critical letter to the editor that appeared in the *Gazette* of Little Rock, Arkansas. But when the author of the letter, "H. H. Greer," could not be found in the phone book, Southwestern Bell managers accused the paper of poor journalistic practice for failing to check facts.[111] The sources do not indicate that Bell managers complained about poor journalistic practice when editors participated in space grabbing.

In at least one case, a utility manager appears to have gone as far as influencing the hiring and firing of an editor. In 1925, an Ohio Bell manager bragged to AT&T executive E. K. Hall that he "had a little something to do with" getting the editor of the *Cleveland Press* fired. The editor's boss was a "close personal friend of mine," the Bell manager gossiped. Along with this bit of intrigue, the manager sent Hall a pro-utility article written by the new editor of the *Cleveland Press*.[112]

Over the course of the 1920s, the control of the press by utility managers steadily expanded. During this time, an unknown number of articles critical of utilities never reached the eyes of readers, while tens of thousands of articles that promoted corporate utilities and vilified government ownership flooded the papers. Under these circumstances it became difficult for Americans to hold an informed public discussion about the merits of corporate monopolies.

Anonymous Authorship

The overwhelming majority of the articles planted by utility publicists appeared before readers without any attribution to their original source. This was by design. Publicists and editors colluded together to hide the true origins of the articles written by utility employees. Leon Bradley, the director of the Alabama information committee, told NELA officials in 1926 that he had planted hundreds of articles, but that, regarding his authorship, there was "nothing to show it most of the time." According to Bradley, editors understood that the material would be more convincing if it seemed to readers that it came from the newspapers. Yet editors knew who wrote the articles because Bradley's name and organization appeared on his clipsheets. "Sometimes, I suggested to the newspapers that it would be more effective not to quote my name," Bradley admitted to FTC investigators.[113]

Other utility publicists operated in the same way. When an FTC investigator asked the assistant director of the Illinois publicity committee if some of the anonymous articles he sent out were published, the following exchange occurred:

> Yes, sir.
> Without any advertisement mark on it?
> Without any advertisement mark; yes, sir.
> With nothing to show where it originated?
> As the editor uses it, if the editor uses it, as we write it, there is nothing to show that reproduction.
> That happens a good many times in the course of a year?
> Yes, sir . . .
> That is one or two things you are organized to do, isn't it?
> Yes, sir.[114]

Editors sometimes cooperated with utilities because they agreed with their politics. In 1927, when the Alabama Power Co. wanted to take over a municipal plant in Dothan, Alabama, the company turned to Leon Bradley, who was an experienced space grabber. Bradley, a former reporter, went to Dothan and penned several anonymous articles based on interviews with customers and supplied the articles free of charge to the Dothan *Eagle*. The paper knew Bradley was in the pay of the Alabama Power Company, yet published the articles anyway because the paper's editor opposed municipal ownership. But shortly after the articles appeared, the rival paper, the *Wiregrass Journal*, outed Bradley's identity and ruined the scheme. Yet Bradley should have known better. Before working for the Alabama utility information committee, he taught journalism at Auburn.[115]

Similar though longer-lasting relationships existed elsewhere. In 1914, the American Light & Traction Company faced municipal ownership agitation in Grand Rapids, Michigan, so it hired experienced political operative Fred Gordon, who published anonymous articles and gave dozens of speeches opposing government ownership. Gordon spoke at civic clubs, furniture factories, and even on street corners. When speaking, Gordon admitted that he was employed by the traction company, but not when writing. For a single month's work in Grand Rapids, Gordon made $2,000—a good middle-class salary for an entire year at the time.[116]

From 1915 through 1917, Gordon employed similar methods for the large Byllesby utility company during municipal ownership fights in Fort Smith, Arkansas; Sioux Falls, South Dakota; and Muskogee, Oklahoma. Then in 1919, when the state of Massachusetts threatened to spend millions to take over the state's entire electricity network, NELA hired Gordon full-time for $2,000 annually. It must have seemed like a poor salary to Gordon, but later that year, the AGA added another $1,600 and sent Gordon to Minnesota to fight the Nonpartisan League. "That was perhaps the most tremendous fight [against socialism] we had in this country," Gordon recalled with relish in 1929. "I worked myself out of a job because I licked those fellows out there."[117]

Gordon's effectiveness as a speaker may have come from the fact that he was a recovering socialist, having worked as a paid organizer for the Socialist Labor Party before, as he put it, "I educated myself out of it." Yet Gordon's effectiveness in print may have come from the fact that he published anonymously. "I have probably written a thousand articles in opposition of municipal socialism and State socialism and international socialism," Gordon boasted. But regarding putting his name and the name of his corporate employers on these articles, Gordon admitted that "many of the articles did not refer to it at all."[118]

Planting Articles

Whether carried out by publicists or local utility managers, space grabbing was delicate business. For that reason, it was not typically carried out through the mail. That would have been too impersonal and less effective. Instead, utility managers were required to visit local editors, develop relationships with them, and eventually plant articles. Several companies had written policies about the process. A 1924 memo by the Pacific Telephone & Telegraph Company (PT&T) revealed that first, ads and articles were prepared at the corporate headquarters or divisional level. Then, "in all cases . . . copy is sent directly to the local manager with instructions to take up the advertising or other publicity with the local papers." This was done "to maintain as close a contact as possible between local manager and the papers of his district." Editors would then accept the material and bill the local manager, not headquarters, for the advertising purchases. That way editors knew who controlled the purse.[119]

Making the News   181

Other utilities, including AT&T, also had explicit policies.[120] An AT&T memo entitled "The Publicity Policy of the Bell System" declared that "the publicity job is not done by advertising alone" and that "the news and editorial columns of the newspapers may be and should be utilized." The memo instructed employees to give news to editors.[121] Space grabbing was clearly not the activity of a few rogue managers in the 1920s; it was the explicit policy of major corporations.

The problem with these procedures was that they required tact, which not all managers possessed. In one poorly conceived attempt to plant an article, a Southwestern Bell employee subscribed, on credit, to the *Campbell Citizen* of Campbell, Missouri, for one month, then sent the editor $10 worth of publicity, and asked him to publish it for free. According to the paper's editor, all this occurred on the same day that Southwestern Bell raised the paper's telephone rates. The editor told readers all about it in "Here Is a Hot One on the Citizen," published in the *Campbell Citizen* on September 7, 1923, issue. After the flap, Southwestern Bell quickly resumed its advertising with the paper, after having canceled it several months earlier. The first of the new ads was appropriately titled "Giving the Telephone Life."[122]

To avoid such embarrassing episodes, experienced managers counseled their less experienced colleagues how to plant articles without offending editors. When the publicity committee of AERA sent out a clipsheet to members, it urged managers not to simply "request editors to print it." Instead, the committee advised managers to strike up a conversation with editors and ask the editors for advice about "helpful editorials, both to the newspapers and to the companies."[123] One manager advised other managers that they should get to know editors "intimately and personally . . . so that these stories could be filtered into the press."[124] The ultimate goal of all this, an Ohio Bell manager taught colleagues in 1923, was to become "so well acquainted with the newspaper man that you can slap him on the back and say, 'Listen, old man, here are the facts.'"[125]

When managers succeeded in planting an article this way, they boasted about it to their colleagues. In 1923, the president of Michigan Bell mailed a favorable newspaper article to AT&T vice president E. S. Wilson with a note stating that "we do this through the local managers keeping in touch with the local newspapers."[126] In 1927 the publicity director for the National Utility Association mailed a colleague three planted articles, which he described with satisfaction as first, "a splendid editorial . . . written and printed through a personal appeal made to the editor"; second, an AP news story published

Small-Town Editors and Walter Lippmann

"due to the influence and acquaintance of one individual journalistically known in his State"; and third, another "editorial . . . of major importance and . . . a splendid result from personal contact."[127] Behind the thousands of utility ads and articles that appeared in newspapers, a tremendous amount of personal contact took place.

Small-Town Editors and Walter Lippmann

Small-town editors were particularly susceptible to space grabbing since they operated in markets where subscription numbers were smaller than in big cities and advertising revenue was lower. Money from corporate utilities could make a big difference to a small-town editor's income. As Samuel MacQuarrie of the New England bureau explained to an FTC examiner, a rural editor was a "poor newspaper man who has to have adverting to live, and I don't blame him, to put up the proposition that if we want any favors we would have to buy space from him." "I thought the newspapers were expected to give news?" the FTC examiner replied. "Little country newspapers are in a little different category from the daily newspapers," MacQuarrie answered.[128]

MacQuarrie was not alone in his analysis of small-town papers. In 1924, John Sheridan of the Missouri information committee wrote to a publicity manager in Nebraska that the value of the country press was "beyond calculation" and marveled that its editors were "'God's fools,' grateful for the smallest and most insignificant service or courtesy."[129] Another utility executive wrote to a colleague in 1927 that he was "very much surprised by the readiness with which the editors of these small country papers accept these editorials and run them in their papers." The Hofer Service did not even bother sending its clipsheets to big-city papers and instead only targeted "the rural press and small city dailies."[130]

The desperation for advertising dollars among rural editors supports one of commentator Walter Lippmann's observations about newspapers. In *Public Opinion*, published in 1922, Lippmann noted that the traditional argument among theorists was that the democratic experiment could not survive without an informed electorate. The task of informing that electorate was usually assigned to the press, Lippmann noted. But the press could not perform this task because it did not have enough money, he argued. Americans, Lippmann marveled, were willing to pay a fair price for almost any product, except news. For some reason, Americans believed that news should be free, or nearly so. As a result, newspaper editors were beholden to advertisers, and an informed electorate, the sine qua non of a healthy democracy, could not come into existence.[131]

It is not known if utility executives read Lippmann's *Public Opinion*, but they certainly subscribed to his belief that editors were dependent on advertisers. "Without advertising, a newspaper cannot exist," stated Samuel MacQuarrie in 1924.[132] And utility publicists reminded editors of this.[133] Publicists specifically targeted small-town editors because of their dependency. When Joe Carmichael founded the Iowa Committee on Public Utility Information in 1922, he immediately increased utility advertising by 1,000 percent and made sure to spread the money around to the small-town papers. Before that time, most utility advertising money in Iowa had gone to the big-city papers.[134]

The immense space-grabbing effort of utility publicists also indicates that they subscribed to another of Lippmann's beliefs, which was that "public opinions must be organized for the press if they are to be sound, not by the press as is the case today."[135] An executive in Michigan told peers that "newspapers do not make news; they gather news. If public utilities want the newspapers to print news about public utilities, they have got to make the news for them."[136] Eventually, making the news is exactly what happened. Utility publicists discovered that if they literally manufactured the news in the form of boiler plates and distributed these plates to newspapers, the articles would get published more often than if the material had to be typeset by the papers. "We have found this plate matter to be very effectively and freely used in the papers that would not, or could not, set our material," observed an Illinois publicist.[137] His experience was widely shared.[138] And when distribution of the plates exceeded one hundred papers, the cost per story came to just 50¢.[139]

Eventually, the utilities' relationship with the press became so close that rather than sending reporters to cover utility news, utilities simply sent reporters completed articles, which the utilities had written. In 1927, a publicity manager for the Ohio Bell bragged that "Columbus newspapers and press associations do not send reporters to cover [rate] hearings but accept our stories as written."[140] In 1928, the Texas bureau director, William C. Grant, observed that he was "daily receiving requests from papers and magazines for information, news stories, and articles."[141] Letters from editors to Grant confirm this observation.[142] The editors "now almost unconsciously look for public utility news," Grant noted. In 1926, a Michigan Bell manager understated the conclusion: "We have got pretty good relations with the press."[143]

One result of the utilities patronizing small newspapers was that the message of corporate utilities reached a large variety of readers in many different places. In 1920, PT&T advertised in hundreds of small-town papers in California, Oregon, Washington, Nevada, and even in several high school papers.[144] The Southern California Edison Company (SCE) advertised in 140 papers in its operating territory, and the Peoples Gas Light & Coke Company in the Chicago area advertised in 112 local papers.[145] Utilities also advertised in papers aimed at various racial, ethnic, and religious groups, including African Americans, immigrants, and Jews.[146]

The utilities also advertised in large circulation journals, including many rural publications. NELA purchased goodwill advertising in popular magazines such as *Collier's*, *Literary Digest*, and *National Weekly*, and it also heavily advertised in popular farm journals such as *Breeder's Gazette*, *Farm and Home*, and *Progressive Farmer*.[147] *Progressive Farmer* had once been the southern organ of the Populist Party, which supported government ownership of monopolies.[148] But by the 1920s, the journal was supported by the corporate monopolies themselves.

William Allen White, perhaps the best-known small-town editor of the first third of the twentieth century, noticed the change in rural papers that accompanied the increase in advertising money. In the early 1890s, when White started as a cub reporter for the Kansas City *Star*, his editor maintained a five-year crusade against the local gas company, and also criticized the streetcar and electricity companies. Yet by the early 1920s, when White had his own paper, the *Gazette* of Emporia, Kansas, he noted that it was "a different organization from what I had come to a generation before" and that "from the East came thousands of dollars in advertising." White claimed that his advertisers did not care about his paper's politics, but that was not quite true. Utilities cared about a paper's politics very much, yet they advertised in unfriendly papers in hopes of softening them up. White may not have known this because he criticized Populists, not corporate monopolies.[149]

White's observation of the money involved in the 1920s helps explain how utility publicists managed to plant so many articles. Although it had been profitable to attack monopolies in the Progressive Era, in the 1920s utility publicists sought to reverse that equation. Bringing about this change was not cheap, but it was not expensive either. In 1921, Bell spent $1.9 million on advertising, a fraction of a percent of its gross telephone revenues. Yet this spending afforded Bell monthly ads in magazines with a total circulation of twenty-eight million, or 168 million ads, at just over a penny per ad.[150] For that small amount, Bell received not only ads, but also news space. In April 1924, PT&T spent approximately $9,200 on advertising and succeeded in planting 362 articles in northern California newspapers for an average cost of $25.32 per article.[151] In 1927, Missouri utilities spent $972 on advertising per news column, if one divides their advertising expenditures by the amount of news space they grabbed.[152] That year, articles planted from Hofer's news service cost utilities just $4.54 per page, or 56¢ a column, a pretty good deal.[153] In the 1920s, news space was not only for sale, it was cheap.

Whatever the cost, it was all passed on to customers. Regulatory boards permitted utilities to include reasonable advertising expenses in their overall operating costs. These operating costs were then used by the boards to set utility rates for customers. Editors and publicists never failed to remind managers to spend freely since it would not come out of corporate profits, and utility managers followed their advice.[154] Once the newspapers were printed with planted articles, the federal government, at taxpayer expense, subsidized the distribution of the papers through media mail discounts.[155]

Did Space Grabbing Work?

Did the nationwide space-grabbing effort of utilities work? The ads-for-articles scheme certainly worked in planting articles. But did these planted articles sway the political sentiments of readers toward favoring corporate utilities? In some ways, no. Neither space grabbing, nor any other public relation strategy of utilities, stopped the Swing-Johnson Act from passing in 1928.[156] Nor were the utilities able to stop the FTC and FCC hearings from occurring.

Yet many people, both inside and outside the utility industry, believed that space grabbing succeeded in several vital areas. Information committees produced "genuine, concrete, plain-to-be-seen results," noted the director of the Rocky Mountain committee in 1923. Committee activities "have been convincingly reflected in the changing attitude of the newspapers, state regulatory bodies, the people in general, and even the law makers," he added.[157] Planted editorials "have undoubtedly had far-reaching results in helping to shape favorable public opinion," echoed the publicity director for the New England bureau in 1922.[158] In 1922, Samuel Insull testified to a group of streetcar executives that "the effect" of the Illinois committee's space-grabbing efforts "has been tremendous throughout the state."[159]

Articles published from the Hofer Service also had their intended effect, according to utility executives. Philip Gadsden of the United Gas Improvement

Company told another executive how Hofer's "editorials . . . week by week, through the country newspapers, are laying the foundation for a better understanding by the people of this country of the basic economic principles upon which all business rests."[160]

People outside the utility industry confirmed the insiders' view that public relations had improved due to print. "Some years ago," the mayor of Lupton, Colorado, stated in 1923, "we all were, more or less, suspicious of our public utilities . . . but in recent years the utilities have pursued a policy of publicity of their acts, and since then we have come to feel that we have a personal interest in their affairs, and they in ours."[161]

Specific incidents also indicate that the newspaper publicity of utilities improved public opinion. In 1922, the president of the Louisville Railway Company told peers that Louisville aldermen had recently threatened to issue a franchise to a nickel bus line in order to force his streetcar company to retract its court petition for a fare hike. The aldermen claimed that nineteen of the twenty-four aldermen were in support of the bus line, and that the Louisville Railway Company would be forced to settle for a 5¢ fare. But the company and the Kentucky Committee on Public Utility Information continuously supplied the Louisville newspapers with their side of the story and, eventually, the city council backed down and accepted the 7¢ fare. "A [utility] bulletin . . . will find a warm reception in all proper quarters, and can but be productive of marked improvement in public understanding of the industry," the executive summarized from experience.[162]

News stories also helped turn the tide in other specific political fights. In 1923, the state publicity committee in Georgia hired E. H. Griffin, a former Georgia house member and the owner of four newspapers, to fight a waterpower bill proposed by the Municipal League of Georgia. Griffin authored a bulletin and sent it to twenty thousand people in the state, including many newspaper editors. The bulletin was widely read and reprinted by editors. In 1927, in a memo headed "Please do not quote directly," the executive secretary of the Georgia information committee described the "remarkable success" that Griffin had in changing the "extremely hurtful anticorporation sentiment which has existed in Georgia" to "sentiment favorable to the utilities in every town" and "strong sentiment against the [public power] bills." According to the secretary, it was "freely admitted by persons most familiar with Georgia politics" that Griffin's work was "the sole reason why these bills are not now law."[163]

John Sheridan also identified specific positive results from space grabbing. In a speech given to Missouri editors in late 1924 or early 1925, he declared that "the dangerous movement of the farmers and others toward socialism had been definitely checked." Sheridan was probably referring to the 1924 defeat of a state constitutional amendment that would have eliminated the state regulatory commission that protected the corporate utilities. Sheridan credited the country newspapers with defeating the amendment.[164]

Quantitative Data

Quantitative data also indicates that newspaper coverage of utilities improved over the 1920s. The Pacific Bell, Southwestern Bell, and Northwest Bell companies all performed careful surveys of newspaper content between 1926 and 1930. The Northwestern Bell survey alone covered 534 newspapers that circulated in its operating territory. In 1926, these Bell companies collectively identified over thirty-three thousand articles and editorials, out of which no less than 95 percent were favorable. In 1930, the amount of favorable press grew to 97 percent of the total number of articles referring to utilities.[165]

As the Depression hit, editors became more negative, but overall coverage remained positive. From 1931 through 1935, Northwest Bell, as well as Illinois

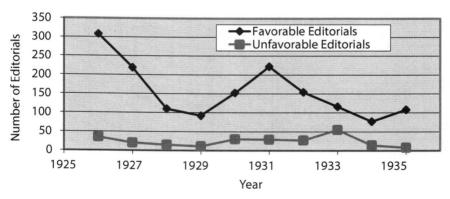

Northwestern Bell Survey of 534 Newspapers for Editorials Regarding Bell Operating Practices. Northwestern Bell Telephone Company, "Item 6: Editorial Comments relating Directly or Indirectly to Telephone Business, Years 1926 to 1935, Inclusive, Northwestern Bell Telephone Company," in *Information Relating to Publicity and Advertising Supplied in Accordance with Federal Communications Commission's Letter of Dec. 11, 1936 to A.T.&T. Co.*, January 7, 1937, Box 41, Ex. 1354, FCC Records.

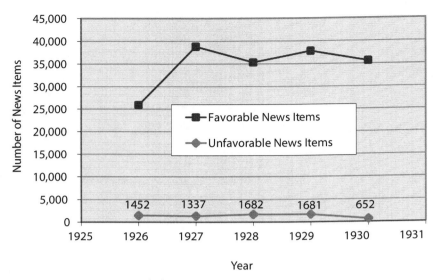

Pacific Bell Survey of News Items. Pacific Bell Telephone and Telegraph Companies, "Item 6: Report of Local News Items," in *Information Requested by Federal Communications Commission through American Telephone and Telegraph Company, December 11, 1936* (January 7, 1937), Box 41, Ex. 1358, FCC Records.

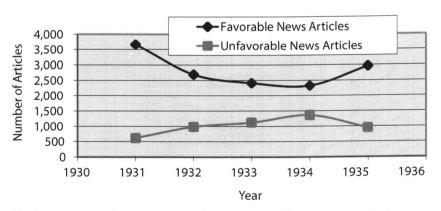

Illinois Bell Survey of Newspaper Articles. G. K. McCorkle, "Survey of Published Newspaper Articles and Editorials," Box 41, Ex. 1353, FCC Records; FCC, "Appendix 2: Survey of Published Newspaper Articles and Editorials, Illinois Bell Telephone Company 1931 to 1935, Inclusive," in *Telephone Investigation* (1937).

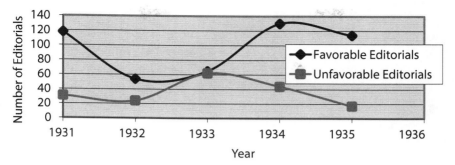

Illinois Bell Survey of Newspaper Editorials. G. K. McCorkle, "Survey of Published Newspaper Articles and Editorials," Box 41, Ex. 1353, FCC Records; FCC, "Appendix 2: Survey of Published Newspaper Articles and Editorials, Illinois Bell Telephone Company 1931 to 1935, Inclusive," in *Telephone Investigation* (1937).

Bell, analyzed over fifteen thousand news items, and classified any item as "negative" if it contained even the slightest criticism. Yet in no year did favorable coverage dip below 64 percent.[166]

Backfire

The strategy of space grabbing also had negative consequences for utilities, however. The strategy obviously backfired somewhat since much of the evidence for this chapter comes from FTC and FCC investigations. These investigations revealed the practice of space grabbing to the nation in the late 1920s and 1930s. Newspapers carried reports of the investigations, while politicians and policy activists who favored government ownership used these revelations to their advantage. In 1930, Senator George Norris of Nebraska thundered that the FTC investigation proved the utilities "had been deceiving and robbing the American people." Norris had previously declared that "a gigantic [electricity] trust . . . has fastened its fangs upon the people."[167] As a result of the bad press and the Depression, utilities disbanded their information committees in the 1930s. By that point, executives found more use for them dead than alive.[168]

Despite some bad press, the response to the government investigations by the general public proved largely muted. Most Americans simply shrugged. A 1938 textbook on public relations published by *Business Week* praised the Bell System for being "an outstanding example of long-range public relations." For proof, the book noted that "confidence in the Bell System is so universal that the Federal Communications Commission couldn't make up its mind after its three-year investigation of the company."[169] A history committee at Illinois Bell looked back from the 1950s on the FCC investigation and concluded that "strangely enough, the most expensive and exhaustive investigation of a private industry in American history had brought increased respect and good will to the Bell System."[170] This was probably an exaggeration, but Bell executives ably defended their right to tell their company's story during the hearings.

Although utility executives dissolved their information committees, these executives did not go into hiding. Some became more outspoken, partly because they no longer had publicity agents to do the talking. Sometimes executives tried to turn the tables on their critics by claiming that any criticism against corporations was an attack on America itself. In 1931, Martin Insull implored executives not to sit around "pussyfooting while those who would upset those national policies that have built the nation, are . . . making breaches in the ranks of our defense." Then, referring to information committees, Insull misquoted Marshal Foch as saying, "My right has crumpled, my left is in retreat, I am attacking with my center."[171] These histrionics were only rivaled by W. C. Mullendore, a vice president at SCE, who in 1931 bellowed before his peers that "we must become crusaders" and that "our cause is the cause of American institutions—a struggle for the birthright of all our people."[172] Mullendore also singled out Senator Norris and municipal socialist Carl D. Thompson for their "onslaught upon American industry and American institutions." Utility executives were regrouping; their attack against New Deal electricity projects would soon follow.[173]

The Importance of Being Frank and the Definition of Propaganda

Mullendore's comments represented a popular communication style among executives by the early 1930s, which they called being "frank." Being frank meant speaking in a direct and straightforward manner that signaled honesty yet also boldness, and even swagger. Speaking frankly to the public allowed executives to unapologetically declare their material interests and receive praise for their honesty, rather than condemnation for their materialism. "Confide in the public with all frankness," enjoined *Public Service Magazine*, and "abandon apology."[174]

Most executives discovered the importance of being frank in the early twentieth century. In 1910, William G. McAdoo observed that "for a long time railroad companies refused to give information to passengers about anything . . . particularly about accidents," but that only created "hordes of enemies." So McAdoo provided immediate information about accidents and other corporate matters, even when it was unflattering. In 1909, when McAdoo eliminated the women's-only cars for lack of demand, he recalled that "our frankness in giving complete and truthful information about the whole matter commended itself to the press, and we received nothing but praise."[175] Following McAdoo's lead, Samuel MacQuarrie advised executives in 1926 that news should be given to the press as long as it was "frank in every respect." "There is nothing to be gained by concealment," he said, whereas "frankness earns good-will and understanding."[176]

But how could MacQuarrie—a consummate space grabber—claim to be frank? One way was that he and others believed in private enterprise so much that they justified their actions as necessary to save America from socialism. In doing so, they saw themselves as frankly communicating the truth, even though their communication disguised its true source. Corporate enterprise preserved American individualism, rewarded initiative, and promoted freedom, MacQuarrie and other publicists believed and taught in their articles. Just because some underhanded activities were going on did not mean insiders like MacQuarrie thought corporate monopolies were a scam, or one big racket. Quite the opposite. Many publicists believed in their message so much they viewed using questionable tactics as legitimate and warranted.

This justification shaped their definition of the word *propaganda*. In the 1920s, the word had two competing definitions: one that MacQuarrie and some others used, and another, more widely used definition, that went back to before World War I. Before the war, *propaganda* simply meant communicating information to shape public opinion. Many people, especially practitioners, thought propaganda was entirely legitimate, and the term did not have a negative connotation. The Populists, for example, maintained a Propaganda Committee.[177] The word suffered some loss of prestige during World War I, because American practitioners such as George Creel depicted their German counterparts as deceitful propagandists.[178] Yet even after the war, the term *propaganda* had not been fully besmirched. It was still possible in the 1920s to hear businessmen urge one another to produce corporate propaganda.[179] In 1922, Walter Lippmann did not imply an entirely negative view of the word when he asked: "What is propaganda, if not the effort to alter the picture of which men respond, to substitute one social pattern for another?"[180] The public relations agent Edward Bernays even called himself a propagandist, and in 1928 he published a book entitled *Propaganda* with the belief that the term's reputation could still be burnished into serviceable form.

The definition of *propaganda* that Bernays and many others used had two types: one that was bad because it was deceptive and another that was good because it was transparent to its audience. As Jack Levin, a critic of utility propaganda, wrote in 1931, "There are two kinds of private propaganda: revealed and concealed propaganda."[181] The editor of the *Chicago Tribune* shared this definition, arguing in 1928 that the utilities had "overdone it with camouflaged propaganda," though he had no objections to an "open and above board" campaign against "public ownership propaganda spread by groups of theorists among college professors."[182]

This widely used twofold definition of *propaganda* was not the one used by some utility publicists. They defined *propaganda* as anything false or un-American; in short, anything that smacked of socialism. For them, the defining attribute of propaganda was that it contained false statements, regardless of whether it was disseminated in an open or concealed manner. The claim that municipal ownership of utilities was superior to corporate ownership was not true in their mind, therefore it was propaganda. All assertions of socialists were propaganda because the assertations were false, regardless of how they were made. In contrast, the statements of utility publicists were not propaganda, even if they were made in deceptive ways, because the arguments were true, in the mind of their creators.

This definition of propaganda explains how William C. Grant of the Texas bureau could flatly deny that space grabbing was propaganda and then, almost in the same breath, criticize "extreme socialistic propaganda," which he claimed could be found in school textbooks.[183] This also explains how the superintendent of Rochester, New York, public schools could argue that utility-authored textbooks, which he used in his schools, did not contain any propaganda. What he meant was that the books' arguments were not false in his view.[184] It did not matter whether or not the books acknowledged their true authorship. The material was true, American, and patriotic; therefore it was not propaganda.

Morality of Space Grabbing

Most utility officers could not see anything wrong with the massive amount of space grabbing in which they engaged. An FTC investigator asked Samuel MacQuarrie of the New England bureau if he would agree that "when your local company advertises extensively in the newspapers . . . that things do get into the news columns because you want them there . . . ?" MacQuarrie agreed, replying, "I think that they very often do, and I think it is a perfectly

Making the News 193

legitimate reason why they should go in."[185] When an FTC investigator asked William C. Grant of the Texas bureau and AP if he would continue space grabbing, Grant affirmed that he would. The investigator incredulously responded by asking: "Anything to influence public opinion on economic questions—do you mean to get that printed in some way?" "Yes," Grant defiantly answered. "And to utilize the same friendships and connections that you have used in the past for the same purpose?" the investigator followed. "More of them," Grant replied. Amazed by his unapologetic attitude, an FTC commissioner who was not leading the questioning broke in and demanded: "Don't you recognize any distinction between . . . the matter of advertising and propaganda? Speaking ethically now, can you not see a distinction in that? . . . Is not that going entirely beyond the business proprieties?" "Oh, I think not at all, Mr. Commissioner," Grant replied.[186] Grant was being frank.

Other utility executives defended their publicity practices in ways that were much harder to dismiss. During one FCC hearing, an FCC examiner tried to make Southern Bell manager Evelyn Harris look bad, but Harris skillfully defended his practice of giving news to editors. Why shouldn't a legitimate business offering an important service give press releases to editors? Harris wanted to know. Why should not America's largest corporation provide news when it was doing something newsworthy? Harris asked when an FCC examiner tried to paint him into a corner. Were socialists and others the only ones with the right to promote their views to the public? Did not everyone have freedom of speech? Of course Bell executives wanted the goodwill of editors, Harris acknowledged during a line of questioning. They wanted the goodwill of "everybody else" too.[187]

Only John Sheridan in Missouri, the most zealous space grabber of them all, expressed doubts about the ethics of his actions. He first revealed his change of heart to his old friend John Colton, who edited the American Electric Railway Association magazine. Colton did not look highly on everything that was going on in the utility industry either. In 1927, Sheridan wrote to Colton to congratulate him for resisting a plan hatched by utility executives in New York to label every advocate of municipal ownership a Bolshevik. Sheridan fumed in his letter that "possession of property breeds liars and cowards. The man who invented private ownership was a moral enemy of the human race." Colton replied that "the thing about the utility industry that disgusts me is the lying, trimming, faking, and downright evasion of trust, or violation of trust, that marks the progress toward enormous wealth of some of the so-called big men in the industry." Colton added that "when I see some of these fellows waving the flag, I am filled with not only disgust but rage, for they are anything but patriots." Colton estimated that only 10 percent of the utility industry's activities were honest, though Sheridan thought the number was at least a bit higher.

Still, Sheridan did not like everything he saw and did. "There were certain things about it that bothered me and that I did worry about," Sheridan admitted to an FTC examiner regarding space grabbing. Sheridan also suffered from personal attacks from editors. In one instance, an editor wrote to Sheridan, who was himself a former editor: "Sorry you swapped real service, for the privilege of disseminating utility propaganda." The comment must have cut deep. "What profiteth it for a man to gain the whole world if he loses his own soul?" Sheridan agonized to Colton, quoting the Bible. After working for the utilities for five years, Sheridan was through. "Damn it all, John," Sheridan wrote to Colton in 1927. "T'ell mit 'em." Three years later, after the FTC had exposed Sheridan's work, he was admitted to a Los Angeles hospital for "nervous trouble." In April 1930, while in the hospital, Sheridan hanged himself.[188]

Conclusion

This chapter has demonstrated that utility managers purchased newspaper ads largely to plant articles written by utilities. As a result of this practice, readers consumed thousands of articles that appeared to be written by journalists but were actually written by utility employees. These planted articles were ads in the sense that they were produced by utilities and promoted utilities, yet they were unlike ads because they lacked acknowledgment of their true source. What these articles sold was the idea that corporate utility monopolies were superior to overregulation or government ownership. Although deceptive, some utility employees did not see a problem with them. They believed that by defending corporate America they were defending America itself.

CHAPTER SIX

Subverting Civics

On April 8, 1925, a handpicked committee of utility managers met in Louisville, Kentucky, to discuss ways to rid American classrooms of textbooks that criticized corporate utilities. Every utility industry appointed a representative to the committee. The National Electric Light Association (NELA) sent Fred Jenkins of the Chicago Central Station Institute; the American Gas Association sent its vice president, Bernard Mullaney, who was also a close associate of Samuel Insull; the American Telephone & Telegraph Company (AT&T) sent J. L. Spellman, a publicity manager at Illinois Bell; and the American Electric Railway Association (AERA) appointed Edward Dana of the Boston Elevated Railway Company, though Dana could not attend the meeting.

The committee members shared the same goal of purging offensive textbooks from classrooms, but they could not agree on the right way to do it. Jenkins wanted face-to-face meetings with publishers, while Spellman counseled caution. In the end, Jenkins's position carried the day, and, as the meeting adjourned, the committee agreed to confront publishers, point out the error of their ways, and suggest that they rewrite their textbooks or face the combined opposition of all four utility industries.[1]

Amazingly, just a few days after the meeting, Jenkins ran into an old acquaintance, O. J. Laylander, who happened to be an executive at one of the largest textbook publishers in the country. Having just decided to confront publishers about their textbooks, Jenkins recognized this meeting, which occurred at a Chicago athletic club, as serendipitous. Laylander's firm, Ginn & Company, published the nation's best-selling civics textbook, *Community Life and Civic Problems*, which severely criticized corporate utilities, and Jenkins's desperately wanted to remove the book from before the eyes of impressionable school children. The book's chapter on utilities related a sordid history of stock-watering, city council bribery, and rate gouging, with specific examples taken from Chicago and Toledo.[2] The book even pointed out that utilities had "at times . . . misled public opinion by controlling the newspapers through their advertising." Such abuses had "caused many people to become advocates of government ownership," the text alarmingly continued, adding that under government ownership in Europe "rates are lower, services are better, and politics are purer than under private ownership."[3] At least one hundred thousand copies of the book had been sold each year since it was first published in 1922, buoyed by the fact that its author, Howard Copeland Hill, headed the Social Sciences Department at the University of Chicago Laboratory School, an institution founded by none other than famed educator and philosopher John Dewey.[4]

Having just run into Laylander, and seeing the main chance, Jenkins decided to ask his old acquaintance for a bit of professional advice. "Assuming that you were in a business about which the publishers published a considerable number of textbooks which contained incomplete, inaccurate information," Jenkins queried, "what means would you take, or what would you do about it?" "You certainly should go to the publishers and tell them about it," Laylander assured him. The reply put Laylander in an awkward position when he learned that the publisher in question was himself. Exactly one month after Jenkins's textbook committee agreed to confront publishers, Jenkins and Mullaney were sitting down with Laylander and another executive at Ginn & Company to review the accuracy of Ginn & Company's *Community Life and Civic Problems.*[5]

During the meeting the executives at Ginn & Company promised to submit future editions of Hill's book to Jenkins, not only to improve the book's accuracy, but because it would be "a good business proposition for them."[6] After the meeting, Jenkins reported to the director of NELA that the committee had made a "good start" and that "after the large publishers were straightened out and were working with you the smaller publishers would naturally fall into line."[7] Jenkins also informed John Sheridan, the secretary of the Missouri Committee on Public Utility Information, about the outcome of the meeting, but cautioned him to keep it a secret since "it might embarrass the publishers."[8]

This chapter reveals that the editing of Hill's book was just one part of a larger strategy to control the content of textbooks. The purpose of this strategy was to shape the opinions of young people toward utilities. That way, the students would grow up to support corporate monopolies. This chapter further analyzes several other publicity strategies that utilities used, including writing their own textbooks and giving them away for free to schools, paying authors to write popular and academic books on utility history, and hiring professors to influence college curriculums regarding utility subjects.

This chapter also reveals that utility publicists sought to shape public opinion in ways that extended far beyond the printed page. Executives knew the power of face-to-face communication at the customer service counter, and they extended this idea to include communication outside the commercial office. Utility employees gave thousands of face-to-face speeches at local civic clubs, purged socialists from the Chautauqua speaking circuit, and spoke on the circuit themselves. Utility employees also produced radio shows, live cooking shows, and traveling plays that demonstrated utility technology and highlighted utility contributions. Finally, utility managers produced popular movies that were syndicated by major theater chains and consumed by millions of Americans. In most cases, viewers had no idea the films were produced by utility companies. Altogether, these strategies sought to improve public opinion toward corporate utilities by educating young people and adults about the virtues of corporate monopolies.

Textbooks

Utilities received a great deal of cooperation from others when executing these public relations strategies. This proved especially true when it came to controlling textbook content. Publishers such as Ginn & Company cooperated readily, and for good reason. They simply could not compete with the organized efforts of utilities to influence texts. Since the early 1920s, utility managers had waged a highly organized and successful effort to purge negative textbooks from classrooms. To do this, they first surveyed economics, civics, and government textbooks, and identified offending passages. Then, managers determined which schools used these books. With that information, local managers visited the schools and pressured their teachers, principals, school boards, and parent-teacher associations to remove the offensive books from classrooms.

Utilities also offered their own utility-authored textbooks for free to any teacher, principal, or superintendent who wanted them. In a typical example, the Iowa Committee on Public Utility Information sent high school principals copies of a utility-authored booklet, along with a letter asking them to review the text and order free copies for their school. Principals who did not order copies received a personal visit from a local utility manager to find out why not. The committee also offered its texts to teachers and kept a list of who ordered them and who did not. Teachers who failed to place an order likewise received a personal visit from a local utility manager. By 1927, over twenty thousand copies of Iowa's booklet were being sent out on a biweekly basis.[9] Similar activities occurred in other states.[10]

These personal and detailed lobbying methods were no match for Ginn & Company, so the company decided to cooperate. Initially, Jenkins and Mullaney wanted executives at Ginn & Company and other publishers to serve as intermediaries between utility managers and textbook authors so that utility personnel could operate behind the scenes. But Jenkins and Mullaney soon got over their timidity. By their second meeting with Ginn & Company in December of 1925, the publishing executives dragged their star author, Howard Hill, to a meeting to sit face-to-face with his critics. He did not say much, according to reports. But by 1928, when Hill was working on a new edition of his book, he dutifully submitted drafts of the manuscript to Jenkins and Mullaney, who edited them and sent them back to Hill with their own suggestions for material to be included.[11] As at many newspapers by this time, utility personnel were now in charge of a major textbook publisher.

When Hill's retitled *Vocational Civics* was published, all mention of utility bribery and stock-watering had been eliminated. Hill did slip in one mention of a questionable campaign contribution, but instead of discussing government corruption and eternal monopoly bills, Hill's new book taught that corporate utilities were regulated by the government in every state but one. And rather than asking students to debate public vs. private ownership—in other words, think critically—students were merely asked to define a natural monopoly, name some in their community, and "tell who owns and controls them." All of the questions had explicit answers in the book. A nearly identical assignment appeared in a utility-authored textbook, though by this point it was difficult to tell the difference.[12]

Entering the Schools

The goal of controlling textbook content was to "fix the truth about the utilities in the young person's mind before incorrect notions become fixed there," the utility publicist Mullaney explained in a memo to executives in the early 1920s.[13] This was necessary, according to publicists Sheridan, because "the prospect of the privately-owned public utilities having in 20,000,000

Subverting Civics   199

children in the United States, 20,000,000 future citizens prejudiced against them, is appalling."[14]

This long-range view was widely shared by utility executives. A Pacific Telephone & Telegraph Company (PT&T) executive informed managers that "the schoolchildren of today will become our customers of tomorrow," which made it "advantageous" to educate them about the telephone.[15] When a Federal Trade Commission (FTC) examiner asked NELA official and state publicity director Thorne Browne why he was meddling in the education of students, Browne summarized the thinking of the entire utility industry: "They are the next voters," Browne flatly replied.[16] With that view in mind, utility executives set out to edit the educational materials used in schools, or author the materials themselves.

When writing their own textbooks, utilities made sure the books could be used in a wide range of grade levels and classes. Utility authors created texts for economics, physics, government, English, and current topics classes, as well as for the new civics courses, which had recently been added to school curriculums in the 1890s.[17] Texts also covered all four utility industries, including streetcars, gas, electricity, and telephones, and sometimes appeared in four-volume sets so students could study each industry one by one.[18] Utilities offered these books to public and private schools, and to middle schools, high schools, and vocational schools.[19] One utility organization even produced a color picture book entitled *The Ohm Queen*, designed for kindergarteners. The free book achieved a distribution of four hundred thousand.[20]

For overworked, underpaid, and undertrained teachers, the offer of free books and lesson plans proved very appealing.[21] In many cases, the utilities did not even bother with personal visits because the teachers themselves requested the materials. In 1927 teachers from some three hundred high schools in Texas ordered eighty thousand booklets, including teachers in San Antonio who ordered six thousand booklets.[22]

The demand for texts proved so high that it nearly exceeded supply. In 1927 in Illinois, Mullaney's office had to print over sixty-five thousand pamphlets just to keep up with demand from teachers. Illinois high schools also received copies of clipsheets produced by utilities as well as speeches, such as Mullaney's "Do You Want the Government in Your Business?"[23] In 1926, in New England, managers sent textbook samples to nine hundred public and private schools in five states and nearly one-third of the schools solicited requested additional copies. The New England Bureau of Public Service Information ended up sending out sixty-two thousand textbooks.[24]

The finding that teachers, principals, and superintendents readily cooperated with utility managers to provide business-friendly instruction supports key aspects of the historiography of public schooling during this period. As historians of education have shown, in city after city during the Progressive Era, coalitions of businesspeople, professionals, and politicians centralized control of school boards into the hands of a few educational experts. As a result, the educational interests of business became more prominent in the classroom and students began receiving instruction in the vocational skills that employers wanted in future workers. Supposedly useless subjects, such as Latin, fell by the wayside, while subjects such as English and history shifted their focus from the interpretation and creation of texts to the teaching of basic grammar and the regurgitation of Whiggish narratives. Meanwhile, arithmetic and shop skills needed by business received more attention.

The debate among educational historians is not whether these changes happened, but whether they represented a capitalist coup on public schools, as the revisionists historians argue, or whether working-class parents and their unions also advocated these vocational curriculums, as the progressive historians argue.[25] The finding that utility companies thoroughly influenced classroom instruction gives credence to the revisionist interpretation, while leaving open the possibility that labor did not object.

Unlike some businessmen, however, utility executives wanted something more than just good corporate employees; they wanted good corporate citizens. Utility executives wanted schools to produce, not just well-trained workers, but pro-business, anti-socialist Americans. To accomplish this, utility executives extended their influence across the country and down to even the smallest school districts in ways that other industries are not known to have done. Due to these activities, utilities in the 1920s exercised one of the most extensive amounts of corporate influence in the history of American education. This is true in terms of curricular scope, geographic reach, and the percentage of students contacted.

By inundating school systems with free literature, the utilities reached an exceptionally high percentage of the student population in the United States. In Illinois in 1928, over 75 percent of the high schools used educational material created by the utilities.[26] In Connecticut, 76 percent of high school students used utility texts.[27] And in Missouri, a staggering 97 percent of the total number of enrolled students, or 88,453 pupils, received instruction from utility-authored material.[28]

Subverting Civics   201

All of this occurred just as the number of students enrolled in public schools reached new highs. During the decades surrounding the turn of the century, schooling had been made compulsory in nearly all states through at least the age of sixteen. This change was brought about by progressives seeking to eliminate child labor, as well as by businesspeople who wanting a better-trained workforce.[29] The result was a massive influx of high school students, which strained the ability of school systems to educate pupils, diluted academic standards, and increased the reliance of teachers on outside material, including utility texts.[30]

The educational value of much of the utility material was dubious. When the Information Bureau of Kansas Public Service Companies tried to have its textbook endorsed by the dean of engineering at the University of Kansas, the dean replied that the text was too one-sided and its claims "extravagant." Thirteen thousand copies went out to schoolchildren anyway.[31] Some of the textbook content was offensive, misleading, or inaccurate. One electricity booklet contained a subsection called "Your 'Thirty Slaves,'" which stated that, according to the Smithsonian Institution, electric machinery provided everyone in the country with the work "equivalent of 30 slaves," so that "the average family of 5 has 150 slaves working for it."[32] The text was distributed by NELA to schools nationwide beginning in 1927 and was intended for English and current topics classes, as well as debate teams.[33] The authors of the *Connecticut Public Utility Catechism* claimed that the cost of living in cities with municipally owned power plants was higher than in cities with privately owned plants, and cited the Industrial Conference Board as proof, but the Industrial Conference Board had made no such statement. Dozens of high schoolers in Connecticut received the *Catechism* anyway.[34]

Utility books did contain some educational value, however. A booklet on electricity illustrated the physics behind voltage transformation and included an informative graph on electricity consumption by time of day. The booklet also contained an interesting cut-away view of a coal powerplant and followed the electricity from the plant, through powerlines, to a substation, and finally into a home.[35] Another gas industry booklet described the process of manufacturing and distributing gas, and provided a brief history of chemists going back to the seventeenth century.[36] Financial and policy issues were also touched on in the texts.

Overall, however, the educational content of the utility texts was limited, as their titles indicated. The Colorado committee issued *The Romance of Gas* and *The Romance of the Kilowatt*.[37] The *Connecticut Public Utility Catechism* indoctrinated students in the dogma of corporate utilities, as its title implied. The Missouri committee authored *A Half-Century Miracle*, while AT&T published *The Magic of Communication*, whose cover featured scores of pointy-eared "imps"—apparently representing sound—running in and out of a telephone ear- and mouthpiece. Despite the cover, the text contained some science, but it also contained subtle advertising and arguments against government ownership. A chart in the book showed the large number of telephones in the United States under private operation, compared to the smaller number of phones in Europe under government operation. Another page showed a commercial office "where courteous attendants receive applications for telephones."[38] Copies of the booklet were available to general customers, but a PT&T manager noted that the company "aimed particularly at their distribution in the schools . . . where it will be appreciated." Indeed, teachers requested the material.[39]

Catechisms, magic, miracles, and romance may not seem to today's readers to be appropriate content for public school instruction, but they did not appear that way to many educators and policymakers in the 1920s. Many positively defended their use. In 1928, the superintendent of the Rochester, New York, school system advocated the use of *The Story of Public Utilities*, telling an FTC examiner that it contained no propaganda. This was after the revelation came out that New York utilities contributed $15,000 to publish copies for Rochester school children.[40] In 1920, the governor of Missouri, Sam Baker, who once worked as a school superintendent, declared that citizens should be "educated up to the necessity for public utilities" in order to "do away with some of these little pusillanimous kicks that are made every once in a while without cause." The *St. Louis Globe Democrat* agreed, observing that the people "know nothing" about utilities, so "surely a little education, as Governor Baker suggests, will not be out of place."[41]

Many teachers shared these views. According to a report published in 1929 by the National Education Association, "typical comments" made by teachers regarding corporate material in the schools included "much advertising is simply a matter of useful information, which makes a decided contribution to the general welfare of the child," "I am glad to let pupils secure useful facts regardless of who publishes them," and "no danger in commodity advertising."[42]

But not all educators agreed. In the late 1920s, the National Education Association formed a Committee on Propaganda in the Schools to investigate the remarkable openness of school curriculums to corporate tampering. The committee included college presidents, deans, and high school superintendents from all over the country. Their 1929 report found that only four of the thirty-seven states that responded to their survey had laws against "propaganda or outside materials in the schools," and just five of thirty-three school boards had rules against using corporate material. When the education committee asked superintendents if they "frequently receive requests to endorse commercial or propaganda material for use in the schools," over 80 percent said yes.[43] In the 1920s, schools were wide open to corporate influence, and corporate utilities took full advantage of it.

The Committee on Propaganda in the Schools did not view this as a good thing. Its report noted that a functional democracy required citizens who could gather evidence and weigh arguments, but the committee observed that since "the propagandist's mind is made up on a particular subject, he merely seeks to inculcate one viewpoint." The committee added that the propagandist's material was aimed at children who did not have a choice about whether to attend school and did not have the same discernment as adults. "An adult is not compelled to read advertisements," the report read, but "the child is required by law to attend school, has little choice as to what he will study or do in school, and therefore, must accept the instruction offered."[44]

Some teachers shared the committee's concerns. Several made statements such as "safer to be obstinate in this respect" and "it is too hard to draw the line—better not admit any."[45] A few administrators even took action. In 1934, the director of the Department of Education in Ohio warned his superintendents and principals about the "ill-advised, promiscuous use of advertising, or propaganda . . . distributed 'gratis' to the schools," and asked his teachers to reject these offers.[46] During the Depression, other educators and publishers blamed the economic downturn on business and expressed this anti-business view in their textbooks. Due to this resistance, the openness of schools to free corporate material declined somewhat in the 1930s. But by that point utilities had educated nearly an entire generation.[47]

Utility textbooks taught a particular political viewpoint regarding the role of government in business. Sometimes between the lines, and often explicitly, utility texts deprecated government ownership and celebrated corporate operation of utilities. According to the director of the Nebraska committee during his FTC testimony, utility authors intentionally conveyed that government ownership of utilities would sap individual initiative, reduce efficiency, and eliminate opportunities for individuals to reach their full potential.[48]

In other cases, utility authors deliberately avoided mentioning government ownership, since they did not want to plant any contrary ideas in students' heads. Why confuse the issue? Municipal ownership was "purposely kept out," testified Samuel MacQuarrie, the director of the New England bureau. Avoiding the topic of government ownership required treating the topic of private ownership carefully, since dwelling on it could lead to an unwanted discussion of its alternative. To avoid this, books often dispensed with the public/private distinction altogether.[49]

Utility authors sometimes even avoided the topic of government regulation. In New England, where a large number of municipally owned powerplants operated under government regulation, regulation was not mentioned for fear that it would legitimize those plants.[50] In other areas, such as Texas, where little public ownership existed, government regulation was trumpeted as fair and judicious in order to promote corporate operation.[51] Each utility information committee tailored its texts to its specific location.

Instead of government ownership, pamphlets often discussed customer ownership. Gas companies were not owned by individual capitalists, students learned, but by the "thousands of thrifty investors who have bought securities with their savings."[52] In another pamphlet, students discovered that they owned the streetcar companies, as long as they kept their savings in banks, because banks owned streetcar securities.[53] When learning to accept corporate monopolies, students also learned the economic values of growth and accumulation of capital.

Utility books did not encourage critical thinking. That was not the goal. As the director of the New England bureau stated, "Facts without argument or discussion, for the sole purpose of education, is the Bureau's mission."[54] In 1926, the Connecticut *Catechism* employed this strategy by declaring that "in every case in which a community has attempted to operate a public service industry . . . the costs of the service are higher" compared to a "private corporation."[55] That blanket statement proved too strong, even for its authors, so the next year's edition hedged this by adding "*practically* every case." Yet both editions retained the unimpeachable conclusion: "Connecticut cities do not favor municipal operation . . . neither do the people of the United States."[56] The *Catechism* also declared that "when people in any community criticize adversely their public utilities," they negatively advertise their city and were "thereby retarding its growth."[57] Such criticism of people's views must have stifled discussion in the classroom. This was certainly a far cry from

Hill's original *Community Life and Civic Problems* which invited students to argue for and against municipal ownership.

Did Writing Textbooks Work?

Did the textbook campaign of utilities work? According to many executives, it did. In Iowa, after a textbook survey in 1924, managers pressured school boards in fifteen towns to remove harmful textbooks, and "in nearly every instance," the director of the Iowa committee observed, the books "were removed and placed on the library shelves for use as reference matters only."[58] Seven or eight schools held out, however, mostly in areas with municipally owned electricity plants.[59] In 1927, after successfully proposing the Bell-created "Adventures in Geography" lesson plans to the New York City Board of Education, a Bell System manager triumphantly told his colleagues: "I can see that it is one of the biggest, one of the most effective, one of the best things we have done in an educational way with the adolescent mind."[60] In the mid-1920s, the director of the Rocky Mountain Committee on Public Utility Information rejoiced that "student's [sic] heads are no longer being crammed with municipal, government and state ownership theories."[61]

Lectures and Movies in Public Schools

In addition to controlling the content of textbooks, utility managers also visited schools to lecture to school children. Since students represented a captive audience, utility speakers were able to reach a large number of them. In Wisconsin in 1930, over fifty-six thousand students heard a lecture from a Bell employee.[62] In New England in 1926, utility executives spoke at 132 different schools.[63] Between 1926 and 1935, over 387,000 students in Illinois attended a lecture presented by a Bell employee.[64]

To promote school lectures, executives encouraged managers to cultivate personal relationships with teachers, superintendents, and student organizations. One executive recommended that "the general manager should identify himself with the Boy Scout movement," since that offered a good opportunity "to talk to the boys individually and collectively, to lecture them on good citizenship, and especially on the essentials involved in healthy public relations." The same work should also be done among Girl Scouts, the executive advised.[65] For managers who were leery about talking to kids, they could pick up *How to Talk to Grade School Pupils*, published by the Illinois utility information committee.[66]

206   Chapter 6

Utilities also produced "educational films" aimed at teaching school children the virtues of corporate monopolies. AT&T's most widely distributed film to schools, *Getting Together*, featured an animated imp—AT&T's favorite character—putting together a handset telephone. The idea was to impress students about the complexity of the telephone in order to reduce criticism about malfunctions and telephone handset rental charges.

School systems proved very open to corporate movies, just as they were to corporate textbooks. One Bell manager in Pennsylvania wrote to Hamilton in 1933 that "our pictures have also proven highly acceptable in various schools, notably in Philadelphia, Allentown and Pittsburgh. In these towns the Boards of Education have taken the entire series and shown them to the student bodies."[67] Films reached even more students than textbooks. In 1927 in Illinois, over 115,000 students viewed a movie supplied by Illinois Bell. Over the next several years, the popularity of films in schools increased dramatically. By 1935, an astonishing 3.2 million students in Illinois had viewed an AT&T movie.[68] These numbers were not unusual.[69] In Ohio, over 305,000 students viewed an AT&T film in 1932. The Ohio Bell Company wanted students to see their films so much that they offered to supply both a film projector and a film operator if the schools could not do so itself. The company also drew up a brochure to help teachers pick out which films they wanted to show.[70]

A large number of high school teachers gratefully accepted the offer for free movies. An educator at a junior high in Scranton, Pennsylvania, wrote to AT&T president Walter Gifford in 1930 to thank him for providing AT&T films, stating, "They have done much toward developing a keener understanding of the problems of communication; have developed a civic and national consciousness; and have promoted the idea of service; such as no other medium which we possess could possibly do." Gifford must have received this note with considerable satisfaction since utility executives also wanted to mold the minds of educators.[71]

Colleges Students and Professors

Utility executives also tried to shape the opinions of college students and professors. One way executives did this was by hiring professors to influence teaching on college campuses. One of the most effective academics hired to do this was Clyde O. Ruggles, a Harvard-educated economist, dean at Ohio State, and eventually a professor at Harvard Business School. In 1927, while still at Ohio State, Ruggles led NELA's Committee on Cooperation with Educational Institutions, which sought to remove unfavorable textbooks from college syllabi. The committee operated separately from the textbook committee that contacted Ginn & Company, but their goals and methods were similar. Ruggles and his group surveyed college textbooks on economics, business, law, engineering, and accounting for any negative statements about corporate utilities. The committee then searched college syllabi to find out where these books were assigned. When offensive textbooks were found, Ruggles used his university contacts and reputation to talk to the professors about their textbook choices. Ruggles also reviewed syllabi for case studies that he felt were out of date. He then suggested to professors that they modify their selections to account for recent advances in utility regulation and practice.[72]

Ruggles also hosted academic conferences on utility subjects for business, law, economics, and engineering professors. Any professor willing to attend these events received an all-expenses-paid trip to the conference, courtesy of their state utility information committee. The conferences were well attended. In the summer of 1926, AT&T hosted a conference on engineering education that was attended by professors from prestigious schools such as the University of California, Harvard, Yale, MIT, Columbia, Cornell, the University of Illinois, the University of Wisconsin, Ohio State, the University of Michigan, the University of Pennsylvania, Stanford, and many others.[73] The conference mainly focused on using illustrations when teaching, but before getting to that, AT&T president Walter Gifford took the opportunity to explain how AT&T's universal telephone network was superior to two competing systems, how AT&T favored government regulation not government operation, and how AT&T earned little on its investment yet still managed to pay 9 percent dividends. Gifford added that AT&T stock was widely distributed among customers, making AT&T "really publicly owned."[74]

Most of the academic conferences organized by utilities occurred in the late 1920s, although Ruggles had been associated with NELA's Committee on Cooperation with Educational Institutions since at least 1924.[75] In 1926, Ruggles helped arrange a $90,000 gift over three years from NELA to Harvard for utility research.[76] Two years later, Ruggles moved from Ohio State to Harvard Business School, where he became professor of public utility management.[77] At Harvard, Ruggles now earned $15,000 per year, but that was less than half of what utilities were paying him to continue his work as a consultant.[78]

A year after Ruggles arrived at Harvard, a Massachusetts legislator demanded an investigation into Ruggles's association with the utilities, but the university found nothing wrong with the relationship. Perhaps this was because Ruggles generated so much funding, or because three AT&T executives sat on Harvard's Board of Overseers.[79] Or perhaps it was because Ruggles's utility courses attracted so many students.[80] Whatever the reason, Ruggles remained at Harvard for the rest of his long career, during which time he continued to advise utilities and write on utilities issues.[81]

Executives not only hired professors as consultants, they also influenced the hiring of professors at universities. Utilities wanted to get universities to hire candidates sympathetic to corporate monopolies so that utilities could then hire these professors as consultants and benefit from the consultants' prestige. This would be especially nice, utilities knew, since the university would bear much of the cost of the employment. In Colorado, the Rocky Mountain committee wanted to have a consultant appointed to the faculty of the University of Colorado, so the committee schemed to establish a fellowship at the university and have it filled with an academic sympathetic to the committee's views. George Lewis, the director of the Rocky Mountain committee, explained to an interested colleague in another state how the Colorado utilities managed this. "While the [fellowship] idea originated in the committee," Lewis confided, "it reached the colleges and universities through a man high in educational circles who broached the subject, without mentioning the public utilities as being interested. Therefore, the colleges, on their own volition, developed the idea and the [Colorado utility] committee volunteered to render all possible assistance." The University of Colorado, in consultation with the utilities, then hired Herbert Wolfe as an instructor and economics researcher.[82]

When Wolfe first arrived at the university in 1925, Lewis took it upon himself to give him a "practical" education in corporate utilities. Wolfe had already received university training in utilities subjects, but Lewis found that too "theoretical." Wolfe's practical education included joining the weekly lunch meetings of the Rocky Mountain committee and going on free trips to NELA conventions and industry conferences. At one of these conferences, Wolfe went on what Lewis characterized as a "spree," racking up a $47.65 bill at the Broadmoor Hotel in Colorado Springs.[83] But Lewis reimbursed Wolfe for it anyway. Apparently, this was the type of practical education of which Lewis approved.

In 1922, before Wolfe's appointment, Lewis had already assembled a group of more than a dozen professors from around Colorado to discuss the possibility of establishing university courses on utility subjects. Lewis proposed that the courses would be mainly taught by utility employees. The idea proved overwhelmingly popular among professors. "We can use your speakers as often as you can send them," declared Charles A. Lory, the president of the State Agricultural College. A professor from Colorado College enthusiastically declared that public utility speakers could have a whole term "with college instructors assisting them."[84] The professors at the meeting with Lewis offered to create for-credit semester-length courses complete with assignments and grades. By 1926, Lewis could boast to a utility colleague that, in Colorado, "we now have 24 public utility company executives as members of the university faculty."[85]

Lewis and Wolfe worked together with these executive-instructors to create detailed lessons plans for their courses. "The underlying purpose," an industry magazine reported, was to "inculcate in the student mind the vital importance of the public utility" and to provide "a more accurate perspective of the public service business."[86] Wolfe also taught courses through the University of Colorado's extension program where 99 percent of his students were utility employees. Yet the university paid half of Wolfe's salary, while the utilities paid the other half.[87] Despite this lopsided workload, *Public Service Magazine* adamantly defended such use of taxpayer money for such appointments.[88]

Wolfe and Ruggles were not the only professors employed by the utilities. Theodore F. Grayson, a professor at the University of Pennsylvania's Wharton School of Finance, oversaw utilities courses at Wharton while at the same time serving as the secretary of the New Jersey Public Service Information Bureau. Grayson spoke extensively at engagements arranged for him by NELA, and received $250 to $400 per speech, plus expenses.[89] Another professor, John McCaustland, the dean of engineering at Missouri State University, was paid by the utilities to give lectures at Missouri's teachers colleges. McCaustland only made $75 per lecture, although ten thousand copies of his lectures were printed and distributed to students who could not attend his speeches in person.[90]

When working for the utilities, professors were not paid to talk about whatever they wanted. The contents of McCaustland's speech had been suggested by John Sheridan, but only after Sheridan ran the text by his steering committee, which included a Bell manager, a gas company manager, and an electric company manager named Hillemeyer. Hillemeyer, in turn, passed the proposed speech along to his company's lawyer, who commented that it appeared "too much on the order of propaganda." The lawyer argued that

210   Chapter 6

there was "too much mention made of 'the people,'" which he thought "might be bad, as it might look as if he had prepared some propaganda under the guise of the utility interests." Hillemeyer forwarded the comments to Sheridan, who edited the speech and sent the revised version to Professor McCaustland, carefully framing it as "merely a suggestion." Once the speech was delivered, press releases summarizing its contents were distributed to the press, a standard practice for these kinds of events.[91]

In some ways, these various activities on campuses were not new. Industry influence had never been completely absent from colleges. After all, the Morrill Act of 1862, which had led to the founding of many of these schools, specifically directed that colleges be established "for the benefit of agriculture and mechanic arts." And several private universities, such as Stanford, Carnegie Mellon, Vanderbilt, and the University of Chicago had been founded by industrialists or their heirs. In the late nineteenth century, these industrial patrons sometimes exercised considerable control over the opinions of the faculty, especially when it came to instructors' views on monopoly. In 1895, economics professor Edward Bemis paid for his antimonopoly views by being dismissed from the University of Chicago, an institution that well-known economist Edward Ross called "the Gas Trust University." Five years later, Ross himself had to resign from Stanford after Jane Stanford could no longer tolerate his intellectual crimes, which included advocating municipal ownership.[92]

In the 1920s, although corporate officers sat on university boards, hired professors as consultants, and hosted academic conferences, corporate influence became less overt. Yet if administrative control declined, instruction increasingly began to look like a company training session. And even when utility personnel did not design and teach entire courses, as happened in Colorado, utility executives frequently gave guest lectures to college students.[93] One of the most prolific of these speakers was Nathaniel T. Guernsey, general counsel and vice president of AT&T. Between 1926 and 1933, Guernsey gave scores of talks to law and business students, including talks at elite institutions such as Northwestern, Harvard, Brown, Yale, and the University of Pennsylvania.[94]

Guernsey clearly enjoyed giving these lectures and fished for invitations by writing to local Bell attorneys and asking them to solicit their local law school dean for an invitation. Guernsey's favorite lecture was "Regulation of Public Utilities," in which he argued that the government's "power to regulate is not unrestricted," and that individual states were legally prohibited

Subverting Civics   211

from setting rates that did "not afford a fair return."[95] Guernsey also compiled a list of rate cases that professors used in their utility classes and sent it to AT&T attorneys for scrutiny. The attorneys replied that many of the cases should not be used because they came from a time "when the courts were somewhat confused."[96]

To fully cover his material, Guernsey requested five one-hour class sessions and offered the lectures for free. Many professors obliged and, during some months, Guernsey spoke on more days than not. One professor at the Cincinnati Law School thanked Guernsey for his "inspiration." The professor added that when giving his own lectures, he "carried the essence" of Guernsey's "message to the Transportation Law Class of the University."[97]

Not all administrators were so welcoming. In 1928, Guernsey wanted to speak at the Ohio State Law School, but the dean refused to give him class time. The dean had already heard Guernsey lecture—once while a student at Yale and again while a professor at the University of Kansas. The dean found Guernsey's content to be "thinly veiled propaganda." When these remarks filtered back to Guernsey, he grumbled that he had always been "absolutely open" about his beliefs and that his talks were not propaganda at all.[98]

Yet Guernsey certainly wanted to shape the opinions of his audiences. In 1926, he wrote about his own lectures to Harvard Business School professor Donald K. David: "I cannot help feeling that benefit, not only to them [the business students], but to the utilities, must eventually result," he noted. "If we can start some hundreds of earnest youngsters thinking about these questions along sound lines," he added, "such a result would justify all of us." Shortly thereafter, Guernsey wrote to another Harvard Business School professor, Philip Cabot, about his speeches. "Continuous hammering along these lines must ultimately set at least a few people to thinking, with a start from relatively sound premises," wrote Guernsey. "If it does, in the long run it is going to be worth what it costs."[99]

The friendship between Guernsey and Cabot went back at least to 1926, when Cabot suggested that Guernsey try to meet the young Columbia economics professor James C. Bonbright. In Cabot's diagnosis, Bonbright was "suffering from the academic contagion" of critiquing corporate utilities but had "not wholly succumbed to the disease." It is not known if Guernsey and Bonbright ever met, but Bonbright remained unconverted to Cabot's views. Bonbright believed that AT&T took an "extremely unfair position" when it came to accounting issues involving how depreciation related to rate setting. He thought that "sooner or later" AT&T's view would hurt the company "in the eyes of the public."[100] Cabot disagreed and thought Bonbright was "very weak on all matters of law and . . . on many matters of economics." Bonbright eventually received Harvard Law School's prestigious Ames Prize and became chairman of the New York State Power Authority. He remained critical of corporate utilities at Columbia University, along with his colleague, Gardiner Means.[101]

Although utility executives did not succeed in changing Bonbright's mind, they did change the thinking of other professors. One of them was C. A. Wright of Ohio State. In 1921, Wright authored a pamphlet entitled "The Determination of Telephone Rates," which an AT&T vice president became aware of and informed managers at Ohio Bell. The pamphlet made "harmful" and "misleading, if not incorrect" statements, according to the AT&T executive. Ohio Bell managers immediately began strategizing how they could convince Wright to recall his pamphlet, edit it, and submit the changes to AT&T for approval before republishing it. While planning this, Bell managers stressed the need for "diplomatic handling" of the whole enterprise. With that in mind, Bell managers met with Wright and persuaded him to allow Ohio Bell personnel to rewrite the pamphlet, after which time Wright could read the new document and approve it. After the meeting with Wright, Bell managers reported that Wright "took the discussion of his pamphlet in a proper spirit." Managers then rewrote the pamphlet and submitted it to AT&T for approval. Yet the work was never published because Ohio Bell officials decided it would be better not to publish a second edition for fear of bringing attention to the first.[102]

Wright later relapsed in his thinking, however, which forced another intervention. Again utility managers sought to "correct the false knowledge upon which the professor has based his theory of rate making," as one executive put it.[103] To do this, Ohio Bell executives invited Wright to an engineering conference hosted by AT&T in New York, then buttonholed him about his supposedly erroneous notions. The discussion apparently convinced Wright to cooperate with AT&T. This time, Wright seemed to stay converted. About a year later, Wright agreed, at the suggestion of a Bell manager, to change the topic of his upcoming radio address from rate making to telephone service, which Wright assured the manager would be perfectly innocuous.[104]

In addition to college professors, utility managers also courted the favor of college newspaper editors. Like professors, college editors functioned as opinion makers, according to utility executives, so executives sought to shape their opinions in hopes of influencing others. Utility managers advertised in college newspapers to change the opinions of student editors, just as managers had done with other local newspapers editors. The goal was mainly to influence public opinion, not increase business. In 1925, when considering whether to advertise in seventeen college newspapers, an Ohio Bell manager explained to his vice president that "the increase in business sought or obtained would be secondary to the good will and esteem engendered in the minds of the students."[105]

George Lewis of the Rocky Mountain committee went even further than advertising to secure the goodwill of college editors. In January of 1924, he threw a party at the Orpheum Theater in Denver for members of the College Editorial Association that cost $143. The party became an annual event, and by 1927 the cost had increased to $181 per bash. When FTC examiners questioned Lewis about these events, Lewis blamed the undergrads: "They got me figuratively by the scruff of the neck and said, 'Lewis, you have got to give this theater party.'"[106]

Did Influencing Colleges Work?

The hiring of professors, lecturing of students, and parties for editors worked in shaping the opinions of college students and professors, according to utility operators. In 1927, the president of the Iowa and Nebraska Light & Power Co. wrote to a company manager that the utility industry had "improved" its relationship with the Iowa State and Iowa University to such an extent that "the attitude of these institutions as well as the personnel of the faculties has changed from one of quite open antagonism to one of friendly relations."[107] In 1931, a commercial manager at Ohio Bell recommended the continuation of advertising at Antioch College since "it helps our relations with the school authorities." In 1935, an Ohio Bell manager reported on the success of the company's advertising in college newspapers, stating, "To summarize, we feel that this college advertising has created good will and generated favorable comments at very nominal cost."[108]

Speaking at Civic Clubs

Alongside public relations campaigns targeting students, utilities also sought to influence the opinion of the general public through publicity. To reach this group, utility representatives went wherever the public went: movies, Chautauqua lectures, workplaces, and even homes. One utility publicist even literally got up on a soap box on a street corner and gave a speech about utilities "to reach everybody in the town."[109] Managers also developed radio shows, and rank-and-file employees spoke at all kinds of civic organizations, including chambers of commerce, men's lodges, women's clubs, farm associations, consumers' leagues, boards of trade, church groups, Kiwanis clubs, and Rotary clubs.

Utility employees speaking at civic clubs contrasted sharply with the pin-striped spokesmen who delivered prepared statements to the press in other industries. These spokesmen first became common in the early twentieth century after several chief executives made remarks that indicated their skills lay elsewhere. These included William Vanderbilt's "public be damned" gaff, but there were other unfiltered remarks, such as oil baron John D. Rockefeller's declaration in 1915 that "God gave me my money." To annunciate the corporate message in slightly less metaphysical terms, business leaders began hiring spokesmen. But to the dismay of executives, the spokesmen themselves sometimes became the subject of further ridicule. In 1914, after the Ludlow Massacre in which twenty Rockefeller miners and their family members were killed by strike breakers, the well-known corporate spokesman Ivy Lee tried to spin the incident in favor of the Rockefellers. After that, critiques dubbed him "Poison Ivy."[110] By the early 1920s, utility executives began to wonder if a few calculated remarks from supposedly golden-tongued public relations consultants could really improve public opinion.[111]

Rather than rely on a few highly paid outsiders, utility executives began having their own employees give speeches at local clubs and organizations. Since utilities had more than a half million employees, this made for a large number of potential speakers. And by speaking at neighborhood clubs, these employees could mingle with their fellow club members, personally explain the views and contributions of utilities, and develop the close community relationships that a few outside spokesmen could never obtain. In this way, the personification of the corporation would no longer be the paunchy manipulator of political cartoons, but the likeable member of the local club.

To assist employees in giving speeches, utility publicists wrote speakers' handbooks that provided outlines of speeches or complete drafts. In a typical example, the Michigan committee produced a thirty-page handbook entitled *Telling the Public Utility Story*, which contained outlines of a variety of speeches.[112] Northwestern Bell provided entire speeches, including one that summarized the history of technology from when "manlike creatures . . . presumably inhabited the earth 250,000 years ago" to the invention of the

Subverting Civics   215

telephone, all in just thirty minutes. A speech by the Illinois committee featured a slightly less sweeping narrative explaining how utility service had ended the age of the horse and buggy, kerosene lamp, and messenger boy in twenty-five years.[113] These prepared speeches sometimes included suggestions for anecdotal introductions, such as: "Before coming here tonight I met a friend. He said to me . . . ," or, "Friends: On my way here, a little fable came to my mind that I want to repeat."[114]

To properly deliver these speeches, publicists coached utility employees in the art of elocution. To do this, George Lewis, the enterprising information director in Colorado, established a "speakers' so-called college." Lewis hired a professor who instructed employees in public speaking and critiqued their performances. Each semester, the course had twenty to forty students who paid a quarter of their own tuition.[115] Once employees had received the training, they could join the state's utility speakers' bureau and speak for their company.

Executives specifically encouraged their female employees to join clubs and speak at them. Many utilities established specific programs to instruct women employees how to give speeches. The Middle West Utilities Company organized a Women's Committee, whose "chairman"—a woman—helped prepare "the women of the organization to represent the company in their community."[116] The state publicity director in Iowa authored a pamphlet that provided women employees with pointers on what to talk about. Many women utility employees spoke at clubs, and some lectured at colleges.[117]

To organize these speaking efforts, publicity directors in each state established a speakers' bureau, divided their state into districts, and assigned a utility manager to each district. The district manager then cultivated local contacts, secured speaking invitations, and assigned available speakers to each engagement.[118] In some states, district managers received quotas for the number of talks they needed to schedule each month, and statistics were kept down to the county level.[119] To encourage club leaders to book speakers, utilities produced a pamphlet called "How about Your Programs?"[120] To keep track of the speaking at the national level, NELA's Public Speaking Committee divided the country into regions, and recorded the number of talks and attendance in each.

The work of public speaking began slowly yet grew rapidly. In 1924, NELA's Public Speaking Committee recorded only six thousand talks nationwide. But the next year that number increased to ten thousand talks reaching 1.25 million people.[121] In 1927, utilities employees delivered thirty-one thousand talks to over 3.8 million Americans. New York speakers led the way, giving 9,720 speeches to 456,000 people, though electricity employees spoke in less populated areas as well. Employees in Oklahoma, for example, gave 2,450 talks.[122] Telephone employees, whose talks were counted separately, also reached a large number of Americans. From 1926 through 1929, Illinois Bell employees spoke to 680,000 people.

Overall, utility employees reached an astonishing percentage of the American population. In 1929 alone, electricity employees delivered thirty-six thousand talks to 4.6 million Americans. Employees that year may have been motivated by the European vacation NELA offered for the best speech. Despite these numbers, some managers still complained that the talks only reached 3.2 percent of the US population.[123] Between 1924 and 1929, utility employees spoke to at least 17.2 million Americans. Since the US population in 1930 was 123 million, if these speeches did not include any audience overlap, utility representatives presented their pro-corporate message to 14 percent of Americans, a staggering percentage to reach face-to-face.[124]

It was precisely this direct, personal contact that motivated utility executives to promote public speaking. In 1922, the president of the Georgia Power Company urged streetcar managers to give speeches, promising that "it will bring you into contact with your customers. It will personify the railroad to them in your own individuality."[125] In 1924, AT&T vice president E. S. Wilson told colleagues that "by systematically cultivating the acquaintance of leading officials and active members of these [civic] associations our companies . . . can . . . effectively place before the membership, educational facts that will permit better understanding of telephone company problems and motives."[126]

The idea that public speaking would improve public relations appeared to be true. During several rate cases in Oklahoma, business groups and civic clubs actually wrote letters to the utility commission urging it to raise utility rates.[127] "The destructive force of silence is no longer at work in the Public Utility Industry," exalted a New England publicity manager in 1922. Speeches, he said, were creating "an entirely different public opinion in regard to our industry."[128]

This may have been because in many cases the utility speaker was literally a member of the club. Executives maintained memberships in a number of civic clubs and encouraged their employees to do the same. In 1921, AT&T president H. B. Thayer explained the reasoning behind joining clubs in a speech entitled "Mobilization of the Forces for Better Public Relations."

Subverting Civics 217

Memberships in "civic organizations of every description," observed Thayer, "afford unusual opportunities for establishing contacts with the leaders in general public activities and those who are molding public sentiment."[129]

Many other executives shared this idea. "Do you realize," asked a Massachusetts executive in 1922, "that the public utility with its employees touches practically all social, fraternal, club, church and industrial activities in the community? Do you know that if all these employees . . . got themselves 'in solid' and each one accumulated a real circle of friends, no politician would ever dare to attack the company. . . . Can you imagine anyone who valued his political success attacking the American Legion? He would stand about as much chance as a Republican in Georgia."[130] This logic, if not this exact speech, may explain why two years later, the Peoples Gas Light & Coke Company, known as Peoples Gas in Chicago, counted 236 employees as members of the American Legion.[131]

To encourage club membership, club dues for employees were often paid by the utilities. Between 1924 and 1934, the Bell System spent $4.8 million on memberships for thousands of workers; a cost that was ultimately borne by telephone users.[132] State publicity directors also billed NELA for their club memberships.[133] A large number of employees, not just executives and publicists, could expense their club memberships. Assistant managers and above received country club memberships at the Southern Bell Company. The company also paid the president down to the assistant district managers to maintain membership in their local chamber of commerce. Unit supervisors, customer service clerks, and women employees had to settle for the "Jr. Chamber of Commerce."[134] These memberships existed in big cities and small towns.

When utility employees spoke at one of these clubs, they often explicitly attacked government ownership. Unlike when speaking at high schools, utility employees at civic clubs gave full voice to their anti–government ownership views. "There are some who would overturn our entire program of government and scheme of life," a Bell employee warned an audience in New York, before arguing that Bell needed a rate increase.[135] In a speech given to the Present Day Club of Riverside, California in 1921, the general manager of Riverside's local power company, A. B. West, declared that the "municipality movement" was nothing less than a plot to socialize the country. The movement, West detailed, included the recent proposal in California to build state-owned hydroelectric plants, which the mayor of Riverside supported. The whole thing was "insidious, a step here, a step there," he decried. "Only a few decades back, the movement started with the acquirement of municipal water works. Next came city traction lines, gas works, local lighting plants, and so on until today we have in many of our cities municipal markets, municipal theaters, municipal warehouses, grain elevators, docks, slaughter houses." "Where will it stop," West implored. "Yes, this will be the last step—the farms."[136]

Tracking Socialists

West's idea that publicly owned power represented the thin edge of the socialist wedge was not a construct of his imagination. Rather, it was the explicit policy of American socialists in the 1920s. After their disastrous experiences during and right after World War I, American socialists sought to rebuild public support by electing politicians who would advocate public ownership of electricity plants. These plants, according to the plan, would provide a "yardstick" on electricity rates and definitively demonstrate that government ownership was cheaper than private ownership. This was why both socialists and corporate executives took every municipal-ownership fight so seriously. Once they had their yardstick, socialists believed, government ownership would gain widespread support, and Americans would convert en masse to socialism. Following that, other aspects of society would easily become socialized.

One of the strategy's chief architects, author and activist H. S. Raushenbush, called the strategy "encroaching control," which contrasted to "cataclysmic socialism," which he believed was impossible in the post–World War I political climate.[137] Another major advocate of encroaching control was Carl D. Thompson, who explained in a pamphlet published by the Socialist Party that elected representatives would "take over one after the other of their public utilities . . . and finally the nation will take . . . mines, railroads, interurban electric lines, power plants, telegraph and telephone systems, waterways, forests. And all this may be done by methods perfectly legal and constitutional."[138] West's view of socialists was therefore not uninformed, just antagonistic.

Aside from the socialists themselves, utility executives were some of the best-informed people about socialism during the 1920s. Utility executives knew all about Raushenbush, Thompson, and many others because executives maintained name lists of known socialists, tracked their movements, and sent employees to spy on their gatherings.[139] Executives also exchanged "confidential" intelligence reports with each other, drew up bibliographies of

Subverting Civics 219

socialist literature, and followed socialist activities on college campuses; a place where executives were never able to fully stamp out the socialist presence.[140] To further their expertise, NELA hired the former socialist organizer and author F.G.R. Gordon, to serve as its in-house policy expert. Gordon, who had recanted his old beliefs, now advised NELA executives during municipal ownership fights, and counseled employees who were "investigating and writing" about socialism.[141]

In urgent cases, executives called high-level meetings with representatives from across the industry to respond to specific socialist threats. In February of 1925, NELA's executive manager, Merlin Aylesworth, and its information director, George Oxley, along with several others, met to discuss claims being made by Pennsylvania governor Gifford Pinchot and Nebraska senator George Norris, both of whom advocated publicly owned electricity projects. The executives decided to hire Bruce Barton, one of the most famous advertising agents of the time, to produce a series of "envelope stuffers" explaining the utilities' position.[142] Barton received $5,000 for his labor. In 1926, over nine million copies of Barton's pamphlets went out to customers, making it "the largest distribution of a direct message to the public ever made," according to Aylesworth.[143]

Although executives clearly understood the beliefs of socialists, they did not typically confront socialists on the basis of their ideas. Instead, executives tarred socialists with the red brush of communism. This proved a particularly effective strategy after the Red Scare of 1919. Executives also smeared any politician or private citizen, socialist or not, who so much as hinted that they might favor government ownership. In the mid-1920s, when a utility publicist was asked by his boss how to defeat the Swing-Johnson Bill and the proposal in Congress to investigate the power companies, he responded: "My idea would not be to try logic, or reason, but to try to pin the Bolshevik idea on my opponent."[144] A short time later, the same publicist did exactly that by circulating a pamphlet among Illinois utility executives that insinuated a link between municipal-ownership advocates and Bolsheviks.[145]

In another case, when socialist Carl D. Thompson secured a series of speaking engagements on the Chautauqua circuit, John Sheridan of the Missouri utility information committee recommended that the utilities not fight Thompson on the terrain of his ideas but "through the local Chautauqua committees." And "if it comes to a showdown and he gets too gay," Sheridan advised, "fight him, not upon the private vs. public ownership question, but on the Socialist, Communists, single tax, [and] land nationalization record.

As I know the farmers of Missouri, they hate the Socialist, Communist, single taxer, and land nationalizer as they hate the devil."[146] Why engage in rational debate, when guilt by association was easier and more effective?

In many ways, the Russian Revolution was the best thing that ever happened to corporate utility executives. When a public-power proposal called the California Water and Power Act was placed on the California referendum in 1922, the supposedly grass-roots Greater California League issued the pamphlet "Shall California be Sovietized? Facts about the Proposed Water and Power Act and Bond Issue of 500 Millions." The pamphlet declared that the proposal represented "the most gigantic experiment in state socialism ever suggested in the US," and that it was "comparable only to the disastrous venture forced on North Dakota by the Non-Partisan League and to the insane political and economic scheme that has ruined Russia."[147]

After the Water and Power Act went down to disastrous defeat in 1922, the utilities' main political operative, lawyer Eustace Cullinan, admitted to the California Senate Investigating Committee that the Pacific Gas & Electric Company and other northern California utilities had paid him to create the Greater California League, hire influential speakers to campaign against the act, purchase advertising space, and mail flyers to every voter in northern California. The total bill, Cullinan divulged, came to nearly $250,000, an unprecedented sum to spend on a referendum at the time. Yet that was not the half of it.[148] A similar organization in southern California spent even more.[149] Supporters of the California Water and Power Act hoped that these revelations would help them gain support, so they placed the same measure on the ballot again in 1924 and 1926. But each time the public-power initiative failed miserably.[150]

Utility representatives also used anti-communist rhetoric in many other locations. In 1927 in Stanberry, Missouri, as a referendum approached regarding whether or not to build a municipally owned power plant, John Sheridan wrote a pamphlet asking: "Are the people of Stanberry prepared to forswear the basic principles of the Constitution which has made America great and, without any compelling reason, substitute for these principles the doctrine of Karl Marx, the outstanding example of which is Soviet Russia . . . ?" The bond measure passed despite these inquiries, but it was declared illegal on a technicality and a second vote was scheduled. But before Sheridan could travel to Stanberry to once again campaign against the act, the FTC called him to Washington to testify about his publicity activities. The power companies had failed to block the FTC investigation and now the investigation was

taking valuable time from Sheridan and others in their fight against municipal socialism.[151]

Taking Over the Chautauqua Circuit

In other instances, however, utility operatives defeated their public power
opponents. In the summer of 1924, Carl D. Thompson of the Public Ownership
League was scheduled to speak on the Chautauqua circuit in the Midwest,
but Sheridan organized a campaign to stop him. The Chautauqua circuit
brought speakers, entertainers, and authors to millions of Americans. These
speakers discussed early twentieth-century issues with an audience with
early twentieth-century attention spans. In early 1924, celebrated economist
Irving Fisher lauded the Chautauqua for having "done more toward keeping American public opinion informed, alert, and unbiased than any other
movement."[152] Then Sheridan got involved.

In the summer of 1924, Thompson had 103 lecturers booked on the Chautauqua circuit.[153] But Sheridan and utility executives found local Chautauqua subscribers to write to the circuit organizer, Keith Vawter, to protest
Thompson's appearance. Some subscribers even canceled their subscriptions to the lecture series.[154] A few newspaper editors wrote editorials attacking Thompson's appearance on the circuit.[155]

The pressure to remove Thompson from the Chautauqua circuit became
so intense that in July of 1924 Vawter met with Sheridan and other utility
executives to discuss the issue. Vawter informed the executives that he had
received ten times more complaints about Thompson in Missouri than from
any other state in which Thompson appeared. It is not clear if Vawter understood that the men he was speaking to were responsible for this. Vawter
suggested that perhaps Thompson could eliminate some of the more objectionable aspects of his speech. As executives knew, the most damaging part
of Thompson's address was when he compared the low rates for government-
produced electricity in Ontario, Canada, to the high rates for corporate electricity in Detroit, Michigan, right across the border. Some utility executives
were inclined to accept Vawter's compromise, but Sheridan wanted Thompson removed altogether. "That is a pretty definite instance of the suppres-
sion of free speech?" an FTC examiner asked Sheridan regarding this. "I do
not know," Sheridan shrugged, "at that time I did not look at it that way."[156]

Thompson ended up modifying his lectures, but in several cities his invitation was rescinded anyway.[157] In Edina, Missouri, in July of 1924 residents
uninvited Thompson after a utility manager brought up the matter with the

local Kiwanis club, which protested, as did a banker and a local editor through his newspaper. The town had just decided not to renew a corporate electricity contract and was about to vote on whether to build a municipal power plant. Two weeks after Thompson's nonappearance, the referendum for the municipal plant failed to pass.[158] But a utility manager in Edina was still not happy. He wrote to Sheridan that Thompson was really a "land nationalizer, single taxer, [and] socialist" and that "the best way would have been to have him thrown in a ditch."[159]

Thompson was denied permission to speak in several other places as well, according to Bernard Mullaney's Illinois committee, which tracked Thompson's speeches.[160] By December 1924, Thompson decided to go South, but utility workers followed him. Sheridan contacted a colleague in Alabama who organized opposition to Thompson there too.[161] By the end of 1924, George Oxley, NELA's information director, reported to Sheridan that, in his estimate, Thompson's career on the Chautauqua circuit was over.[162]

With that, utility executives began envisioning speaking on the Chautauqua circuit themselves. In 1927, Mullaney, who had played a large role in forcing Thompson off the circuit, spoke on the circuit himself. Mullaney told his audience that "those who are in favor of public ownership, if they do not think they are traveling in the direction of eventual communism, are either fooling themselves or trying to fool us." Mullaney further warned that "advocates of red or communist information stood in behind every municipal ownership enterprise. . . . Some in the minority are communists of deepest Russian red . . . others are part socialist, red shading into parlor pink." For those who missed the speech, the Illinois committee printed nineteen thousand copies.[163] By the late 1920s, any public forum for rational informed debate about public utility policy had been largely replaced by a new orthodoxy created by the corporate utility executives.

Radio Shows, Tours, and Demonstrations

To further communicate their message, utility employees also developed radio programs and demonstration shows. Some of these programs specifically targeted the opinions of women. Samuel Insull's gas and electric companies in Chicago created one of the most extensive programs for women through what was known as the Home Service Department. The main talent at the Home Service Department was Anna J. Peterson, who hosted cooking and home economics demonstrations.[164] During these presentations,

"Mrs. Peterson," as she was known, taught women how to use the latest cooking and homemaking devices, such as gas and electric ranges, as well as dishwashers and washing machines. Peterson also offered tips on household chores such as removing stains.

To expand Peterson's audience, Insull innovatively broadcast her presentations on the radio, itself a new electrical device. In what became even clearer with President Roosevelt's Fireside Chats in the 1930s, radio was a warm, almost personal method of building public trust. Mrs. Peterson and the Home Service staff also toured Chicagoland, giving talks at women's clubs, churches, and high school home science classes.[165]

Peterson's presentations proved a huge success. Thousands of women flocked to see her demonstrations live at the Peoples Gas auditorium in downtown Chicago, while thousands more listened to her on the radio at 11:30 weekday mornings, and 9:30 Saturday evenings. In 1929 alone, Peterson lectured in-person to over a quarter of a million customers, as well as an estimated daily radio audience of one hundred thousand.[166] In 1923, so many listeners responded to Peterson's invitation to join her "Children's Radio Christmas Party" that the three-thousand-seat auditorium at the Peoples Gas headquarters reached maximum capacity and fans had to be turned away at the door. Listeners also warmly responded to Peterson's free recipe offers. The Home Service Department distributed three million recipe cards in 1928, or ten thousand a day, either in person at utility offices or through the mail.[167] Several other companies also hosted radio shows and home service demonstrations, and some even offered the irresistible perk of free babysitting during the demos.[168]

Although the Home Services Department was designed to increase appliance use and sell more service, these were not the only goals. As the 1930 Peoples Gas *Yearbook* explained, the Home Service Department was "not merely to further the use of gas for cooking but to obtain complete public confidence."[169] This explains why the Women's Committee of Insull's Middle West Utilities taught housewives how to bake with an electric range as well as the "principles and economics of the industry."[170] Courting the opinion of women made sense considering that newly enfranchised female customers were often the member of the household who signed up for utility service, inspected the monthly utility bill, and paid it. What women thought about their local utility mattered politically. Simply put, fans of Mrs. Peterson were less likely to vote against her employer.

Thousands of women and children, as well as a few men, gather at the Peoples Gas Building in Chicago for Mrs. Peterson's "Children's Radio Christmas Party" in 1923. "Home Service Department," *Peoples Gas Year Book, 1924,* 29. Courtesy of Loyola University Chicago Archives and Special Collections.

Three thousand women attend a cooking demonstration presented by the Home Services Department of the Public Service Company of Northern Illinois at a high school in Cicero, near Chicago, 1930. "Merchandise, Sales and Home Service," *Public Service Company of Northern Illinois Year Book 1929,* 18, Box 55, Folder 8, Insull Papers. Courtesy of Loyola University Chicago Archives and Special Collections.

To reach even more customers, utilities developed touring demonstrations. Bell companies in particular created elaborate demonstrations that traveled from town to town in an effort to humanize the company and reduce dissatisfaction. The demonstrations began in the early 1920s, and typically included a short welcome by a local manager highlighting the accomplishments of the Bell System, followed by a speech by a telephone operator emphasizing the complexities of switchboards and why calls were sometimes dropped. Then, several operators presented a play, which illustrated "in a laughable way, the mistaken notion some subscribers have of what goes on in an operating room," according to an employee magazine.[171] Some shows also included a short film and Q&A. Before and after each show, cast and crew members would "mix and talk with the audience," which helped "create a very good impression," according to one manager.[172]

To enhance the shows, Bell technicians built portable switchboards that could place live telephone calls during the demonstrations. Technicians at a gas company also developed a portable machine that could make gas from

A scene from a 1921 Southern Bell touring play. "Showing the Subscriber a Switchboard in Service: A Demonstration That Shows the Public What Takes Place When a Call is Put In," *Southern Telephone News*, December 1921, 13, AT&T-TX. Courtesy of AT&T-TX.

charcoal for demonstrations. Other employees painted scenery.[173] Utility employees performed these live commercials at civic clubs, fraternal societies, churches, schools, and state fairs.[174] Presenting the shows required ten to twenty employees, most of whom did not get paid for these evening events. "I generally buy them a $2-dinner," boasted one publicity manager to a colleague, "—all they get, by the way, for coming out. . . . *And we convert from 100 to 3,000 people!*"[175]

Managers selected the most "attractive operators" from throughout their territory to present the demonstrations. The caption below one photograph of these women referred to them as "the committee of pretty operators." Perhaps this explains why audiences found the presentations "gratifying" and of "genuine interest."[176]

Did Demonstrations Work?

Utility managers lauded the public relations value of these demonstrations. An AT&T advertising manager declared that demonstrations had "immense value" after witnessing the rapt attention of audiences.[177] In 1922, one Southern Bell manager concluded that demonstrations "undoubtedly do a great deal of good in giving the public a better understanding of our business, and so securing their cooperation."[178] Another employee reported that, after seeing a demonstration, a customer exclaimed: "I don't think I ever will lose my temper with the operator again, now that I know more about what a telephone call involves."[179]

Executives also credited specific political victories to demonstrations. The president of Michigan Bell stated that demonstrations helped turn around public opinion regarding the company. In 1919, the company had poor public relations and had been refused a rate increase. In response, Michigan Bell launched a demonstration tour. By 1922, some 250,000 people had seen the demonstration, and, according to the company's president, public opinion had improved as a result.[180]

Utility employees also produced other events such as musicals and talent shows. Several companies produced minstrel shows that included white workers in blackface. Bell companies produced these shows in the South and the North, and some occurred as late as the 1950s. These events functioned mostly as company-sponsored recreation activities for white employees, though they also engaged community members, both as participants and as audience members.[181] The public opinion of black Americans appears not

Subverting Civics   227

to have been a concern of utility managers, perhaps because many were disenfranchised.

Popular Movies

Speeches, radio shows, and demonstrations represented major strategies by which utility executives shaped the opinions of customers. Yet as movies became increasingly popular, executives quickly adopted this medium for popular audiences. Eventually, utility films reached an enormous number of people. Between 1926 and 1935, the Bell System counted 436.8 million film viewers. In 1931 alone, Bell claimed that more than seventy-four million people saw one of their films.[182] That number may be high, but if accurate and there was no audience overlap, it amounted to 60 percent of the US population in 1931.[183]

These films effectively communicated a positive message regarding corporate telephone service to viewers. After screening the AT&T film *A Modern Knight*, a member of the Advertising Club of Montreal observed that the film represented "one of the most subtle and powerful forms of propaganda ever demonstrated to the club."[184] Most viewers of the film had no idea that AT&T made the film, since telephone use was only incidental to the plot, and no mention of AT&T was made in the credits.[185] Instead the credits indicated that the film was produced by Audio Cinema.[186] AT&T only began claiming production credit for its films in 1934.[187]

One strategy AT&T used to increase viewership was to make their films nearly indistinguishable from contemporary Hollywood films. The plot of the twenty-two-minute-long *Modern Knight*, for instance, centered around the kidnapping of a girl and the demand for ransom, which sets off an international manhunt. Detectives collaborate by placing international calls from New York City to Scotland Yard in London and even to a detective aboard a steamer in the middle of the Atlantic using a radio phone. Detectives also send out bulletins to police stations around the United States using an AT&T teletype machine. The kidnapped girl is eventually found safe and sound, thanks to clever detective work and modern telephone technology.

According to reports, popular audiences literally applauded at the end of the movie.[188] It was "very much appreciated by those who had the pleasure of seeing it," noted a theater manager in Washington, DC, to a Bell manager.[189] The early film columnist Caroline A. Lejeune wrote in the London *Observer* that she instinctively distrusted industrial films, but that she was "ready to stand up and cheer" when the kidnappers were caught in *A Modern Knight*. "We leave the theatre convinced that the telephone is the greatest power for security and justice that science has ever discovered," she wrote. As a result of watching the film, she added, the "next time our own cursed black machine gets us out of bed in the middle of the night for a wrong number, we look at it with a less malicious eye."[190] Even professors liked it. Columbia lecturer on film Frances Taylor Patterson praised *A Modern Knight* in *Printer's Ink*.[191]

AT&T executives expected Bell managers to personally place films with theater managers, a task for which managers proved themselves highly capable. In January and February 1932, nearly all of the sixty-eight Loews theaters in Manhattan, Brooklyn, the Bronx, Westchester County, and Long Island were screening *A Modern Knight*. In Philadelphia, the Fox, Keith, and Warner Brothers theater chains also carried AT&T films.[192]

A detective aboard a steamship in the Atlantic takes a radio call from her New York boss in *A Modern Knight*. AT&T, "A Modern Knight," 1931, AT&T Tech Channel, video, http://techchannel.att.com/play-video.cfm/2011/7/27/AT&T-Archives-A-Modern-Knight.

If any managers had trouble convincing theater owners to show AT&T films, J. M. Hamilton, the director of AT&T's Motion Picture Bureau, sent Bell managers the pamphlet called "An Imaginary Conversation with a Motion Picture Theatre Manager." The tract contained scripted replies to potential objections from theater managers. If a manager resisted showing a film on the grounds that it was propaganda, Bell managers were instructed to reply: "Well, it's a good kind of propaganda because the information is all true, and therefore no one considers it offensive."[193]

Utility companies produced scores of movies for consumption at movie theaters, civic clubs, and schools. AT&T alone produced at least fifty-six films from the mid-1920s through the 1930s.[194] As early as 1914, the Commonwealth Edison Company created a public relations film, and presented it for free at an exposition in Chicago. Eighty-five thousand peopled watched the movie, which depicted how electrical appliances eliminated household drudgery.[195] NELA also created several movies that were screened in public theaters in the 1920s, including *Yours to Command*, which NELA estimated 1.25 million people viewed. NELA found that the production cost per viewer amounted to just seven-tenths of a penny, which members agreed was an excellent value. The American Electric Railway Association (AERA) also created publicity movies, as did electric utilities in Boston, Chicago, and Philadelphia.[196]

A major goal of these films was to influence people's political views. In 1927, the Public Service Company of Northern Illinois created a series of films collectively entitled *Highways and Byways of Northern Illinois*. The company screened the films at public theaters and community meetings, and boasted that the films were in "constant demand."[197] The series title seemed apolitical, but the purpose of the series was to communicate to the public that "public utilities must be privately owned," as one of producer stated. The producer promised that "after viewing them the people will understand . . . why they should cooperate with the private ownership of the public utility which serves them."[198] AT&T managers also declared the public relations goal of their films. During the Federal Communications Commission hearings, discussed in the previous chapter, an examiner led his witness, J. M. Hamilton, by asking: "These pictures have played an important part in the good will of the public toward the Bell System, have they not?" "I hope they have," Hamilton confidently replied. Hamilton believed his films worked. In 1933, he wrote his boss, George Banning, that the widely distributed AT&T film *Getting Together* had "silenced" a great deal of criticism.[199]

Trade Press Books

Utility executives also hired authors to write books on the history of the utility industry for popular consumption. The utilities then distributed these books to editors, large shareholders, and public and university libraries. The first of these books was Herbert Casson's *History of the Telephone*, published by A. C. McClurg & Company in 1910. Casson had served as an editor for the *New York World* and *Munsey's*, and received $8,400 to produce the work.[200] The book described the invention and technical improvement of the telephone, but also argued against government ownership by comparing the number of telephones in the United States under private ownership to the number of telephones in Europe under government ownership.

Bell employees distributed over ten thousand copies of the book to libraries, reviewers, and others. Free copies included a slip of paper pasted into the inside front cover notifying readers that McClurg & Company had provided the book as a gift. The publisher asked AT&T vice president J. D. Ellsworth if the notice should come from the publisher or from AT&T. Ellsworth replied that "the slips to libraries, etc., should also go over your company's signature" since libraries "do not connect your company with the matter in any way."[201] The copy of Casson's book in this author's university library included this gift slip from McClurg & Company.

AT&T produced several other books in this genre. One of the most widely distributed of them was *The Telephone Idea* by Arthur Pound, published in 1926. While writing the book for AT&T, Pound worked for the Atlantic Monthly Press and as an editor for the *Independent* magazine. Yet not everything Pound wrote was independent. When he completed a draft of his book, he submitted it to AT&T executive, J. D. Ellsworth, who edited it, and sent back a new typed manuscript. AT&T paid Pound $2,200 to write the book, a fact that did not make it into the text.[202]

In *The Telephone Idea*, Pound raised propaganda to new literary heights. The text featured a breathless account of the development of telephone service and cast the telephone as a central part in the timeless drama of human communication. In Pound's portrayal, AT&T was an all-for-the-greater-good service corporation and its employees selfless public servants.[203] Pound's account also managed to harmonize monopoly with the "American way," by defining the latter as including "voluntary cooperation," not just "individual initiative," which might have conflicted with Bell's monopoly.[204]

Subverting Civics   231

Despite Pound's eloquence, he found it difficult to find a publisher. His first choice was Macmillan Company, but they demurred, explaining that "while the propaganda or publicity elements are very skillfully constituted, the book still is propaganda or publicity, and while perfectly legitimate in its own field, would seem a bit out of place on a general publisher's list." Undeterred, Pound approached the publishers Payson and Clarke, yet they too rejected the manuscript, calling it "too obviously propaganda." Finally, Pound settled for Greenberg, Inc., which held none of the literary pretensions of its peers. Greenberg agreed to publish the book, but in an unusual arrangement, Greenberg simply allowed its name to appear on the book, carried the title on its list, shipped the book, and collected the money. AT&T sourced the printer and binder, and handled the marketing.[205]

Ellsworth wanted the book to serve as "a means of some favorable publicity," so when it was completed he sent it out to Bell publicity managers with instructions to distribute the copies to editors, regulatory commissioners, and university libraries. His managers followed his orders. The copy of the book in the library of the University of California, Berkeley, has "Gift of American Telephone and Telegraph" hand-scrolled into its title page, while the University of Michigan copy bears the inscription "Mr. J. J. Kelly, Gift, 10-3-1927." Kelly was a Bell manager in Ann Arbor.[206] Thousands of other copies were given to libraries and friends so that by 1935, some 8,500 copies of *The Telephone Idea* had been distributed.[207]

Utilities also produced policy books. AT&T paid James Mavor, a professor of political economy at the University of Toronto, to write *Government Telephones: The Experience of Manitoba, Canada*, published in 1916. In the conclusion, Mavor stated that his goal was to make "the public realize that the proper function of government is not the conduct of industries but the impartial inspection of them under intelligent laws."[208] This was a timely argument, since at the time the postmaster general, Albert Burleson, wanted to take over the nation's telephone network.[209] Nowhere in the book did Mavor acknowledge that AT&T paid him $2,050 for his labors, a project which Mavor stated was "as impartial as possible.[210]

Later, electric utilities employed Mavor to write a book condemning the Ontario Hydroelectric Commission, which oversaw the government-owned power system in Ontario, Canada. NELA provided research materials and funds. Publication occurred in 1925 and was heavily promoted by the utilities. Over ten thousand copies went out to libraries, newspaper editors, and

232   Chapter 6

reviewers.[211] Just as in his previous work, Mavor made no mention of the source of his funding.[212]

Envelope Stuffers, Window Displays, and Philanthropy

To reach Americans who might not be inclined to read books, utilities disseminated an enormous array of direct mail, advertising brochures, and signs. These included posters on streetcar platforms, pamphlets left by meter readers, and envelope stuffers for customers to discover inside their monthly utility bills.[213] Some of this material was aimed at selling products, but much of it was aimed at improving public relations. In 1927, meter readers for the American Gas & Electric Company dropped off at the front door of fifty-five thousand customers a booklet entitled "Government Fails in Industry" and an editorial opposing government ownership from the *New York American*.[214]

To reach pedestrians, utilities created elaborate window displays designed to attract attention and improve public relations. During "Electrical Prosperity Week" in 1916, PT&T kept a live person in a Los Angeles window display doing nothing but splicing cables from 9 A.M. to 10 P.M.[215] One popular Bell window display featured a telephone disassembled into 136 pieces. The display was supposed to impress customers about the complexity of the telephone, though one wag wanted to know: "Which part of it is always busy?"[216]

These displays appeared in prominent locations and in some cases attracted crowds. Peoples Gas in Chicago maintained intricate window displays at their company headquarters on Michigan Avenue, a street famous for its Christmas window displays. Other utilities with less prominent locations leased windows from downtown hotels or retailers in order to increase their exposure to customers.[217] Windows displays may have been "small things in and of themselves," a PT&T executive admitted to managers in 1925, "but in the aggregate they are important because of the impression they create in the minds of our customers as to our performance in bigger matters."[218] As another telephone employee accurately observed, "No opportunity is ever overlooked . . . to cultivate further the cordial relations already existing between the company and the public."[219]

To further promote cordial relations, managers donated money to various charities and groups. In 1920s and early 1930s, Southern Bell donated to a host of groups, including the Community Chest, Police Relief Association, the Georgia Association for the Blind, the Episcopal Orphanage in Savannah, the Utility Milk Fund, several different Boy Scout troops, the Sisters of St. Francis, Salvation Army, twenty different YMCA and YWCAs, and a synagogue. Donations ranged from $3 to the Episcopal Orphans Home in Savannah to $7,500 to the Community Chest in Atlanta. Donations in 1934 totaled $23,600.[220]

Bell donations were not always disinterested. The president of Southwestern Bell made a $2,500 donation to the Houston YWCA in 1920 because, as he put it, "we got our rates increased at Houston . . . [so] I feel that it is necessary to make the donation of $2500 to the YWCA." This did not pave the way for future rate increases, however. So the next year the president of Southwestern Bell had to make another donation, to "enlist the support of some of the influential citizens who are behind the YWCA." According to a Southwestern Bell vice president, this was part of the president's "endeavor to get rid of the rate litigation at Houston."[221] The extent and diversity of the various philanthropic and publicity methods so amazed one FTC examiner that he asked a NELA official incredulously: "Do you know of any means of publicity that has been neglected?" The NELA official blithely replied: "Only one and that is sky writing."[222]

Influencing Regulators

What is remarkable about all of these public relations tactics is how thoroughly they targeted regular citizens, rather than legislators or regulators. Yet utility executives still occasionally backslid into their old Gilded Age habit of bribing legislators and regulators. In 1931, for example, the Southern Bell Telephone Company placed South Carolina state legislator E. H. Brown on retainer, after which time he flip-flopped from being an ardent advocate of lower utility rates to a defender of the existing rates. The year after Brown was put on retainer, he sat shoulder to shoulder with Southern Bell attorneys, defending the company at the very rate hearings Brown himself had earlier demanded.[223]

In other cases, utilities provided regulators with free telephone service, sometimes because the regulators asked for it. In 1924, the chairman of the Arkansas Railroad Commission asked Bell's general attorney if Southwestern Bell "would extend to him the courtesy" of its long-distance lines during the commissioner's reelection campaign. The Bell attorney replied that the company would "make some satisfactory arrangement." It is not known exactly what the arrangement entailed but in August 1924 Southwestern Bell wrote off over $7,000 in uncollectable bills incurred by politicians.[224] Similar provision of free service existed elsewhere, including in the Carolinas where utility-board commissioners and their staff, all the way down to the stenographers, received free telephone service for years, not just at their offices, but also at their homes.[225]

Either as a result of these friendly gestures, or for other reasons, commissioners sometimes worked with telephone managers to present utility issues to the public. A "confidential & to be destroyed" memo that failed to remain confidential or get destroyed reveals that in 1932 a Southern Bell manager strategized with a North Carolina utility commissioner on how to manage rate hearings in a way that would benefit Bell. The commissioner and manager agreed to have two sets of hearings: one for the public and one for the commission. At the public hearing where a large number of customers and reporters were expected, Bell would present a general accounting report emphasizing the high expenses and low earnings of the company. The commissioner advised Bell that the company should "appeal as far as possible to the public in this hearing," according to the memo, which was authored by the general counsel of the Southern Bell Company and found in the files of the general counsel of AT&T. At the second, unadvertised hearing, Bell managers would offer a more detailed accounting report for the commissioners. Despite the friendly commissioner, the utility board was "bombarded" by letters calling for a reduction in telephone rates due to the Depression, so the commission ultimately voted to reduce handset charges from 50¢ to 25¢.[226] Working with commissioners did not always work, but that does not mean it was not tried.

Telephone executives also colluded with state regulators to get friendly utility commissioners elected. In 1930, a utility board commissioner in Mississippi wrote to a Southern Bell manager concerning a rate issue brewing in Jackson. "If there is anything I can do to assist you," the commissioner wrote, "I will be glad to do it. This letter is written [to] you in strict confidence." The Bell manager replied, "I appreciate your attitude in connection with our rate case and will thank you for any assistance you can render." A few months later, the commission granted a rate increase for commercial rates.[227]

Other utility operatives offered money and alcohol to legislators to influence them. In the early 1920s, Robert Prather, the secretary for the Great Lakes division of NELA, asked Merlin H. Aylesworth, the executive director of NELA, to bring him a half-dozen bottles of whisky to "sweeten the palate" of Illinois legislators. "The legislature is in session here and it looks like a very stormy session," Prather wrote to Aylesworth. "I could use very handily a little J. Walker to very good advantage." It is not known what specific political errand Prather was on, but in 1928 the Illinois legislature rejected a bill to promote municipal ownership, which Prather, of course, also opposed.[228] By the time Prohibition ended a few years later, Aylesworth had become the founding president of the National Broadcasting Company.[229]

Illinois legislators may have drank their whisky to the memory of Illinois politician and former regulator, Frank L. Smith. Smith's political career ended abruptly in 1927 after a US Senate investigation discovered that utility mogul Samuel Insull had contributed $125,000 to Smith's Senate campaign.[230] Other utility executives also contributed money to Smith, although Insull, as one of the largest utility operators in the country, made the largest donation. Insull's political fixer testified before Congress that Insull had called him one day, told him that he wanted to support Smith, and added: "When you want the money, come and get it." In true Cook County fashion, Insull handed his power broker envelopes of cash for Smith's campaign on several occasions.[231] At the time Insull made the donations, he was fighting municipal ownership in several towns in Illinois, and trying to monopolize the streetcar system in Chicago.[232] But when the Senate heard the revelations about Smith receiving the donations, they refused to seat him and he was ultimately forced to resign. Perhaps protesting too much, Insull later wrote that he did not give Smith money "because of favors I had received from him when he was Chairman of the Illinois Commerce Commission," the state's utility regulatory board.[233]

Insull's contributions to Smith backfired in more ways than one. Not only was Smith forced to resign, but public confidence in utility regulation declined. The property commissioner of Springfield, Illinois, testified that, due to Insull's donations, "the cities of Illinois no longer have any confidence in regulation by our commission" and that "regulation of utilities by commission in Illinois has become a scandalous and almost tragic failure."[234]

What is most surprising about these cases of political influence is not that they occurred, but how little of it executives appear to have engaged in after the first decade of the twentieth century. There was probably more of it than is currently known, but utility executives, even when communicating among themselves, frequently stated that bribery and other forms of corruption could no longer be relied upon to secure franchise permits and rate increase if public opinion opposed the measures. Executives instead believed that the decisions of government officials ultimately had to conform to public opinion or the decisions would not stand. While occasional gifts or bribes functioned as an expedient here and there, the main strategies of utility executives had fundamentally changed by the 1920s. Customers and their opinions became the primary focus.

Conclusion

Public relations of utilities shifted during the Progressive Era from bribing the few to persuading the many, including students, professors, club members, housewives, moviegoers, readers, and pedestrians. As the number of people that utilities needed to influence increased, the scope of utility publicity increased as well. Eventually it covered not just advertisements and articles, but also textbooks, college courses, public speeches, radio programs, movies, traveling demonstrations, and "envelope stuffers." Utility managers certainly took AT&T executive E. S. Wilson's public relations directive to heart: "Make sure we are leaving no stone unturned." Wilson's statement, made in 1920, characterized the view of corporate utility operators for the entire decade.[235]

Overall, these wide-ranging publicity activities appear to have improved public opinion toward monopolies. In 1929, Ohio State business professor Charles Dice observed, "The common folks . . . no longer look upon the captains of industry as magnified crooks." This was precisely how customers viewed utility operators around 1910 and before. "Have we not heard their voices over the radio?" inquired Dice. "Are we not familiar with their thoughts, ambitions, and ideals as they have expressed them to us almost as a man talks to his friend?"[236] Dice accurately identified a shift in public opinion regarding big business and linked it to corporate public relations. Yet in the case of utilities, Dice was only half right. Public opinion had improved but not only because "common folk" heard the voices of "captains of industry" but also because common people heard the voice of Mrs. Peterson and many other regular employees, in person, on the radio, and during demonstrations. Americans had studied from utility textbooks, viewed utility movies, and heard speeches from neighborly and friendly utility employees. All of this, along with an avalanche of literature in newspapers and popular books, communicated the utilities' message to Americans, and helped dissipate antimonopoly sentiment.

Conclusion

One day, while doing research for this book, I received an email from the Pacific Gas & Electric Company (PG&E), which supplied electricity to my Berkeley apartment. Would I like to join their "online community" called "Customer Voice" in order to help them improve their service? My first thought was that I did not want to be bothered by these ridiculous emails. After all, the company had not been nearly so solicitous the first time I requested access to their archives. But my second thought was: Of course I want to see how the PG&E's public relations has evolved in the twenty-first century. I replied to the "online community manager" of PG&E's "customer experience team," and filled out a lengthy survey about my age, education, income, and consumption habits. I never heard from them again. A few years later, the company went bankrupt.[1]

PG&E's lack of response indicated that, unlike earlier efforts, the company no longer cared about shaping the opinions of college students and academics. But in other ways, PG&E's desire for feedback was not new. William G. McAdoo had invited his subway customers to complain directly to him as early as 1908, and hundreds of other utility executives followed. This feedback, executives knew, would help them improve their service, especially by increasing employee conformance to the demands for courteous capitalism. Customers had targeted monopolies for reform, so monopolies targeted customers for feedback in a counter-reform of courtesy. Stuck in the middle, clerks grasped at the ever-decreasing autonomy of their newly bureaucratized souls.

In addition to providing courtesy, managers sought to improve public opinion by redesigning their commercial offices, selling stock to customers, and exchanging advertisements for articles. Utility employees also influenced the content of textbooks, spoke at civic clubs, canceled Chautauqua speakers, and produced radio programs and popular movies. These activities in the 1920s represented the largest nongovernmental public relations campaign Americans had ever seen.

As detailed in the "Did ____ Work?" sections of the preceding chapters, the public relations efforts of utilities proved effective, at least to a degree. Negative opinions still existed regarding corporate monopolies, and these were amplified by people like Senator George Norris. Yet utility executives, employees, and outside observers, including critical ones, agreed that public opinion toward corporate utility monopolies had improved during the 1920s. These individuals credited the four strategies of courteous capitalism, open offices, customer stock ownership, and publicity with bringing about this change.

One question that may be asked about this campaign is: Did one strategy work better than the others? Executives viewed all four public relations strategies as very important, yet they viewed courtesy as the most important method of all. Customers liked the comfortable and well-appointed open offices, yet these offices still required courteous clerks. The removal of bars and frosted glass facilitated courteous service but could not replace it.

Customer stock ownership also improved public opinion, yet it did so mostly for those who purchased stock. Although utility employees valiantly sold stock to 20 percent of the total number of shareholders in the United States by 1930, that number was still small compared to the total US population. The value of the two million customer shareholders should not be discounted, nor overemphasized. Some of these shareholders were concentrated in areas that had formerly been hotbeds of municipal ownership. In some areas, such as regions of California, utility shareholders represented 10 percent of the voting population. Rather than seeing themselves as adversaries of corporate monopolies, as the Populists once had, many citizens, including rural and working-class Americans, now considered themselves partners with corporate monopolies.

Yet the numbers converted through customer stock ownership were small compared to those who interacted with courteous clerks. Consider just how many people contacted clerks face-to-face. By the end of the 1920s, almost every urban household had utility service of some kind, and signing up and paying for service often had to be done in person. In 1928, when the US population was some 130 million, Bell estimated its clerks interacted with over one hundred million customers face-to-face. In 1923, an electricity executive

Conclusion 239

stated that 95 percent of customers knew the people who worked at the local utility office.[2] If these clerks had routinely offended customers, as railroad workers had in the Gilded Age, the clerks could have easily undone all the goodwill created by customer stock ownership, and then some. This justifies the strong emphasis executives placed on courtesy. It was not that customer stock ownership did not have an impact; it certainly did. But courtesy reached a much larger number of people.

Space grabbing and the other publicity methods involving textbooks, speeches, radio, and movies also improved the public relations of utilities. Testimonies from people involved in these strategies stated that the methods worked. Specific municipal-ownership bills in California, Georgia, Kentucky, and Minnesota were also defeated at least in part because of publicity. Members of the public also noted that that these strategies improved public opinion.

Quantitative evidence supports these observations. As presented in chapter 6, the number of critical articles about utilities declined during the 1920s. This, and the fact that utility managers stopped many negative articles from appearing in the first place, must have influenced readers. How could Americans even learn about the ideas of people like municipal socialist Carl D. Thompson when publicists like John Sheridan had expelled Thompson from the Chautauqua circuit and eliminated the mention of him from so many Missouri newspapers? Sheridan and his colleagues could not persuade every single editor, but they influenced a substantial portion, and this proved true in many other states as well. Careful and conservative surveys by utilities indicated that newspaper participation in space grabbing ranged from 70 to over 90 percent in several multistate regions of the country. This resulted in the publication of tens of thousands of column inches' worth of articles that flattered corporate monopolies.

Utility publicists also expunged negative material from schools and placed their own books before school children. In states such as Illinois and Connecticut, over 70 percent of high schoolers received instruction from utility-authored books, while in Missouri the number reached well over 90 percent. Speeches, radio programs, and movies also reached vast numbers of Americans. It is difficult to imagine Americans applauding utilities as they did after seeing *A Modern Knight* if utilities had not zealously produced and distributed this kind of publicity.

Yet executives still viewed courtesy as even more effective than publicity, and for good reason. After discussing movies, speeches, demonstrations, and plant tours, a Pacific Telephone & Telegraph (PT&T) manager declared that "day-to-day contacts are undoubtedly the greatest single factor in maintaining and promoting good mutual understanding."[3] "Our advertising, our display windows, and other methods of publicity are useful in educating the public," stated an editor of a Bell employee magazine in 1922, "but, greater than all of these, is the fact that there are thousands of people on our payrolls who come in contact every day with the public."[4] This idea of the primacy of courtesy was widely shared. "There is no more splendid vehicle to carry the message of the company to the public than the man on the cars," echoed a streetcar executive at an industry conference. "The story they tell—more effectively by their course of conduct than by any other means—is one of the greatest agencies in informing the general public of the actual attitude of management."[5] These managers knew about the other public relations strategies, yet specifically singled out courtesy as "the greatest single factor."[6]

Even those not directly employed by utilities argued that courtesy was the most influential method in shaping sentiment regarding utility ownership. Psychologist and business consultant J. David Houser summarized thousands of interviews his firm had conducted with utility customers by emphatically declaring that courtesy mattered more than anything else. "The treatment of the utility customer, as he comes into our office . . . determines to an overwhelming extent what the customer will say and feel about the service as a whole," Houser concluded from his research. "And the way that customer feels about service as a whole . . . is far and away the largest single influence on the way he feels about the matter of private or public ownership."[7] A stronger and more informed statement could not have been made.

Executives specifically appraised courtesy as more valuable than advertising. "We advertise, of course, in the mediums at our command," wrote the editor of a Bell employee magazine, "but our service is our greatest advertisement."[8] "Render a service which will impress," echoed a National Electric Light Association (NELA) report, "that is the best kind of advertising we can secure."[9] A Boston electricity executive put it succinctly in 1920: "Actions speak louder than words."[10] Countervailing voices could occasionally be heard, especially by executives promoting one of the other three strategies, but, in general, executives strongly promoted courtesy as the most effective public relations strategy.[11]

Print did not even rank second to courtesy in terms of its public relations effectiveness, in the minds of many executives. These executives believed that any kind of face-to-face interaction, such as speeches and demonstra-

Conclusion 241

tions, was more effective than advertising. "The spoken word is much more convincing than the written word," emphasized the president of the Georgia Railway and Power Company at an American Electric Railway Association (AERA) meeting. This executive authorized hundreds of thousands of dollars in advertising and philanthropy annually, but he still put spoken messages above printed ones.[12] PT&T also ranked face-to-face interaction above print. In a reading assignment for employees, the company observed that "no matter how much advertising space we fill with type and pictures . . . and no matter how many bulletins and pamphlets we may print . . . the finest and most effective form of advertising is the personally spoken recommendation of one person to another."[13]

Some executives downplayed print matter because they believed that the public did not read much. Samuel Kennedy, the vice president for public relations at the Southern California Edison Company (SCE), told peers that "the average individual does not read the printed literature that comes to him, and it is pretty hard to send a personal letter to each individual. Even a personal letter," Kennedy opined, may be read, "but the benefit is infinitesimal compared to the personal contact."[14]

Other managers argued that customers sometimes did not believe what they read. One PG&E employee observed that individual customers often came in to complain about the company. "As proof positive" of the [company's] faults, the employee noted, "the kicker will cite articles he has read in the newspapers, showing up the corporation's base methods. Yet when questioned closely as to his general belief in the truth of many statements made on other subjects by the press, he will frankly acknowledge his doubts."[15] Managers who questioned print may have been in the minority, but no manager could be heard debating the effectiveness of courtesy. Department store magnate John Wanamaker famously quipped that half his money on advertising was wasted but he did not know which half, yet utility executives were even more skeptical about the power of ads.

Some observers ranked courtesy as second only to delivering quality physical service at a decent price. One newspaper editor acknowledged that utilities already provided good physical service at a good price, then told utility executives that "added to this primary requisite must be a courteous, obliging, considerate corps of officials, managers, superintendents and employees. With these, your utility is not likely to experience any great amount of unfavorable public sentiment. Without these, the case is absolutely hopeless." And this came from someone with an interest in selling ads. According to this editor, "persistent and consistent publicity" functioned only as a "final ingredient."[16]

Many industry insiders even ranked courtesy higher than providing quality physical service. In 1922, a regulatory commissioner observed that "it is not poor engineering practice or plant troubles which irritate the gas-consuming public today, but uncivil treatment at the hands of clerical employees in the gas company's offices."[17] A 1929 NELA report concluded that "most people judge companies with which they deal, more largely through the employees with whom they come in contact than through any other single factor." The report downplayed print and even physical utility service by declaring that "neither advertising nor the general policies of the company, nor the physical service of the companies has any effect as that of the direct personal contact."[18]

Scholars have been less keen than executives to recognize the public relations impact of face-to-face interaction. Dealing primarily with written sources, academics have naturally emphasized the importance of print. But some students of the media have gone so far as to imply that, due to all the advertising done by corporations in the 1920s, a large-scale brainwashing of the American public took place. Stuart Ewen's book *PR! A History of Spin*, for example, traced the idea of manipulating public opinion through various theorists, then focused on the well-known practitioner of public relations, Edward Bernays. Bernays claimed to be able to influence public opinion using sentimental and colorful advertising images. Consumers must be made to feel, he taught, following his predecessors. Bernays and his predecessors dismissed the Enlightenment notion of a rational public, and instead asserted that "the crowd" could be manipulated through print-based appeals to emotion. The rational public was dead, they argued, and publicists could skip trying to rationally appeal to consumers. But whatever Bernays may have claimed about "engineering consent"—the title of one of his books—most utility executives did not share his belief that the majority of Americans would go hook, line, and sinker for the claims of advertisers.[19] Although Bernays and others claimed massive print-based manipulation, the evidence for it was thin gruel.

Consumers were simply not as pliable as Ewen and his social theorists believed. Americans understood that advertisements were paid for by corporations and intended to appeal to consumers. Simply put, ads were transparent to American readers. Utility publicists and executives recognized this and deprecated an overreliance on ads for that reason. In 1927, Robert

Hofer of the Hofer Service, discussed in chapter 5, wrote to an utility executive that "the greatest value of our service to the utilities is the fact that the people are reading something about public service companies other than what is sent out directly by such companies."[20] An electricity executive told colleagues that "clever publicity articles in the press and other publications and public speeches by officials of the company create a certain amount of good will and friendliness," but "due to the very fact that such utterances emanate from the executive heads of the company, they are often taken with more than a 'grain of salt.'" The executive then added that a "majority never hear the speeches or read the articles. Their usefulness, therefore, is somewhat limited." Rather than ads, articles, or even speeches, this executive stressed courteous service: "When a customer has encountered a friendly attitude toward him, time after time, in his contact with nearly all of the company's employees, he . . . feels that the company is fair and trustworthy, and he is prompted to reciprocate."[21]

If clerks provided courteous service, then advertising could complement that effort, according to executives. But if employees failed to mind their manners, then advertising would fail no matter what. "Advertising is not a magic wand to be successfully wielded by whomever may buy it," declared the advertising director of AERA, "rather it is a hoe with which one may till the soil of public sentiment." The director cautioned managers that "seeds of empty promises, sprung from years of poor service and general indifference, never will produce bountiful crops. But when the seed is good the hoe will help."[22] In other words, advertising and articles could only help if customers received courteous service. After studying the question "Does Advertising Pay?" an AERA committee concluded that "advertising and publicity alone will not bring prosperity to the electric railway or any other industry. There must also be good service." The commercial manager of the Pittsburgh Railways Company added a similar condition to advertising: "I am convinced that we can, through the medium of advertising, reduce expenses, increase business, and materially improve public relations, if the written word is backed up by performance."[23] "It pays to advertise," Samuel Kennedy summarized, *"but you've got to have the goods."*[24]

The extraordinary skepticism with which utility executives viewed print, and their strong emphasis on the actual behavior of clerks, explains why companies often advertised their own courtesy when they did advertise. PG&E ads frequently featured the company's the motto: "Courteous Continuous Service." AERA produced stock advertisements showing a conductor helping an old woman onto a car, with the words "Courteous Electric Railway Employees Make Riding a Pleasure." The Greenville Gas Company advertised its motto, "Courtesy, Service and Co-Operation," while SCE advertised its own maxim, "Courteous Treatment, Good Service, Square Dealing." These ads reveal how deeply executives wanted customers to identify their company with courteous service.

Executives also used this courtesy advertising to control clerks. By informing customers about how employees were supposed to behave, customers could demand the advertised courtesy, or report the offending clerk. And since employees knew that customers understood the behavioral standards, employees were more likely to perform in the advertised manner. "We tell the people that they have a right to fair and courteous treatment from us at all times," explained the president of the Rochester Gas & Electric Company. "By so doing, we exert a salutary influence upon the operations of our employees who follow our publicity very closely and who are therefore repeatedly reminded of what is expected of them in their dealings with the public."[25] In 1928, an AERA committee found that "newspaper advertising can be utilized to advantage in a systematic display program, portraying the

"Courteous Continuous Service," the motto of PG&E, was emblazoned on the company's seal, as seen in this 1922 advertisement. *Journal of Electricity and Western Industry*, August 15, 1922, 14, Box 440, Folder 8, SCE Records.

A stock advertising image that was heavily used by AERA members in the early 1920s. "Report of Committee on Publicity," *AERA Proceedings* (1922) 189.

The emblem of the Edison Club of SCE, which featured the company's motto since 1905: "Courteous Treatment, Good Service, Square Dealing." Call No. 02 10606, SCEPN.

duties of the individual employee and designed to promote friendly cooperation between the trainmen and the public."[26]

When utilities failed to advertise in the approved manner, they could be chastised by the industry. In 1916, the editors at *System: The Magazine of Business* criticized a gas company for spending large sums of money to advertise that its executives were moral. "Such an effort must have come from . . . a reluctance to look squarely at the basic fact that the reputation of a service company is made or lost at the complaint counter," opined *System* magazine.[27] At the same time as readers witnessed a shift from producer-centered ads to consumer-centered ads, consumers also experienced a shift from clerk-centered service to customer-centered service.[28]

No single public relations method or political strategy can fully explain why corporate monopolies survived the first third of the twentieth century. Executives spent millions on open architecture, customer stock ownership, and publicity, and strongly believed in each of these strategies. Yet executives never believed that these methods could replace courtesy when it came to improving public opinion. Open and inviting architecture could not improve customer relations if the offices remained staffed by rude clerks. Nor could customer stock ownership dissipate antimonopoly sentiment all by itself. And print could not improve public relations if the claims made in print were not backed up by courtesy at the customer service counter. While scholars have credited store architecture, personal finance, and print with everything from fashioning consumers to forming nations, when it came to forming enduring corporate monopolies, courtesy mattered most.

NOTES

Abbreviations

AERA. American Electric Railway Association

AERA Proceedings. Proceedings of the American Electric Railway Association (New York: American Electric Railway Association). References to specific publication years can be found in the notes.

AGA. American Gas Association

AT&T. American Telephone & Telegraph Company

AT&T, *Annual Report. Annual Report of the Directors of American Telephone & Telegraph Company to the Stockholder for the Year Ending* [date] (Boston: Geo. Ellis Co.). References to specific publication years can be found in the notes.

AT&T-TX. AT&T Archives and History Center, San Antonio, Texas

Bell Securities, *Annual Report. Annual Report of the Bell Telephone Securities Company, Incorporated, For the Year Ending* [date] (New York). References to specific publication years can be found in the notes.

Ex. Exhibit

FCC Records. Records of the Federal Communications Commission, National Archives, College Park, Maryland

FTC Letter. Letter from the Chairman of the Federal Trade Commission Transmitting in Response to Senate Resolution No. 83 a Monthly Report on the Electric Power and Gas Utilities Inquiry, No. [number], *Filed with the Secretary of the Senate,* [date] (Washington, DC: Government Printing Office, 1928), [page number]. References to specific letter no., date, and page number can be found in the notes.

FTC Records. Records of the Federal Trade Commission, National Archives, College Park, Maryland

Insull Papers. Samuel Insull Papers, Loyola University Chicago Archives and Special Collections

McAdoo Papers. William Gibbs McAdoo Papers, Huntington Library, San Marino, California

NELA. National Electric Light Association

NELA Proceedings. Proceedings of the National Electric Light Association, [numbered] *Convention,* [date] (New York: National Electric Light Association). References to specific publication years can be found in the notes.

Peoples Gas, *Year Book. The Peoples Gas Light & Coke Company Year Book*

PG&E. Pacific Gas & Electric

PT&T. Pacific Telephone & Telegraph Company

Public-Contact-Training Methods and Principles. Public-Contact-Training Methods and Principles: Experiences of Member Companies Presented and Discussed at the Chicago Conference, September, 1929: A Report of the Industrial Relations Committee, Public Relations National Section (1929). This obscure source was bound together with other booklets as *Special Publications, 1929,* published by NELA and found in the University of California, Berkeley Library under call no. TK 1 N 24, 1929:3.

RG. Record Group

SCE. Southern California Edison Company

SCEPN. Southern California Edison Photographs and Negatives, Huntington Library, San Marino, California

SCE Records. Southern California Edison Records, Huntington Library, San Marino, California

Telephone Investigation (1937). *Telephone Investigation, Special Investigation Docket No. 1: Report on Control of Telephone Communications (Pursuant to Public Resolution No. 8, 74th Congress)* (June 15, 1937)

Introduction

1. "Editorial Comment: I Pray Thee Have Me Excused," *Stone & Webster Journal,* June 1921, 475; F.G.R. Gordon, reprint of "Concisely Expressed in Cleveland," *Haverhill Record,* June 4, 1922, Box 3853, Ex. 2976, Series: Economic Investigations Files, 1915–1938, Subject: Power and Gas, RG 122: Records of the Federal Trade Commission, National Archives, College Park, Maryland; hereafter FTC Records.

2. "Address of M. H. Aylesworth, Executive Manager, National Electric Light Association," National Association of Railway and Utilities Commissioners, *Proceedings of the Thirty-Third Annual Convention, Atlanta Georgia, October 11–14, 1921* (New York: State Law Reporting, 1921), 323.

3. Samuel Kennedy, "Transforming Public Opinion: An Address by Mr. Samuel M. Kennedy, Vice-President Southern California Edison Co., Los Angeles, California, before the Convention of Managers and Executives of the Management Division of Stone & Webster Inc., Held in Boston, October 10–18, 1921," Box 389, Folder 26,

Southern California Edison Records, Huntington Library, San Marino, California; hereafter SCE Records.

4. Kennedy, "Transforming Public Opinion," 6, 9, 24–25, 45.

5. Discussion after Kennedy, "Transforming Public Opinion," 45.

6. N. C. Kingsbury, *Publicity: A Paper Presented May 7, 1912, before the Philadelphia Telephone Society*, Folder: Publicity, Box 1, RG 6: Publications, 1893–1912, Collection 6: AT&T Corp, AT&T Archives and History Center, San Antonio, Texas; hereafter AT&T-TX.

7. Samuel M. Kennedy, *Winning the Public*, 2nd ed. (New York: McGraw-Hill, 1921), 123.

8. By *executives*, here and throughout this book, I generally mean directors, vice presidents, and above. By *managers*, I mean those below directors, such as commercial office managers. In some cases, the terms were, and therefore, are, used interchangeably. For example, John Sheridan variously styled himself as the "manager" and "director" of the Missouri Committee on Public Utility Information. His position gave him a lot of power and influence, yet he did not officially oversee very many people.

9. Italics in original. "Address of Mr. Insull before the First Annual Meeting of the Co-Operative Council of the Public Service Company of Northern Illinois, Chicago, December 7, 1921," 19–20, Folder 20–8, Samuel Insull Papers, Loyola University Chicago Archives; hereafter Insull Papers; Richard E. Smith, "The Fellow in the Street," *Edison Current Topics* 8, no. 8 (August 1919): 91, Box 308, Folder 7, SCE Records; William G. McAdoo, "The Relations between Public Service Corporations and the Public," lecture delivered before the Graduate School of Business Administration of Harvard University, April 6, 1910 (New York: Alexander Hamilton Institute, 1910), 19. Italics in original.

10. Kennedy, *Winning the Public*, 106; P. H. Gadsden, "The Committee Chairman's Viewpoint," *Proceedings of the Forty-Seventh Convention of the National Electric Light Association* (New York: NELA, 1924), 152–155; hereafter *NELA Proceedings* (1924); similar citations will be similarly abbreviated; Smith, "The Fellow in the Street"; Paul C. Rawson, "Prize-Winning Article in Forbes Contest," *NELA Proceedings* (1924), 178; G. C. Staley and F. C. Jordan, "The Utility Customer," *Journal of the American Water Works Association*, November 1926, 645; W. P. Graef, Chief Salesman Pasadena District, "The Electrical Salesman," *Edison Current Topics*, May 1912, 19–21, Box 308, Folder 1, SCE Records.

11. John M. Mulvihill, "Popularizing Utility Companies," *Public Service*, December 1908, 171.

12. Arlie Russell Hochschild, *The Managed Heart: Commercialization of Human Feeling* (Berkeley: University of California Press, 1983), 5–7.

13. For emotional labor in other settings, see Susan Porter Benson, *Counter Cultures: Saleswomen, Managers, and Customers in American Department Stores, 1890–1940* (Champaign: University of Illinois Press, 1988); Dorothy Sue Cobble, *Dishing It Out: Waitresses and Their Unions in the Twentieth Century* (Urbana: University of Illinois Press, 1991); Jack Santino, *Miles of Smiles, Years of Struggle: Stories of Black Pullman Porters* (Urbana: University of Illinois Press, 1991), 8.

14. Andrew Jackson, "Veto Message," July 10, 1832, Avalon Project, http://avalon .law.yale.edu/19th_century/ajveto01.asp.

250 Notes to Pages 4–7

15. Elizabeth Sanders, *Roots of Reform: Farmers, Workers, and the American State, 1877–1917* (Chicago: University of Chicago Press, 1999), 37, 267–268, 387–388; Charles Postel, *The Populist Vision* (Oxford: Oxford University Press, 2007), 277.

16. David M. Kennedy, "Overview: The Progressive Era," in *Historian* 37, no 3 (May 1975)": 453–468; Gabriel Kolko, *The Triumph of Conservatism: A Re-interpretation of American History, 1900–1916* (New York: Free Press, 1963); James Weinstein, *The Corporate Ideal in the Liberal States: 1900–1918* (Boston: Beacon Press, 1968); Robert H. Wiebe, *The Search for Order, 1877–1920* (New York: Hill and Wang, 1967), 212.

17. David E. Nye, *Electrifying America: Social Meanings of a New Technology, 1880–1940* (Cambridge, MA: MIT Press, 1990); Claude S. Fischer, *America Calling: A Social History of the Telephone to 1940* (Berkeley: University of California Press, 1992).

18. Roland Marchand has blazed the trail in asking and answering some of these questions through his analysis of corporate advertising, but many questions still remain. Roland Marchand, *Creating the Corporate Soul: The Rise of Public Relations and Corporate Imagery in American Big Business* (Berkeley: University of California Press, 1998).

19. Alfred D. Chandler, *The Visible Hand: The Managerial Revolution in American Business* (Cambridge, MA: Belknap Press of Harvard University Press, 1977). Scholars valiantly struggled at "bringing the state back in" after the social turn of the 1960s. The present volume seeks to bridge these two interests.

20. I refer here to roughly the first two decades of the twentieth century, or about the period from 1900 to the end of World War I in November 1918. I am aware of the debate surrounding the term "Progressive Era," but find using it in this way less cumbersome than spelling out the dates each time.

21. Louis D. Brandeis, "How Boston Solved the Gas Problem," *American Review of Reviews* 36, no. 5 (November 1907): 592.

22. Theodore Roosevelt, "The New Nationalism," August 31, 1910, Teaching American History, http://teachingamericanhistory.org/document/the-new -nationalism/.

23. Woodrow Wilson, *The New Freedom: A Call for the Emancipation of the Generous Energies of a People* (New York: Doubleday, Page, 1913), 172.

24. Henry Marison Byllesby, *The Responsibilities of Electrical Engineers in Making Appraisals, an Address Delivered before the Members of the American Institute of Electrical Engineers in Annual Convention, Hotel Sherman, Chicago, Illinois, June 27, 1911*, 3rd ed. (1911), 17.

25. *Annual Report of the Directors of American Telephone & Telegraph Company to the Stockholder for the Year Ending December 31, 1916* (New York: AT&T, 1917), 44; hereafter AT&T, *Annual Report, 1916*; similar citations will be similarly abbreviated.

26. William E. Leuchtenburg asked "What killed progressivism?" in *The Perils of Prosperity, 1914–1932* (Chicago: University of Chicago Press, 1958), 120–121; Arthur S. Link asked, "What Happened to the Progressive Movement in the 1920s?," *American Historical Review* 64, no. 4 (July 1959): 833–851.

27. Harold Platt has argued that poor service was one cause of the Progressive movement. Harold Platt, *City Building in the New South: The Growth of Public Services in Houston, Texas, 1830–1910* (Philadelphia: Temple University Press, 1983), 96–97.

28. Postel, *The Populist Vision.*

29. Ray Morris, *Railroad Administration* (New York: D. Appleton, 1910), 202–203, 210; Alan R. Raucher, *Public Relations and Business, 1900–1929* (Baltimore: Johns Hopkins University Press, 1968), 39–40. Workers may have behaved rudely toward customers because they no longer needed to prove their individual character to generate business, because they did not know proper etiquette, or what may be more likely, because they enjoyed being occasionally spiteful to their economic superiors who had long looked down their noses at them and were now powerless to do anything about it.

30. Howard Elliot, *The Truth about the Railroads* (New York: Houghton Mifflin, 1913), xii.

31. Hamilton W. Mabie to William McAdoo, April 7, 1909, Box 12, McAdoo Scrapbook, Vol. 1, William Gibbs McAdoo Papers, Huntington Library, San Marino, California; hereafter McAdoo Papers.

32. Richard Hofstadter, *The Age of Reform: From Bryan to F.D.R.* (New York: Vintage Books, 1955), 131–173.

33. Norbert Elias, *The Civilizing Process: The Development of Manners: Changes in the Code of Conduct and Feelings in Early Modern Times,* translated by Edmund Jephcott (New York: Urizen Books, 1978).

34. Richard L. Bushman, *The Refinement of America: Persons, Houses, Cities* (New York: Vintage Books, 1992).

35. John F. Kasson, *Rudeness and Civility: Manners in Nineteenth-Century Urban America* (New York: Hill and Wang, 1990), 157, 93, 6, 141.

36. Stanley Coben, *Rebellion against Victorianism: The Impetus for Cultural Change in 1920s America* (New York: Oxford University Press, 1991).

37. Richard L. Bushman, "The Genteel Republic," *Wilson Quarterly* 20, no. 4 (Autumn 1996): 14–23; Thorstein Veblen, *Theory of the Leisure Class: An Economic Study of Institutions* (New York: Macmillan, [1899] 1912); Sven Beckert, *The Monied Metropolis: New York City and the Consolidation of the American Bourgeoisie, 1850–1896* (New York: Cambridge University Press, 2001), 1.

38. Elias, *The Civilizing Process*; Peter N. Stearns with Carol Z. Stearns, "Emotionology: Clarifying the History of Emotions and Emotional Standards," *American Historical Review* 90 (October 1985): 813–836; Anne Schmidt and Christoph Conrad, "The Role of Emotions in the Production of Capitalist Subjects: An Introduction," in *Bodies and Affects in Market Societies,* ed. Anne Schmidt and Christoph Conrad (Tübingen, Germany: Mohr Siebeck, 2016), 1–22.

39. Paula S. Fass, *The Damned and the Beautiful: American Youth in the 1920's* (New York: Oxford University Press, 1977); Coben, *Rebellion against Victorianism*; Frederick Lewis Allen, *Only Yesterday: An Informal History of the Nineteen-Twenties* (New York: Harper & Row, 1931); Daniel T. Rodgers, *The Work Ethic in Industrial America, 1850–1920* (Chicago: University of Chicago Press, 1978), 27; Lendol G. Calder, *Financing the American Dream: A Cultural History of Credit* (Princeton, NJ: Princeton University Press, 1999).

40. Carol Z. Stearns and Peter N. Stearns, *Anger: The Struggle for Emotional Control in America's History* (Chicago: University of Chicago Press, 1986), 11, 39, 69, 110.

252 *Notes to Pages 12–18*

41. Kasson, *Rudeness and Civility*, 157, 93, 6, 141.

42. See the writings of Louisa May Alcott, for example, though William Dean Howells also shows that fitting in socially also mattered. William Dean Howells, *The Rise of Silas Lapham* (New York: Houghton, Mifflin, 1884).

43. "New Edison Building Beautiful and Modern," *Edison Current Topics*, January 1919, 4, Box 308, Folder 7, SCE Records.

44. Architectural historian Louise A. Mozingo is one exception to this. She has focused on suburban corporate campuses and estates rather than skyscrapers. Louise A. Mozingo, *Pastoral Capitalism: A History of Suburban Corporate Landscapes* (Cambridge, MA: MIT Press, 2011).

45. D. C. Thomas, "New Type Business Office Has No Counters," *Southern Telephone News*, January 1929, 9-10, AT&T-TX; Robert J. Donovan and John R. Rossiter, "Store Atmosphere: An Environmental Psychology Approach," *Journal of Retailing* 58, no. 1 (1982): 39; Albert Mehrabian, *Public Spaces and Private Spaces: The Psychology of Work, Play and Living Environments* (New York: Basic Books, 1976), 19, 287, 289, 293.

46. See the personal accounts of *Wall Street Journal* publisher Clarence W. Barron in *They Told Barron* and *More They Told Barron*, edited by Arthur Pound and Samuel Taylor Moore (New York: Harper & Brothers, 1930 and 1931, respectively). See also Richard White, "Information, Markets, and Corruption: Transcontinental Railroads in the Gilded Age," *Journal of American History* 90, no. 1 (June 2003): 19–43.

47. Examination of Robert M. Hofer, manager, E. Hofer & Sons, in *Letter from the Chairman of the Federal Trade Commission Transmitting in Response to Senate Resolution No. 83 a Monthly Report on the Electric Power and Gas Utilities Inquiry, No. 7, Filed with the Secretary of the Senate, October 15, 1928* (Washington, DC: Government Printing Office, 1928), 245; hereafter *FTC Letter No. 7* (1928); similar citations will be similarly abbreviated.

48. Examination of J.M. Hamilton in *Official Report of the Proceedings before the Federal Communications Commission at Washington, D. C., June 4, 1936*, 2202-2206, Box 3, Vol. 17, Record Group 173, "Records of the Federal Communications Commission," National Archives, College Park, Maryland (hereafter FCC Records); J.A. Callahan, Manager, Warner Bros. Theatres, Capital Theatre, Danbury, CT, to T.H. Tuohy, Manager, S.N.E. Telephone Co., Danbury, CT, January 12, 1933, in J. M. Hamilton, *Annual Report of Motion Picture Activities, 1932* (AT&T, Feb. 1, 1933), Box 17, Ex. 220, FCC Records.

49. Elihu Katz and Paul F. Lazarsfeld, *Personal Influence: The Part Played by People in the Flow of Mass Communications* (Glencoe, IL: Free Press, 1955), 32–33, 138.

50. Katz and Lazarsfeld, *Personal Influence*, 138, 222.

Chapter 1 • *Courteous Capitalism Begins*

1. "Address of Mr. W. G. McAdoo, President, to the Train Employees of the Hudson & Manhattan Railroad Company, at Hoboken Station, New Jersey, February 21, 1908," 4, Box 12, Vol. 1, McAdoo Papers.

2. Paul E. Johnson, *A Shopkeeper's Millennium: Society and Revivals in Rochester, New York, 1815-1837* (New York: Hill and Wang, 1978), 38–60; William Cordes, "Keep in Touch with John and Jim," in *Handling Men: Selecting and Hiring, How to Hold*

Notes to Pages 19–23   253

Your Men, Breaking In and Developing Men, Putting More Than Money in Pay Envelopes, ed. Edward Butler, Frank Disston, James A. Farrel, and John Wanamaker (Chicago: A. W. Shaw, 1917), 108–111.

3. William G. McAdoo, "The Relations between Public Service Corporations and the Public," lecture delivered before the Graduate School of Business Administration of Harvard University, April 6, 1910 (New York: Alexander Hamilton Institute, 1910), 19, 21.

4. McAdoo's subway received immense ridership from commuters traveling from New Jersey to Manhattan and back. "Opening of the Hudson and Manhattan Railroad's Tunnels," *Wall Street Journal,* February 18, 1908, Box 12, Vol. 1, McAdoo Papers.

5. John Morton Blum, *Woodrow Wilson and the Politics of Morality* (Boston: Little, Brown, 1956), 43–45, 49–50.

6. Isaac F. Marcosson, "A Curb on Corporation Abuses," *Saturday Evening Post,* January 11, 1908, 4.

7. W. A. Rogers, "Interborough Rattled Transit," *New York Herald,* March 24, 1905.

8. Marcosson, "A Curb on Corporation Abuses," 12.

9. Burton J. Hendrick, *The Age of Big Business: A Chronicle of the Captains of Industry* (New Haven, CT: Yale University Press, 1919), 146–147.

10. Ray Morris, *Railroad Administration* (New York: D. Appleton, 1910), 222.

11. Lincoln Steffens, *Shame of the Cities* (New York: Hill & Want, 1960), 27–37.

12. Sidney I. Roberts, "Portrait of a Robber Baron: Charles T. Yerkes," *Business History Review* 35, no. 3 (Autumn 1961): 352.

13. John A. Fairlie, "The Street Railway Question in Chicago," *Quarterly Journal of Economics* 21, no. 3 (May 1907): 384.

14. "A Section of Hades in Los Angeles" (clipping from unidentified newspaper), E. L. Stephens Scrapbook, Los Angeles Railway Records, Huntington Library, San Marino, California.

15. Jon C. Teaford, *The Unheralded Triumph: City Government in America, 1870–1900* (Baltimore: Johns Hopkins University Press, 1984), 237.

16. "Address of Mr. W. G. McAdoo," 4; McAdoo's first recorded use of the phrase "public be pleased" occurred five months after his February 1908 speech, in July 1908, when he opened his second tunnel. William G. McAdoo, *Crowded Years: The Reminiscences of William G. McAdoo* (New York: Houghton Mifflin, 1931), 105.

17. "Vanderbilt in the West: The Railroad Millionaire Expresses Himself Freely," *Chicago Daily Tribune,* October 9, 1882, 8; "Vanderbilt in the West: The Railroad Millionaire Expresses Himself Freely," *New York Times,* October 9, 1882, 1; "A Talk with Vanderbilt: The Railroad Magnate Freely Unbosoms," *San Francisco Chronicle,* October 9, 1882, 3; "The Vanderbilt Interview," *New York Times,* October 13, 1882, 5"; "'The Public Be Damned,'" *International Railway Journal,* April 1922, 12; Richard S. Tedlow, *Keeping the Corporate Image: Public Relations and Business, 1900–1950* (Greenwich, CT: JAI Press, 1979), 5.

18. Nella Braddy Henney, *The Book of Business Etiquette* (New York: Doubleday, 1922), 17.

19. McAdoo, *Crowded Years,* 104.

20. Hamilton W. Mabie to William McAdoo, April 7, 1909, Box 12, McAdoo Scrapbook, Vol. 1, McAdoo Papers.

21. "One Subway Best, Mayor's Board Finds," *New York Times,* December 29, 1910, 4.

254   *Notes to Pages 23–26*

22. McAdoo, *Crowded Years*.

23. S. C. Haver, "Uses of the Little Red Book," *Edison Current Topics*, June 1912, 15–16, Box 308, Folder 1, SCE Records.

24. W. J. Phillips, Division Commercial Superintendent, "The Employee's Part in Public Relations," *Pacific Telephone Magazine*, November 1914, 6, AT&T-TX.

25. Prof. H. V. Bozell, "Legislation Affecting Public Utilities, Changes Brought about by Introduction of Commissions," *Public Service*, July 1913, 16.

26. *The North Chicago Street Railroad Company and Its Lines* (Chicago: North Chicago Street Railroad, 1889), 10, Newberry Library, Chicago. The North Chicago Street Railroad Company tried to argue that rude treatment was a thing of the past, precisely because it wasn't. A curious video of a streetcar in Berkeley, California, shows a conductor and others beating a man for standing in the tracks (c. 1906); see Library of Congress, "A Trip to Berkeley, Cal.," YouTube, July 28, 2010, video, 3:23, https://www.youtube.com/watch?v=wBslZUau0NE.

27. John A. Fairlie, "The Street Railway Question in Chicago," *Quarterly Journal of Economics* 21, no. 3 (May 1907): 378.

28. Josiah L. Lombard, *The Yerkes Bill: Answer of the Chicago Committee of One Hundred* (Chicago: [Chicago Committee of One Hundred], 1897), Newberry Library, Chicago; Steffens, *Shame of the Cities*, 34–37.

29. "A Blow at a Corrupt System," *San Francisco Chronicle*, March 29, 1879; "New Gas Company Threatened: If It Comes It Will Raise the Price of Light All Over the City," *San Francisco Chronicle*, May 20, 1909; "Spreckels Sells, and So Lighting War Is Ended," *San Francisco Chronicle*, July 2, 1903.

30. Henry Marison Byllesby, *The Responsibilities of Electrical Engineers in Making Appraisals, An Address Delivered before the Members of the American Institute of Electrical Engineers in Annual Convention, Hotel Sherman, Chicago, Illinois, June 27, 1911*, 3rd ed. (1911), 14–16; David E. Nye, *Electrifying America: Social Meanings of a New Technology, 1880–1940* (Cambridge, MA: MIT Press, 1990), 56.

31. NELA, *Political Ownership and the Electric Light and Power Industry (Published for the Information of Member Companies)* (1925), 91.

32. Bureau of the Census, US Department of Commerce, *Historical Statistics of the United States, 1789–1945* (Washington, DC: Government Printing Office, 1949), table: Series G 191–193—Power—Electricity Energy, Industrial Use: 1902–1945, 157.

33. John Coffee Hays, *Hydroelectric Power as Applied to Irrigation* (American Institute of Electric Engineers, 1910), 554–555, California State Archives, Sacramento, California; "Electricity Pays Its Bill Twice on New York Farms," *PG&E Progress*, August 1928, 3; "Efficiency and Comfort on California Farms," *California Cultivator*, September 9, 1922, 257.

34. Bureau of the Census, *Historical Statistics of the United States*, 157; "Electricity Pays Its Bill Twice on New York Farms"; "Efficiency and Comfort on California Farms."

35. Ruth Schwartz Cowan has argued that, ironically, in the long run, new ovens and cleaning appliances increased expectations for multi-dish meals instead of one-pot ones, and raised cleaning standards. Therefore, these electrical devices and appliances created "more work for mother." Ruth Schwartz Cowan, *More Work for Mother: The Ironies of Household Technology from the Open Hearth to the Microwave* (New York: Basic Books, 1983). Leah S. Glaser has argued that consumers of electrical products

Notes to Pages 27–29   255

knew how much efficiency in their daily life such devices would bring, and made their purchasing decision accordingly. Leah S. Glaser, *Electrifying the Rural American West: Stories of Power, People, and Place* (Lincoln: University of Nebraska Press, 2009), 67–68, 125. The present volume engages with these scholars by arguing that, at least initially, urban consumers saw some work-reducing value in their purchases.

36. Nye, *Electrifying America*, 139, 239.

37. Robert MacDougall, *The People's Network: The Political Economy of the Telephone in the Gilded Age* (Philadelphia: University of Pennsylvania Press, 2013), 195, 197.

38. AT&T *Annual Report, 1910*, 22.

39. Samuel Insull, "The Gas Industry's Biggest Task," speech before the Annual Convention of AGA, Chicago, November 11, 1921, 4, Folder 20-8, Insull Papers.

40. "A Memorable Speech on Public Relations," *Southern Telephone News,* January 1922, 3, AT&T-TX.

41. W. L. Willkie, General Counsel, Northern Ohio Power and Light Company, "At the Public's Service," *Proceedings of the American Electric Railway Association, 1929* (New York: AERA, 1929), 18–21, hereafter *AERA Proceedings, 1929*; similar citations will be similarly abbreviated.

42. AT&T, *Annual Report, 1910*, 22.

43. N. C. Kingsbury, *Publicity: A Paper Presented May 7, 1912, before the Philadelphia Telephone Society*, Folder: Publicity, Box 1, RG 6: Publications, 1893–1912, Collection 6, AT&T-TX.

44. Nye, *Electrifying America*, 261.

45. William P. Banning, "Advertising Technique and Copy Appeal," presented at a Bell System Publicity Conference, 1921, 4, File: Publicity Folder, 1916–1929, Box 56: Presidential Office Files, RG 5, Collection 3, AT&T-TX.

46. Samuel M. Kennedy, *Winning the Public*, 2nd ed. (New York: McGraw-Hill, 1921), 5.

47. Olin J. Clark, Acting District Traffic Chief, Flint, "Courtesy in One's Work Indicates Good Breeding and Refinement," *Mouthpiece* (Detroit, MI), March 1924, 13–14, AT&T-TX.

48. "Portland Chooses Courteous Operators," *Pacific Telephone Magazine,* March 1925, 25–26, AT&T-TX.

49. Samuel Insull, "Satisfy Your Customers," speech given at the banquet of H. M. Byllesby & Company and affiliated companies in Chicago on January 20, 1911, in *Central-Station Electric Service: Its Commercial Development and Economic Significance as Set Forth in the Public Addresses (1897–1914) of Samuel Insull* (Chicago: Privately printed, 1915), 179.

50. J. David Houser, "Employee-Customer Relations," AGA, *Twelfth Annual Convention, October 13–17, 1930* (New York: AGA, 1930), 737.

51. Charles Postel, *The Populists Vision* (Oxford: Oxford University Press, 2007); Frank Norris, *The Octopus: A Story of California* (New York: Doubleday, Page, 1901); Eustace Cullinan, *Some Questions about the Proposed California Water and Power Act Answered by Facts* (San Francisco: Greater California League), 10–11; NELA, *Electric Light and Power: Facts and Figures on the Development and Scope of the Industry in the United States, Prepared, as the Statistical Section of the N.E.L.A. Handbook, by the Association's Statistical Department, March, 1928* (New York, 1928), 21–31; Ohio Bell

256 Notes to Pages 29–32

Telephone Company, Plant Department, Main District, *Tentative Course for All Employees on Public Relations* (1936), 19, Box 16, Ex. 177, RG 173: Records of the Federal Communications Commission, National Archives, College Park, Maryland; hereafter FCC Records.

52. Nye, *Electrifying America*, 93, 303; MacDougall, *The People's Network*, 143, 147; Harry W. Laidler and H. S. Raushenbush, *Power Control* (New York: New Republic, 1928), 88–116, 169, 171–172; Alvin C. Reis, Member, Wisconsin Legislature, *Ontario Points Way to Cheap Electricity with an Introduction by Franklin Hichborn* (1928[?]), 4–5, Bancroft Library, University of California, Berkeley.

53. "To Improve the Telephone's Usefulness," *Pacific Gas and Electric Magazine* 1, no. 11 (April 1910): 474.

54. George E. Mowry, *The California Progressives* (Berkeley: University of California Press, 1951), 74, 83, 118, 278; William A. Myers, *Iron Men and Copper Wires: A Centennial History of the Southern California Edison Company* (Glendale, CA: Trans-Anglo Books, 1983), 147–148; "Assembly Passes Railroad Bill," *San Francisco Chronicle*, December 13, 1911.

55. "Keep Business Out of Politics, Says Wilson," *Public Service*, January 1911, 2.

56. "Editorial Comment: The True Thought of the People," *Stone & Webster Public Service Journal*, April 1921, 301.

57. Nye, *Electrifying America*, 261.

58. Walter Dean Burnham, "The Changing Shape of the American Political Universe," *American Political Science Review* 59, no. 1 (March 1965), 11.

59. R. A. Balzari, Westinghouse Electric and Manufacturing Company, "Courteous Service Clubs," *Service Suggestions*, no. 32 (March 1925), republished in "Report on Commercial Service and Relations with Customers Committee," *NELA Proceedings* (1925), 500.

60. "Address of Mr. Insull before the First Annual Meeting of the Co-Operative Council of the Public Service Company of Northern Illinois, Chicago, December 7, 1921," 19[?], Folder 20-8, Insull Papers.

61. William Graham Sumner, *What Social Classes Owe to Each Other* (New York: Cosimo Classics, [1883] 2007); Andrew Carnegie, *The Gospel of Wealth* (Cambridge, MA: Harvard University Press, [1889] 1962)

62. Alfred D. Chandler Jr., *The Visible Hand: The Managerial Revolution in American Business* (Cambridge, MA: Belknap Press of Harvard University Press, 1977).

63. *Manual of Organization and Policies: Middle West Utilities Company, 1927*, 19, Folder 54-2, Insull Papers.

64. Insull, "Satisfy Your Customers," 179.

65. H. L. Donaldson, Philadelphia Company and Affiliated Corporations, "Appendix A: Training for Better Public Contact," in *Public-Contact-Training Methods and Principles: Experiences of Member Companies Presented and Discussed at the Chicago Conference, September, 1929: A Report of the Industrial Relations Committee, Public Relations National Section* (1929), 7. This obscure source was bound together with other booklets as *Special Publications, 1929*, published by NELA and found in the University of California, Berkeley Library under call no. TK 1 N 24, 1929:3; hereafter *Public-Contact-Training Methods and Principles*.

Notes to Pages 32–34   257

66. Samuel Kennedy, "Transforming Public Opinion: An Address by Mr. Samuel M. Kennedy, Vice-President Southern California Edison Co., Los Angeles, California, before the Convention of Managers and Executives of the Management Division of Stone & Webster Inc., Held in Boston, October 10–18, 1921," 24, Box 389, Folder 26, SCE Records.

67. "Appendix O—Report of the Committee on Employee—Customer Contact," *Proceedings of the American Electric Railway Association, 1928* (New York: AERA, 1929), 231.

68. Paul C. Rawson, "Prize-Winning Article in Forbes Contest," *NELA Proceedings* (1924), 178.

69. David B. Sicilia, "Selling Power: Marketing and Monopoly at Boston Edison, 1886–1929" (PhD diss., Brandeis University, 1990), 448–449.

70. Balzari, "Courteous Service Clubs," 500.

71. John M. Mulvihill, "Popularizing Utility Companies," *Public Service*, December 1908, 171.

72. "Address of Mr. W. G. McAdoo," 4.

73. "Organizing Courtesy to Build Good Will," *Electrical World*, May 21, 1921, 1158.

74. Mulvihill, "Popularizing Utility Companies," 171.

75. William Hamilton Burquest, "Marking Courtesy an Asset," *Business: A Magazine for Office, Store, and Factory*, January 1912, 10.

76. Mulvihill, "Popularizing Utility Companies," 172.

77. "Courtesy to the Public," *Principles of Public Utility Management: Extracts from Public Addresses by Samuel Insull Compiled for the Information of Employees of the Companies under His Management*," Folder 22-7, Insull Papers. This address was given to the Chicago Central Station Institute on May 7, 1915.

78. Charles Heston Peirson, "From Every Man," *Edison Current Topics*, August 1919, 106, Box 308, Folder 7, SCE Records.

79. H. N. Sessions, Commercial Engineer, "Company Thrift," *Edison Current Topics*, February 1913, 18, Box 308, Folder 2, SCE Records.

80. B. C. Forbes, "Why Creed Puts Service above Money-Making: P.G. & E. President Says "'Business is Business' No Longer Reflects National Sentiment"—His Life is an Ideal Illustration of This Evolution," *Forbes Magazine*, 98, April 28, 1923, Box 440, Folder 8, SCE Records.

81. Katherine M. Schmitt, "Memoir of a Telephone Operator, 1930," in *Major Problems in the History of American Technology*, ed. Merritt Roe Smith and Gregory Clancey (New York: Houghton Mifflin, 1998), 240.

82. Frances Swenson quoted in Studs Terkel, *Working: People Talk about What They Do All Day and How They Feel about What They Do* (New York: New Press, 1974), 32–33. The recollection comes from the mid-1970s, but work and work experience are applicable to earlier times.

83. Quoted in MacDougall, *The People's Network*, 245. Italics in original quote.

84. Schmitt, "Memoir of a Telephone Operator," 240, 338.

85. Balzari, "Courteous Service Clubs," 500.

86. Kennedy, "Transforming Public Opinion," 42.

87. "Training for Better Public Contact—Its Necessity and Importance," *NELA Proceedings* (1928), Public Relations National Section, Tuesday, June 5, 1928, 281.

258 *Notes to Pages 34–37*

88. Kennedy, "Transforming Public Opinion," 9.

89. "The Era of Better Understanding," *Edison Current Topics*, January 1917, 119, Box 308, Folder 6, SCE Records.

90. Kennedy, *Winning the Public*, 106.

91. Italics in original. Verne Ray, "Public Relations Committees and the Pink Ticket Plan," in *Conference of Personnel Group, Bell System, April 18–25, 1922*, 2, Box 88, RG 4, Collection 6, AT&T-TX.

92. McAdoo, "The Relations between Public Service Corporations and the Public," 18–19.

93. Karen Halttunen, *Confidence Men, Painted Women: A Study of Middle-Class Culture in America, 1830–1870* (New Haven, CT: Yale University Press, 1982).

94. Halttunen, *Confidence Men, Painted Women*.

95. Mark H. Rose, *Cities of Light and Heat: Domesticating Gas and Electricity in Urban America* (University Park: Pennsylvania State University Press, 1995), 114–116; C. L. Campbell, Treasurer, Connecticut Light & Power Company, "Broadening the Accountant's Duties," *NELA Proceedings* (1926), 297; "Future Executives Get Diplomas," *Busy Buttons' Bulletin* [1], no. 3 (August 1928), Box 461, Folder 4, SCE Records. Some low-level employees did rise to a management role; see, for example, Rose, *Cities of Light and Heat*, 114–116.

96. Campbell, "Broadening the Accountant's Duties."

97. Edward F. Trefz, "Judgment, Enthusiasm, Obedience and Loyalty," *Edison Current Topics* 4, no. 9 (September 1915): 171, Box 308, Folder 4, SCE Records.

98. F. Scott Fitzgerald, *This Side of Paradise* (New York: Scribner, 1920), 170, 213.

99. Daniel T. Rodgers, *The Work Ethic in Industrial America, 1850–1920* (Chicago: University of Chicago Press, 1978), 24–27.

100. Ida. M. Tarbell, *All in the Day's Work: An Autobiography* (New York: Macmillan, 1939), 283.

101. Hon. Frank West Rollins, "The Value of a Smile Transmuted Into Dollars," *Edison Current Topics*, February 1913, 3, Box 308, Folder 2, SCE Records.

102. Rollins, "The Value of a Smile," 5.

103. Lois Holloway, Operator, "Courtesy Counts," *Southern Telephone News*, January 1922, 12, AT&T-TX.

104. Kennedy, *Winning the Public*, 20.

105. J. B. McClary, "Establishing Friendly Relations," *Public Service*, January 1909, 5.

106. "Training for Better Public Contact—Its Necessity and Importance," 281; Susan Porter Benson, "'The Clerking Sisterhood': Saleswomen's Work Culture," in *Counter Cultures: Saleswomen, Managers, and Customers in American Department Stores, 1890–1940* (Champaign: University of Illinois Press, 1988), 232.

107. SCE, *Rules and Instructions for Substation Operators in Los Angeles District* (1913), 5, Box 472, Folder 7, SCE Records; SCE, *Annual Report to the Stockholders of Southern California Edison Company Ltd. For the Year 1949*, 18, Box 11, Folder 4, SCE Records; SCE, *You and Your Company: A Handbook for Employees*, 13, 1953, Box 88, Folder 2, SCE Records; "B1.21—New Edison Building," Call No. 02 17319, Southern California Edison Photographs and Negatives, Huntington Library, San Marino, California; hereafter SCEPN.

108. "Training for Better Public Contact—Its Necessity and Importance," 281.

Notes to Pages 37–40   259

109. "Kennedy, "Transforming Public Opinion," 9.

110. *Public-Contact-Training Methods and Principles*, 3.

111. H. R. Halsey and J. David Houser & Associates, "Good and Bad Customer Relations Practices," in AGA, *Twelfth Annual Convention*, 1876.

112. "Errors Checked, Manners Improved," *The Peoples Gas Light & Coke Company Year Book, 1926*, 21, Folder 54-13, Insull Papers; hereafter Peoples Gas, *Year Book, 1926*; similar citations will be similarly abbreviated. Kennedy, *Winning the Public*, 18.

113. Halsey, "Good and Bad Customer Relations Practices," 1876.

114. Italics in original. Wm. A. Durgin, Commonwealth Edison Company, Chicago, "Appendix C (Continued): Public-Contact Training and Measurement of Results by Service Sampling," in *Public-Contact-Training Methods and Principles*, 18.

115. "Relations to Consumers Discussed by Neelands," *Edison Current Topics*, May 1915, 92–93, Box 308, Folder 4, SCE Records.

116. MacDougall, *The People's Network*, 239.

117. Sicilia, "Selling Power," 465.

118. Lucien Kellogg, "'Visitors are Welcome': How a Western Utility Brings Together Four Factors in Its Sales-and-Service Plan," *Business*, May 1925, 23, Box 440, Folder 8, SCE Records.

119. Peoples Gas, *Year Book, 1923*, 28; "New Class In Psychology," *Pacific Electric Magazine*, April 10, 1929, 12; Sicilia, "Selling Power," 529.

120. "Relations to Consumers Discussed by Neelands," 92.

121. Peoples Gas, *Year Book, 1928*, 23; Halsey, "Good and Bad Customer Relations Practices," 1876–1877.

122. "Appendix O," 229–230.

123. Kennedy, "Transforming Public Opinion," 9.

124. Halsey, "Good and Bad Customer Relations Practices," 1876.

125. "Opening of Conference: Talk by E. K. Hall," in *Bell System Educational Conference, 195 Broadway, New York City, August 18–23, 1924*, 8–9, Box 88, RG 4, Collection 6, AT&T-TX; "Public Relations and Publicity: A Reading Assignment," 2nd ed., in *Employees General Training Course: The Pacific Telephone and Telegraph Company, 1927*, 11, Collection 3, RG 5, Box 3, File: Public Relations and Publicity, AT&T-TX.

126. Miss Rose G. Stone, Editor, *Ohio Oil & Gas Men's Journal*, "The Part Every Utility Employee Plays in Rendering Utility Service," in AGA, *Tenth Annual Convention, October 8–12, 1928* (New York: AGA, 1930), 168.

127. "Appendix O," 233, 231.

128. "Address of Mr. W. G. McAdoo," 4; Butchuk2007, "Re: Pacific Electric Training Film—1914," YouTube, May 16, 2008, video, 2:16, http://www.youtube.com/watch?v=iCTyMo8vak4; Donaldson, "Appendix A," 10.

129. "Training for Better Public Contact—III, *NELA Proceedings* (1929), 1541; S. M. Kennedy, Vice President, SCE, *A Pleasing Personality*, 3, Box 449, Folder 5, SCE Records.

130. B. J. Bowen, General Superintendent of Traffic, New England Telephone and Telegraph Company, "Personal Service Committees," in *Conference of Personnel Group, Bell System, April 18–25, 1922*, 7, Box 88, RG 4, Collection 6, AT&T-TX; Burquest, "Marking Courtesy an Asset," 11; Labert St. Clair, "Getting the Public Eye and Ear," *American Gas Association Monthly*, January 1922, 30.

260 *Notes to Pages 40–44*

131. "No Stock Quotas," *Busy Buttons' Bulletin* 1, no. 1 (February 1928), Box 461, Folder 4, SCE Records.

132. *Public-Contact-Training Methods and Principles*, 3.

133. "The Speech-Weaver's School," *Pacific Telephone Magazine*, December 1916, 11, AT&T-TX.

134. W. H. Hamilton, discussion about S. M. Kennedy's pamphlet "Service," Second General Session, May 20, 1920, *NELA Proceedings* (1920), 57.

135. Cromwell Childe, "The Customer," *Public Service*, April 1912, 134.

136. Houser, "Employee-Customer Relations," 736.

137. Stephen H. Norwood, *Labor's Flaming Youth: Telephone Operators and Worker Militancy, 1878–1923* (Urbana: University of Illinois Press, 1990), 43; "The Speech-Weaver's School," 10.

138. "The Speech-Weaver's School," 10.

139. M. B. French, Traffic Engineer, "Review of Bell System Traffic Operations, 1930," in *Operating Papers Conference—Absecon, New Jersey, Year 1931*," 4, File: Conference, 1926, 1931, Box 10, RG 5, Collection 3, AT&T-TX; "Opening of Conference: Talk by E. K. Hall," in *Bell System Educational Conference, 195 Broadway, New York City, August 18–23, 1924*, 8, Box 88, RG 4, Collection 6, AT&T-TX.

140. The Dartnell Corporation, Chicago, *Special Investigation: Training Clerical Employees, Report No. 578*, n.d., Box 7, Folder 3, Alfred W. Uhrich Papers, Huntington Library, San Marino, California, 13.

141. Kennedy, "Transforming Public Opinion," 18–19, 32; Kennedy, *Winning the Public*, 7; "Training for Better Public Contact—III," *NELA Proceedings* (1929), 1541.

142. "Address of Mr. W. G. McAdoo," 4.

143. "The Counter," *Pacific Telephone Magazine*, February 1920, 3, AT&T-TX.

144. *Public-Contact-Training Methods and Principles*, 1.

145. "Among the Employees," *Public Service Company of Northern Illinois Year Book 1929*, 24, Box 55, Folder 8, Insull Papers.

146. S. M. Kennedy, Vice President, SCE, *A Pleasing Personality*, 3, Box 449, Folder 5, SCE Records.

147. Kennedy, "Transforming Public Opinion," 44.

148. "Training For Better Public Contact—III," *NELA Proceedings* (1929), 1539.

149. Kennedy, *Winning the Public*, 7.

150. Sarah Eisenstein, *Give Us Bread but Give Us Roses: Working Women's Consciousness in the United States, 1890 to the First World War* (Boston: Routledge & Kegan Paul, 1983), 108–109.

151. McAdoo, "The Relations between Public Service Corporations and the Public," 19.

152. Henney, *The Book of Business Etiquette*, 280.

153. Clark, "Courtesy in One's Work," 13.

154. Edward H. Mulligan, "Courteous Service," *Edison Current Topics* 4, no. 7 (July 1915): 128, Box 308, Folder 4, SCE Records; Norbert Elias, *The Civilizing Process: The Development of Manners: Changes in the Code of Conduct and Feelings in Early Modern Times*, trans. Edmund Jephcott (New York: Urizen Books, 1978).

155. Bell System, "Training for Service," 1926, AT&T Tech Channel, video, http://techchannel.att.com/play-video.cfm/2013/7/3/AT&T-Archives-Training-For-Service.

Notes to Pages 44–47   261

156. W. J. O'Connor, "The Why and How of Personnel Work in the Bell System," in *Conference of Personnel Group, Bell System, April 18–25, 1922*, 12, Box 88, RG 4, Collection 6, AT&T-TX.

157. "Commercial Department, No. 3 of a Series, September 1, 1954," Box 470, Folder 6, SCE Records.

158. Ralph L. Mahon, "The Telephone in Chicago, 1877–1940," typescript, 146, AT&T-TX.

159. Venus Green, *Race on the Line: Gender, Labor, and Technology in the Bell System, 1880–1980* (Durham, NC: Duke University Press, 2001), 210, 217.

160. "The Speech-Weaver's School," 10.

161. Hamilton, discussion about S. M. Kennedy's pamphlet, 58.

162. "The Speech-Weaver's School," 10.

163. "Medical Record" (form) in A. M. Boyd, "Judging and Adjusting the Office Worker," in "Report of Committee on Office Personnel," AGA, *Twelfth Annual Convention*, insert between pp. 1856 and 1857.

164. "Boyd, "Judging and Adjusting the Office Worker," 1836, 1857.

165. Public Speaking Committee, Public Relations National Section, *Serial Report* (New York: NELA, May 1929), 2.

166. J. E. Dozier, General Manager, Nahant & Lynn Street Railway Co., Lynn, MA, "Complaint Superintendents," *AERA*, February 1914, 716.

167. "Report of Bell System Commercial Operations, 1930, Compiled by the Commercial Engineer, American Telephone and Telegraph Company," in *Operating Papers Conference—Absecon, New Jersey, Year 1931*, 7, File: Conference, 1926, 1931, Box 10: Company Leaders, Presidential Office Files, Complaints of Service—Northern California Conferences, RG 5, Collection 3, AT&T-TX; Phillips, "The Employee's Part in Public Relations," 5; "The Work of the Commercial Department: Part I: A Reading Assignment," in *Employees General Training Course*, 4; "Report of Committee on Commercial Service and Relations with Customers," *NELA Proceedings* (1920), 254.

168. Peoples Gas, *Year Book, 1929*, 24.

169. "Organization Diagram," October 1913, Box 470, Folder 6, SCE Records.

170. *Commerce Journal* 4, no. 1 (August 1923): 5–8, Box 470, Folder 6, SCE Records. Although this organizational chart is from 1923, Kennedy referred to himself by this title in speeches and in his book *Winning the Public* as early as 1921.

171. PG&E, *Outstanding Features of Pacific Service* (San Francisco, 1924), 5, Box 440, Folder 8, SCE Records.

172. "Training for Better Public Contact—Its Necessity and Importance," 281.

173. Paul A. Walker, *Proposed Report, Telephone Investigation (Pursuant to Public Resolution No. 8, 74th Congress)* (Washington, DC: Government Printing Office, 1938), 563.

174. *Statistical Supplement to the 'Electric Light and Power Industry in the United States': Prepared, as the Statistical Section of the N. E. L. A. Handbook, by the Statistical Research Department of the Association, Revised to January 1, 1929: Supplement to the N.E.L.A. Publication 289-14* (1929), 3.

175. Peoples Gas, *Year Book, 1928*, 23.

176. AT&T, *Annual Report, 1934*, 25; Claude S. Fischer, *America Calling: A Social History of the Telephone to 1940* (Berkeley: University of California Press, 1992), 44;

Nye, *Electrifying America*, 261; R. T. Duncan, "Report of Customer Relations Committee," *NELA Proceedings* (1927), Commercial National Session, 408.

177. "Report of Bell System Commercial Operations, 1930," 7; AT&T, *Annual Report, 1928*, 6.

178. "Service to Our Customers," Peoples Gas, *Year Book, 1927*, 15; "Customer Satisfaction as an Asset in Public Utility Business," Peoples Gas, *Year Book, 1926*, 20. Peoples Gas, *Year Book, 1927*, 15; "Customer Satisfaction as an Asset in Public Utility Business," 20.

179. "Customer Satisfaction as an Asset in Public Utility Business," 20.

180. "Training for Better Public Contact—Its Necessity and Importance," 282; R. H. Burcher, Assistant Vice President, AT&T, "Operating Objectives of the Bell System and How and Where Personnel and Public Relations Activities Can Help Attain Them," in *Conference of Personnel Group, Bell System, April 18–25, 1922*, 21, Box 88, RG 4, Collection 6, AT&T-TX.

181. "Relations with Customers," Peoples Gas, *Year Book, 1924*, 25.

182. Peoples Gas, *Year Book, 1927*, 15.

183. Floyd W. Parsons, "You and the Public Utilities: The Part They Play in the Everyday Life of Every Citizen," *The World's Work*, May 1922, 100, 104.

184. In 1927 there were 22 billion telephone conversations compared to 15 billion letters sent through the mail. This brought telephone companies, via switchboard operators, into more personal contact with customers than the post office, though not face-to-face. M. S. Sloan, President of the Brooklyn Edison Company, *A Problem of Human Nature (1925)*, 6, Box 449, Folder 6, SCE Records; Rocky Mountain Committee on Public Utility Information, "Public Utility Service, 1927, The Telephone, Its History and Methods of Operation: For Use of School Students, English and Current Topics Classes, and Debating Clubs," 10, Box 485, Folder 1, SCE Records.

185. Balzari, "Courteous Service Clubs," 500.

186. Balzari, "Courteous Service Clubs," 500.

187. "Co-Operation—'Say It With Action,'" *Bell Telephone News* (Chicago) February 1924, 5, AT&T-TX

188. Clark, "Courtesy in One's Work," 13–14.

189. C. Y. Ferguson, "How to Get the Best Results from Workmen," *Pacific Gas and Electric Magazine* 1, no. 9 (February 1910): 389.

190. Quoted by Richard Gillespie, *Manufacturing Knowledge: A History of the Hawthorne Experiments* (Cambridge: Cambridge University Press, 1991), 27.

191. William A. Prendergast, Chairman, Public Service Commission of the State of New York, "Regulative Problems," AGA, *Tenth Annual Convention*, 121–122.

192. Green, *Race on the Line*, 270.

193. A few cities retained the right to set rates. Charles David Jacobson, *Ties That Bind: Economic and Political Dilemmas of Urban Utility Networks, 1800–1990* (Pittsburgh: University of Pittsburgh Press, 2000), 100.

194. Richard R. John, *Network Nation: Inventing American Telecommunications* (Cambridge, MA: Belknap Press of Harvard University Press, 2010), 359–363; MacDougall, *The People's Network*, 217.

195. Richard F. Hirsh, *Power Loss: The Origins of Deregulation and Restructuring in the American Electric Utility System* (Cambridge, MA: MIT Press, 1999), 23; John,

Notes to Pages 50–56   263

Network Nation, 343–344; Robert Britt Horwitz, *The Irony of Regulatory Reform: The Deregulation of American Telecommunications* (New York: Oxford University Press, 1989), 11, 101.

196. Examination of John B. Sheridan, Secretary, Missouri Committee on Public Utility Information, in *FTC Letter No. 5* (1928), 48; Examination of Eugene S. Wilson in *Official Report of the Proceedings before the Federal Communications Commission at Washington, D.C., January 26, 1937*, 5338–5345, Box 5, Vol. 39, FCC Records; hereafter Wilson in *Proceedings before the FCC, January 26, 1937*; similar citations will be similarly abbreviated.

197. Floyd W. Parsons, "You and the Public Utilities: The Part They Play in the Everyday Life of Every Citizen," *World's Work*, May 1922, 99.

198. William A. Prendergast, Chairman, Public Service Commission of the State of New York, "Regulative Problems," AGA, *Tenth Annual Convention*, 122.

199. "Public Relations and Publicity: A Reading Assignment," 5.

200. Kennedy, *Winning the Public*, 123.

201. "Draft of Address Written by John Sheridan for J. F. Hull's Speech to the Missouri Public Utilities Association on May 4, 1922, Ex. 2744, Box 3851, Series: Economic Investigations Files, 1915–1938, Subject: Power and Gas, FTC Records.

202. Wilson in *Proceedings before the FCC, June 4, 1936*, 2033. Wilson was referring to the early 1920s.

203. Max Weber, *The Theory of Social and Economic Organization*, trans. A. M. Henderson and Talcott Parsons (Glencoe, IL: Free Press, 1947), 339–341, 337, 373, 204–205. The book was first published in German in 1920.

204. Robert H. Wiebe, *The Search for Order, 1877–1920* (New York: Hill and Wang, 1967), 148; Samuel P. Hays, *The Response to Industrialism, 1885–1914*, 2nd ed. (Chicago: University of Chicago Press, 1957).

205. Sloan, *A Problem of Human Nature*, 7–8.

206. P. H. Gadsden, "The Committee Chairman's Viewpoint," *NELA Proceedings* (1924), 155.

Chapter 2 • *Courteous Capitalism Intensifies*

1. Wm. A. Durgin, Commonwealth Edison Company, Chicago, "Appendix C (Continued): Public-Contact Training and Measurement of Results by Service Sampling," in *Public-Contact-Training Methods and Principles*, 18. This obscure source was bound together with other booklets as *Special Publications, 1929*, published by the National Electric Light Association and found in the University of California, Berkeley, library under call no.: TK 1 N 24, 1929:3.

2. Byron F. Field, "Appendix C: Public-Contact Training," in *Public-Contact-Training Methods and Principles*, 15.

3. Durgin, "Appendix C (Continued)," 18–19.

4. Field, "Appendix C," 16.

5. D. C. Thomas, "New Type Business Office Has No Counters," *Southern Telephone News*, January 1929, 9, AT&T-TX.

6. "Report of Bell System Commercial Operations, 1930," 15, File: Conference, 1926, 1931, Box 10: Company Leaders, Presidential Office Files, Complaints of Service—Northern California Conferences, RG 5: PT&T, Collection 3, AT&T-TX.

7. "Appendix O—Report of the Committee on Employee—Customer Contact," *AERA Proceedings, 1928*, 226.

8. "Let Us Talk It Over—and Be Fair About It," *Public Service*, December 1915, 164.

9. David B. Sicilia, "Selling Power: Marketing and Monopoly at Boston Edison, 1886–1929" (PhD diss., Brandeis University, 1990), 435–436.

10. John M. Mulvihill, "Popularizing Utility Companies," *Public Service*, December 1908, 172.

11. Samuel Kennedy, "Transforming Public Opinion: An Address by Mr. Samuel M. Kennedy, Vice-President Southern California Edison Co., Los Angeles, California, before the Convention of Managers and Executives of the Management Division of Stone & Webster Inc., Held in Boston, October 10–18, 1921," 24–25, Box 389, Folder 26, SCE Records; Sicilia, "Selling Power," 526.

12. Kennedy, "Transforming Public Opinion," 29–30.

13. "Chart I," *Commerce Journal* 4, no. 1 (August 1923): 5, Box 470, Folder 6, SCE Records.

14. Kennedy, "Transforming Public Opinion," 44.

15. Sicilia, "Selling Power," 526.

16. W. R. McGovern, General Manager, Wisconsin Telephone Company, to E. S. Wilson, Vice President, AT&T, July 27, 1920, Ex. 142, Box 15, Series: Special Investigations of the Bell System, FCC Records.

17. "Mrs. Crete Herlihy, "Subscribers' Instruction," in *Fifth Annual Chief Operators Conference, Los Angeles, February 15th, 1929*, 56, File: Conference, 1926, 1931, Box 10: Company Leaders, Presidential Office Files, Complaints of Service—Northern California Conferences, RG 5, Collection 3, AT&T-TX.

18. Herlihy, "Subscribers' Instruction," 55–56.

19. Herlihy, "Subscribers' Instruction," 57.

20. "Errors Checked, Manner Improved," Peoples Gas, *Year Book, 1926*, 21.

21. *Public-Contact-Training Methods and Principles*, 4.

22. *Training for Better Public Contact—Measurement of Results Obtained by a Public Contact Training Program: Serial Report of the Industrial Relations Committee 1928–1929, Public Relations National Section, July 1929* (New York: National Electric Light Association, 1929), 2.

23. Southwest Bell Telephone and Telegraph Companies, "7-a. Forecasts and Actual Results as to Certain Customer Relations Activities," in *Response to Federal Communications Commission's Inquiry Dated December 11, 1936, Relative to Certain Advertising, Publicity and Information Activities for the Years 1926 to 1936, Inclusive*, Box 41, Ex. 1355, FCC Records.

24. Northwestern Bell Telephone Company, "Item 7a: 1926 Commercial Program," in *Information Relating to Publicity and Advertising Supplied in Accordance with Federal Communications Commission's Letter of Dec. 11, 1936, to A.T.&T. Co.*, January 7, 1937, Box 41, Ex. 1354, FCC Records.

25. Sanford M. Jacoby, "Employee Attitude Testing at Sears, Roebuck and Company, 1938–1960," *Business History Review* 60, no. 4 (Winter 1986): 605–606.

26. J. David Houser & Associates, "Employee-Customer Relations," *American Gas Association, Twelfth Annual Convention, October 13–17, 1930* (New York: AGA, 1930), 736.

Notes to Pages 59–63   265

27. Houser, "Employee-Customer Relations," 736–737.

28. Durgin, "Appendix C (Continued)," 19.

29. "Report of Bell System Commercial Operations, 1930," 15. Bell set a very high bar for what constituted a defect-free interaction. In some cases, operators may not have used the exact right phrase, but customers may not have noticed.

30. Durgin, "Appendix C (Continued)," 17.

31. Edward F. Trefz, "Judgment, Enthusiasm, Obedience and Loyalty," *Edison Current Topics*, September 1915, Box 308, Folder 4, SCE Records.

32. Paul Lüpke, "Expanded Loyalty," *NELA Proceedings* (1912), Seattle, Washington, June 10–13, 1912 (New York: James Kempster Printing, 1912), 1:179–180.

33. Charles Heston Peirson, "Duty," *Edison Current Topics*, May 1917, 99, Box 308, Folder 6, SCE Records.

34. "The Business of Winning the War," *Edison Current Topics*, December 1917, 239, Box 308, Folder 6, SCE Records.

35. Lüpke, "Expanded Loyalty," 180.

36. John F. Kasson, *Rudeness & Civility: Manners in Nineteenth-Century Urban America* (New York: Hill and Wang, 1990), 141.

37. Angel Kwolek-Folland, *Engendering Business: Men and Women in the Corporate Office, 1870–1930* (Baltimore: Johns Hopkins University Press, 1994), 188–189.

38. Katherine M. Schmitt, "Memoir of a Telephone Operator, 1930," in *Major Problems in the History of American Technology*, ed. Merritt Roe Smith and Gregory Clancey (New York: Houghton Mifflin, 1998), 240.

39. "Electricity May Prevent Lines in Face Which Paris Hats and Cosmetics Are Bought to Cure—Says Helen E. Steiner," *Public Service Management*, March 1927, 85.

40. Mary E. Dillon, Manager, Brooklyn Borough Gas Company, "Humanizing a Gas Company," *Gas Industry* 24, no. 12 (December 1924): 457.

41. Emily Post, "Etiquette in Business and Politics," in *Etiquette in Society, in Business, in Politics, and at Home* (New York: Funk & Wagnalls, 1922), 530–539.

42. The Pullman Company was the largest corporate employer of black men in the country in the 1920s. Jack Santino, *Miles of Smiles, Years of Struggle: Stories of Black Pullman Porters* (Urbana: University of Illinois Press, 1991), 8. These porters were required to be courteous. See the disciplinary records of porters for "discourtesy" and other offenses, for example: "Allen, Fred B.," RG 06: Employee and Labor Relations Department; Subgroup 02: Personnel Administration Department; Series 03: Employee Service Records, 1890–1969; Box 21: Conductors Out of Service prior to 1935, A-Fors; Pullman Company Archives, Newberry Library, Chicago. See also Evelyn Nakano Glenn, "From Servitude to Service Work: Historical Continuities in the Racial Division of Paid Reproductive Labor," *Signs* 18, no. 1 (August 1992): 1–43.

43. Eric Foner, *Free Soil, Free Labor, Free Men: The Ideology of the Republican Party before the Civil War* (1970).

44. Clark Davis, *Company Men: White Collar Life and Corporate Culture in Los Angeles, 1892–1941* (Baltimore: Johns Hopkins University Press, 2000), 227.

45. Edward H. Mulligan, "Courteous Service," *Edison Current Topics*, July 1915, 128, Box 308, Folder 4, SCE Records.

46. "The Era of Better Understanding," *Edison Current Topics*, January 1917, 119, Box 308, Folder 6, SCE Records.

47. "The Big Men," *Edison Current Topics*, February 1915, 22, Box 308, Folder 4, SCE Records; the poem was also published in *The Gleaner*, February 1914, 516; *Lumber World Review*, August 10, 1918, 35; *Railroad Men*, June 1914, 244; *Shop Review*, March 1914, 127; and *Technograph*, January 1918, 91.

48. H. N. Sessions, Commercial Engineer, "Company Thrift," *Edison Current Topics* 2, no. 10, February 1913, 18, Box 308, Folder 2, SCE Records.

49. "Criticism—Good and Bad," *Southern Telephone News*, March 1921, 1, AT&T-TX.

50. Proverbs 15:1; Kennedy, "Transforming Public Opinion," 25–27; *Pacific Electric Magazine*, August 10, 1916.

51. John A. Britton, "'Policy of Public Service Corporations: Address before San Francisco Section A. I. E. E.,' The American Institute of Electrical Engineering, Given Friday Feb. 27, 1914," *Pacific Service Magazine*, April 1914, 373–374.

52. Miss Margaret Lindley, "Training," in *Fifth Annual Chief Operators Conference, Los Angeles, February 15th, 1929*, 39, Collection 3: Pacific Telesis Group, RG 5, Box 10, AT&T-TX.

53. Matthew Josephson, *The Robber Barons: The Great American Capitalists, 1861–1901* (New York: Harcourt, Brace, 1934), 319–320, 374; Elizabeth A. Fones-Wolf, *Selling Free Enterprise: The Business Assault on Labor and Liberalism, 1945–1960* (Urbana: University of Illinois Press, 1994), 219; Frederick Lewis Allen, *The Big Change: America Transforms Itself 1900–1950* (New York: Bantam Books, 1952), 229.

54. Mulligan, "Courteous Service," 127–128. No employee that this author has found brought up the Bible's critique of the systemizing of the "souls of men" as brought up in Revelation 18:11–13.

55. Émile Durkheim, "What Is a Social Fact?," in *The Rules of the Sociological Method*, ed. Steven Lukes, trans. W. D. Halls (New York: Free Press, 1982), 50–59.

56. "Round Table on Customer Ownership Problems," *NELA Proceedings* (1924), 219; Samuel M. Kennedy, *Winning the Public*, 2nd ed. (New York: McGraw-Hill, 1921), 127; George A. Damon, Dean of Engineering, Throop Polytechnic Institute, Pasadena, California, "Public Regulation," *Edison Current Topics*, December 1912, 7, Box 308, Folder 1, SCE Records, 7; *Addresses, Papers, and Interviews by Walter S. Gifford*, vol. 1, "Address by Mr. W.S. Gifford, President American Telephone and Telegraph Company, at Philadelphia, October 27, 1926," (New York: AT&T, 1928), 180.

57. "The Land of Flowers," *Southern Telephone News*, February 1922, 1, AT&T-TX.

58. *Telephone People: Their Relationships and Activities: Reading Assignment: Employees' General Training Course*, PT&T, 1928, 4–5, Box 6, RG 5, Collection 3, AT&T-TX.

59. Kennedy, *Winning the Public*, 127.

60. "Address of M. H. Aylesworth," *National Association of Railway and Utilities Commissioners, Proceedings of the Thirty-Third Annual Convention, Atlanta Georgia, October 11–14, 1921* (New York: State Law Reporting, 1921), 323.

61. William G. McAdoo, "The Relations between Public Service Corporations and the Public," lecture delivered before the Graduate School of Business Administration of Harvard University, April 6, 1910 (New York: Alexander Hamilton Institute, 1910), 18–19.

62. *Telephone People*, 15.

Notes to Pages 65–67   267

63. R. T. Barrett, "The Changing Years as Seen from the Switchboard," *Bell Telephone Quarterly*, October 1935, 289. This was a retrospective article about changes in customer service over the years.

64. W. P. Banning, Information Department, AT&T, "Motion Pictures for Employees and the Public," in *Conference of Personnel Group, Bell System, April 18–25, 1922*, 6, Box 1, RG 4, Collection 6, AT&T-TX; Barrett, "The Changing Years," 289.

65. "The New Home of the Bell System," *Southern Telephone News*, December 1922, 12, AT&T-TX; Barrett, "The Changing Years," 289.

66. Max Weber, *The Protestant Ethic and the Spirit of Capitalism*, trans. A. M. Henderson and Talcott Parsons (New York: Charles Scribner's Sons, 1958), 181. Originally published in German in 1905.

67. E. K. Hall, Vice President, AT&T, "Summary of Conference and Objectives of Personnel and Public Relations Work for the Next Twelve Months," in *Conference of Personnel Group, Bell System, April 18–25, 1922*, 74, Box 88, RG 4, Collection 6, AT&T-TX.

68. W. E. Wood, President, Virginia Electric and Power Company, Richmond, Virginia, "Men and Machinery," *AERA Proceedings, 1929*, 25.

69. *Annual Report of the Directors of American Telephone & Telegraph Company to the Stockholder for the Year Ending December 31, 1917* (New York: AT&T, 1918), 36; hereafter AT&T, *Annual Report, 1917*. "Report of the Committee on Education," *AERA Proceedings, 1922*, 289.

70. AT&T, *Annual Report, 1923*, 40.

71. Barrett, "The Changing Years," 290–291.

72. *Telephone People*, 15.

73. Sara A. Carr, General Traffic Staff, "The Personality Back of the Voice: A Little Talk to Operators," *Southern Telephone News*, November 1923, 24, AT&T-TX.

74. Hall, "Summary of Conference," 74.

75. J. W. Spalding, Manager, New England Telephone and Telegraph Company, "The Spirit of Service in Springfield," in *Conference of Personnel Group, Bell System, April 18–25, 1922*, 8, Box 88, RG 4, Collection 6, AT&T-TX; "Report of the Committee on Education," *AERA Proceedings, 1922*, 289, 219; "The Land of Flowers," 1; Kennedy, *Winning the Public*, 127; "South Central Gas Association," *Gas Age-Record*, September 3, 1921, 265; Hall, "Summary of Conference," 74.

76. Michel Foucault, *The History of Sexuality*, vol. 1, trans. Robert Hurley (New York: Vintage Books, 1990), 75–132.

77. W. J. O'Connor, "The Why and How of Personnel Work in the Bell System," in *Conference of Personnel Group, Bell System, April 18–25, 1922*, 3, Box 88, RG 4, Collection 6, AT&T-TX.

78. Verne Ray, "Public Relations Committees and the Pink Ticket Plan," in *Conference of Personnel Group, Bell System, April 18–25, 1922*, 4, Box 88, RG 4, Collection 6, AT&T-TX.

79. Arlie Russell Hochschild, *The Managed Heart: Commercialization of Human Feeling* (Berkeley: University of California Press, 1983), 33, 35, 38–48.

80. The so-called Stockholm Syndrome is one example. In less shocking terms, historian of emotions Christina Kotchemidova, in another cultural context, cited Antonio Gramsci's similar observation specifically regarding monopoly capitalism.

268   Notes to Pages 68–70

Christina Kotchemidova, "Why We Say 'Cheese': Producing the Smile in Snapshot Photography," *Critical Studies in Media Communication* 22, no. 1 (March 2005): 3.

81. B. J. Bowen, General Superintendent of Traffic, New England Telephone and Telegraph Company, "Personal Service Committees," in *Conference of Personnel Group, Bell System, April 18–25, 1922*, 8, 12, Box 88, RG 4, Collection 6, AT&T-TX; Stephen H. Norwood, *Labor's Flaming Youth: Telephone Operators and Worker Militancy, 1878–1923* (Urbana: University of Illinois Press, 1990), 129, 151, 169.

82. Miss Margaret Lindley, "Training," in *Fifth Annual Chief Operators Conference, Los Angeles, February 15th, 1929*, 39, Collection 3: Pacific Telesis Group, RG 5, Box 10, AT&T-TX.

83. Summary of E. K. Hall's speech, "Review of the Previous Conference—Program of the Work to Date—Personnel Work in Other Industries—Importance of Morale," in *Conference of Personnel Group, Bell System, April 18–25, 1922*, 14, Box 88, RG 4, Collection 6, AT&T-TX.

84. Ray, "Public Relations Committees," 7.

85. Norwood, *Labor's Flaming Youth*, 203.

86. *Pacific Electric Magazine*, August 10, 1916.

87. Historians and psychologists both seek to explain why humans have acted the way they have, and this author sees no reason why the two disciplines should maintain such distinct barriers. Social psychological phenomena seem admissible when the culture of the subjects is reasonably similar, as in this case. J. Merrill Carlsmith, Barry E. Collins, and Robert L. Helmreich, "Studies in Forced Compliance I. The Effect of Pressure for Compliance on Attitude Change Produced by Face-to-Face Role Playing and Anonymous Essay Writing," *Journal of Personality and Social Psychology* 4, no. 1 (1966): 1–13; Kennedy, "Transforming Public Opinion," 21–22.

88. Insull stated in 1919 that 75 percent of his workforce, some twelve thousand employees, made about $100 a month; see "Meeting of the Public Service Section of the National Electric Light Association at Elks Clubhouse, 6 P.M., Thursday, October 23, 1919," 18, Folder 20-6, Insull Papers; Sharon Hartman Strom, *Beyond the Typewriter: Gender, Class, and the Origins of Modern American Office, Work, 1900–1930* (Urbana: University of Illinois Press, 1992), 206–208; Kenneth Lipartito, "When Women Were Switches: Technology, Work and Gender in the Telephone Industry, 1890–1920," *American Historical Review* 99, no. 4 (October 1994): 1087.

89. These findings aligned with William James's earlier argument that emotions follow from bodily changes. James wrote: "Sit all day in a moping posture, sigh, and reply to everything with a dismal voice, and your melancholy lingers." William James, "What Is an Emotion?" *Mind* 9, no. 34 (April 1884): 188–205, esp. 189–190 and 198. See also James D. Laird, "The Real Role of Facial Response in Experience of Emotion: A Reply to Tourgangeau and Ellsworth, and Others," *Journal of Personality and Social Psychology* 47, no. 4 (October 1984): 909–917; Sandra E. Duclos, James D. Laird, Eric Schneider, Melissa Sexter, Lisa Stern, and Oliver Van Lighten, "Emotion-Specific Effects of Facial Expressions and Postures on Emotional Experience," *Journal of Personality and Social Psychology* 57, no. 1 (1989): 100–108; Carroll E. Izard, *Human Emotions* (New York: Plenum Press, 1977), 106–107.

90. Sylvester Baxter, "The Telephone Girl," *Outlook*, May 26, 1906, 231.

Notes to Pages 70–72 269

91. Examination of J. B. Sheridan, Secretary of the Missouri Committee on Public Utility Information, in *FTC Letter No. 5* (1928), 77.

92. Richard E. Smith, Executive Assistant, SCE, "Father and Son: A Study in Public Relations," 4, reprinted from *Electrical World*, April 11, 1936, Box 449, Folder 7, SCE Records.

93. Norwood, *Labor's Flaming Youth*, 35–36; Sheridan in *FTC Letter No. 5* (1928), 77.

94. Stuart D. Brandes, *American Welfare Capitalism, 1880–1940* (Chicago: University of Chicago Press, 1976), 8; Sanford M. Jacoby, *Modern Manors: Welfare Capitalism since the New Deal* (Princeton, NJ: Princeton University Press, 1997), 15–18.

95. Sicilia, "Selling Power," 442, 446, 448–450.

96. R. F. Estabrook, "Carrying Out the Public Relations and Personnel Relations Policies in Traffic Work," in *Conference of Personnel Group, Bell System, April 18–25, 1922*, 9, Box 88, RG 4, Collection 6, AT&T-TX.

97. Summary of E. K. Hall's speech, "Review of the Previous Conference," 15.

98. For an interpretation of a more direct influence, see Andrea Tone, *The Business of Benevolence: Industrial Paternalism in Progressive America* (Ithaca, NY: Cornell University Press, 1997), 8.

99. E. K. Hall quoted in Estabrook, "Carrying Out the Public Relations," 33.

100. Ralph L. Mahon, "The Telephone in Chicago, 1877–1940," typescript, 77, AT&T-TX; Estabrook, "Carrying Out the Public Relations," 26; Summary of E. K. Hall's speech, "Review of the Previous Conference," 12; "Comprehensive Educational Work Carried On," Peoples Gas, *Year Book, 1924*, 31; Mary K. Cochran, Division Instructor, "Talks for Supervisors," *Southern Telephone News*, May 1922, 8, AT&T-TX; John E. Lewis in *FTC Letter No. 4* (1928), 364.

101. "Pacific Service Club Courts Are Dedicated," *San Francisco Chronicle*, November 27, 1914; Kennedy, "Transforming Public Opinion," 21–22.

102. William E. Oliver, Assistant District Manager, Los Angeles, to Vice President and General Manager R. H. Ballard, April 1, 1921, Box 83, Folder 9: Masonic Club Records, SCE Records.

103. "Lunch and Rest Rooms for Edison Women," *Edison Current Topics*, August 1919, 79–81, Box 308, Folder 7, SCE Records; *Southern Telephone News*, May 1921, 21, AT&T-TX; "New Homewood Office Opened," *Bell Telephone News* (Chicago), July 1927, 11.

104. Franklin C. Webber, "Are You a Member?," *Edison Torch*, June 1922, 1, Box 333, Folder 14, SCE Records.

105. Kennedy, "Transforming Public Opinion," 22.

106. "Association Parties," *Mouthpiece* (Detroit, MI), March 1924, ii, AT&T-TX.

107. A. Emory Wishon, "Now and Tomorrow with Customer Ownership," in "Popular Ownership of Property: Its Newer Forms and Social Consequences," ed. William L. Ransom and Parker Thomas Moon, special issue, *Proceedings of the Academy of Political Science in the City of New York* 11, no. 3 (April 1925): 414.

108. AT&T, *Annual Report, 1916*, 20–21.

109. Richard Gillespie, *Manufacturing Knowledge: A History of the Hawthorne Experiments* (Cambridge: Cambridge University Press, 1991), 17–18, 26.

110. AT&T, *Annual Report, 1916*, 49, 57.

111. Sicilia, "Selling Power," 442, 448–450.

112. "Public Relations and Publicity: A Reading Assignment," 2nd ed., in *Employees General Training Course: The Pacific Telephone and Telegraph Company, 1927*, 12, Collection 3, RG 5, Box 3, File: Public Relations and Publicity, AT&T-TX.

113. *Pacific Telephone Magazine*, February 1908, 7, AT&T-TX.

114. "Address of Mr. Insull before the First Annual Meeting of the Co-Operative Council of the Public Service Company of Northern Illinois, Chicago, December 7, 1921," 19–20, Folder 20-8, Insull Papers.

115. Barrett, "The Changing Years," 278.

116. Pearl Heyser, Battle Creek Commercial Association, "Associations and Public Relations," *Mouthpiece* 5, no. 4 (Detroit, MI), April 1924, 12, AT&T-TX.

117. Susan Strasser, "Customer to Consumer: The New Consumption in the Progressive Era," *OAH Magazine of History* 13, no. 3 (Spring 1999), 10–14.

118. Richard White, *Railroaded: The Transcontinentals and the Making of Modern America* (New York: W. W. Norton, 2011), chap. 3.

119. *Public Service Management* 30, no. 5 (May 1921), iii.

120. "To Improve the Telephone's Usefulness," *Pacific Gas and Electric Magazine* 1, no. 11 (April 1910): 474.

121. Bowen, "Personal Service Committees," 4.

122. "Organizing Courtesy to Build Good Will," *Electrical World*, May 21, 1921, 1157.

123. Robert MacDougall, *The People's Network: The Political Economy of the Telephone in the Gilded Age* (Philadelphia: University of Pennsylvania Press, 2013), 245.

124. "Nine Counter-Men Had to Run," *Pacific Gas and Electric Magazine*, April 1910.

125. "Conducting a Public Utility Complaint Department," *Public Service*, April 1913, 130; *How Customers Departments Promote Good Will: A Report of the Customers' Records Committee Accounting National Section* (New York: NELA, 1929), 2.

126. Henry H. Bradlee in Kennedy, "Transforming Public Opinion," 48.

127. Quoted in MacDougall, *The People's Network*, 245.

128. W. H. Dempster, "An Opportunity for Cooperation" *Pacific Electric Magazine*, July 10, 1916; "Conductors Happy; Company Provides Seats, Ease for Tired Feet Brings Smiles of Joy," *Los Angeles Examiner*, August 24, 1912, E. L. Stephens Scrapbook, Los Angeles Railway Records, Huntington Library, San Marino, California.

129. McAdoo, "The Relations between Public Service Corporations and the Public," 19–20.

130. Schmitt, "Memoir of a Telephone Operator, 1930," 240.

131. "Organizing Courtesy to Build Good Will," *Electrical World*, May 21, 1921, 1157.

132. W. J. Driscoll, "At Your Service—Verse," *Pacific Gas and Electric Magazine*, July 1909, 40, PG&E Archives, San Francisco, CA.

133. Susan Porter Benson, *Counter Cultures: Saleswomen, Managers, and Customers in American Department Stores, 1890–1940* (Champaign: University of Illinois Press, 1988), 95.

134. Lendol G. Calder, *Financing the American Dream: A Cultural History of Credit* (Princeton, NJ: Princeton University Press, 1999), 98.

135. "P.G. and E. Progress," January 1928, cartoon reprinted from a 1927 *Saturday Evening Post*, Box 440, Folder 8, SCE Records.

Notes to Pages 78–84 271

136. Andrew P. Russell, "Keeping Tabs on Rising Costs," *System: The Magazine of Business*, December 1914, 622.

137. "Not the Kind We Use," *Southern Telephone News*, January 1921, 5, AT&T-TX.

138. Charles Smallwood, *The White Front Cars of San Francisco* (Glendale, CA: Interurbans, 1978), 46–59.

139. "An Interview with Our New Vice President," *Inside Track* 4, no. 11 (January 1926), in Ira L. Swett, ed., *Market Street Railway Revisited: The Best of "The Inside Track"* (South Gate, CA: Interurbans, 1972), 84. The book is an edited collection of the company's employee magazine.

140. Swett, *Market Street Railway Revisited*, 99.

141. "A Transcript of a Conversation with Mrs. Barbara Kahn Gardner," transcript of an oral history conducted May 29, 2004, by Walter and Lauretta Rice (Bay Area Electric Railway Association), The Cable Car Home Page, http://www.cable-car-guy .com/html/ccmrsg.html.

142. Swett, *Market Street Railway Revisited*, 99.

143. Smallwood, *The White Front Cars*, 61.

144. The company was the Spring Valley Water Company. William Issel and Robert W. Cherny, *San Francisco, 1865–1932: Politics, Power, and Urban Development* (Berkeley: University of California Press, 1986), 184.

145. Martin J. Insull, President, Middle West Utilities Company, "Community Development and Public Relations," *NELA Proceedings* (1927), Public Relations Sessions, 264, 265.

146. M. S. Sloan, President of the Brooklyn Edison Company, *Our Selves and the Public* (lecture before the Kentucky Public Utilities Association, 1925), 5–6, Box 449, Folder 6, SCE Records.

147. Kennedy, "Transforming Public Opinion," 35.

148. "Public Relations under Public Regulation: Address by Lester S. Ready, Chief Engineer, Railroad Commission of the State of California before the Public Relations Section, Pacific Coast Electrical Association. Los Angeles, June 11, 1926," 6–7, Box 449, Folder 6, SCE Records.

149. Kennedy, "Transforming Public Opinion," 36.

150. "Pleasant Letters from Pleased Patrons," *Edison Current Topics*, April 1913, 15, Box 308, Folder 2, SCE Records.

151. W. M. Mehan, "The Claim Department," *How Commonwealth Edison Company Works* (Commonwealth Edison, 1914), 40, Folder 55-1, Insull Papers.

152. MacDougall, *The People's Network*, 218–19; Norwood, *Labor's Flaming Youth*, 162–164, 169, 193–194, 203.

153. Charles A. Willis, 2908 S. St., Sacramento, California, to Hon. Wm. McAdoo, Secretary of the Treasury, Washington, DC, September 14, 1918, File "Complaints— Misc, 1914–1918," Box 9, RG 5, Collection 3, AT&T-TX.

154. Division Commercial Superintendent to General Commercial Superintendent, October 16, 1918, File "Complaints—Misc, 1914–1918," Box 9, RG 5, Collection 3, AT&T-TX; General Commercial Superintendent to Division Commercial Superintendent, October 10, 1918, File "Complaints—Misc, 1914–1918," Box 9, RG 5, Collection 3, AT&T-TX.

155. E. R. Ringo, 1312 Northwestern Bank Building, Portland, Oregon, to Post Masters General, Washington, DC, October 2, 1918, File "Complaints—Misc, 1914–1918," Box 9, RG 5, Collection 3, AT&T-TX.

156. A. S. Burleson, "Order Relating to Courtesy and Service," *Pacific Telephone Magazine*, 23, December 1918, AT&T-TX.

157. According to one customer in the nineteenth century, "Post office clerks are models of unconcern if not rudeness, all the country over." David M. Henkin, *The Postal Age: The Emergence of Modern Communications in Nineteenth-Century America* (Chicago: University of Chicago Press, 2006), 80. A writer about business courtesy stated in 1922 that the Post Office was "notorious for haughty and arrogant behavior." Nella Braddy Henney, *The Book of Business Etiquette* (New York: Doubleday, 1922), 19.

158. H. D. Pillsbury to N. C. Kingsbury, New York, September 26, 1918, File "Complaints—Misc, 1914–1918," Box 9, RG 5, Collection 3, AT&T-TX; Telegram to N. C. Kingsbury, Vice President, AT&T, 195 Broadway, New York City, from H. D. Pillsbury, San Francisco, October 7, 1918, File "Complaints—Misc, 1914–1918," Box 9, RG 5, Collection 3, AT&T-TX.

159. George K. Stocker, S. 508 Monroe St, Apartment D, Spokane, Washington, to Post Office Department, Spokane, Washington, September 20, 1918, File "Complaints—Misc, 1914–1918," Box 9, RG 5, Collection 3, AT&T-TX.

160. Letter, September 14, 1918, File: Conference, 1925, Box 10, RG 5, Collection 3: Pacific Telesis Group, AT&T-TX.

161. General Commercial Superintendent, San Francisco, to Division Commercial Superintendent, October 29, 1918, File: Complaints—Misc, 1914–1918, Box 9, RG 5, AT&T-TX; Mrs. Herbert L. Kent, Alameda, California to First Assistant Postmaster, Washington, DC, October 8, 1918, File: Complaints—Misc, 1914–1918, Box 9, RG 5, Collection 3, AT&T-TX.

162. Richard R. John, *Network Nation: Inventing American Telecommunications* (Cambridge, MA: Belknap Press of Harvard University Press, 2010), 403, 401; see also J. Warren Stehman, *The Financial History of the American Telephone and Telegraph Company* (Boston: Houghton Mifflin, 1925), 220.

Chapter 3 • The Architecture of Consent

1. Michael Zakim, "Producing Capitalism: The Clerk at Work," in *Capitalism Takes Command: The Social Transformation of Nineteenth-Century America*, ed. Michael Zakim and Gary J. Kornblith (Chicago: University of Chicago Press, 2012), 229.

2. "Selling a Utility Company to the Public," *Southern Telephone News*, June 1922, 6, AT&T-TX.

3. B. C. Forbes, "What the Customer Is Thinking," *NELA Proceedings* (1926), 55.

4. Labert St. Clair, Director, Advertising Section, AERA, "Getting the Public Eye and Ear," *American Gas Association Monthly*, January 1922, 25.

5. "Draft of Address Written by John Sheridan for J. F. Hull, for Hull's Speech to the Missouri Public Utilities Association on May 4, 1922," Ex. 2744, Box 3851, Series: Economic Investigations Files, 1915–1938, Subject: Power and Gas, FTC Records.

6. "New Edison Building Beautiful and Modern," *Edison Current Topics*, January 1919, 4, Box 308, Folder 7, SCE Records.

Notes to Pages 89–91   273

7. Louise A. Mozingo is an exception to this. She has focuses on suburban corporate campuses and estates rather than skyscrapers. Louise A. Mozingo, *Pastoral Capitalism: A History of Suburban Corporate Landscapes* (Cambridge, MA: MIT Press, 2011).

8. "Alameda Exchange Has Club House," *Pacific Telephone Magazine*, December 1914, AT&T-TX.

9. AT&T, *Annual Report, 1934*, 25; Claude S. Fischer, *America Calling: A Social History of the Telephone to 1940* (Berkeley: University of California Press, 1992), 44. Bell had five million subscribers in 1910.

10. David E. Nye, *Electrifying America: Social Meanings of a New Technology, 1880–1940* (Cambridge, MA: MIT Press, 1990), 261; R. T. Duncan, "Report of Customer Relations Committee," *NELA Proceedings* (1927), Commercial National Session, 408.

11. Lucien Kellogg, "'Visitors Are Welcome': How a Western Utility Brings Together Four Factors in Its Sales-and-Service Plan," *Business*, May, 1925, 25, Box 440, Folder 8, SCE Records.

12. Warren R. Voorhis, Vice President, American Water Works & Electrical Company, New York, "The Girl at the Window" (*Electrical World*, August 4, 1923), 1, Box 449, Folder 5, SCE Records.

13. Samuel Kennedy, "Transforming Public Opinion: An Address by Mr. Samuel M. Kennedy, Vice-President Southern California Edison Co., Los Angeles, California, before the Convention of Managers and Executives of the Management Division of Stone & Webster Inc., Held in Boston, October 10–18, 1921," 17–18, Box 389, Folder 26, SCE Records; "Merchandise Sales," *Public Service Company of Northern Illinois Year Book 1928*, 22, Box 55, Folder 8, Insull Papers.

14. The Bell System operated 6,017 central offices in 1925, at least four hundred of which were "open offices" by 1930. Bell Telephone Securities Company, *Bell Telephone Securities Reference Tables and Descriptions for the Use of Investors, Investment Houses, and Bankers, with a Brief Introductory Statement of the Organization and Financing of the American Telephone and Telegraph Company and Associated Companies* (New York, 1935), 21; "Report of Bell System Commercial Operations, 1930, Compiled by the Commercial Engineer, American Telephone and Telegraph Company," in *Operating Papers Conference—Absecon, New Jersey, Year 1931*, 13–15, File: Conference, 1926, 1931, Box 10, RG 5: PT&T, Collection 3, AT&T-TX; R. S. Masters, R. C. Smith, and W. E. Winter, *An Historical Review of the San Francisco Exchange* (San Francisco: PT&T, 1927), 104–106; "Building for Service," *Bell Telephone Quarterly* 7, no. 2 (April 1928), 78; Richard Storrs Coe, "Bell System Buildings—an Interpretation," *Bell Telephone Quarterly*, July 1929, 205; Kennedy, "Transforming Public Opinion," 17–18; "Merchandise Sales," 22.

15. "The Work of the Commercial Department: Part II: A Reading Assignment," in *Employees General Training Course: The Pacific Telephone and Telegraph Company, 1927*, 3, Collection 3, RG 5, File: Public Relations and Publicity, AT&T-TX.

16. "The Work of the Commercial Department: Part I: A Reading Assignment," in *Employees General Training Course*, 11.

17. Kennedy, "Transforming Public Opinion," 38; "Selling a Utility Company to the Public," *Southern Telephone News*, June 1922, 6, AT&T-TX.

274   *Notes to Pages 91–95*

18. See "Edison Electric Company Office Staff, Long Beach," 1905, Call No. 01 00784, SCEPN; and Call Nos. 02 00595, 01 00784, 02 00218, 02 00228, 02 01453, 02 00210, 02 00213, 02 00204, 02 001928, 02 00225.

19. "New Edison Building Beautiful and Modern," 4.

20. Charles Heston Peirson, "Service," *Edison Current Topics*, March 1914, 460, Box 308, Folder 3, SCE Records.

21. Kennedy, "Transforming Public Opinion," 17–18.

22. Peirson, "Service," 17–18.

23. "Organization Diagram," October, 1913, Box 470, Folder 6, SCE Records; "Stock Salesmen Meeting, October 8, 1921," 3, 8, Box 114, Folder 8, SCE Records; G. Haven Bishop, "Pomona Local Office—Interior," 1923, Call No. 02 08845, SCEPN; Kennedy, "Transforming Public Opinion," 17–18; *Commerce Journal* 4, no. 1 (August 1923): 5–8, Box 470, Folder 6, SCE Records; "El Centro Has New Business Office," *Pacific Telephone Magazine*, August 1929, 9, AT&T-TX; Photograph 13706, Folder: Pacific Bell—California Prints—by Exchange—Oakland—Buildings and Facilities—3545 E. 14th St. Business Office, 1927–1930, Box 88, RG 4, Collection 6, AT&T-TX.

24. "Spokane's Newly Completed Business Office," *Pacific Telephone Magazine*, January 1927, 30, AT&T-TX; "Believed to Be the Accounting Dept at the Los Angeles Local Business Office," 1906, Call No. 01 00592, SCEPN; "Edison Electric Company Office Staff, Long Beach," 1905, Call No. 01 00784, SCEPN; "Office at Wisconsin Traction, Light, Heat & Power Co., 1908," Early Office Museum, https://www .officemuseum.com/1908_Office_6_Workers_Hidden_Burroughs.jpg; "Spokane's Newly Completed Business Office," 30.

25. Angel Kwolek-Folland, *Engendering Business: Men and Women in the Corporate Office, 1870–1930* (Baltimore: Johns Hopkins University Press, 1994), 106; Dell Upton, *Architecture in the United States* (New York: Oxford University Press, 1998), 207.

26. "El Centro Has New Business Office," 9; Photograph 13706; "The Work of the Commercial Department: Part II," 4.

27. Photograph 13707: FJ Marshall Dist Com. Mgr, Counterless Business Office," Folder: Pacific Bell—California Prints—by Exchange—Oakland—Buildings and Facilities—2545 E. 14th St. Business Office, 1927–1930, Box 88, RG 4, Collection 6, AT&T-TX.

28. "The Work of the Commercial Department: Part II," 4, 12.

29. [Ohio Bell Telephone Company], *Commercial Department, Public Relations Conference, Outline for Training All Commercial Employees* [1934], 7, 9, Box 16, Ex. 177A, FCC Records.

30. Robt. E. Power, "Business Office Management," in *Meeting of Managers* (San Francisco: PT&T, March 30, 1926), 1, 8; File: Pacific Bell Company Leaders Executive Office Files, Conference, 1925, 2 of 8; Box 10; RG 5, AT&T-TX.

31. Samuel M. Kennedy, *Winning the Public*, 2nd ed. (New York: McGraw-Hill, 1921), 8–9; C. Wright Mills, *White Collar: The American Middle Classes* (New York: Oxford University Press, 1951), 190; Cindy Sondik Aron, *Ladies and Gentlemen of the Civil Service: Middle-Class Workers in Victorian America* (New York: Oxford University Press, 1987), 163.

32. "Spokane's Newly Completed Business Office," 30.

33. Clark Davis, *Company Men: White Collar Life and Corporate Culture in Los Angeles, 1892–1941* (Baltimore: Johns Hopkins University Press, 2000), 225–227;

Notes to Pages 95–96 275

Oliver Zunz, *Making America Corporate, 1870–1920* (Chicago: University of Chicago Press, 1990), 202.

34. Thomas Welskopp, "Sons of Vulcan," in *Bodies and Affects in Market Societies,* ed. Anne Schmidt and Christoph Conrad (Tübingen: Mohr Siebeck), 23–40.

35. J. P. Ingle, Manager, Haverhill Gas Light Company, Haverhill, Massachusetts, "Seeing Ourselves as Others See Us," *American Gas Association Monthly,* March 1922, 153.

36. "Alameda Exchange Has Club House."

37. Max Weber, *The Protestant Ethic and the Spirit of Capitalism,* trans. A. M. Henderson and Talcott Parsons (New York: Charles Scribner's Sons, 1958), 181; "Bank Buildings," special issue, *Architectural Review,* March 1905; John M. Anderson, "The Man in the Cage: Some Things That Happen in the Day's Work of the Paying Teller," *Saturday Evening Post,* February 1, 1908, 5; *Illinois Merchant Bank Building* (Chicago: Illinois Trust Safety Deposit, 1922); D. C. Thomas, "New Type Business Office Has No Counters," *Southern Telephone News,* January 1929, 9, AT&T-TX; Kwolek-Folland, *Engendering Business,* 109.

38. Naomi R. Lamoreaux, *Insider Lending: Banking Personal Connections, and Economic Development in Industrial New England* (Cambridge: Cambridge University Press, 1994), photographic insert between pp. 83 and 84.

39. Alfred Hopkins, *The Fundamentals of Good Bank Building* (New York: Bankers Publishing, 1929), 75.

40. Kennedy, "Transforming Public Opinion," 17–18. Banks at the time Kennedy worked for them did not enjoy a great degree of public trust, despite the bars; see Christopher W. Shaw, *Money, Power, and the People: The American Struggle to Make Banking Democratic* (Chicago: University of Chicago Press, 2019), 57–59.

41. Louis Sullivan took hesitant steps toward the open office in the 1910s by designing banks with open counters for employees not dealing directly with cash, though tellers still remained behind bars. Sullivan's goal was the same as utility executives', to dispel the secrecy and suspicion surrounding big business institutions and improve customer service. In 1928, a bank president named John Poole patented an open bank counter "to bring the bank officials and those dealing with them into more intimate contact thereby contributing to the art of making friends," the patent read. The open office idea spread slowly, but by the mid-1950s, banks in Manhattan designed by architectural firm Skidmore, Owings & Merrill boasted that customers could transact business "over the tops of open counters free from bars and grille work." See the open designs in Ann-Christine Frandsen, Tammy Bun Hiller, and Elton G. McGoun, *Money Reloaded: The Architecture of Trust* (Warwick, UK: Architectural Press, 2012), 9; John Poole, "Bank Counter," US Patent 1,673,639, filed November 19, 1927, and issued June 12, 1928; Manufactures Trust Company, New York, "Welcome . . . to Our New Fifth Avenue Office," October, 1954, 5, pamphlet included with Manufactures Trust Company, New York, *A New Concept in Bank Design* (New York: W. E. Rudge's Sons, 1954), Environmental Design Library, University of California, Berkeley; Ann-Christine Frandsen, Tammy Bun Hiller, Janice Traflet, and Elton G. McGoun, "From Money Storage to Money Store: Openness and Transparency in Bank Architecture," *Business History* 55, no. 5 (2013): 696.

42. "Vallejo Office Tries Innovation," *Pacific Telephone Magazine,* March 1929, 24, AT&T-TX.

43. John P. Ingle, Haverhill Gas Light Company, speaking in the post-speech discussion in Kennedy, "Transforming Public Opinion," 32.

44. Kennedy, "Transforming Public Opinion," 32.

45. "Vallejo Office Tries Innovation," 24.

46. "The Unit Plan: Bill Simmons Thought We Should Get Closer to Subscribers—and That's What We Are Doing," *Southern Telephone News*, January 1922, 7, AT&T-TX.

47. "The Unit Plan," 8.

48. Richard Gillespie, *Manufacturing Knowledge: A History of the Hawthorne Experiments* (Cambridge: Cambridge University Press, 1991), 13–15.

49. Whether or not the author of the article made up this quote from someone called "Bill Simmons," it still reveals the thinking of company managers in adopting the unit plan. "The Unit Plan: Bill Simmons Thought We Should Get Closer to Subscribers—and That's What We Are Doing," *Southern Telephone News*, January 1922, 7, AT&T-TX.

50. "The Unit Plan," 7.

51. "New Seattle Business Office a Source of Pride," *Pacific Telephone Magazine*, April 1922, 26, AT&T-TX.

52. "San Francisco's New Business Office," *Pacific Telephone Magazine*, July 1925, 20, AT&T-TX.

53. "New Seattle Business Office a Source of Pride," 26.

54. "Spokane's Newly Completed Business Office," 30; "Big Pasadena Job Successfully Accomplished," *Pacific Telephone Magazine*, September 1927, 3–6, AT&T-TX.

55. There's no direct evidence that the Atlanta office adopted the open office after learning about it from SCE, but there is a lot of photographic evidence showing that many Bell offices were closed offices with grilles and grating in the 1910s.

56. "Further Steps Taken toward Greater 'Teamwork for Service' in Chicago," *Bell Telephone News* (Chicago), August 1927, 2, AT&T-TX.

57. "New Telephone Home for Southern California," *Pacific Telephone Magazine*, October 1930, 14, AT&T-TX.

58. "Alhambra's Counterless Office," *Pacific Telephone Magazine*, February 1929, 28, AT&T-TX.

59. "Further Steps Taken," 2.

60. "Report of Bell System Commercial Operations, 1930," 14.

61. Bancroft Gherardi, Vice President, AT&T, New York, to H. D. Pillsbury, President PT&T, San Francisco, June 24, 1927, 3–4, File: Conference, 1925–1933, Box 10, RG 5, AT&T-TX.

62. Erving Goffman, *The Presentation of Self in Everyday Life* (New York: Anchor Books, 1959).

63. Kennedy, *Winning the Public*, 79–80.

64. Thomas, "New Type Business Office Has No Counters," 9.

65. "Training for Better Public Contact—Its Necessity and Importance," *NELA Proceedings* (1928), Public Relations National Section, Tuesday, June 5, 1928, 281.

66. Kennedy, "Transforming Public Opinion," 21, 25; W. H. Hamilton, discussion about S. M. Kennedy's pamphlet "Service," Second General Session, May 20, 1920, *NELA Proceedings* (1920), 58–59; Samuel Insull, speech given at the annual meeting of the NELA, Commonwealth Edison Company Section, held in Customers Hall, Edison

Building, Chicago, October 30, 1919, 10, Folder 20-6, Insull Papers; Power, "Business Office Management," 4; "The Counter," *Pacific Telephone Magazine*, February 1920, 3, AT&T-TX.

67. Call No. 01 00592, SCEPN.

68. Thomas, "New Type Business Office Has No Counters," 9.

69. C. L. Campbell, Treasurer, Connecticut Light & Power Company, "Broadening the Accountant's Duties," *NELA Proceedings* (1926), 297.

70. This fact fit remarkably well into what Henri Lefebvre called the "illusion of transparency." See Henri Lefebvre, *The Production of Space*, trans. Donald Nicholson-Smith (Malden, MA: Blackwell Publishing, [1974] 1991), 27–28.

71. Thomas, "New Type Business Office Has No Counters," 9.

72. "The Work of the Commercial Department: Part I," 9–10.

73. David F. Noble, *Forces of Production: A Social History of Industrial Automation* (New York: Oxford University Press, 1986); Michael Burawoy, *Manufacturing Consent: Changes in the Labor Process under Monopoly Capitalism* (Chicago: University of Chicago Press, 1979), 81–82; Kempster B. Miller, "Modern Telephone Engineering," lecture delivered before the New York Electrical Society, February 14, 1901 (New York: New York Electrical Society, 1901), 4; John E. Kingsbury, *The Telephone and Telephone Exchanges: Their Invention and Development* (London: Longmans, Green, 1915), 212, 365; Venus Green, *Race on the Line: Gender, Labor, and Technology in the Bell System, 1880–1980* (Durham, NC: Duke University Press, 2001), 26, 34, 43–45; Kenneth Lipartito, "When Women Were Switches: Technology, Work and Gender in the Telephone Industry, 1890–1920," *American Historical Review*, October 1994, 1082, 1096–1097.

74. Norwood, *Labor's Flaming Youth*, 31, 37; Miller, "Modern Telephone Engineering," 2, 9; Arthur Vaughan Abbott, *Telephoney: A Manual of Design, Construction, and Operation of Telephone Exchanges* (New York: McGraw, 1903), 26; F. Barrows Colton, "The Miracle of Talking by Telephone, *National Geographic Magazine*, October 1937, 407, Box 485, Folder 1, SCE Records.

75. "Spokane's Newly Completed Business Office," *Pacific Telephone Magazine*, January 1927, 30, AT&T-TX; Kennedy, "Transforming Public Opinion," 17; Robt. E. Power, "Business Office Management," in *Meeting of Managers* (San Francisco: Pacific Telephone and Telegraph Company, March 30, 1926), 1, 8, Pacific Bell Company Leaders Executive Office Files, Conference, 1925, 2 of 8, box 10, record group 5, AT&T-TX; Michel Foucault, *Discipline and Punish: The Birth of the Prison*, trans. Alan Sheridan (New York: Vintage, 1979).

76. "The Reality—a Typical Exchange," *Pacific Telephone Magazine*, October 1914, 14; "The Work of the Traffic Department: Part I," *Organization, Employment & Training, Operator's Quarters, Local Operating, and Toll Operating: Reading Assignment: Employees' General Training Course, The Pacific Telephone and Telegraph Company, 1928*, 4, Collection 3, RG 5, Box 6, AT&T-TX.

77. R. T. Barrett, "The Changing Years as Seen from the Switchboard," *Bell Telephone Quarterly*, April 1935, 113; Colton, "The Miracle of Talking," 410; "General Operating Department, Western Union Telegraph Building, New York," photograph (1875), Library of Congress Control N. 2002706683, Library of Congress. https://www.loc.gov/item/2002706683/; "'Switch' General Operating Department, Western Union

Telegraph Building, New York," photograph (1875), Library of Congress; Green, *Race on the Line*, 29; "Barclay Telegraph Instruments, Showing Instruments on Stand with Women Operators; One Handling the Receiving Tape," Cincinnati, Ohio, photograph (1908), Library of Congress; *Bell Telephone Quarterly*, July 1925, 211; Kingsbury, *The Telephone and Telephone Exchanges*, 232–233.

78. F. A. Pickernell, "Some General Remarks on Telephone Exchange Construction and Equipment," in *Twelfth Meeting of the National Telephone Exchange Association . . . September 9th and 10th, 1890* (Brooklyn, NY: Eagle, 1890), 67–68; this statement was partly self-plagiarized by Pickernell from a paper he gave the year before; see A. S. Hibbard, J. J. Carty, and F. A. Pickernell, "The New Era in Telephony," in *Eleventh Meeting of the National Telephone Exchange Association . . . September 10th and 11th, 1889* (Brooklyn, NY: Eagle, 1889), 34–43; see also Green, *Race on the Line*, 57, 29, 45; Miller, "Modern Telephone Engineering," 2–3.

79. Kingsbury, *The Telephone and Telephone Exchanges*, 385–386; Barrett, "Changing Years as Seen from the Switchboard," 117; M. D. Fagen, ed., *A History of Engineering and Science in the Bell System*, vol. 1, *The Early Years, 1875–1925* (New York: Bell Telephone Laboratories, 1975), 501–502; Stephen H. Norwood, *Labor's Flaming Youth: Telephone Operators and Worker Militancy, 1878–1923* (Urbana: University of Illinois Press, 1990), 34, 37; Green, *Race on the Line*, 45; Lipartito, "When Women Were Switches," 1096–1097; AT&T, "Her Right Place," AT&T Tech Channel, video, 1929, http://techchannel.att.com/play-video.cfm/2013/7/1/AT&T-Archives-Her -Right-Place.

80. Norwood, *Labor's Flaming Youth*, 31, 37.

81. Masters et al., *An Historical Review of the San Francisco Exchange*, 62; Colton, "The Miracle of Talking," 407.

82. Coe, "Bell System Buildings," 204.

83. Voorhees, Walker, Smith, Smith & Haines, *Telephone Buildings since 1885* (New York, 1961), 21.

84. *Commonwealth Edison Company Yearbook, 1929*, 22, Folder 49-17, Insull Papers.

85. Masters et al., *An Historical Review of the San Francisco Exchange*, 82.

86. "Telephone Central Office Buildings in the Small Communities," *Architecture and Building* 67, no. 2 (February 1930): 59.

87. Coe, "Bell System Buildings," 204.

88. *Commonwealth Edison Company Yearbook, 1929*, 22.

89. "In Behalf of Home Comfort," *Commonwealth Edison Company Yearbook, 1930*, 18, Folder 49-17, Insull Papers.

90. "Telephone Central Office Buildings in the Small Communities."

91. "Telephone Central Office Buildings in the Small Communities."

92. O.J. Cooper, "The Sub-Station Department: Scope and System," *How Commonwealth Edison Company Works* (Commonwealth Edison, 1914), 5, Box 55, Folder 1, Insull Papers.

93. Kennedy, "Transforming Public Opinion, "15.

94. Kennedy, "Transforming Public Opinion," 15–16; *Commonwealth Edison Company Yearbook, 1929*, 22.

95. Armonk, New York, office in "Telephone Central Office Buildings in the Small Communities"; "Casa Grande, Arizona, 1928," in Voorhees, Walker, Smith, Smith &

Haines *Telephone Buildings*; "All Forces Cooperated in Sales and Other Activities during 1928," *Southern Telephone News*, January 1929, 7, AT&T-TX.

96. "Telephone Central Office Buildings in the Small Communities."

97. The article might have been planted, as chapter 5 indicates was common. Philip Hampson, "Mixes Utility, Beauty; Raises Realty Values," *Chicago Tribune*, January 20, 1929.

98. Coe, "Bell System Buildings," 213–214.

99. "Additional Field Headquarters for More Efficient Operation," *Public Service Company of Northern Illinois Year Book 1931*, 11, Box 55, Folder 8, Insull Papers.

100. "New Telephone Home for Southern California," 24.

101. Joseph P. Baloun, "The Usefulness of a Photo Department," *Pacific Gas and Electric Magazine* 1, no. 11 (April 1910): 460; "New Telephone Home for Southern California," 24; NELA, Committee on Commercial Service and Relations with Customers, "Acknowledgement of Application for Service," *Service Suggestions* 1, no. 5 (December 1921), republished in "Report on Commercial Service and Relations with Customers Committee," *NELA Proceedings* (1922), 1:360; Power, "Business Office Management," 2; David B. Sicilia, "Selling Power: Marketing and Monopoly at Boston Edison, 1886–1929" (PhD diss., Brandeis University, 1990), 442.

102. G. Haven Bishop, "Local Offices A–Z," Call No. 02 03642, SCEPN; Ingle, "Seeing Ourselves as Others See Us," 153.

103. For an account of the development of single-family homes and their geographic separation from commercial areas, see the subsection "Neighborhoods" beginning on p. 48 in Paul E. Johnson, *A Shopkeeper's Millennium: Society and Revivals in Rochester, New York, 1815–1837* (New York: Hill and Wang, 1978).

104. Bethany Moreton, *To Serve God and Wal-Mart: The Making of Christian Free Enterprise* (Cambridge, MA: Harvard University Press, 2009), 88–89; William Leach, *Land of Desire: Merchants, Power, and the Rise of a New American Culture* (New York: Pantheon Books, 1993).

105. Katherine C. Grier, *Culture and Comfort: Parlor Making and Middle-Class Identity, 1850–1930* (Washington, DC: Smithsonian Institution Press, 1997); Richard L. Bushman, *The Refinement of America: Persons, Houses, Cities* (New York: Vintage Books, 1992).

106. Harry W. Laidler and H. S. Raushenbush, *Power Control* (New York: New Republic, 1928), 88–116, 169, 171–172; Robert MacDougall, *The People's Network: The Political Economy of the Telephone in the Gilded Age* (Philadelphia: University of Pennsylvania Press, 2013), 116, 143, 147; Nye, *Electrifying America*, 261, 303.

107. "Merchandise Sales," 22.

108. "Home Service Aids Modern Trend," Peoples Gas, *Year Book* (1930), 24.

109. L. D. Mathes, ed., "The Display Room," *NELA Proceedings* (1908) 1:667.

110. "New Stores Opened," *Public Service Company of Northern Illinois Year Book 1929*, 18, Box 55, Folder 8, Insull Papers.

111. Mathes, "The Display Room," 667.

112. "New Stores Opened," 18; "Merchandise Sales," 22.

113. "Preview Electrical Home, St. Francis Wood, Will Open Today," *San Francisco Chronicle*, June 11, 1920; "Home Service: Organization and Operation," *NELA Proceedings* (1930), 1290–1300; Sicilia, "Selling Power," 452.

280   *Notes to Pages 113–117*

114. Lipartito, "When Women Were Switches," 1087. For a contemporary description of typical middle-class family rooms, see Robert S. Lynd and Helen Merrell Lynd, *Middletown: A Study in Contemporary American Culture* (New York: Harcourt, Brace, 1929), 100–101.

115. *Southern Telephone News*, May 1921, 21, AT&T-TX.

116. "New Homewood Office Opened," *Bell Telephone News* (Chicago), July 1927, 11.

117. Wisconsin Telephone Company, *Information for Federal Communications Commission, Cost and Other Data relating to the Advertising, Publicity, Information and Promotion Activities of the Wisconsin Telephone Company*, "Answer to 12, Page 1 and 4," Box 41, Ex. 1352, FCC Records; Southwest Bell Telephone and Telegraph Companies, "12. Certain Subscriptions to Papers, Periodicals and Magazines," in *Response to Federal Communications Commission's Inquiry Dated December 11, 1936 relative to Certain Advertising, Publicity and Information Activities for the Years 1926 to 1936, Inclusive*, Box 41, Ex. 1355, FCC Records; Pacific Bell Telephone and Telegraph Companies, "Item 12: Magazine Purchased for Operators' Rest Rooms," in *Information Requested by Federal Communications Commission through American Telephone and Telegraph Company, December 11, 1936* (January 7, 1937), Box 41, Ex. 1358, FCC Records.

118. "The Average Subscriber's Idea of a Telephone Exchange," *Pacific Telephone Magazine*, October 1914, 23, AT&T-TX.

119. Green, *Race on the Line*, 39.

120. M. B. French, Traffic Engineer, "Review of Bell System Traffic Operations, 1930," in *Operating Papers Conference—Absecon, New Jersey, Year 1931*," 9, File: Conference, 1926, 1931, Box 10, RG 5, Collection 3, AT&T-TX.

121. Norwood, *Labor's Flaming Youth*, 34, 38, 61.

122. Studs Terkel, *Working: People Talk about What They Do All Day and How They Fell about What They Do* (New York: New Press, 1974), 32–33.

123. "The Speech-Weaver's School," *Pacific Telephone Magazine*, December 1916, 11, AT&T-TX; Terkel, *Working*, 34.

124. *The Story of a Telephone Operator* (1912), 9, RG 6, Collection 6: AT&T Corp, AT&T-TX.

125. "Showing the Subscriber," *Southern Telephone News*, December 1921, 1, AT&T-TX.

126. "Tell Our Story," *Pacific Telephone Magazine*, December 1916, 4, AT&T-TX.

127. Bell Telephone Company of Pennsylvania, *Pennsylvania Rate Publicity Program*, 1920, Ex. 142, Box 15, FCC Records; SW Bell T&T Companies, "Information Pamphlets and Similar Material," in *Response to Federal Communications Commission's Inquiry Dated December 11, 1936*; PT&T Companies, "Item 5: Statement of Press Releases," in *Information Requested by Federal Communications Commission through American Telephone and Telegraph Company, December 11, 1936*; Wisconsin Telephone Company, *Information for Federal Communications Commission*, "Answers to Question 5, Page 3."

128. R. F. Estabrook, "Carrying Out the Public Relations and Personnel Relations Policies in Traffic Work," in *Conference of Personnel Group, Bell System, April 18–25, 1922*, 27, Box 88, RG 4, Collection 6, AT&T-TX.

Notes to Pages 117–121   *281*

129. "Completed Building Publicly Inspected," *Pacific Telephone Magazine*, July 1927, 18, AT&T-TX; "The Speech-Weaver's School," 10.

130. "Showing the Subscriber," 1.

131. FCC, "Appendix 5, Sheet 2: Illinois Bell Telephone Company, Commercial Department Report of Customer Relations Activities, Years 1926 to 1935 Inclusive," in *Telephone Investigation, Special Investigation Docket No. 1: Report on Control of Telephone Communications (Pursuant to Public Resolution No. 8, 74th Congress)* (June 15, 1937); hereafter FCC, *Telephone Investigation* (1937); SW Bell T&T Companies, "7-a. Forecasts and Actual Results as to Certain Customer Relations Activities," in *Response to Federal Communications Commission's Inquiry Dated December 11, 1936*.

132. FCC, "Appendix 5, Sheet 3: The Ohio Bell Telephone Co., Report of Customer Relations Activities, 1930," in *Telephone Investigation* (1937).

133. *Memorandum on the Work of the Illinois Committee on Public Utility Information*, 2, Box 3810, Ex. 167, FTC Records.

134. Kellogg, "'Visitors Are Welcome'" 55.

135. Pacific Gas & Electric Company, *A Visit to Pacific Gas and Electric Company's Pit River Hydro-Electric Development, Shasta County, California*, [1922?], The Bancroft Library, University of California, Berkeley.

136. Sicilia, "Selling Power," 452.

137. "Completed Building Publicly Inspected," 17. This article quoted articles from the Portland *Telegram* and the Portland *News*.

138. "Seeing Is Believing," *Southern Telephone News*, May 1922, 1, AT&T-TX.

139. "Satisfactory Service Comes from Growing Sense of Responsibility among Telephone People," *Southern Telephone News* (Detroit, MI), April 1924, 2, AT&T-TX.

140. "New Exchange at Tifton, Ga., Opened: Big Reception Attended by over Five Hundred Visitors," *Southern Telephone News* (Detroit, MI), September 1921, 17, AT&T-TX.

141. "Kokomo Entertains at 'Open House,'" *Bell Telephone News* (Indianapolis), June 1924, 22, AT&T-TX.

142. Richard R. John, *Network Nation: Inventing American Telecommunications* (Cambridge, MA: Belknap Press of Harvard University Press, 2010), 217; MacDougall, *The People's Network*, 12, 24.

143. Sicilia, "Selling Power," 434–435.

144. "Housewarming at New Main Office Building, Seattle," *Pacific Telephone Magazine*, March 1922, 3, AT&T-TX.

145. "Opening of New Exchange at Aberdeen, Wash.," *Pacific Telephone Magazine*, December 1912, 3, AT&T-TX; "Preview Electrical Home, St. Francis Wood, Will Open Today," *San Francisco Chronicle*, June 11, 1920; Sicilia, "Selling Power," 452.

146. Lipartito, "When Women Were Switches," 1095.

147. "Big Pasadena Job Successfully Accomplished," 3–6.

148. Abraham H. Maslow and Norbett L. Mintz, "Effects of Esthetic Surroundings: I. Initial Short-Term Effects of Three Esthetic Conditions upon Receiving 'Energy' and 'Well-Being' in Faces," in *People and Buildings*, ed. Robert Gutman (New York: Basic Books, 1972), 219.

149. Thomas, "New Type Business Office Has No Counters," 9–10.

150. H. W. Dennis, Constructor Engineer, "New Edison Building: A Broadway Feature," *Edison Current Topics*, June 1917, 113, Box 308, Folder 6, SCE Records.

151. "New Telephone Home for Southern California," 14.

152. Maslow and Mintz, "Effects of Esthetic Surroundings," 212–219.

153. Albert Mehrabian, *Public Places and Private Spaces: The Psychology of Work, Play, and Living Environments* (New York: Basic Books, 1976), 289.

154. Thomas, "New Type Business Office Has No Counters," 9.

155. "El Centro Has New Business Office," 9.

156. "East Bay Opens New District Office," *Pacific Telephone Magazine*, July 1930, 37, AT&T-TX.

157. John Bakewell, "Architectural Treatment of the Building," *Pacific Service Magazine*, July 1925, 147, PG&E Archives.

158. Kennedy, *Winning the Public*, 9–10.

159. Kennedy, "Transforming Public Opinion," 17.

160. Robert J. Donovan and John R. Rossiter, "Store Atmosphere: An Environmental Psychology Approach," *Journal of Retailing* 58, no. 1 (1982): 39; Mehrabian, *Public Spaces and Private Spaces*, 19, 287, 289, 293.

161. "Report of Bell System Commercial Operations, 1930," 14. The development of quiet offices was not unique to utilities; see Emily Thompson, *The Soundscape of Modernity: Architectural Acoustics and the Culture of Listening in America, 1900–1933* (Cambridge, MA: MIT Press, 2002).

162. "Spokane's Newly Completed Business Office," 30.

163. Thomas, "New Type Business Office Has No Counters," 10.

164. Thompson, *The Soundscape of Modernity*, 171, 197, 203, 217, 220. This muting of sound but enhancing of vision ushered indoors a nineteenth-century project of segregating the senses; see Jonathan Crary, *Techniques of the Observer: On Vision and Modernity in the Nineteenth Century* (Cambridge, MA: MIT Press, 1994), 19; Dell Upton, *Another City* (New Haven, CT: Yale University Press, 2008), 3.

165. Mary E. Dillon, Manager, Brooklyn Borough Gas Company, "Humanizing a Gas Company," *Gas Industry* 24, no. 12 (December 1924): 456.

166. Thomas, "New Type Business Office Has No Counters," 9–10.

167. Coe, "Bell System Buildings," 211, 213.

168. NELA, "Acknowledgement of Application for Service," *Service Suggestions*, December 1921.

Chapter 4 • *Customer Stock Ownership as Corporate Political Strategy*

1. "Blazing the Trail for Popular Partnership in 'Pacific Service,'" *Pacific Service Magazine*, October 1929, 322. Portions of this chapter have been adapted from Daniel Robert, "Customer Stock Ownership as Monopoly Utility Political Strategy in the 1910s and 1920s," *Enterprise & Society* 18, no. 4 (December 2017): 893–920. Reprinted with permission.

2. Charles Remington, "Consumers Given Stock Privilege," *San Francisco Chronicle*, July 28, 1914; Janette Rutterford and Dimitris P. Sotiropoulos, "The Rise of the Small Investor in the United States and United Kingdom, 1895 to 1970," *Enterprise & Society* 18, no. 3 (September 2017): 491.

Notes to Pages 125–128   283

3. Roland Marchand, *Creating the Corporate Soul: The Rise of Public Relations and Corporate Imagery in American Big Business* (Berkeley: University of California Press, 1998), 74–83; Julia Ott, *When Wall Street Met Main Street: The Quest for an Investors' Democracy* (Cambridge, MA: Harvard University Press, 2011), 151, 153, 163; N. R. Danielian, *AT&T: The Story of Industrial Conquest* (New York: Vanguard Press, 1939), 184.

4. "Capital Grows through 'Customer-Ownership Plan,'" *Wall Street Journal*, October 6, 1921; John B. Miller, President, SCE., "Customer Ownership on the Pacific Coast," *NELA Proceedings* (1924), 207.

5. Ott, *When Wall Street Met Main Street*, 2, 4, 115, 126, 129, 134, 139, 149, 151, 163. Thomas Nixon Carver did not "inspire" customer stock ownership, nor was he the "originator" of it, as Ott argued. For more on this, see Robert, "Customer Stock Ownership." See also Thomas Nixon Carver, *The Present Economic Revolution in the United States* (Boston: Little, Brown, 1925), 139. Ott notes that as late as March 1919, Carver was still not advocating customer stock ownership (*When Wall Street Met Main Street*, 108).

6. Cedric B. Cowing, *Populists, Plungers, and Progressives: A Social History of Stock and Commodity Speculation, 1890–1936* (Princeton, NJ: Princeton University Press, 1965), 155–157, 165–171, 177–178; John Kenneth Galbraith, *The Great Crash 1929* (Boston: Hughton Mifflin, 1955), 24, 37, 51–52, 174.

7. William A. Myers, *Iron Men and Copper Wires: A Centennial History of the Southern California Edison Company* (Glendale, CA: Trans-Anglo Books, 1983), 147–149; SCE, *Annual Report to the Stockholders of Southern California Edison Company for the Year 1914*, 7–8, Folder 3, Box 11, SCE Records.

8. *Eight Annual Report of the Pacific Gas and Electric Company for the Fiscal Year Ended December 31, 1913*, 26.

9. William Issel and Robert W. Cherny, *San Francisco, 1865–1932: Politics, Power, and Urban Development* (Berkeley: University of California Press, 1986), 175.

10. *Annual Report to the Stockholders of Southern California Edison Company for the Year 1914*, 7–8, Folder 3, Box 11, SCE Records; Charles Remington, "Consumers Given Stock Privilege: Pacific Gas and Electric Company Invites Patrons to Purchase Shares," *San Francisco Chronicle*, July 28, 1914.

11. *Nineteenth Annual Report of the Pacific Gas and Electric Company for the Fiscal Year Ended December 31, 1924*, 12, Bancroft Library, University of California, Berkeley.

12. "Blazing the Trail," 322.

13. Charles Remington, "Banker Predicts Pacific Gas Bonds Will Sell Much Higher," *San Francisco Chronicle*, June 9, 1914.

14. "The Government and Utilities," *Pacific Telephone Magazine*, December 1914, 6, AT&T-TX; "Difficulties in Regulation of Utilities," *Living Church*, December 12, 1914, 192; John M. Eshleman, "Control of Public Utilities in California," *California Law Review* 1, no. 2 (January 1914): 104–123.

15. "Editorial," *Pacific Service Magazine*, August 1915, 101.

16. Charles Remington, "Consumers Taking Pacific Gas Stock," *San Francisco Chronicle*, August 9, 1914.

17. Charles Remington, "Hockenbeamer's Plan Unequaled," *San Francisco Chronicle*, December 10, 1914.

18. "Blazing the Trail," 322.

19. A. F. Hockenbeamer, "The Financial Side of 'Pacific Service," *Pacific Service Magazine,* August 1915, 97.

20. "Utilities and the Small Investor," *Pacific Telephone Magazine,* December 1916, 10–11, AT&T-TX.

21. "Customer Ownership Committee Session," Thursday, June 7, 1923, *NELA Proceedings* (1923), 220.

22. "Customer Ownership Committee," Public Relations National Section, Tuesday, June 7, 1927, *NELA Proceedings* (1927), 215–237.

23. AT&T, *Annual Report, 1921,* 15.

24. Miller, "Customer Ownership on the Pacific Coast," 208; Summary of D. F. Houston's speech, "Telephone Financing and Sale of Preferred Stock to Subscribers," in *Conference of Personnel Group, Bell System, April 18–25, 1922,* 61, Box 88, RG 4, Collection 6, AT&T-TX; Samuel Insull, "Modern Financial Problems of Utilities," speech at luncheon of the Bond Men's Club of Chicago at Hotel La Salle, November 15, 1923, in *Public Utilities in Modern Life: Selected Speeches, 1914–1923* (Chicago: Privately printed, 1924), 389; Danielian, *AT&T,* 191; Marchand, *Creating the Corporate Soul,* 79; Jay Brigham, *Empowering the West: Electrical Politics before FDR* (Lawrence: University Press of Kansas, 1998), 139; Ott, *When Wall Street Met Main Street,* 151–153.

25. Fred H. Scheel, A. H. Grimsley, and Percy H. Whiting, "Sales Manual for Public Utility Employees: Prepared by Subcommittee for Use in Customer Ownership Campaigns," *NELA Proceedings* (1922), 1:81.

26. Samuel Insull, "Production and Distribution of Electric Energy in the Central Portion of the Mississippi Valley," Cyrus Fogg Brackett Lecture delivered at Princeton University, December 1, 1921, 42–44, Folder 20-8, Insull Papers.

27. See *NELA Proceedings* (1927), xi, for example.

28. *NELA Bulletin* 9, no. 1 (January 1922), 26; Miller, "Customer Ownership on the Pacific Coast," 207; "Customer Ownership Committee," *NELA Proceedings* (1927), 218–223.

29. "Customer Ownership," *NELA Proceedings* (1921), 1:146, 1:148.b

30. Samuel Kennedy, "Transforming Public Opinion: An Address by Mr. Samuel M. Kennedy, Vice-President Southern California Edison Co., Los Angeles, California, Before the Convention of Managers and Executives of the Management Division of Stone & Webster Inc., Held in Boston, October 10–18, 1921," 39, Box 389, Folder 26, SCE Records.

31. Myers, *Iron Men and Copper Wires,* 149–151.

32. For examples of utility cooperative associations, see Tulare County Power Co., *How to Own Your Own Power* (Porterville, CA: Messenger Print, August, 1911), 15, California Public Utilities Commission Collection, California State Archives, Sacramento, California; Leah S. Glaser, *Electrifying the Rural American West: Stories of Power, People, and Place* (Lincoln: University of Nebraska Press, 2009), 38–39; Claude S. Fischer, *America Calling: A Social History of the Telephone* (Berkeley: University of California Press, 1992), 43; Robert MacDougall, *The People's Network: The Political Economy of the Telephone in the Gilded Age* (Philadelphia: University of Pennsylvania Press, 2013), 110, 136, 140, 143.

33. NELA, *Electric Light and Power: Facts and Figures on the Development and Scope of the Industry in the United States, Prepared, as the Statistical Section of the*

N.E.L.A. Handbook, by the Association's Statistical Department, March, 1928 (New York, 1928), 21–31; David B. Sicilia, "Selling Power: Marketing and Monopoly at Boston Edison, 1886–1929" (PhD diss., Brandeis University, 1990), 480–481; Brigham, *Empowering the West*, 135; Charles David Jacobson, *Ties That Bind: Economic and Political Dilemmas of Urban Utility Networks, 1800–1990* (Pittsburgh: University of Pittsburgh Press, 2000), 103.

34. David M. Kennedy, *Over Here: The First World War and American Society* (New York: Oxford University Press, 1982), 253.

35. Although the telephone network was also nationalized during the war, the reasons for this were more largely political rather than operational; see Richard R. John, *Network Nation: Inventing American Telecommunications* (Cambridge, MA: Belknap Press of Harvard University Press, 2010), 395–396.

36. For discussions of Bell's operator training and procedures, see the first chapter of Stephen H. Norwood, *Labor's Flaming Youth: Telephone Operators and Worker Militancy, 1878–1923* (Urbana: University of Illinois Press, 1990), and the first two chapters of Venus Green, *Race on the Line: Gender, Labor, and Technology in the Bell System, 1880–1980* (Durham, NC: Duke University Press, 2001).

37. *Stenographic Report of Mr. Gifford's Talk at the Operating Conference (Seaview), May 7, 1930*, File: Conferences, 1925–1933, 5–6, Box 10, Collection 3, RG 5, AT&T-TX; Mahon, "The Telephone in Chicago, 1877–1940," typescript, 75–76, AT&T-TX; Robert W. Garnet, *The Telephone Enterprise: The Evolution of the Bell System's Horizontal Structure, 1876–1909* (Baltimore: Johns Hopkins University Press, 1985), 133.

38. Kenneth Lipartito, *The Bell System and Regional Business: The Telephone in the South, 1877–1920* (Baltimore: Johns Hopkins University Press, 1989), 201–202; Green, *Race on the Line*, 14–15; Garnet, *The Telephone Enterprise*, 153–154, 157. MacDougall correctly shows that even Kingsbury himself did not view his commitment as the end of Bell's problems. MacDougall, *The People's Network*, 242.

39. This is a paraphrase written in a summary of Hall's speech, "Review of the Previous Conference—Program of the Work to Date—Personnel Work in Other Industries—Importance of Morale," in *Conference of Personnel Group, Bell System, April 18–25, 1922*, 9, Box 88, RG 4, Collection 6, AT&T-TX.

40. *Stenographic Report of Mr. Gifford's Talk*, 5–6.

41. Ott, *When Wall Street Met Main Street*, 163–164; Marchand, *Creating the Corporate Soul*, 74; A. Emory Wishon, "Now and Tomorrow with Customer Ownership," in "Popular Ownership of Property: Its Newer Forms and Social Consequences," ed. William L. Ransom and Parker Thomas Moon, special issue, *Proceedings of the Academy of Political Science in the City of New York* 11, no. 3 (April 1925): 408, 410; AT&T, *Comments Submitted to Federal Communications Commission by American Telephone and Telegraph Company on Commission Ex. 230: Ownership of American Telephone and Telegraph Company* (AT&T, November 19, 1937), 4–6, AT&T-TX.

42. AT&T, *Comments Submitted to the FCC, Ex. 230*, 6; Marchand, *Creating the Corporate Soul*, 74; Ott, *When Wall Street Met Main Street*, 153. For a discussion of monopoly privileges in exchange for low rates, see John, *Network Nation*, 407.

43. "Scarcity of Capital," *Pacific Telephone Magazine*, June 1920, 3, AT&T-TX.

44. Pillsbury to Gifford, February 20, 1925, 1, File: PT&T Co.–Stock Issue, 1925 [2 of 3], Box 49, RG 5, Collection 3, AT&T-TX.

45. "Blazing the Trail," 322.

46. Paul A. Clapp in *Report, Telephone Investigation (Pursuant to Public Resolution No. 8, 74th Congress)* (Washington, DC: Government Printing Office, 1938), 563; NELA, *Statistical Supplement to the 'Electric Light and Power Industry in the United States'* (New York: NELA, 1929), 3.

47. F. L. Devereux, "The Development of the Ownership of the Bell System," in "Popular Ownership of Property," 420.

48. Scheel, Grimsley, and Whiting, "Sales Manual for Public Utility Employees," 1:74, 78–79.

49. Scheel quoting Insull from the 1921 NELA convention in Scheel, Grimsley, and Whiting, "Sales Manual for Public Utility Employees," 1:74; Percy H. Whiting, Chairman, A. H. Grimsley, and Fred H. Scheel, "Appendix 2: Successful Methods and Practices for Customer Ownership Campaigns Prepared by Subcommittee," *NELA Proceedings* (1922), 1:88.

50. Whiting, Grimsley, and Scheel, "Appendix 2," 1:88.

51. "Report of the Customer Ownership Committee," *AERA Proceedings, 1925*, 205.

52. Whiting, Grimsley, and Scheel, "Appendix 2," 1:88–89; "How I Sold Fifty Shares of Stock," *Pacific Telephone Magazine*, October 1925, 33, AT&T-TX.

53. C. E. Rolfe, W. J. O'Connor, J. T. Sheafor, and J. C. Koons, "Getting Information to Employees," in *Bell System Personnel Conference, Washington, D. C. October 23–30, 1929*, 5, Box 88, RG 4, Collection 6, AT&T-TX.

54. Scheel, Grimsley, and Whiting, "Sales Manual for Public Utility Employees," 1:81.

55. "Report of the Customer Ownership Committee, Appendix A: Customer Ownership Methods," *AERA Proceedings, 1925*, 205.

56. "'I Can and I Will,' Says Mr. Brommage," *Pacific Telephone Magazine*, January 1925, 23, AT&T-TX.

57. Rolfe et al, "Getting Information to Employees," 5.

58. SCE, "Securities Department" (1917): 4, Box 114, Folder 4, SCE Records; "Putting More E's in Stock Sales," *Pacific Telephone Magazine*, April 1926, 35, AT&T-TX.

59. "Round Table on Customer Ownership Problems," *NELA Proceedings* (1924), 219–220.

60. "Round Table on Customer Ownership Problems," 218; "Report of the Customer Ownership Committee, Appendix A," 202, 205.

61. Whiting, Grimsley, and Scheel, "Appendix 2," 1:84; "Round Table on Customer Ownership Problems," 219.

62. *Answers to Customer Ownership Questionnaire*, 1930, 66, Box 116, Folder 4, SCE Records.

63. "Report of the Customer Ownership Committee," 205.

64. SCE, "Important Special Stock Sales Bulletin, January 1, 1926," 1, Box 115, Folder 4, SCE Records.

65. Miller, "Customer Ownership on the Pacific Coast," 208.

66. "Stock Salesmen Meeting Held in Assembly Room, Edison Building on November 5, 1921," 2, Box 114, Folder 8, SCE Records.

67. *Pacific Telephone Magazine*, November 1925, 22, AT&T-TX; "Ramona Office Wins Two Banners," *Pacific Telephone Magazine*, April 1926, 19, AT&T-TX; *Answers to*

Customer Ownership Questionnaire, 69; "How I Sold Fifty Shares of Stock," *Pacific Telephone Magazine*, October 1925, 33, AT&T-TX; "Report of the Customer Ownership Committee, Appendix A," 206.

68. "No Stock Quotas," *Busy Buttons' Bulletin*, February 1928, Box 461, Folder 4, SCE Records.

69. "Round Table on Customer Ownership Problems," 219.

70. J. C. Rourke Jr., "How's This for a Sales Record? John H. Schrodt of Thibodaux Has Made 208 Sales of 704 Shares," *Southern Telephone News*, February 1927, 19, AT&T-TX.

71. "Stock Salesmen Meeting, October 8, 1921," 7–8, Box 114, Folder 8, SCE Records.

72. "Report of the Customer Ownership Committee," 200, 203–204.

73. "Stock Salesmen Meeting, October 8, 1921," 1.

74. T. H. Dawson, "12,000 See Our Demonstration at Big Copper Country Fair," *Mouthpiece* (Detroit, MI), November 1924, 5, AT&T-TX.

75. SCE, "Securities Department," 7.

76. Miller, "Customer Ownership on the Pacific Coast," 208–209; Ott, *When Wall Street Met Main Street*, 73, 75–100; "Blazing the Trail," 322–323.

77. Percy H. Whiting, Manager, Securities Department, Central Maine Power Company, "Intensive Sales of Public Utility Securities," *Electrical World*, May 28, 1921, 1296; Kennedy, "Transforming Public Opinion."

78. "Stock Salesmen Meeting . . . November 5, 1921," 12; "Transforming Public Opinion," 33.

79. Miller, "Customer Ownership on the Pacific Coast," 208–209.

80. Scheel, Grimsley, and Whiting, "Sales Manual for Public Utility Employees," 1:72–74.

81. Marchand, *Creating the Corporate Soul*, 77–78, 214.

82. SCE, "Securities Department," 5.

83. Miller, "Customer Ownership on the Pacific Coast," 208.

84. William Z. Ripley, *Main Street and Wall Street* (Boston: Little, Brown, 1927), 345.

85. *Annual Report of the Bell Telephone Securities Company Incorporated for the Year Ending December 31, 1928* (New York, 1929), 6; hereafter Bell Telephone Securities, *Annual Report 1928*; similar citations will be similarly abbreviated.

86. Bell Telephone Securities, *Annual Report, 1923*, 11.

87. Whiting, Grimsley, and Scheel, "Appendix 2," 1:85–86; "An Intelligent Thief," *Public Service Management*, January 1923, 26.

88. Bell Telephone Securities, *Annual Report of the Bell Telephone Securities Company, Incorporated, For the Year Ending December 31, 1924* (New York: 1925), 11.

89. AT&T, *Annual Report, 1922*, 15.

90. MacDougall, *The People's Network*, 110; *FTC Letter No. 4* (1928), 447.

91. Summary of D. F. Houston's speech, "Telephone Financing and Sale of Preferred Stock to Subscribers," in *Conference of Personnel Group, Bell System, April 18–25, 1922*, 60–61, Box 88, RG 4, Collection 6, AT&T-TX.

92. Summary of D. F. Houston's speech, "Telephone Financing," 60.

93. AT&T, *Annual Report, 1921*, 14.

94. MacDougall, *The People's Network*, 68–69.

95. "Customer Ownership Committee," *NELA Proceedings* (1927), 225.

96. "Customer Ownership Committee," *NELA Proceedings* (1927), 225.

97. Bell Telephone Securities, *Annual Report, 1924*, 14.

98. David P. Thelen, *Robert M. La Follette and the Insurgent Spirit* (Boston: Little, Brown, 1976), 190.

99. *Bell Telephone Quarterly*, October 1923, 261–266.

100. H. Blair-Smith, "The 1926 Stock Issue of the American Telephone and Telegraph Company," *Bell Telephone Quarterly*, October 1926, 265; "1928 Stock Offer of the American Telephone and Telegraph Company," *Bell Telephone Quarterly*, October 1928, 262, 264, 261, photograph opposite p. 264.

101. In 1925, there were 6,017 "central offices" within the Bell System. Bell Telephone Securities, *Bell Telephone Securities Reference Tables and Descriptions for the Use of Investors, Investment Houses, and Bankers, with a Brief Introductory Statement of the Organization and Financing of the American Telephone and Telegraph Company and Associated Companies* (New York, 1935), 21.

102. Richard Storrs Coe, "Bell System Buildings—an Interpretation," *Bell Telephone Quarterly*, July 1929, 205.

103. H. Blair-Smith, "1929 Convertible Bond Offer of the American Telephone and Telegraph Co.," *Bell Telephone Quarterly*, October 1929, 320.

104. Bell Telephone Securities, *Annual Report, 1925*, 9; *1926*, 9; *1927*, 8; *1928*, 8; *The Stock of the American Telephone and Telegraph Company* (New York: Bell Telephone Securities, September [1923]), 6, Box 4, RG 6, Collection 6, AT&T-TX; "Customer Ownership Committee," *NELA Proceedings* (1923), 220.

105. "Report of the Customer Ownership Committee—1931," *NELA Proceedings* (1931), 1093; "Report of the Customer Ownership Committee, Appendix A," 202–203; Whiting, Grimsley, and Scheel, "Appendix 2," 1:85.

106. "Customer Ownership Committee," *NELA Proceedings* (1927), 227; Bell Telephone Securities, *Annual Report, 1928*, 5.

107. Twenty percent is a conservative estimate. The number was obtained using the following methodology: For the years from 1923 through 1929, NELA member companies gave the total number of new shareholders obtained through customer stock-ownership programs and the percentage of these shareholders who were customers, employees, and others. The numbers of shareholders gained in these three categories were therefore easily calculable. For the years prior to 1923, an average percentage for each category was obtained from the years 1923–1929 and applied to the years 1914–1922. The NELA data includes numbers for many, but not all, electricity and gas companies. At the end of 1929, AT&T counted approximately 289,000 of their 469,801 shareholders as coming directly from the company's customer stock-ownership plans. Adding this number to the total number of customer and employee shareholders gained specifically through customer ownership campaigns leads to slightly more than two million people who purchased utility stock directly through customer stock-ownership programs. Taking a percentage of that number to ten million, gives 20.1 percent. If one excludes all utility employees who purchased stock through customer ownership programs, utility shareholders still comes to 18.39 percent of the total number of shareholders by the crash of 1929. Many streetcar companies are not included in these numbers. See the Customer Stock Ownership

Notes to Pages 144–145 289

Committee reports in *NELA Proceedings* (1922), 1:70; (1924), 199; (1925), 209; (1926), 323; (1927), 227; (1928), 254; (1929), 1509; (1930), 1253; Edwin H. Robnett, "Report of Committee on Customer Ownership," *American Gas Association Proceedings 1930*, 119; Bell Telephone Securities, *Annual Report, 1929*; AT&T, *Annual Report, 1929*, 11. One executive estimated that customer stock ownership added 2.5 million shareholders to utility companies by November 1928. William H. Hodge, Vice President, Sales and Advertising, H. M. Byllesby & Co., "What Should Shareholder Contact Be?" *American Gas Association Monthly*, November 1928, 727.

108. Walter A. Friedman estimates ten million shareholders in the United States by 1930. Walter A. Friedman, *Fortune Tellers: The Story of America's First Economic Forecasters* (Princeton, NJ: Princeton University Press, 2014), 8; and N. R. Danielian also estimates ten million shareholders by 1930 based on reasonable assumptions and published data. Danielian, *AT&T*, 185. Estimates vary, however. Edwin J. Perkins estimated five million in *Wall Street to Main Street: Charles Merrill and Middle-Class Investors* (Cambridge: Cambridge University Press, 1999), 86; Ott estimated eight million in *When Wall Street Met Main Street*, 2, 170, 56–57; Gardiner C. Means estimated eighteen million stockholders in 1928 in "The Diffusion of Stock Ownership in the United States," *Quarterly Journal of Economics* 44, no. 4 (August 1930): 565.

109. Bell Telephone Securities, *Annual Report, 1923*, 5.

110. Blair-Smith, "The 1926 Stock Issue," 261; AT&T, *Comments Submitted to FCC, Ex. 230*, 9; "Annual Meeting of the NELA Commonwealth Edison Company Section Held in Customers Hall, Edison Building, Chicago, October 30, 1919," Folder 20-6, Insull Papers; "Report of Customer Ownership Committee," *NELA Proceedings* (1922), 1:67; "A Welcome to a New Stockholder," *Pacific Telephone Magazine*, October 1925, 23–24, AT&T-TX; Ripley, *Main Street and Wall Street*, 345; Wishon, "Now and Tomorrow with Customer Ownership," 413; "Blazing the Trail," 323; Rourke Jr., "How's This for a Sales Record?," 19. AT&T defined all married women, designated as "Mrs." on their stock forms, as a housewife, though this was certainly not the case. See *General Information of Interest to Employees Relative to the Employees' Stock Plan of the American Telephone and Telegraph Company* (New York: AT&T, July 1, 1922), 2, Box 4, RG 6, Collection 6, AT&T-TX; AT&T, *Comments Submitted to FCC, Ex. 230*, 6–9; "Customer Ownership Committee," *NELA Proceedings* (1925), 192–194; "Logic of Customer Ownership," *Public Service Management*, March 1927, 67.

111. Blair-Smith, "The 1926 Stock Issue," 261; AT&T, *Comments Submitted to FCC*, 9; "Annual Meeting of the NELA Commonwealth Edison Company."

112. Ripley, *Main Street and Wall Street*, 345.

113. "Report of Customer Ownership Committee,"" *NELA Proceedings* (1922), 1:67.

114. "A Welcome to a New Stockholder," 23–24. This article also contains a picture of Taylor handing over the cash. Genealogical evidence shows that Taylor did, in fact, exist; see "Thomas L. Taylor," People Search, accessed March 15, 2023, http://www.faqs.org/people-search/thomas-l-taylor/. The Thomas L. Taylor born December 15, 1909, may be the same Taylor as in the article.

115. *FTC Letter No. 22* (1930), 1200–1201; FCC, *Telephone Investigation* (1937), 4:23a–23b; Lucien Kellogg, "'Visitors Are Welcome': How a Western Utility Brings Together Four Factors in Its Sales-and-Service Plan," *Business*, May 1925, 54, Box 440, Folder 8, SCE Records.

116. *FTC Letter No. 22* (1930), 1183.

117. "Round Table on Customer Ownership Problems," 221–222.

118. *NELA Bulletin* 9, no. 1 (January 1922), 61.

119. "Round Table on Customer Ownership Problems," 220.

120. *Employees' Stock Plan: A Plan for Subscriptions for Stock of the American Telephone and Telegraph Company* (New York: AT&T, May 1, 1921), 1, Box 3, RG 6, Collection 6, AT&T-TX.

121. B. C. Forbes, "Why Creed Puts Service above Money-Making: P.G. & E. President Says "'Business is Business' No Longer Reflects National Sentiment"—His Life Is an Ideal Illustration of This Evolution," *Forbes Magazine*, 97, April 28, 1923, Box 440, Folder 8, SCE Records.

122. "Playing 'One Night Stands' in Jersey," *American Gas Association Monthly*, June 1922, 342.

123. Miller, "Customer Ownership on the Pacific Coast," 209.

124. Henry L. Stimson, "The Effects of Popular Ownership on Public Opinion," in "Popular Ownership of Property," 490.

125. Quoted in "Blazing the Trail," 323.

126. Wishon, "Now and Tomorrow with Customer Ownership," 412–413.

127. "Report of the Customer Ownership Committee," *AERA Proceedings, 1925*, 199.

128. "Capital Grows through 'Customer-Ownership Plan.'"

129. John Spargo, "Letter of Confession and Challenge," *Outlook*, October 29, 1924, 328; Taylor, "The Spirit Which Permeates the Service of Our Utilities," *NELA Proceedings* (1925), 1722; M. S. Sloan, President of the Brooklyn Edison Company, *Our Selves and the Public* (lecture before the Kentucky Public Utilities Association, 1925), 5–6, Box 449, Folder 6, SCE Records.

130. "Meeting of Engineering Department," [1923], 4, Box 114, Folder 11, SCE Records.

131. Insull, "Modern Financial Problems of Utilities," 390.

132. Wishon, "Now and Tomorrow with Customer Ownership," 408. Socialism declined in the 1910s and 1920s because it split from within, was suppressed from the above, and was supplanted from the bottom by customer ownership.

133. Sheridan in *FTC Letter No. 5* (1928), 57–58.

134. Herbert Markle, Division Manager, Appalachian Electric Power Co., in *FTC Letter No. 22* (1930), 403–404

135. Wishon, "Now and Tomorrow with Customer Ownership," 414. Voting numbers come from Frank C. Jordan, *Statement of Vote at General Election Held on November 7, 1922, in the State of California* (Sacramento, California State Printing Office, 1923).; *Customer Ownership Committee*; and *NELA Proceedings* (1927), 222.

136. "Report of Customer Ownership Committee," *NELA Proceedings* (1922), 1:66; FCC, *Telephone Investigation* (1937), 4:23a–23b.

137. Ott, *When Wall Street Met Main Street*, 164; Marchand, *Creating the Corporate Soul*, 74; Wishon, "Now and Tomorrow with Customer Ownership," 408, 410; AT&T, *Comments Submitted to FCC, Ex. 230*, 4–6.

138. David E. Nye, *Electrifying America: Social Meanings of a New Technology, 1880–1940* (Cambridge, MA: MIT Press, 1990), 261.

139. "Customer Ownership Committee," *NELA Proceedings* (1928), 225.

Notes to Pages 150–154   *291*

140. Insull, "Public Relations," speech before AERA, Claypool Hotel, Indianapolis, Indiana, February 28, 1922, 9, Folder 21-1, Insull Papers.

141. Insull, "Modern Financial Problems of Utilities," 391. The story is almost identical to the one that mentions Minneapolis found in Insull, "Public Relations."

142. "Capital Grows through 'Customer-Ownership Plan.'"

143. Kennedy, "Transforming Public Opinion," 41.

144. Ripley, *Main Street and Wall Street*, 293; Galbraith, *The Great Crash*, 52.

145. The use of the term "shareholders' democracy" here is not intended to refer to the term coined by Julia Ott. Ott did not argue that corporations were, in fact, democratic. Rather, she argued that certain individuals promoted a vision of a country filled with shareholders who would express their approval or disapproval of a company by buying or selling its shares. Ott, *When Wall Street Met Main Street*, 151.

146. Galbraith, *The Great Crash*, 52–55.

147. Green, *Race on the Line*, 12.

148. AT&T, *Annual Report, 1905*, 31–32; *1925*, 22.

149. Roger Babson, for example, predicted the economic downturn of late 1929 and in the early twentieth century had worked selling utility bonds until he came to believe that many of the firms were more interested in making money through financing than through providing service. See Friedman, *Fortune Tellers*, 43–44, 80, 16.

150. B. C. Forbes, "What the Customer Is Thinking," *NELA Proceedings* (1926), 56–57.

151. John Sheridan to Thorne Browne, Middle West Division, NELA, Lincoln, Nebraska, August 12, 1927, Box 3853, Ex. 2968, FTC Records.

152. Ripley, *Main Street and Wall Street*, 1927; Ott views Ripley as being a "loyal critic" of customer stock ownership, but this is implausible. Ott, *When Wall Street Met Main Street*, 131–132, 152. Ripley fiercely criticized the prevailing corporate financial practices in a way that could only make investors bearish.

153. AT&T, *Comments Submitted to FCC, Ex. 2114*, 4, 9.

154. "Dividend and Stock Split History," PG&E Corp., accessed June 20, 2014, http://www.pgecorp.com/investors/shareholders/dividend_history.shtml; SCE, *Annual Report to the Stockholders of Southern California Edison Company Ltd. for the Year 1949*, 7, Box 11, Folder 4, SCE Records.

155. T. E. Butler, 222 N. Genesee St, Waukegan, Illinois, to Samuel Insull Jr., August 18, 1930, Box 15, Folder 1, Insull Papers.

156. Stock in Insull's Insull Utilities Investments, Middle West Utilities Company, Corporation Securities Company of Chicago, and Peoples Gas Light & Coke Company all became worthless. "Cyrus Eaton and Insull Group Stock, Draft of Passage," Folder 18-13, 1–5, Insull Papers; Page 38A-1, 7/23/34, Box 18, Folder 11, Insull Papers; Annie Brady, 7236 Champlain Ave., Chicago, Illinois, to Samuel Insull, May 9, 1936, Box 15, Folder 1, Insull Papers; Bernard A. Klusen, 5708 S. Sangamon St, Chicago, Illinois, to Samuel Insull, June 19, 1939, Box 15, Folder 2, Insull Papers; Forrest McDonald, *Insull* (Chicago: The University of Chicago Press, 1962), 301; John F. Wasik, *The Merchant of Power: Samuel Insull, Thomas Edison, and the Creation of the Modern Metropolis* (New York: Palgrave Macmillan, 2006), 189–190, 199–201, 208.

157. Brady to Insull, May 9, 1936.

158. Mary V. Cullen, 4256 North Lamon Ave., Chicago, Illinois, to Samuel Insull, December 20, 1932, Box 15, Folder 1, Insull Papers.

292   Notes to Pages 154–158

159. Butler to Insull Jr., August 18, 1930, and December 19, 1930, Box 15, Folder 1, Insull Papers.

160. Insull to Violet Coad, February 26, 1932, Box 15, Folder 1; Insull Jr. to Klusen, June 23, 1939, Box 15, Folder 2, Insull Papers.

161. Page 22A-1, 7/11/34, Box 18, Folder 11, Insull Papers.

162. "Cyrus Eaton and Insull Group Stock," 1–5.

163. Wasik, *The Merchant of Power*, 242; Page 38A-1, 7/23/34.

164. Page 69A-1, Folder 18-11, Insull Papers.

165. "Death Closes Remarkable Career," *PG&E Progress*, December 1935, 5.

Chapter 5 • Making the News

1. John Sheridan to H. R. Beck, November 15, 1922, Ex. 2904, Box 3853, Series: Economic Investigations Files, 1915–1938, Subject: Power and Gas, FTC Records; Sheridan in *FTC Letter No. 5* (1928), (National Archives, College Park, Maryland) 133–134, xx. The masthead of the *Poplar Bluff American* declared itself an "independent" newspaper; see, for example, *Popular Bluff American*, Friday, December 1, 1922, 1, microfilm, State Historical Society of Missouri, Columbia.

2. Sheridan in *FTC Letter No. 5* (1928), 82–83, xiv; J. B. Sheridan, "Copy of Address Delivered by J. B. Sheridan to the Missouri Press Association," [February 10, 1922], Ex. 2736, Box 3851, FTC Records; J. B. Sheridan to C. C. Hellmers, February 9, 1922, Ex. 2734, Box 3851, FTC Records; J. B. Sheridan to J. F. Hull, February 11, 1922, Ex. 2737, Box 3851, FTC Records; John Sheridan, *Weekly Report of the Manager—Missouri Committee on Public Utility Information, February 6–11, 1922*, 2–3, Ex. 2735, Box 3851, FTC Records.

3. Sheridan, *Weekly Report of the Manager . . . February 6–11, 1922*, 4–5.

4. Examination of John B. Sheridan, Secretary of the Missouri Committee on Public Utility Information in *FTC Letter No. 5* (1928), 84.

5. "The Read Value of Public Utilities," *Excelsior Springs Daily Standard*, June 15, 1923, 1, microfilm, State Historical Society of Missouri, Columbia; J. B. Sheridan to S. W. Henderson, June 13, 1923, Ex. 2908, Box 3853, FTC Records; J. B. Sheridan to Wiley Corl, June 13, 1923, Ex. 2911, Box 3853, FTC Records; Sheridan in *FTC Letter No. 5* (1928), 135–136, 121; North Missouri Power Company, "Announcing a 7 Per Cent Non-Taxable Investment," *Excelsior Springs Daily Standard*, June 12, 1923, 3; "The Read Value of Public Utilities," *Excelsior Springs Daily Standard*, June 15, 1923, 1; "North Missouri Power Company, "Pave Your Path to Wealth" (advertisement), *Excelsior Springs Daily Standard*, June 15, 1923, 4, microfilm, State Historical Society of Missouri, Columbia.

6. I have used the conservative *Boston Herald* conversion factor for all such conversions in this book, since the New England Bureau of Public Service Information, which operated much like Sheridan's committee, used a conversion factor of 168.3 column inches per page based on the size of the *Boston Herald*. Joseph B. Groce, Director, New England Bureau of Public Service Information, *Report of First Year's Work, 1922*, 4, Box 3817, Ex. 687, FTC Records; Sheridan in *FTC Letter No. 5* (1928), 43, 38.

7. "The Read Value of Public Utilities," 1; Sheridan in *FTC Letter No. 5* (1928), 135–136, 121; David E. Nye, "Public Relations as Covert Political Communication: The Debate over Public vs. Private the United States," *American Studies in Scandinavia* 16 (1984): 28.

Notes to Pages 158–161   293

8. Between the advent of central station electricity service in 1882 and 1925, over 860 municipally owned power plants closed, many in small towns. NELA, *Political Ownership and the Electric Light and Power Industry (Published for the Information of Member Companies)* (1925), 91; Bernard J. Mullaney, "Space Grabbing in the Newspapers," address to AGA, 1927, *FTC Letter No. 2* (1928), xii, xxvii; Examination of Rob Roy McGregor, Assistant Director, Illinois Committee on Public Utility Information, in *FTC Letter No. 2* (1928), 159; Examination of Samuel T. MacQuarrie, Director, New England Bureau of Public Service Information; Chairman, Public Relations, National Electric Light Association (NELA); Chairman, Public Speaking Committee, NELA; Chairman, Organization of Information Bureau Committee, NELA and similar position in American Gas Association, in *FTC Letter No. 2* (1928), 170.

9. David E. Nye is an exception; see Nye, "Public Relations," 21–35.

10. Paul F. Lazarsfeld and Robert F. Merton, "Mass Communication, Popular Taste, and Organized Social Action," in *The Communication of Ideas, a Series of Addresses*, ed. Lyman Bryson (New York: Institute of Religious and Social Studies, 1948), 95–118.

11. Nye, "Public Relations," 21–35; David B. Sicilia, "Selling Power: Marketing and Monopoly at Boston Edison, 1886–1929" (PhD diss., Brandeis University, 1990), 531–539; Stuart Ewen, *PR! A Social History of Spin* (New York: Basic Books, 1996); Ernest Gruening, *The Public Pays: A Study of Power Propaganda* (New York: Vanguard Press, 1931); Jack Levin, *Power Ethics: An Analysis of the Activities of Public Utilities in the United States, Based on a Study of the U.S. Federal Trade Commission Records* (New York: Alfred A. Knopf, 1931); M. L. Ramsay, *Pyramids of Power: The Story of Roosevelt, Insull and the Utility Wars* (New York: Bobbs-Merrill, 1937); H. S. Raushenbush and Harry W. Laidler, *Power Control* (New York: New Republic, 1928); Carl D. Thompson, *Confessions of the Power Trust: A Summary of the Testimony Given in the Hearings of the Federal Trade Commission on Utility Corporations Pursuant to Resolution No. 83 of the United States Senate Approved February 15, 1928* (New York: D. P. Dutton, 1932).

12. J. F. Hull to J. B. Sheridan, January 6, 1922, 2, Ex. 2726, Box 3851, FTC Records; Sheridan, "Copy of Address."

13. Examination of George F. Oxley, Director of the Department of Public Information, NELA, in *FTC Letter No. 3* (1928), 20–21; Examination of Willis J. Spaulding, Commissioner of Public Property, City of Springfield, Illinois, in *FTC Letter No. 2* (1928), 10; McGregor in *FTC Letter No. 2* (1928), 130, 143; Examination of George E. Lewis, Director, Rocky Mountain Committee on Public Utility Information, in *FTC Letter No. 4* (1928), 386, 389; Examination of Thorne Browne, Supervisor, Nebraska Utilities Information Bureau; Managing Director, Secretary, and Treasurer, Middle West Division, NELA, in *FTC Letter No. 4* (1928), 86, 94, 103; Gruening, *The Public Pays*, 25.

14. J. Leonard Bates, *Senator Thomas J. Walsh of Montana: Law and Public Affairs, from TR to FDR* (Urbana: University of Illinois Press, 1999), 205, 210, 257–259; Josephine O'Keane, *Thomas J. Walsh, a Senator from Montana* (Francestown, NH: M. Jones, 1955), 197–199; Spaulding in *FTC Letter No. 2* (1928), 10; Mullaney, in *FTC Letter No. 2* (1928), 87.

15. "Limits Utilities Hearing," *New York Times*, January 17, 1928, 31.

16. Bates, *Senator Thomas J. Walsh*, 259; "Senate Votes, 46-31, for Power Inquiry by the Trade Board," *New York Times*, February 16, 1928, 1, 10.

294   *Notes to Pages 161–164*

17. *FTC Letter No. 3* (1928), vi–vii; McGregor in *Response to Senate Resolution No. 83 a Monthly Report on the Electric Power and Gas Utilities Inquiry, No. 2, Filed with the Secretary of the Senate, April 16, 1928* (1928), 69; B. F. Weadock, Special Counsel, "Federal Trade Investigation," *NELA Proceedings* (1930), 68.

18. *FTC Letter No. 73* (1935), ix; *FTC Letter No. 77* (1935), 15, 121.

19. FCC, *Telephone Investigation* (1937), 4:1.

20. "Roosevelt Orders Telephone Inquiry: He Signs Resolution Granting $750,000 for a Sweeping Investigation of Industry," 21, *New York Times*, March 16, 1935.

21. "Gifford Says A.T.&T. Has No Fears of FTC [*sic*] Investigation," 1, *Wall Street Journal*, November 19, 1934.

22. Samuel Insull, "Public Relations," speech before AERA, Claypool Hotel, Indianapolis, Indiana, February 28, 1922, 6–7, Folder 21-1, Insull Papers.

23. "Samuel Insull and the State Council of Defense of Illinois in the World War of 1917–1918," 9, Folder 19-15: State Council of Defense of Illinois, 1917–1919, Insull Papers.

24. Ernest Palmer, Chicago Chairman, Los. A. Rushton, Secretary, "Certified Copy of Letter Addressed to Mr. Samuel Insull and Resolution Adopted by the Governing Committee of the Four Minute Men in Chicago, at Their Final Meeting, December 19, 1918," Folder 19-15, Insull Papers.

25. Mullaney in *FTC Letter No. 2* (1928), 75, 100.

26. Mullaney in *FTC Letter No. 2* (1928), 102.

27. Mullaney in *FTC Letter No. 2* (1928), 74–75.

28. Mullaney in *FTC Letter No. 2* (1928), xii, 87; McGregor in *FTC Letter No. 2* (1928), 140.

29. Willard Cope, Vice President and Executive Secretary, Utilities Information Committee of Georgia, in *FTC Letter No. 3* (1928), 526; Sheridan in *FTC Letter No. 5* (1928), 39; Examination of Leon C. Bradley, Director, Alabama Public Utilities Information Bureau, in *FTC Letter No. 10* (1929), 1; "Here and There with the Section," *American Gas Association Monthly*, March 1922, 157.

30. Oxley in *FTC Letter No. 3* (1928), 20–21.

31. Examination of Joe Carmichael, Director, Iowa Committee on Public Utility Information, in *FTC Letter No. 4* (1928), 6; Browne in *FTC Letter No. 4* (1928), 88; Examination of William C. Grant, Director, Texas Public Service Information Bureau, in *FTC Letter No. 4* (1928), 442; Sheridan in *FTC Letter No. 5* (1928), 40–41.

32. Examination of J.S.S. Richardson, Director, Department of Information of the Joint Committee, National Utility Association, in *FTC Letter No. 3* (1928), 404.

33. Grant in *FTC Letter No. 4* (1928), 460–461, 467.

34. Although the names of these organizations appeared restrictive to one industry, in practice they included members from all four utility industries, and in some cases the same people chaired publicity committees in more than one association. Robert V. Prather in *Response to Senate Resolution No. 83*; Oxley in *FTC Letter No. 3* (1928), 20–21; Spaulding in *FTC Letter No. 2* (1928), 10; McGregor in *FTC Letter No. 2* (1928), 130, 143; Lewis in *FTC Letter No. 4* (1928), 386, 389; Browne in *FTC Letter No. 4* (1928), 86, 94, 103; Gruening, *The Public Pays*, 25.

35. Grant in *FTC Letter No. 4* (1928), 461, Sheridan in *FTC Letter No. 5* (1928), 141–142.

36. Rocky Mountain Committee on Public Utility Information, Resume of Three Years' Activities [1924?], Ex. 1845, Box 3841, FTC Records.

Notes to Pages 164–169   295

37. Meeting minutes from the organization refer to this; see Richardson in *FTC Letter No. 3* (1928), 400.

38. Examination of Eugene S. Wilson, Vice-president, AT&T in *Proceedings before the FCC, January 26, 1937*, 5338–5345.

39. Missouri Committee on Public Utility Information, *List of Subscribers for Year 1927–1928*, Box 3853, Ex. 2972, FTC Records.

40. Examination of Fred R. Jenkins, Chairman, Educational Committee of NELA in *FTC Letter No. 4* (1928), 616–617.

41. Examination of Arthur W. Page, Vice President, Information Department, AT&T, in *Proceedings before the FCC, January 25, 1937*, 5189.

42. Sheridan in *FTC Letter No. 5* (1928), 104.

43. Carmichael in *FTC Letter No. 4* (1928), 31–32.

44. Sheridan in *FTC Letter No. 5* (1928), 95.

45. Sheridan in *FTC Letter No. 5* (1928), 83.

46. Theodore N. Vail, *At the Opening of the Annual Conference of the Bell System*, New York, October 1913, 3, Box 2, RG 6, Collection 6, AT&T-TX.

47. W. L. Willkie, General Counsel, Northern Ohio Power and Light Company, "At the Public's Service," *AERA Proceedings, 1929*, 19–20.

48. *The Big Problem of the Future: Synopsis of an Address by E.K. Hall, Vice-President, American Telephone and Telegraph Company, at Meeting of Men Employees of the Illinois Bell Telephone Company, Hotel LaSalle, Chicago, Illinois, March 21, 1923*, 8, Box 4, RG 6, Collection 6, AT&T-TX.

49. C. H. Markham, President, Illinois Central Railroad Company, "What Small Customers Can Do for a Business," *System: The Magazine of Business*, June 1922, 666.

50. F. Lauriston Bullard, Chief Editorial Writer, *Boston Herald*, "The Newspaper Man's View of Public Relations," *NELA Proceedings* (1924), 146.

51. MacQuarrie in *FTC Letter No. 2* (1928), 176.

52. Fred W. Mitchell, *Daily Standard* publisher, to Missouri Committee on Public Utility Information, January 5, 1922[?], Ex. 2890, Box 3853, FTC Records.

53. Examination of Evelyn Harris, Assistant to the President in Charge of Public Relations, Southern Bell Telephone and Telegraph Company, in *Proceedings before the FCC, January 13, 1937*, 4747–4749.

54. Sheridan in *FTC Letter No. 5* (1928), 86–87, xvii.

55. Sheridan in *FTC Letter No. 5* (1928), 86–90, xvii.

56. FCC, *Telephone Investigation* (1937), 4:63–67.

57. FCC, *Telephone Investigation* (1937), 4:63–64.

58. Underlining in original. Harris in *Proceedings before the FCC, January 13, 1937*, 4759–4761.

59. Harris in *Proceedings before the FCC, January 13, 1937*, 4842–4846.

60. Harris in *Proceedings before the FCC, January 13, 1937*, 4764–4766.

61. "Draft of Address Written by John Sheridan for J. F. Hull, for Hull's Speech to the Missouri Public Utilities Association on May 4, 1922," Ex. 2744, Box 3851, FTC Records.

62. Harris in *Proceedings before the FCC, January 13, 1937*, 4720–4734.

63. FCC, *Telephone Investigation* (1937), 4:45–48. The *Evening Telegram* was published in Rocky Mount, North Carolina.

64. FCC, *Telephone Investigation* (1937), 4:48, 46–47.

65. Edward Bemis to George Lewis, January 30, 1926, Ex. 1973, Box. 3843, FTC Records; Lewis in *FTC Letter No. 4* (1928), 421–422.

66. Grant in *FTC Letter No. 4* (1928), 447; W. C. Grant, Director, Texas Public Service Information Bureau, to R. B. Still, General Manager, Gulf States Telephone Co., November 23, 1927, Box 3843, Ex. 2023, FTC Records.

67. Quoted in Upton Sinclair, *The Brass Check: A Study of American Journalism* (Pasadena, 1919), 294.

68. Richard White, "Information, Markets, and Corruption: Transcontinental Railroads in the Gilded Age," *Journal of American History* 90, no. 1 (June 2003): 19–43.

69. Examination of Mrs. John D. Sherman, President, General Federation of Women's Clubs, in *FTC Letter No. 10* (1929), 34–44. Mrs. Sherman was not related to John Sherman, the publicity director for the Missouri state committee.

70. FCC, *Telephone Investigation* (1937), 4:74–75; Page in *Proceedings before the FCC, January 25, 1937,* 5271.

71. Page in *Proceedings before the FCC, January 25, 1937,* 5262–5270.

72. Sheridan in *FTC Letter No. 5* (1928), 131.

73. Harlin F. Clark, *Cass County Democrat*, December 9, 1921, Ex. 2887, Box 3853, FTC Records.

74. George F. Smith, Advertising Manager, *Scurry County Times-Signal*, Snyder, Texas, "Notice to the Free Publicity Hounds of the Universe," Box 3843, Ex. 2038, FTC Records.

75. Harris in *Proceedings before the FCC, January 13, 1937,* 4753–4754.

76. Harris in *Proceedings before the FCC, January 13, 1937,* 4856–4857.

77. J. B. Sheridan to C. C. Hellmers, January 21, 1922, 1, Ex. 2730, Box 3851, FTC Records.

78. Examination of Arthur F. Herwig, Director, Wisconsin Public Utility Information Bureau, in *FTC Letter No. 5* (1928), 470, xlviii.

79. "Suggestions for Letter to Newspapers," Ex. 2739B, Box 3851, FTC Records.

80. Sheridan in *FTC Letter No. 5* (1928), 125.

81. E. Hofer & Sons, *The Manufacturer*, Ex. 3847, FTC Records.

82. Robert M. Hofer, managing editor, E. Hofer & Sons, in *FTC Letter No. 7* (1928), 229, 231, 245–46.

83. Robert M. Hofer in *FTC Letter No. 7* (1928), 224, 233, 237, 240, 251; FCC, *Telephone Investigation* (1937), 4:77; *Proceedings before the FCC, January 26, 1937,* 5294.

84. Page in *Proceedings before the FCC, January 25, 1937,* 5272–5280.

85. Northwestern Bell Telephone Company, "Payments Made to Subscriptions to Papers, Periodicals, or Magazines, Years 1926 to 1935 Inclusive," in *Information relating to Publicity and Advertising Supplied in Accordance with Federal Communications Commission's Letter of Dec. 11, 1936 to A.T.&T. Co.,* January 7, 1937, Box 41, Ex. 1354, FCC Records; FCC, *Telephone Investigation* (1937), 4:76–77; G. K. McCorkle, Vice President, Illinois Bell Telephone Company, "Statement of Payments Made to Newspaper Men, Radio Commentators, College Professors, Scientists, Lecturers, or Writers," in *Information as to Advertising, Publicity, Information Department Activities, and Other Matters in Response to Request of the Federal Communications Commission,* December 10, 1936, Box 41, Ex. 1353, FCC Records; FCC, *Telephone Investigation* (1937), 4:76–77.

Notes to Pages 174–177 297

86. Robert M. Hofer in *FTC Letter No. 7* (1928), 239–240, 245, xviii.

87. Joseph B. Groce, Director, New England Bureau of Public Service Information, *Report of Second Year's Work, 1923*, 6, Box 3817, Exs. 687–688, FTC Records.

88. Connecticut Committee on Public Service Information, reports for four years between April 1, 1924, and April 1, 1928, Box 3830, Exs. 1046–1050, FTC Records.

89. *Memorandum to Mullaney*, January 9, 1926, Box 3815, Ex. 541, FTC Records; McGregor in *FTC Letter No. 2* (1928), 157.

90. Grant in *FTC Letter No. 4* (1928), 470.

91. *Working Manual of Texas Public Service Information Bureau*, January 1, 1928, 11–12, Box 3843, Ex. 2028, FTC Records.

92. H. M. Lytle, Associate Director, Illinois Committee on Public Utility Information, to C. G. Willard, Executive Secretary, Connecticut Committee on Public Service Information, March 31, 1925, Box 3815, Ex. 540, FTC Records.

93. MacQuarrie in *FTC Letter No. 2* (1928), 168.

94. Texas Public Service Information Bureau, *Press Matter Data*, October 23, 1926, Box 3843, Ex. 2030, FTC Records.

95. FCC, *Telephone Investigation* (1937), 4:35–37.

96. Groce, *Report of First Year's Work, 1922*, 4.

97. Robert Hofer used a conversion factor of 120 column inches per newspaper page. This is less conservative than the 168.3 column inches per page that the New England bureau used, based on the size of the *Boston Herald*. I have used the conservative *Boston Herald* conversion factor for all calculations in this book. Robert M. Hofer in *FTC Letter No. 7* (1928), 242–245, 248.

98. Robert M. Hofer in *FTC Letter No. 7* (1928), 248, 250, 240.

99. Grant in *FTC Letter No. 4* (1928), 459.

100. *Memorandum to Mullaney*, January 9, 1926; Richardson in *FTC Letter No. 3* (1928), 399–400; Sheridan in *FTC Letter No. No. 5* (1928), 127; Connecticut Committee on Public Service Information, editorials republished between April 1, 1924, and April 1, 1928, Box 3830, Ex. 1050, FTC Records.

101. Louis Galambos searched issues of *Wallace's Farmer* from 1895 to 1932 and issues of *Progressive Farmer* from 1926 to 1940. NELA advertised in both these magazines, at least in 1922, and GE advertised in *Progressive Farmer* in the 1920s. See Louis Galambos, *The Public Image of Big Business in America, 1880–1940: A Quantitative Study in Social Change* (Baltimore: Johns Hopkins University Press, 1975), 34, 191–221; "Address of Chairman of Public Relations National Section, Martin J. Insull," *NELA Proceedings* (1922), 1:10; David E. Nye, *Image Worlds: Corporate Identities at General Electric, 1890–1930* (Cambridge, MA: MIT Press, 1985), 126.

102. "Bulletin 1" in *Bulletins of the Rocky Mountain Committee on Public Utility Information*, (bulletins issued between 1923–1928), Ex. 1938, Box 3842, FTC Records.

103. John Sheridan to H. H. Kuhn, Kansas City Power & Light Company, June 6, 1925, Box 3853, Ex. 2961, FTC Records.

104. FCC, *Telephone Investigation* (1937), 4:42.

105. The *Raleigh* in "sending to *Raleigh*" has been italicized by this author. Harris in *Proceedings before the FCC, January 13, 1937*, 4802–4805.

106. Page in *Proceedings before the FCC, January 25, 1937*, 5206–5208.

107. Several editors sent clippings of their articles to Sheridan or their local utility manager, possibly in a bid to receive extra advertising revenue. Sheridan in *FTC Letter No. 5* (1928), 116.

108. FCC, *Telephone Investigation* (1937), 4:49; Examination of Vincent M. Carroll, Vice President, Southwestern Bell Telephone Company, *Proceedings before the FCC, January 28, 1937*, 5433–5435.

109. Carroll in *Proceedings before the FCC, January 28, 1937*, 5451–5462; FCC, *Telephone Investigation* (1937), 4:51–52.

110. Carroll in *Proceedings before the FCC, January 28, 1937*, 5446–5449.

111. Carroll in *Proceedings before the FCC, January 28, 1937*, 5463–5465.

112. Page in *Proceedings before the FCC, January 25, 1937*, 5203.

113. Bradley in *FTC Letter No. 10* (1929), 14–16.

114. McGregor in *FTC Letter No. 2* (1928), 130.

115. Bradley in *FTC Letter No. 10* (1929), 8–10, 2, 7.

116. The real price of $2,000 in commodities using the consumer price index from 1914 and 2014 is $48,100; the income value of $2,000 in 1914 converts to $285,000; these and subsequent comparisons were made using the "Purchasing Power Calculator" available at MeasuringWorth.com. F.G.R. Gordon, publicist and policy advocate, in *FTC Letter No. 9* (1929), 50–52.

117. Gordon in *FTC Letter No. 9* (1929), 54–57.

118. Daniel De Leon, "F.G.R. Gordon—And There Are Others," *Daily People*, Monday, July 11, 1910, http://www.slp.org/pdf/de_leon/eds1910/jul11_1910.pdf; Gordon in *FTC Letter No. 9* (1929), 51, 63.

119. PT&T, *Publicity and Advertising*, May 1924, 2, File: Publicity Folder, 1916–1929, Box 56: Presidential Office Files, RG 5, Collection 3, AT&T-TX.

120. Harris in *Proceedings before the FCC, January 13, 1937*, 4698, 4606–4610, 4713–4715; Samuel Kennedy, "Transforming Public Opinion: An Address by Mr. Samuel M. Kennedy, Vice-President Southern California Edison Co., Los Angeles, California, before the Convention of Managers and Executives of the Management Division of Stone & Webster Inc., Held in Boston, October 10–18, 1921," 19, Box 389, Folder 26, SCE Records.

121. *Memorandum: The Publicity Policy of the Bell System*, July 13, 1921, 2, File: Publicity Folder, 1916–1929, Box 56: Presidential Office Files, RG 5, Collection 3, AT&T-TX.

122. "Here Is a Hot One on the Citizen," *Campbell Citizen*, September 7, 1923, 2, microfilm, State Historical Society of Missouri, Columbia; Editorial, "Here Is a Hot One on the Citizen," [*Campbell Citizen*], September 7, 1923, Ex. 2913, Box 3853, FTC Records; Sheridan in *FTC Letter No. 5* (1928), 137; Southwestern Bell Telephone Company, "Your Voice Is You," advertisement, *Campbell Citizen*, January 26, 1923, 3; Southwestern Bell Telephone Company, "The Joy of Hearing a Voice," advertisement, *Campbell Citizen*, March 3, 1923, 2; Southwestern Bell Telephone Company, "This Sign Means You're Near Home," advertisement, *Campbell Citizen*, March 3, 1923, 2; microfilm, State Historical Society of Missouri, Columbia; Southwestern Bell Telephone Company, "Giving the Telephone Life," advertisement, *Campbell Citizen*, January 25, 1924, microfilm, State Historical Society of Missouri, Columbia.

123. "Report of Committee on Publicity," *AERA Proceedings, 1927*, 319.

Notes to Pages 181–184   299

124. The representative was Frank Whittenmore, of Akron, Ohio, District Commercial Manager, Ohio Bell Telephone Company, to C. F. McGuire Jr., Division Commercial Manager, Ohio Bell, August 30, 1933, Box 4, Folder: Exhibits 101 to 122, Part 1, Ex. 108, FCC Records.

125. Page in *Proceedings before the FCC, January 25, 1937*, 5189.

126. Page in *Proceedings before the FCC, January 25, 1937*, 5203–5204.

127. Examination of Rob Roy McGregor, in *FTC Letter No. 2* (1928), 141. During the examination parts of the letter J.S.S. Richardson to R. R. McGregor, October 31, 1927, were read into the record. The letter was cited in FTC *Letter No. 2* on page xix as Ex. 380.

128. MacQuarrie in *FTC Letter No. 2* (1928), 176.

129. Sheridan in *FTC Letter No. 5* (1928), 116.

130. Robert M. Hofer in *FTC Letter No. 7* (1928), 245, 231.

131. Walter Lippmann, *Public Opinion* (New York: Macmillan, 1922), 31–32; 322–323.

132. Samuel T. MacQuarrie, Director, New England Bureau of Public Service Information, *Report of Third Year's Work, 1924*, 5, Box 3817, Ex. 689, FTC Records.

133. Herwig in *FTC Letter No. 5* (1928), 470, xlviii; "Suggestions for Letter to Newspapers."

134. Carmichael in *FTC Letter No. 4* (1928), 32.

135. Lippman, *Public Opinion*, 32.

136. Quoted by Bernard J. Mullaney, Peoples Gas Light & Coke Co., Chicago, "The State Committees on Public Utility Information," *American Gas Association, Fourth Annual Convention, October 23–28, 1922* (New York: AGA, [1922?]), 271–272.

137. R. R. McGregor, Assistant Director, Illinois Committee on Public Utility Information, to J. B. Sheridan, February 24, 1927, Box 3815, Ex. 538, FTC Records.

138. "Meeting—Missouri Committee on Public Utility Information," St. Louis, May 27, 1925, Box 3853, Ex. 2960, FTC Records; McGregor to Sheridan, February 24, 1927; Carmichael in *FTC Letter No. 4* (1928), 31; *FTC Letter No. 3* (1928), xxxv.

139. "Meeting—Missouri Committee on Public Utility Information."

140. FCC, *Telephone Investigation* (1937), 4:38.

141. W. C. Grant, Director, Texas Public Service Information Bureau, to Ray Baumgardner, Associated Press, Dallas, Texas, March 24, 1928, Box 3843, Ex. 2033, FTC Records.

142. Grant in *FTC Letter No. 4* (1928), 482, 460, 487, xxxix.

143. FCC, *Telephone Investigation* (1937), 4:41.

144. *Advertising Expenditure, the Pacific Telephone and Telegraph System, 1920*, File: Publicity Folder, 1916–1929, Box 56, RG 5, Collection 3, AT&T-TX.

145. "Service and Public Relations," *Public Service Company of Northern Illinois Year Book 1928*, 24, Box 55, Folder 8, Insull Papers; Kennedy, "Transforming Public Opinion," 19.

146. Mark H. Rose, *Cities of Light and Heat: Domesticating Gas and Electricity in Urban America* (University Park: Pennsylvania State University Press, 1995), 162.

147. Also *Farm Journal* and *Successful Farming*. "Address of Chairman of Public Relations National Section, Martin J. Insull," *NELA Proceedings* (1922), 1:10–11.

148. Charles Postel, *The Populist Vision* (Oxford: Oxford University Press, 2007), 277.

149. William Allen White, *The Autobiography of William Allen White*, 2nd ed., ed. and abridged by Sally Foreman Griffith (Lawrence: University Press of Kansas, 1990), 329.

150. William P. Banning, "Advertising Technique and Copy Appeal," presented at a Bell System Publicity Conference, 1921, 2, File: Publicity Folder, 1916–1929, Box 56, RG 5, Collection 3, AT&T-TX.

151. This cost per article estimate is conservative, since the number of articles placed in regions other than Northern California is unknown. The $9,200 per month is an approximation using the yearly total for 1923 divided by twelve. Expenses for 1924 are not known. PT&T, *Summary of Results Obtained from Use of Telephone Press Service Bulletins, Coast Division, Month Ending—April 30, 1924*, File: Publicity Folder, 1916–1929, Box 56, RG 5, Collection 3, AT&T-TX; PT&T, *Publicity and Advertising*, 8; *Advertising Expenditure, the Pacific Telephone and Telegraph System, 1920*.

152. This calculation uses a 21-inch newspaper column. Sheridan in *FTC Letter No. 5* (1928), 124, 77.

153. Eighty-four thousand dollars in 1927 converts to $1.13 million in 2013 dollars using the consumer price index from these years at MeasuringWorth.com. Robert M. Hofer in *FTC Letter No. 7* (1928), 228.

154. This is why Ernest Gruening entitled his critique of the electricity industry *The Public Pays: A Study of Power Propaganda*; J. F. Hull, "Press Association President Talks before Utility Men," May 4, 1922, Ex. 2745, Box 3851, FTC Records; "Draft of Address"; "Suggestions for Letter to Newspapers"; Wilson in *Proceedings before the FCC, June 4, 1936*, 2101.

155. Richard R. John, *Spreading the News: The American Postal System from Franklin to Morse* (Cambridge, MA: Harvard University Press, 1995), 31.

156. Utilities still managed to profit by distributing the dam's power, however. Tom Sitton, *John Randolph Haynes: California Progressive* (Stanford, CA: Stanford University Press, 1992), 118; Jay Brigham, *Empowering the West: Electrical Politics before FDR* (Lawrence: University Press of Kansas, 1998), 124; Dean Witter & Co. Municipal and Corporation Bonds, *Southern California Edison Company, Ltd.* (1936), Box 271, Folder 13, SCE Records; "Letter from W. C. Mullendore, Executive Vice-President, Southern California Power Company to the Honorable City Council of Los Angeles, City Hall, Los Angeles, California, September 2, 1932," 1, Box 116, Folder 6, SCE Records.

157. George E. Lewis, Executive Manager, Rocky Mountain Committee on Public Utility Information, "National Electric Light Association Convention Resume," 1923, Box 3843, Ex. 2020, FTC Records.

158. Groce, *Report of First Year's Work, 1922*, 4.

159. Insull, "Public Relations," 6–7.

160. Robert M. Hofer in *FTC Letter No. 7* (1928), 245.

161. "Colorado Mayor Finds Ideal Standard of Government in Public Utilities," *Public Service Magazine*, January 1923, 15.

162. James P. Barnes, President, Louisville Railway Company, "The Value of Public Utility Information Committees," *AERA Proceedings 1922*, 170–171.

163. Willard Cope, Utilities Information Committee of Georgia, from a letter dated April 4, 1923, quoted in *FTC Letter No. 3* (1928), 527–529.

164. Sheridan in *FTC Letter No. 5* (1928), 104; Missouri Digital Heritage, Missouri Constitutions, 1820–1945, http://cdm16795.contentdm.oclc.org/cdm/landingpage /collection/p16795coll1. See the details on the 1922 Missouri constitution.

Notes to Pages 187–191   301

165. Pacific Bell Telephone and Telegraph Companies, "Item 6: Report of Local News Items," in *Information Requested by Federal Communications Commission through American Telephone and Telegraph Company, December 11, 1936*, January 7, 1937, Box 41, Ex. 1358, FCC Records; Southwest Bell Telephone and Telegraph Companies, "Published Newspaper Articles or Editorials relating to the Business of Respondent during the Years 1926 to 1935, Inclusive," in *Response to Federal Communications Commission's Inquiry Dated December 11, 1936 Relative to Certain Advertising, Publicity and Information Activities for the Years 1926 to 1936, Inclusive*, Box 41, Ex. 1355, FCC Records; Northwestern Bell Telephone Company, "Item 6: Editorial Comments Relating Directly or Indirectly to Telephone Business, Years 1926 to 1935, Inclusive, Northwestern Bell Telephone Company," in *Information relating to Publicity and Advertising Supplied in Accordance with Federal Communications Commission's Letter of Dec. 11, 1936 to A.T.&T. Co.*.

166. G. K. McCorkle, "Survey of Published Newspaper Articles and Editorials," in *Information as to Advertising, Publicity, Information Department Activities, and Other Matters in Response to Request of the Federal Communications Commission*, December 10, 1936, Box 41, Ex. 1353, FCC Records. The Ohio Bell Telephone Company also conducted a survey in 1934, and claimed that they received "10,000 favorable comments and less than 100 unfavorable comments." Ohio Bell Telephone Company, Plant Department, North Eastern Area, *Public Relations Conference, Outline of Data for Conference Leader* (1935), "Appendix VIII—Advertising," 2, Box 16, Ex. 177, FCC Records.

167. Congressional Record, January 2, 1925, 69th Congress, 2nd Session, 1101–1107, quoted in Thompson, *Confessions of the Power Trust*, xvii; W. C. Mullendore, *The Power Industry and Political Sabotage*, 5–6, reprint from speech at Pacific Coast Electrical Association, February 5, 1931, Box 449, Folder 7, SCE Records.

168. Martin J. Insull, President, Middle West Utilities Company, *Public Contracts*, 7, reprint of speech delivered at the award ceremony for winners of Employees' Public Speaking Contest, NELA, June 10, 1931, Box 449, Folder 7, SCE Records; Richardson in *FTC Letter No. 3* (1928), 402, xxxv.

169. Business Week, *Public Relations for Industry: A Presentation of the Imperative Need of Mutual Understanding in the Conduct of Our Daily Work* (New York: McGraw-Hill, 1938), Box 449, Folder 7, SCE Records.

170. Ralph L. Mahon, "The Telephone in Chicago, 1877–1940," typescript, 123, AT&T-TX.

171. M. J. Insull, *Public Contracts*, 6–7.

172. Mullendore, *The Power Industry and Political Sabotage*, 14.

173. [Ohio Bell Telephone Company], *Commercial Department, Public Relations Conference, Outline for Training All Commercial Employees* [1934], 4, Box 16, Ex. 177A, FCC Records.

174. Arthur W. Park, "Why Discriminate against the Public Utilities?" *Public Service Management*, May 1921, 146.

175. William G. McAdoo, "The Relations between Public Service Corporations and the Public," lecture delivered before the Graduate School of Business Administration of Harvard University, April 6, 1910, 28.

176. Samuel T. MacQuarrie, Director, New England Bureau of Public Service Information, *Report of Fifth Year's Work, 1926*, 8, Box 3818, Ex. 691, FTC Records.

302   Notes to Pages 191–198

177. C. Vann Woodward, *Origins of the New South, 1877–1913* (Louisiana State University Press, 1951), 195.

178. Edward L. Bernays, *Biography of an Idea: Memoirs of Public Relations Counsel Edward L. Bernays* (New York: Simon and Schuster, 1965), 287–288; Mark Crispin Miller, introduction to *Propaganda* by Edward L. Bernays, (New York: Ig Publishing, 2005), 14–15.

179. Alan R. Raucher, *Public Relations and Business, 1900–1929* (Baltimore: Johns Hopkins University Press, 1968), 68.

180. Lippmann, *Public Opinion*, 26.

181. Jack Levin, *Power Ethics: An Analysis of the Activities of Public Utilities in the United States, Based on a Study of the U.S. Federal Trade Commission Records* (New York: Alfred A. Knopf, 1931), 13–14.

182. Editor, *Daily Oklahoman* and *Oklahoma City Times*, "Customer Ownership," *American Gas Association, Tenth Annual Convention, October 8–12, 1928* (New York: AGA, [1928?]), 117. The article quoted the editor of the *Chicago Tribune*.

183. Grant in *FTC Letter No. 4* (1928), 506–508.

184. "Underwrote Rochester Text Book," *New York Times*, May 30, 1928, 21.

185. MacQuarrie in *FTC Letter No. 2* (1928), 170.

186. Grant in *FTC Letter No. 4* (1928), 506–07. Ellipses in the original.

187. Harris in *Proceedings before the FCC, January 13, 1937*, 4736–4739.

188. J. B. Sheridan to John W. Colton, June 24, 1927, Ex. 2723, Box. 3851, FTC Records; John W. Colton to J. B. Sheridan, October 17, 1927, Ex. 2724, Box. 3851, FTC Records; Sheridan in *FTC Letter No. 5* (1928), 76–78, xiii; James Bush, Editor of *Montrose Tidings*, to John Sheridan, January 9, 1922, Ex. 2898, Box 3853, FTC Records; J. B. Sheridan to John W. Colton, Editor, *A.E.R.A*, New York, June 14, 1927, Box 3851, Ex. 2721, FTC Records; Gruening, *The Public Pays*, 247; "Veteran Writer on Sports Hangs Self," *Los Angeles Times*, April 16, 1930, 22.

Chapter 6 • Subverting Civics

1. Examination of Fred R. Jenkins, Chairman, Educational Committee of NELA, in *FTC Letter No. 4* (1928), 615–617, 624; FCC, *Telephone Investigation* (1937), 4:131.

2. Jenkins in *FTC Letter No. 4* (1928), 618, 620, 632, lviii.

3. Howard C. Hill, *Community Life and Civic Problems* (New York: Ginn, 1922), 410.

4. Jenkins in *FTC Letter No. 4* (1928), 629, 632, 620.

5. Jenkins in *FTC Letter No. 4* (1928), 618–620.

6. This is the FTC examiner's paraphrasing of the minutes of the meeting. Jenkins in *FTC Letter No. 4* (1928), 625.

7. Jenkins in *FTC Letter No. 4* (1928), 626.

8. Jenkins's words during the FTC examination. Jenkins in *FTC Letter No. 4* (1928), 625.

9. Examination of Joe Carmichael, Director, Iowa Committee on Public Utility Information, in *FTC Letter No. 4* (1928), 11–12.

10. Examination of J. S. S. Richardson, Director, Department of Information of the Joint Committee, National Utility Association, in *FTC Letter No. 3* (1928), 398.

11. Jenkins in *FTC Letter No. 4* (1928), 620, 634.

Notes to Pages 198–200 303

12. Howard C. Hill, *Vocational Civics* (New York: Ginn, 1928), 121–125; Samuel T. MacQuarrie, Director, New England Bureau of Public Service Information; Chairman, Public Relations, NELA; Chairman, Public Speaking Committee, NELA; Chairman, Organization of Information Bureau Committee, NELA, similar position in the American Gas Association, in *FTC Letter No. 2* (1928), 177; Connecticut Committee on Public Service Information, *Catechism* [1926], 10, Box 3830, Exhibit 1052, Series: Economic Investigations Files, 1915–1938, Subject: Power and Gas, FTC Records.

13. *Memorandum on the Work of the Illinois Committee on Public Utility Information*, 2, Box 3810, Ex. 167, FTC Records; Examination of Bernard J. Mullaney, Director, Illinois Committee on Public Utility Information, Vice President, American Gas Association, Vice President, Peoples Gas Light & Coke Co., in *FTC Letter No. 2* (1928), 78.

14. Examination of John B. Sheridan, Secretary of the Missouri Committee on Public Utility Information, in *FTC Letter No. 5* (1928), 58.

15. "Public Relations and Publicity: A Reading Assignment," 2nd ed., in *Employees General Training Course: The Pacific Telephone and Telegraph Company, 1927*, 14, Collection 3, RG 5, Box 3, File: Public Relations and Publicity, AT&T-TX.

16. Examination of Thorne Browne, Supervisor, Nebraska Utilities Information Bureau; Managing Director, Secretary, and Treasurer, Middle West Division, NELA, in *FTC Letter No. 4* (1928), 73.

17. Rocky Mountain Committee on Public Utility Information, "Public Utility Service, 1927, The Telephone, Its History and Methods of Operation: For Use of School Students, English and Current Topics Classes, and Debating Clubs," 12, Box 485, Folder 1, SCE Records; *FTC Letter No. 2* (1928), 84, xi; Carmichael in *FTC Letter No. 4* (1928), 11; Examination of H. Lee Jones, Information Bureau of Kansas Public Service Companies, in *FTC Letter No. 5* (1928), 265; Robert S. Lynd and Helen Merrell Lynd, *Middletown: A Study in Contemporary American Culture* (New York: Harcourt, Brace, 1929), 189, 198–199.

18. Examination of Samuel T. MacQuarrie in *FTC Letter No. 2* (1928), 165; Sheridan in *FTC Letter No. 5* (1928), 47; Examination of William C. Grant, Director, Texas Public Service Information Bureau, in *FTC Letter No. 4* (1928), 462.

19. MacQuarrie in *FTC Letter No. 2* (1928), 165; Sheridan in *FTC Letter No. 5* (1928), 47; Grant in *FTC Letter No. 4* (1928), 462.

20. "Propaganda by Utilities Is Scored by FTC," *Citizen-Advertiser* (Auburn, NY), November 15, 1934.

21. Edward A. Krug, *The Shaping of the American High School*, vol. 2, *1920–1941* (Madison: University of Wisconsin Press, 1972), 148, 156–163; see also the Lynd's description of typical teachers in Muncie, Indiana in the 1920s in Lynd and Lynd, *Middletown*, 206–207.

22. Grant in *FTC Letter No. 4* (1928), 462.

23. Examination of C. G. Willard, Executive Secretary, Connecticut Committee on Public Service Information, in *FTC Letter No. 3* (1928), 245; MacQuarrie in *FTC Letter No. 2* (1928), 180.

24. MacQuarrie in *FTC Letter No. 2* (1928), 176.

25. Ira Katznelson and Margaret Weir, *Schooling for All: Class, Race, and the Decline of the Democratic Ideal* (Berkeley: University of California Press, 1985), 19,

25–26, 86, 89; Samuel Bowles and Herbert Gintis, *Schooling in Capitalist America: Educational Reform and the Contradictions of Economic Life* (New York: Basic Books, 1976), 179–181, 186–187; Joel Spring, *Education and the Rise of the Corporate State* (Boston: Beacon Press, 1972), 84–87; Thomas Timar and David Tyack, *The Invisible Hand of Ideology: Perspectives from the History of School Governance* (Denver, CO: Education Commission of the States, 1999), 7, 16; Krug, *The Shaping of the American High School*, 2:18–19, 30, 68–69, 82; David F. Noble, *America by Design: Science, Technology and the Rise of Corporate Capitalism* (New York: Oxford University Press, 1977).

26. Mullaney in *FTC Letter No. 2* (1928), 78.

27. Willard in *FTC Letter No. 3* (1928), 252.

28. Sheridan in *FTC Letter No. 5* (1928), 47.

29. Richard Hofstadter, *Anti-Intellectualism in American Life* (New York: Alfred A. Knopf, 1963), 326, 335.

30. Richard Hofstadter and C. DeWitt Hardy, *The Development and Scope of Higher Education in the United States* (New York: Columbia University Press, 1952), 31; Krug, *The Shaping of the American High School*, 2:42–47.

31. Jones in *FTC Letter No. 5* (1928), 265–266.

32. Comparing the work of electricity to slaves was common, but the conversions were usually higher than thirty slaves per person. See Harry L. Brown, "Electric Power Gives Each American 900 Slaves," *Public Service Management*, December 1927, 217; Hon. Albert C. Ritchie, the Governor of Maryland, also cited nine hundred slaves in "Electricity in Politics," *NELA Proceedings 1927*, 187.

33. Statement of Bernard F. Weadock, Counsel, Joint Committee, in *FTC Letter No. 19* (1930), 12; *FTC Letter Nos. 18 & 19* (1930), insert between pp. 218 and 219; *FTC Letter No. 2* (1928), 84, xi.

34. Willard in *FTC Letter No. 3* (1928), 251.

35. Texas Public Service Information Bureau, *Electricity: Its Process of Manufacture and Distribution*, n.d., Box 3843, Ex. 2032, FTC Records.

36. Texas Public Service Information Bureau, *Natural and Manufactured Gas: How This Most Convenient and Flexible Fuel Is Produced and Distributed to Customers*, n.d., 10–11, Box 3843, Ex. 2031, FTC Records.

37. Examination of George E. Lewis, Director, Rocky Mountain Committee on Public Utility Information, in *FTC Letter No. 4* (1928), 347.

38. John Mills, *The Magic of Communication: A Tell-You-How Story* [1922?], 19, Box 4, RG 6, Collection 6, AT&T-TX.

39. PT&T, *Publicity and Advertising*, May 1924, 5–6, File: Publicity Folder, 1916–1929, Box 56, RG 5, Collection 3, AT&T-TX.

40. "Underwrote Rochester Text Book," *New York Times*, May 30, 1928, 21.

41. "Missouri Governor Wants Utilities Studied in Schools," *PG&E Progress*, August 1928, 4.

42. "Report of the Committee on Propaganda in the Schools," presented at the Atlanta meeting of NELA, July 1929, in *FTC Letter Nos. 18 & 19* (1930), 233.

43. "Report of the Committee on Propaganda in the Schools," 230.

44. "Report of the Committee on Propaganda in the Schools," 225, 227.

45. "Report of the Committee on Propaganda in the Schools," 233.

46. FCC, *Telephone Investigation* (1937), 4:155–156.

Notes to Pages 203–205   305

47. In the 1930s, coalitions of power companies published ads opposing the Tennessee Valley Authority and other public power projects. As of 1975, *The Story of Electricity*, which utilities first published in the 1920s, was still in print, courtesy of the Florida Power and Light Company. And SCE continued to use its cartoon character, Reddy Kilowatt, who obtained his own publishing house, Reddy Kilowatt, Incorporated, in 1972. As of 1976, AGA was still distributing *The History of Natural Gas* and several other utilities also continued to publish materials for the classroom. See Ernest Gruening, *The Public Pays: A Study of Power Propaganda* (New York: Vanguard Press, 1931), photo inserts after p. xviii; Sheila Harty, *Hucksters in the Classroom: A Review of Industry Propaganda in Schools* (Washington, DC: Center for Study of Responsive Law, 1979), 41–42, 45–47, 49, 81; SCE, *You and Your Company: A Handbook for Employees*, 13, 1953, Box 88, Folder 2, SCE Records. For 1940s and 1950s efforts, see Elizabeth A. Fones-Wolf, "Educating for Capitalism: Business and the Schools," in *Selling Free Enterprise: The Business Assault on Labor and Liberalism, 1945–1960* (Urbana: University of Illinois Press, 1994), 189–217.

48. Browne in *FTC Letter No. 4* (1928), 74.

49. MacQuarrie in FTC Letter No. 2 (1928), 179; Mullaney in *FTC Letter No. 2* (1928), 81.

50. MacQuarrie in *FTC Letter No. 2* (1928), 179.

51. Texas Public Service Information Bureau, *Electricity: Its Process of Manufacture and Distribution*, n.d., 15–16, Box 3843, Ex. 2032, FTC Records.

52. This is an FTC examiner's quotation. It is likely that the examiner was directly quoting from a document in his hand, but because the court reporter transcribed the testimony from spoken statements, the transcriber did not use quotation marks. MacQuarrie in *FTC Letter No. 2* (1928), 178.

53. MacQuarrie in *FTC Letter No. 2* (1928), 178.

54. Joseph B. Groce, Director, New England Bureau of Public Service Information, *Report of First Year's Work, 1922*, 1, Box 3817, Ex. 687, FTC Records.

55. Connecticut Committee on Public Service Information, *Catechism*, 10–11.

56. Italics added. Connecticut Committee on Public Service Information, *Catechism*, 12–13.

57. Connecticut Committee on Public Service Information, *Catechism*, 6.

58. Carmichael in *FTC Letter No. 4* (1928), 9.

59. Lewis in *FTC Letter No. 4* (1928), 384.

60. FCC, *Telephone Investigation* (1937), 4:122.

61. Rocky Mountain Committee on Public Utility Information, Resume of Three Years' Activities [1924?], Ex. 1845, Box 3841, FTC Records.

62. Wisconsin Telephone Company, *Information for Federal Communications Commission, Cost and Other Data Relating to the Advertising, Publicity, Information and Promotion Activities of the Wisconsin Telephone Company*, "Answer to Question 7.A.," Box 41, Ex. 1352, FCC Records.

63. MacQuarrie in *FTC Letter No. 2* (1928), 183.

64. FCC, "Appendix 5, Sheet 2: Illinois Bell Telephone Company, Commercial Department Report of Customer Relations Activities, Years 1926 to 1935 Inclusive," in *Telephone Investigation* (1937).

65. Sheridan in *FTC Letter No. 5* (1928), xiii, 73.

66. Published in 1927. *FTC Letter No. 2* (1928), 84, xi.

67. FCC, *Telephone Investigation* (1937), 4:28.

68. FCC, "Appendix 5, Sheet 2."

69. Pacific Bell Telephone and Telegraph Companies, "Item 6: Report of Local News Items," in *Information Requested by Federal Communications Commission through American Telephone and Telegraph Company, December 11, 1936,* January 7, 1937, Box 41, Ex. 1358, FCC Records.

70. FCC, *Telephone Investigation* (1937), 4:153–154.

71. FCC, *Telephone Investigation* (1937), 4:157.

72. Browne in *FTC Letter No. 4* (1928), 113, 91.

73. *Bell System Educational Conference, 195 Broadway, New York City, August 18–23, 1924,* 3–4, Box 88, RG 4 Collection 6, AT&T-TX.

74. "Opening of Conference: Talk by Mr. Gifford," in *Bell System Educational Conference,* 2, 4–5.

75. "Education Section," *NELA Proceedings* (1924), 181–194.

76. Examination of Paul A. Clapp, Managing Director of the National Electric Light Association, in *FTC Letter No. 3* (1928), 201, xxii.

77. http://oasis.lib.harvard.edu/oasis/deliver/~bak00155.

78. Fifteen thousand dollars comes to a little more than $200,000 in 2014 dollars using the consumer price index to convert at MeasuringWorth.com.

79. Paul A. Walker, *Proposed Report, Telephone Investigation, (Pursuant to Public Resolution No. 8, 74th Congress)* (Washington, DC: Government Printing Office, 1938), 567.

80. Examination of P. S. Arkwright, President, Georgia Power Co. in *FTC Letter No. 28* (1931), 100.

81. Carter A. Daniel, *MBA: The First Century* (Cranbury, NJ: Associated University Presses, 1989), 110; see the "Biographical Note" on Ruggles here: https://hollisarchives.lib.harvard.edu/repositories/11/resources/568.

82. FTC reports sometimes refer to him as Hubert P. Wolfe. Lewis in *FTC Letter No. 4* (1928), 352–353.

83. Lewis in *FTC Letter No. 4* (1928), 353, 355.

84. Rocky Mountain Committee on Public Utility Information, *Minutes of Educational Committee Meeting, December 8, 1922,* 2, Ex. 1837, Box 3841, FTC Records.

85. Rocky Mountain Committee on Public Utility Information, *Minutes of Educational Committee Meeting,* 1–3.

86. "Public Utility Placed in the Curriculum of Every University in the State of Colorado," *Public Service Management,* February 1923, 43.

87. Lewis in *FTC Letter No. 4* (1928), 351–352, 387, 339–340, 354, xxvi. Other sources indicate that industry paid 63 percent of the salary; see Elmore Petersen, University of Colorado Extension Division, to George E. Lewis, Secretary, Rocky Mountain Committee on Public Utility Information, May 23, 1928, 3, Ex. 1945, Box 3842, FTC Records.

88. "Public Utility Placed in the Curriculum," 43.

89. Two hundred fifty dollars in 1924 comes to $3,460 in 2014 dollars using the consumer price index to convert at MeasuringWorth.com; Richardson in *FTC Letter No. 3* (1928), 387–388.

90. Sheridan in *FTC Letter No. 5* (1928), 54.

Notes to Pages 210–215   307

91. Sheridan in *FTC Letter No. 5* (1928), 54, 56–57, 55.

92. Richard Hofstadter and Walter P. Metzger, *The Development of Academic Freedom in the United States* (New York: Columbia University Press, 1955), 420–421, 438–439; Mary O. Furner, "The Perils of Radicalism," in *Advocacy and Objectivity: A Crisis in the Professionalization of American Social Science, 1865–1905* (Lexington: Published for the Organization of American Historians by the University Press of Kentucky, 1975), 163–204; Jennifer Washburn, *University, Inc.: The Corporate Corruption of American Higher Education* (New York: Basic Books, 2005), 33.

93. Examination of George F. Oxley, Director of the Department of Public Information, NELA, in *FTC Letter No. 3* (1928), 29; Sheridan in *FTC Letter No. 5* (1928), 60; W. Griffin Gribbel, "Report of Committee on Cooperation with Educational Institutions," *American Gas Association, Tenth Annual Convention, October 8–12, 1928* (New York: AGA, [1928]), 54.

94. FCC, *Telephone Investigation* (1937), 4:139, 144, appendix 6, sheets 1–4.

95. How those rates should be determined depended not on what it cost to build the utility infrastructure in the past, minus depreciation, Guernsey argued, but on the current costs of reproducing the network. FCC, *Telephone Investigation* (1937), 4:139–142.

96. FCC, *Telephone Investigation* (1937), 4:147.

97. FCC, *Telephone Investigation* (1937), 4:149.

98. FCC, *Telephone Investigation* (1937), 4:144.

99. FCC, *Telephone Investigation* (1937), 4:146–147, 150.

100. FCC, *Telephone Investigation* (1937), 4:149.

101. "Dr. James C. Bonbright, 93, Ex-Head of Power Authority," *New York Times*, November 14, 1985.

102. FCC, *Telephone Investigation* (1937), 4:134–136.

103. FCC, *Telephone Investigation* (1937), 4:138.

104. FCC, *Telephone Investigation* (1937), 4:134–139.

105. FCC, *Telephone Investigation* (1937), 4:157–159.

106. Lewis in *FTC Letter No. 4* (1928), 360–361. One hundred forty-three dollars is about $2,000 in 2014 dollars using the consumer price index to convert at Measuring-Worth.com.

107. Browne in *FTC Letter No. 4* (1928), 113.

108. FCC, *Telephone Investigation* (1937), 4:157–159.

109. F.G.R. Gordon, publicist and policy advocate, in *FTC Letter No. 9* (1929), 51.

110. Alan R. Raucher, *Public Relations and Business, 1900–1929* (Baltimore: Johns Hopkins University Press, 1968), 20, 28.

111. J. P. Ingle, Manager, Haverhill Gas Light Company, Haverhill, Massachusetts, "Seeing Ourselves as Others See Us," *American Gas Association Monthly*, March 1922, 151.

112. Browne in *FTC Letter No. 4* (1928), 77.

113. "Publicity Happenings," *American Gas Association Monthly*, June 1922, 345.

114. Illinois Committee on Public Utility Information, *Public Opinion and Public Utilities: Speakers' Bulletin No. 1, 1920: The Nature, Development and Service of Public Utility Companies* (Chicago, 1920), 17–18, Box 449, Folder 5, SCE Records; Grant in *FTC Letter No. 4* (1928), 478.

115. Lewis in *FTC Letter No. 4* (1928), 343–344.

308   *Notes to Pages 215–217*

116. *Manual of Organization and Policies: Middle West Utilities Company, 1927,* 22–23, Folder 54-2, Insull Papers.

117. Browne in *FTC Letter No. 4* (1928), 109; Samuel Kennedy, "Transforming Public Opinion: An Address by Mr. Samuel M. Kennedy, Vice-President Southern California Edison Co., Los Angeles, California, before the Convention of Managers and Executives of the Management Division of Stone & Webster Inc., Held in Boston, October 10–18, 1921," 20, Box 389, Folder 26, SCE Records; Carmichael in *FTC Letter No. 4* (1928), 20.

118. Sheridan in *FTC Letter No. 5* (1928), 46.

119. *FTC Letter No. 2* (1928), xvii.

120. MacQuarrie in *FTC Letter No. 2* (1928), 173, 180.

121. MacQuarrie in *FTC Letter No. 2* (1928), 174.

122. "Public Speaking Committee," *NELA Proceedings* (1928), Public Relations National Section, Tuesday, June 5, 1928, 288.

123. "Report of the Public Speaking Committee," *NELA Proceedings 1930,* 1282–1283.

124. Some audience overlap almost certainly occurred, yet much of the data on telephone companies for these years is missing. In many cases, the presenter, audience, talk title, and exact number in attendance were recorded. "Public Speaking Committee," 288–289; "Report of the Public Speaking Committee," 1283; FCC, "Appendix 5, Sheet 2"; G. K. McCorkle, "Commercial Department Record of Customer Relations Activities Years 1926 to 1935, Inclusive," in *Information as to Advertising, Publicity, Information Department Activities, and Other Matters in Response to Request of the Federal Communications Commission,* December 10, 1936, Box 41, Ex. 1353, FCC Records; Mountain States Telephone and Telegraph Companies, "7A—Copies of Commercial Department Progress Reports, 1926–1935," *Response to Inquiries Federal Communications Commission Contained in its Letter of December 11, 1936 to the American Telephone and Telegraph Company,* Box 41, FCC Records; Pacific Bell Telephone and Telegraph Companies, "Item 6: Report of Local News Items"; Southwest Bell Telephone and Telegraph Companies, "7-a. Forecasts and Actual Results as to Certain Customer Relations Activities," in *Response to Federal Communications Commission's Inquiry Dated December 11, 1936 Relative to Certain Advertising, Publicity and Information Activities for the Years 1926 to 1936, Inclusive,* Box 41, Ex. 1355, FCC Records. For population, see "National Intercensal Tables: 1900–1990," US Census Bureau, last modified October 8, 2021, https://www.census.gov/data/tables/time-series/demo/popest/pre-1980-national.html.

125. P. S. Arkwright, "Public Speaking as Publicity Medium," *AERA Proceedings, 1922,* 175.

126. FCC, *Telephone Investigation* (1937), 4:23a.

127. Examination of Earl H. Painter, General Counsel, Southwestern Bell Telephone Company, *Proceedings before the FCC, January 28, 1937,* 5582–5583.

128. Groce, *Report of First Year's Work, 1922,* 7.

129. FCC, *Telephone Investigation* (1937), 4:21–22.

130. Ingle, "Seeing Ourselves as Others See Us," 151–152.

131. "Peoples Gas Club—Popular and Progressive," Peoples Gas, *Year Book, 1924,* 31.

132. FCC, *Telephone Investigation* (1937), 4:20–21.

133. Browne in *FTC Letter No. 4* (1928), 105–106.

Notes to Pages 217–221   309

134. General Auditor, Southern Bell Telephone and Telegraph Company, to Herbert L. Pettey, Secretary, FCC, January 6, 1936, Box 21, Ex. 228, FCC Records.

135. New York Telephone Company, *I Am Here to Tell You about the Telephone Problem in This State*, Ex. 142, Box 15, FCC Records.

136. A. B. West, Vice President and General Manager of the Southern Sierras Power Company, "Speech to the Present Day Club of Riverside," March 28, 1921, 1, 3, Box 285, Folder 12, SCE Records.

137. H. S. Raushenbush, "A Program of Gradual Socialization of Industry," *New Leader*, March 5 and 12, 1927, quoted in Edwin Vennard, *Dangers of the TVA Method of River Control* (Chicago: 1944), 9, Box 485, Folder 5, SCE Records.

138. Quoted by Vennard, *Dangers of the TVA Method of River Control*, 15.

139. Carl D. Thompson, "Is the Chautauqua a Free Platform?" *New Republic*, December 18, 1924, 87.

140. Sheridan in *FTC Letter No. 5* (1928), 70, 127.

141. F.G.R. Gordon, *The Government Ownership of the Railways* (Chicago: Charles H. Kerr, 1898), 3; Daniel De Leon, "F.G.R. Gordon—And There Are Others," *Daily People*, Monday, July 11, 1910, http://www.slp.org/pdf/de_leon/eds1910/jul11 _1910.pdf; "Public Policy Session," in NELA, *Bulletin*, ed. T. C. Martin, May 1919, 224.

142. Sheridan in *FTC Letter No. 5* (1928), 151.

143. Clapp in *FTC Letter No. 3* (1928), 201, xxii.

144. Rob Roy McGregor in *Response to Senate Resolution No. 83 a Monthly Report on the Electric Power and Gas Utilities Inquiry, No. 2, Filed with the Secretary of the Senate, April 16, 1928* (1928), 70–71.

145. Mullaney in *FTC Letter No. 2* (1928), 89–90.

146. Sheridan in *FTC Letter No. 5* (1928), 66.

147. Executive Committee of the Greater California League, *Shall California Be Sovietized? Facts about the Proposed Water and Power Act and Bond Issue of 500 Millions* (San Francisco: Greater California League, n.d.)

148. Two hundred fifty thousand dollars comes to a little more than $3.5 million in 2014 dollars using the consumer price index to convert at MeasuringWorth.com; Benjamin P. Cook, "Spreckels Reveals Secret of His Fight for Water and Power Measure," *San Francisco Chronicle*, January 31, 1923.

149. Thomas Goebel, *A Government by the People: Direct Democracy in America, 1890–1940* (Chapel Hill: University of North Carolina Press, 2002), 161.

150. Frank C. Jordan, Secretary of State, *Statement of Vote at General Election Held on November 4, 1924, in the State of California (Party Registration and Voting Precincts)* (Sacramento, CA State Printing Office, 1928), 36. Frank C. Jordan, Secretary of State, *Statement of Vote at General Election Held on November 2, 1926, in the State of California* (Sacramento, CA State Printing Office, 1926).

151. Sheridan in *FTC Letter No. 5* (1928), 160–162.

152. Prof. Irving Fisher, "An Estimate of Chautauqua," *Lyceum*, March 1924, 39.

153. Thompson, "Is the Chautauqua a Free Platform?" 84.

154. Sheridan in *FTC Letter No. 5* (1928), 61, 65.

155. Thompson, "Is the Chautauqua a Free Platform," 84; F. R. Schofield, editor, *Sentinel*, to Redpath-Vawter Chautauqua System, Cedar Rapids, Iowa, July 12, 1924, Box 3851, Ex. 2672, FTC Records.

310   *Notes to Pages 221–226*

156. Sheridan in *FTC Letter No. 5* (1928), 64.

157. Sheridan in *FTC Letter No. 5* (1928), 61–70, x–xii.

158. Sheridan in *FTC Letter No. 5*, (1928), 67–68; P. B. Linville, Chairman, Bank of Edina, Edina, Missouri, to Redpath-Vawter Chautauqua System, Cedar Rapids, Iowa, New York, July 11, 1924, Box 3851, Ex. 2676, FTC Records; Thompson, "Is the Chautauqua a Free Platform?" 87.

159. J. F. Duncan, North Missouri Power Company, Edina, Missouri, to John Sheridan, August 6, 1924, Box 3851, Ex. 2701, FTC Records.

160. Examination of Alfred Fischer, Former Director, Michigan Committee on Public Information, in *FTC Letter No. 5* (1928), 412.

161. Examination of Frank O. Cuppy, Legislative Agent, Indiana Public Utilities Association, in *FTC Letter No. 5*, (1928), 526.

162. Sheridan in *FTC No. 5* (1928), 70.

163. Mullaney in *FTC Letter No. 2* (1928), 91.

164. Katherine Kelley, "Tribune Cookery Students to See Turkey Roasted," *Chicago Tribune*, 20, November 24, 1933.

165. "Reaching the Company's Women Customers," *Public Service Company of Northern Illinois Year Book 1929*, 20, Box 55, Folder 8, Insull Papers.

166. "Changing Housekeeping to Home-Making," Peoples Gas, *Year Book, 1929*, 21.

167. "Home Service Department," Peoples Gas, *Year Book, 1924*, 29; "Merchandise Sales," *Public Service Company of Northern Illinois Year Book 1928*, 22, Box 55, Folder 8, Insull Papers.

168. Mrs. Marjorie Pidgeon Wardman, Chairman, Brooklyn Borough Gas Company, "Report of Home Service Committee," AGA, *Tenth Annual Convention, 1928*, 559; David B. Sicilia, "Selling Power: Marketing and Monopoly at Boston Edison, 1886–1929" (PhD diss., Brandeis University, 1990), 515; "Home Service: Organization and Operation," *NELA Proceedings* (1930), 1289.

169. "Home Service Aids Modern Trend," Peoples Gas, *Year Book, 1930*, 24.

170. *Manual of Organization and Policies: Middle West Utilities Company, 1927*, 22–23, Folder 54-2, Insull Papers.

171. "Showing the Subscriber a Switchboard in Service: A Demonstration That Shows the Public What Takes Place When a Call Is Put In," *Southern Telephone News*, December 1921, 13, AT&T-TX.

172. C. W. Hungerford, Publicity Manager, Michigan Bell, to J. D. Ellsworth, Advertising Manager, AT&T, December 8, 1920, Box 15, FCC Records.

173. Edward H. Bauer, Providence Gas Co., Providence, Rhode Island, "Portable Demonstrating Water Gas Set," *American Gas Association Monthly*, April 1922, 251.

174. "Telling Our Story to Public an Ever-Continuing Program," *Mouthpiece* (Detroit, MI), November 1924, 4, AT&T-TX; "The Work of the Commercial Department: Part II: A Reading Assignment," in *Employees General Training Course: The Pacific Telephone and Telegraph Company, 1927*, 14–15, Collection 3, RG 5, Box 3, File: The Work of the Commercial Department: Part II, AT&T-TX; Bauer, "Portable Demonstrating Water Gas Set," 251.

175. Underlining in the original. C. W. Hungerford, Publicity Manager, Michigan Bell, *Excerpts from Reports Giving Details of the "Michigan Plan,"* Box 15, FCC Records.

Notes to Pages 226–228   311

176. "Selling a Utility Company to the Public," *Southern Telephone News*, June 1922, 6, AT&T-TX.

177. J. D. Ellsworth, Advertising Manager, AT&T, Memorandum, January 10, 1921, Box 15, FCC Records.

178. "Seeing Is Believing," *Southern Telephone News*, May 1922, 1, AT&T-TX.

179. "Selling a Utility Company to the Public," 6.

180. Franz C. Kuhn, President, Michigan State Telephone Company, "Demonstration Switchboards—Their Usefulness with Employees and the Public," in *Conference of Personnel Group, Bell System, April 18–25, 1922*, 63–65, Box 88, RG 4, Collection 6, AT&T-TX.

181. Polly Lassiter, "Atlanta Traffic Minstrels Make a Hit," *Southern Telephone News*, January 1922, 3, AT&T-TX; "Christmas Comes but Once a Year," *Pacific Telephone Magazine*, January, 1932, AT&T-TX; Venus Green, *Race on the Line: Gender, Labor, and Technology in the Bell System, 1880–1980* (Durham, NC: Duke University Press, 2001), 207.

182. J. M. Hamilton, "Comparative Study—Motion Picture Distribution—1930 to 1932," in *Annual Report of Motion Picture Activities, 1932* (AT&T, February 1, 1933), Box 17, Ex. 220, FCC Records.

183. Bell's methodology for counting movie attendance varied. In 1933, one Bell publicity manager assumed that theatres were half empty when estimating the number of attendees at Bell screenings. This method may have been used before this time and by many publicity managers. Later in 1933, Bell became more conservative and began multiplying theatre seating capacity by 3/8. Still, Bell showed their films around 174,000 times in 1931, which would require each screening to have had some five hundred attendees to reach Bell's viewership estimates, which seems far too high. See Examination of J. M. Hamilton, Motion Picture Director, AT&T, in *Proceedings before the FCC, June 4, 1936*, 2136. This calculation uses the US population in 1930 of 123,076,741 as measured by the US Census; see "National Intercensal Tables: 1900–1990."

184. Hamilton in *Proceedings before the FCC, June 4, 1936*, 2133–2134.

185. A. B. Stearns, Publicity Manager, New Jersey Bell Telephone Company, to J. M. Hamilton, January 20, 1933, 3, in Hamilton, *Annual Report of Motion Picture Activities, 1932*.

186. AT&T, "A Modern Knight," 1931, AT&T Tech Channel, video, http://techchannel .att.com/play-video.cfm/2011/7/27/AT&T-Archives-A-Modern-Knight.

187. J. M. Hamilton to A. F. Hardman, Advertising Manager, Ohio Bell Telephone Company, May 14, 1934, Box 17, Ex. 227-10, FCC Records.

188. Hamilton in *Proceedings before the FCC, June 4, 1936*, 2202–2206; J. A. Callahan, Manager, Warner Bros. Theatres, Capital Theatre, Danbury, Connecticut, to T. H. Tuohy, Manager, S.N.E. Telephone Co., Danbury, Connecticut, January 12, 1933, in Hamilton, *Annual Report of Motion Picture Activities, 1932*.

189. Sidney B. Lust [theatre chain owner], to H. D. Sonnemann, C. & P. Telephone Co., Washington, DC, May 5, 1932, in Hamilton, *Annual Report of Motion Picture Activities, 1932*.

190. J. M. Hamilton, photocopy of C. A. Lejeune, "Two Ports and a Telephone," *Observer*, (London), February 29, 1932, in *Annual Report of Motion Picture Activities, 1932*.

312   *Notes to Pages 228–232*

191. Hamilton in *Proceedings before the FCC, June 4, 1936*, 2202–2206.

192. Hamilton, *Annual Report of Motion Picture Activities, 1932*.

193. FCC, *Telephone Investigation* (1937), 4:27.

194. FCC, *Telephone Investigation* (1937), 4:23c.

195. H. A. Seymour, "How We Advertise, and Why," *How Commonwealth Edison Company Works* (Commonwealth Edison, 1914), 160, Folder 55-1, Insull Papers.

196. Richardson in *FTC Letter No. 3* (1928), 390; MacQuarrie in *FTC Letter No. 2* (1928), 165; "Appendix M. Report of Committee on Publicity," *AERA Proceedings, 1929*, 190.

197. "Service and Public Relations," *Public Service Company of Northern Illinois Year Book 1928*, 23–24, Box 55, Folder 8, Insull Papers.

198. Examination of Rob Roy McGregor, Assistant Director, Illinois Committee on Public Utility Information, in *FTC Letter No. 2* (1928), 137–138.

199. FCC, *Telephone Investigation* (1937), 4:31.

200. Examination of Arthur W. Page, Vice President, Information Department, AT&T, in *Proceedings before the FCC, January 25, 1937*, 5219–5124; $8,400 in 1910 comes to $216,000 in 2014 dollars using the consumer price index to convert at MeasuringWorth.com.

201. FCC, *Telephone Investigation* (1937), 4:81–83; Page in *Proceedings before the FCC, January 25, 1937*, 5224–5230.

202. Page in *Proceedings before the FCC, January 25, 1937*, 5242–5262.

203. FCC, *Telephone Investigation* (1937), 4:81; Walker, *Proposed Report*, 567.

204. Page in *Proceedings before the FCC, January 25, 1937*, 5242–5250.

205. FCC, *Telephone Investigation* (1937), 4:86–90.

206. Arthur Pound, *The Telephone Idea: Fifty Years After* (New York: Greenberg, 1926); digital copies from both libraries obtained through the Hathi Trust's Digital Library; the identity of J. J. Kelly is known through the Michigan Bell employee magazine article "Finding Marshal Foch, by 'Phone for a University," *Mouthpiece* (Detroit, MI), December 1921, 7.

207. Pound, *The Telephone Idea*; FCC, *Telephone Investigation* (1937), 4:85–90; Page in *Proceedings before the FCC, January 25, 1937*, 5242–5262.

208. James Mavor, *Government Telephones: The Experience of Manitoba, Canada* (New York: Moffat, Yard, 1916), 164.

209. "Government Wires Urged by Burleson," *New York Times*, December 14, 1914, 6.

210. Walker, *Proposed Report*, 566; Mavor, *Government Telephones*, vii.

211. Oxley in *FTC Letter No. 3* (1928), 25–27; Clapp in *FTC Letter No. 3* (1928), 201, xxii.

212. James Mavor, *Niagara in Politics: A Critical Account of the Ontario Hydroelectric Commission* (New York: E. P. Dutton, 1925). This strategy of secretly paying experts was used again in the 1990s by PG&E. See David Heath, "How Industry Scientist Stalled Action on Carcinogen," *The Center for Public Integrity*, March 13, 2013, about the scandal at the center of the movie *Erin Brockovich*, starring Julia Roberts.

213. Sheridan in *FTC Letter No. 5* (1928), 151; MacQuarrie in *FTC Letter No. 2* (1928), 166; Arkwright in *FTC Letter No. 28* (1931), 98; Ralph L. Mahon, "The Telephone in Chicago, 1877–1940," typescript, 144, AT&T-TX.

214. *FTC Letter No. 22* (1930), 1182.

Notes to Pages 232–240   313

215. "Los Angeles Window Display," *Pacific Telephone Magazine*, December 1916, 11, AT&T-TX.

216. "Tell 'Em About It," *Southern Telephone News*, October 1921, 1, AT&T-TX.

217. "Peoples Gas Stores," Peoples Gas, *Year Book, 1924*, 24.

218. Robt. E. Power, "Business Office Management," in *Meeting of Managers* (San Francisco: PT&T, March 30, 1926), 3, File: Pacific Bell Company Leaders Executive Office Files, Conference, 1925, 2 of 8, Box 10, RG 5, AT&T-TX.

219. "Selling a Utility Company to the Public," 7–8.

220. General Auditor, Southern Bell Telephone and Telegraph Company, to Herbert L. Pettey, Secretary, January 6, 1936, Box 21, Ex. 228, FCC Records.

221. Painter in *Proceedings before the FCC, January 28, 1937*, 5543–5544.

222. Oxley in *FTC Letter No. 3* (1928), 214.

223. FCC, *Telephone Investigation* (1937), 4:109–113.

224. Painter in *Proceedings before the FCC, January 28, 1937*, 5554–5555, 5563.

225. FCC, *Telephone Investigation* (1937), 4:99–100, 102.

226. FCC, *Telephone Investigation* (1937), 4:91–95.

227. FCC, *Telephone Investigation* (1937), 4:96–97

228. Robert Prather in *Response to Senate Resolution No. 83*, 107–108, 116–117.

229. "Merlin Hall Aylesworth," Advertising Hall of Fame, accessed March 15, 2023, http://advertisinghall.org/members/member_bio.php?memid=528.

230. One hundred twenty-five thousand dollars comes to $1.7 million in 2014 dollars using the consumer price index to convert at MeasuringWorth.com.

231. William Z. Ripley, *Main Street and Wall Street* (Boston: Little, Brown, 1927), 278.

232. Harold Platt, *The Electric City: Energy and the Growth of the Chicago Area, 1880–1930* (Chicago: University of Chicago Press, 1991), 270–271.

233. Folder 18-12, 7/5/34, Insull Papers.

234. Examination of Willis J. Spaulding, Commissioner of Public Property, City of Springfield, Illinois, in *FTC Letter No. 2* (1928), 11.

235. FCC, *Telephone Investigation* (1937), 4:56.

236. John Kenneth Galbraith, *The Great Crash of 1929* (Boston: Houghton Mifflin, 1955), 175.

Conclusion

1. John Woolfolk, "Confused about PG&E's Bankruptcy? Here's What You Need to Know," *Mercury News*, January 23, 2020. The company filed for bankruptcy in January of 2019; it had done so before, in 2001. The first time was related to so-called deregulation and state regulators not allowing PG&E to charge enough to cover costs. The second bankruptcy was primarily related to wildfire liabilities and included the threat of state ownership.

2. AT&T, *Annual Report, 1928*, 6; Warren R. Voorhis, Vice President, American Water Works & Electrical Company, New York, "The Girl at the Window," *Electrical World*, August 4, 1923, 1, Box 449, Folder 5, SCE Records.

3. "The Work of the Commercial Department: Part I: A Reading Assignment," in *Employees General Training Course: The Pacific Telephone and Telegraph Company, 1927*, 18, Collection 3, RG 5, Box 3, File: Public Relations and Publicity, AT&T-TX.

4. "Tell 'Em About It," *Southern Telephone News*, October 1921, 1, AT&T-TX.

314 *Notes to Pages 240–243*

5. C. E. Morgan, General Manager, Brooklyn City Railroad Company, "Telling Your Story through Employees," *AERA Proceedings 1922*, 173.

6. "The Work of the Commercial Department: Part I," 18.

7. J. David Houser, "Employee-Customer Relations," *American Gas Association, Twelfth Annual Convention, October 13–17, 1930* (New York: AGA, [1930]), 737.

8. "Building and Telling of It," *Mouthpiece* (Detroit, MI) 5, no. 3 (March 1924): ii, AT&T-TX.

9. "Report on Commercial Service and Relations with Customers Committee," *NELA Proceedings* (1922), 1:361.

10. W. H. Hamilton, discussion about S. M. Kennedy's pamphlet "Service," Second General Session, May 20, 1920, *NELA Proceedings* (1920), 59.

11. "Report of the Customer Ownership Committee," *AERA Proceedings, 1925*, 198–199; Samuel T. MacQuarrie, Director, New England Bureau of Public Service Information, *Report of Fifth Year's Work, 1926*, 8, Box 3818, Ex. 691, FTC Records; "Suggestions for Letter to Newspapers," Ex. 2739B, Box 3851, FTC Records.

12. P. S. Arkwright, "Public Speaking as Publicity Medium," *AERA Proceedings, 1922*, 175; Examination of P. S. Arkwright, President, Georgia Power Co. *Letter No. 28* (1931), 100.

13. "Public Relations and Publicity: A Reading Assignment," 2nd ed., in *Employees General Training Course: The Pacific Telephone and Telegraph Company, 1927*, 14, Collection 3, RG 5, Box 3, File: Public Relations and Publicity, AT&T-TX.

14. Samuel Kennedy, "Transforming Public Opinion: An Address by Mr. Samuel M. Kennedy, Vice-President Southern California Edison Co., Los Angeles, California, before the Convention of Managers and Executives of the Management Division of Stone & Webster Inc., Held in Boston, October 10–18, 1921," 42, Box 389, Folder 26, SCE Records.

15. James Clements, "Interviewing Dissatisfied Customers," *Pacific Gas and Electric Magazine* 1, no. 9 (February 1910): 405.

16. J. F. Hull, "Press Association President Talks before Utility Men," 1922, Ex. 2745, Box 3851, Series: Economic Investigations Files, 1915–1938, Subject: Power and Gas, FTC Records.

17. J.S.S. Richard, City Editor, *Philadelphia Public Ledger*, paraphrasing an unnamed source during his speech to the Fourth Annual Convention of the AGA, October 29, 1922, "Public Relations," *American Gas Association Monthly*, December 1922, 735.

18. H. L. Donaldson, "Appendix A: Training for Better Public Contact," in *Public-Contact-Training Methods and Principles*, 7.

19. Stuart Ewen, *PR! A Social History of Spin* (New York: Basic Books, 1996), 71–72, 127, 144–145.

20. Examination of Robert M. Hofer, managing editor, E. Hofer & Sons, in *FTC Letter No. 7* (1928), 245–246.

21. Hamilton, discussion about S. M. Kennedy's pamphlet "Service," 58.

22. Labert St. Clair, "Getting the Public Eye and Ear," *American Gas Association Monthly*, January 1922, 24.

23. "Does Advertising Pay?" *AERA Proceedings, 1927*, 327, 324.

24. Italics in original. Kennedy, "Transforming Public Opinion," 8.

Notes to Pages 244–246   315

25. Robert M. Searle, "Seventeen Reasons for Advertising," *American Gas Association Monthly*, June 1922, 345.

26. "Appendix O—Report of the Committee on Employee—Customer Contact," *AERA Proceedings, 1928*, 218.

27. Edward S. Rogers, "Advertising Policies That Hold Customers," *System: The Magazine of Business*, July 1916, 43; Pamela Walker Laird, *Advertising Progress: American Business and the Rise of Consumer Marketing* (Baltimore: Johns Hopkins University Press, 1998), 376.

28. Laird, *Advertising Progress*, 376–379.

INDEX

academic conferences, 207

ads-for-articles scheme. *See* space grabbing

advertisements, 242–43; change over time, 246; to facilitate space grabbing, 15, 156–58, 167–68, 183–85; of stock, 138; as tool to control clerks, 244, 246. *See also* space grabbing

AERA. *See* American Electric Railway Association

African Americans, 45, 62, 78–80, 184, 226–27, 265n42

American Electric Railway Association (AERA), 70, 134, 164, 181, 229, 244

American Federation of Labor, 171

American Gas Association (AGA), 45, 66, 86, 163, 195

antimonopoly sentiment, 4, 142, 176, 186, 236; in American history, 4

architecture, exterior, 105–11

architecture, interior: back region, 100–101; complaint booths, 75; front region, 100–101; surveillance and, 91–95, 102–5

Associated Press (AP), 169, 181

AT&T: and academic conferences, 207; antimonopoly sentiment against, 6; and architecture, 100, 104, 105–6, 143; and civic clubs, 216; and college professors, 202; corporate history, 27, 51, 131, 152; and courtesy, 75; and customer stock ownership, 125, 128–29, 131–33, 137–38, 139–43, 153–54, 207; and FCC investigation, 161; and government operation, 83–86; and movies, 206, 227–29; and public speaking, 210–11, 216; and textbooks, 202, 206; and trade press books, 230–31; and space grabbing, 171, 173–74, 175, 177, 178, 181; and the spirit of service, 66, 68; and state utility information committees, 165, 195; and welfare capitalism, 71–72. *See also* McReynolds Settlement

Aylesworth, Merin, 219, 234

Barton, Bruce, 219

Bell, Alexander Graham, 152

Bell System: and architecture, 99–100, 110, 114, 116; and corporate history, 27; and FCC investigation, 160, 189–90; and operator training, 40; and public opinion, 87–88; and regulators, 233; and space grabbing, 175, 177–78, 187–89; and surveillance, 55; and tours, 119; and the unit plan, 98

Bell Telephone Securities Company, 129, 139–40, 142, 144–45

Bemis, Edward, 210

benefits, employee. *See* welfare capitalism

Bentham, Jeremy, 14, 103

Bernays, Edward, 16, 191, 242

Bible, 9, 64, 194, 266n54. *See also* Christianity

blackface, 226

blue-collar workers, 36

Bonbright, James C., 211

Boston Edison Company, 38, 56–57, 74–76, 118

books: policy books, 231–32; for trade press, 230–31. *See also* textbooks

branch offices, 13, 88–91, 197; customer visits to, 89; with model rooms and model homes, 112–13. *See also* closed offices; open offices

318 *Index*

break rooms. *See* rest rooms
Burleson, Albert, 83–85

California Water and Power Acts, 148, 220
Carver, Thomas Nixon, 126
Chautauqua circuit, 221–22, 239
Christianity, 64–65
clerks: African American, 45, 265n42; dress, 41–44; importance in shaping public opinion, 31–32; job dissatisfaction, 35; physical exams, 45; promotions, 95; rudeness before courteous capitalism, 7, 21, 24, 75, 251n29, 254n26; self-conversion, 66–70; wages, 70, 95, 131, 180, 268n88; work experience, 2, 32–34, 36, 102, 105. *See also* emotional labor; telephone operators
cliometrics, 176
closed offices, 13, 88; customer impressions of, 90; visibility within, 94
Colton, John, 70, 193–94
commercial offices. *See* branch offices
Commonwealth Edison Company: and architecture, 106, 108, 110; and courtesy, 33, 83; and customer stock ownership, 129, 149–50, 155; and movies, 229; and state utility information committees, 162; supervision, 54
communism, 219–20, 222
conductors. *See* clerks
confidence men and painted women, 35
consumer culture, 11, 12, 13, 77
consumption, 7, 246; in small towns, 9, 71, 98
corporate domesticity, 13, 111–15
corruption, 25, 233–36
counterless offices, 99–101
courteous capitalism, 2–9, 11, 12, 13, 28–29, 237; and ads, 237, 243–46; complemented by open offices, 98, 238; effectiveness of, 32, 80–83, 238, 240–46; examples of use, 80–83; within the firm, 49; and government operation, 84; ideological justifications, 60–62; origins in utility industries, 52; and power relations, 77; and rationality, 166; and regulation, 51; relationship to surveillance, 8, 18, 23, 56, 60, 91, 102; religious justifications, 64; and welfare capitalism, 71; and work experience, 34, 36

courtesy, 9, 246; chants and pledges, 38; classes for utility workers, 38; clubs, 47–48; in company mottos, 243–45; early utility courtesy training efforts, 37; enforcement of, 12, 35; and gender, 9, 41–42, 62–63, 69; history of (before courteous capitalism), 9–11; measured by numbers of people contacted, 46–47, 238; political dimension, 4, 30; and race, 78–80; training, 12, 37–41, 44, 46; training movies, 38; within utilities, 48
Creel, George, 161–62, 191
customers: being courteous, 75; being rude, 32–33; complaining, 74–75; finding clerks strange, 9; as "friends," 73–74; giving feedback, 8, 18–19; paying for utility ads, 185; as rational, 30; service experience by age and gender, 59–60; service experience compared to small shops, 70–71
customer service. *See* clerks; customers; emotional labor
customer stock ownership, 14–15, 127, 238, 246; and AERA, 134, 195; and age, 145; and antimonopoly sentiment, 126; at AT&T, 125, 128–29; buy-back service, 144; corporate supply, 126; customer demand, 142; customer reception of, 137; employees purchasing of stock, 72; and ethnicity, 145; and gender, 145; goals of, 129–30; at Insull-related companies, 149–50, 154; and NELA, 129, 195; origins of in utility industry, 125–26, 129; percentage of Americans reached, 126, 144, 238; political views of shareholders, 145–46; quotas, 135; regional aspects, 139–42; sales at branch offices, 136, 143; sales training, 133–35; spread of strategy, 128; and streetcar companies, 137; success of strategy, 146–48, 150; and utility rates, 130–31; and welfare capitalism, 138; and World War I, 125, 128, 130–31; and yields, 132. *See also* holding companies

democracy, 30, 151, 183, 203
demonstrations, 225–27
Depression, 152–55, 187, 203, 234
Durkheim, Émile, 65

Index 319

editors: demanding ads, 172; dependent on advertisers, 172; filtering negative articles, 176–77; paying money to, 170–71; receiving free utility service, 168–69; resisting space grabbing, 171–72; in small towns, 15, 182–84; soliciting ads for column space, 157, 167
education, 198–201
efficiency, 52, 72–73
electricity consumption: of farms and factories, 26
emotional labor, 1–3; commodification of emotions, 3, 33, 36, 69; as desired by managers, 3, 32; emotional freedom, 12, 63; and gender, 9, 62; as political strategy, 3–4; race, 9, 62; and rude customers, 32–33; and sincerity, 34; and worker experience, 33–34, 48
employee magazines, 3, 40, 135
environmental psychology. *See* open offices
Ewen, Stuart, 242
executives, definition of, 249n8

face-to-face interaction, 7; numbers of Americans contacted this way, 16, 47, 55–57, 59, 216, 238, 262n184; public relations importance of, 32, 240–42; relation to architecture, 92–93; relation to stock sales, 139, 146; during speeches, 197, 216; in theories of Paul Lazarsfeld and Robert Merton, 159
Federal Communications Commission (FCC), 160–61, 185, 189, 190, 193
Federal Trade Commission (FTC), 160–61, 185, 189, 199, 220
feedback, 8, 12, 18–19, 56, 58, 75, 86, 237
Fitzgerald, F. Scott: *This Side of Paradise*, 35
Forbes, B. C., 88, 153
frankness in speaking to media, 190–91, 193

Gilded Age, 6, 73, 233, 239
Goffman, Erving, 100
Gompers, Samuel, 171
Gordon, Fred G. R., 179–80, 219
government ownership. *See* municipal ownership
Great Depression. *See* Depression

Harvard Business School, 206, 211
Hochschild, Arlie, 3, 67
Hockenbeamer, A. F., 125, 127, 132–33, 155
Hofer & Sons, 173–75, 182, 185, 186, 243
holding companies, 150–55
Home Services Department, 222–24
Houser, David J., 29, 38, 59, 240

ideology, 9, 60–65; the "spirit of service," 9, 56, 65–66
information committees, 158; goals, 165; joint funding, 163–64; methods, 165; organizational structure, 163–64; origins, 161–63
Insull, Samuel, 29, 58, 108, 129; end of career, 154–55; political donations, 235; and space grabbing, 163; and state information committees, 163; and World War I, 162

Kahn, Samuel, 80–82
Katz, Elihu, 16
Kennedy, Samuel, 1, 57, 69, 91–92, 108, 123, 150, 241, 243

LaFollette, Robert, Jr., 139, 141, 160, 171
LaFollette, Robert, Sr., 6
Lazarsfeld, Paul, 16, 159
lectures, 16, 209–11, 213; at civic clubs, 213–18; by female employees, 215; to students, 154–55. *See also* Chautauqua circuit
Lee, Ivy, 16, 214
Lippmann, Walter, 182–83, 191

managers, 1–3, 8, 14, 16, 45, 52, 66–67, 69, 93, 120, 249n8; and customer stock ownership, 134, 149; and employee discipline, 12, 40, 46, 75, 101; and films, 228–29; and gender, 44–45, 62; and lectures, 205, 215; limits of power, 42, 66–67, 138; and practicing courtesy, 49; and professors, 212; and publicity, 160; and space grabbing, 156, 163, 181, 194; and surveillance, 55, 57, 92, 94; and textbooks, 195, 197–98; and training employees, 38–39
Market Street Railway Company, 80–81
Maslow, Abraham, 120–23
matrons, 117–18
Mavor, James, 231–32

McAdoo, William Gibbs, 18; and customer feedback, 18–19, 56, 237; later career, 23, 84; "the Public Be Pleased," 21–24; relations with press, 190–91

McReynolds Settlement, 49, 131, 152

Means, Gardiner, 212

Merton, Robert, 159

minstrel shows, 226

monopolies, 210; critiques of, 5–6

movies, 35; corporate training movies, 38; for a popular audience, 227–29, 239; for students, 206

Mullaney, Bernard, 195, 222

municipal ownership, 20, 86, 176; in Canada, 221, 231; as compared to corporate utility service, 26, 29–30, 201; and customer stock ownership, 238–39; declining popularity of, 147, 148; efforts by utilities to thwart, 14, 126–28, 193, 204, 205, 235; in Europe, 51, 196, 230; and newspapers, 172–73, 176, 179–80, 186; promotion of, 1, 72, 130, 165, 171, 190, 210, 217–22; in small towns, 15, 158

mystery shoppers, 8, 33, 54–56, 59–60; and checklists, 8

National Electric Light Association (NELA), 37, 129, 161, 164, 206–7, 215–16, 229

New Deal, 161, 190

newspapers. See space grabbing

Nonpartisan League, 180, 220

Norris, George, 189, 190, 219, 238

open houses, 119–20. See also tours of utility buildings

open offices, 13, 88, 90, 246; and banks, 95; and environmental psychology of, 13–14, 120–23, 268n87; gender and seating, 93; layout of employees, 93; reception of by clerks, 96; reception of by customers, 96; seating layout within, 93–94; and sound, 123; visibility within, 91–96

operating rooms, 102–5; customer perceptions of, 116; panopticon, 14, 103; supervision within, 102

Peoples Gas Light & Coke Company: and advertising, 184; and civic clubs, 217; and customer contact, 46–47, 233; and

demonstrations, 223–24; and feedback, 58; and Home Service Department, 223; and Mrs. Peterson, 223; and radio, 223; and training, 46; and window displays, 232

personal interaction. See face-to-face interaction

Peterson, Anna J., 222

philanthropy, 232–33

Pinchot, Gifford, 160, 161, 219

plays. See demonstrations

Populists, 4, 7, 29, 142, 184, 191, 238

Post Office: clerks at, 272n157; contact with the public, 47; operation of telephone network, 83–86

Pound, Arthur, 230, 252n46

print matter, 139, 166, 240–41, 243, 246. See also reading advertisements and articles

professors: as authors for utilities, 231–32; as critiqued by utilities, 192; as guest lecturers, 210–12; influenced by utility managers, 212–13; influencing hiring of, 208; as utility consultants, 206–9

Progressive Era, 5, 73, 116, 168, 184, 236; centrality of utility policy to, 5; definition of, 31, 250n20; and education, 200–201; end of, 7; interpretations of, 4, 52; and progressive reformers, 125

propaganda, 191–92, 209–10, 211, 229–31

public opinion, 1, 28–31, 146, 197, 235–36, 246; definition of, 28; efforts to influence, 160; and franchise permits, 28; importance of, 1, 2; of monopoly utilities, 20, 81, 94, 127, 186; and rates, 28; relation to regulation, 28, 30, 50

Public Ownership League of America, 148

public relations: and architecture, 72, 108, 112; campaigns by utilities, 13, 15, 47, 159; and courtesy, 29, 246; and customer stock ownership, 129, 146; development as a field, 1, 16, 46, 75, 237–41; and films, 229; improvement over time, 80–82; and McAdoo, 23; and monopolies, 7, 26; and publicity, 232; and railroads, 131; and regulatory boards, 51; and welfare capitalism, 71; and World War I, 162

radio shows, 222–23

rationality, 166, 242

Raushenbush, H.S., 218
reading advertisements and articles, 166, 241, 243
Red Scare (1919), 219
regulation, 25, 27, 49–51, 194; courtesy by regulators, 56; historical interpretations of, 4–5; improved regulatory environment for utilities, 81, 185; and lobbying, 233–36; political regulation related to emotional regulation, 11; public critiques of, 60, 187; public demand for, 7, 30; and railroads, 131; of securities, 127–28; in textbooks, 194, 198, 204; of utility rates, 185. *See also* public opinion
rest rooms, 72, 113–16; magazine selection within, 114–15
Ripley, William Z., 152, 160
Ross, Edward, 210
Ruggles, Clyde O., 206–8

Sheridan, John, 196, 198, 209, 221, 239; criticism of utility industry, 70; and customer stock ownership, 148, 153; death of, 194; and space grabbing, 156, 187, 193–94
sincerity, 11–12, 34–35, 86
Smith, Frank L., 235
socialism, 180, 192, 200, 218, 219–20. *See also* municipal ownership
Southern California Edison Company: and advertising, 184, 241; and architecture, 78, 89–90, 121–22; and corporate history, 1–2, 127; and courtesy, 1–2, 23, 34, 57; and customer stock ownership, 125–27, 137–38, 146; and supervision, 57
space grabbing, 15; accuracy of statistics, 176; amount in pages, 158, 174–75; anonymous authorship, 178–80; in college newspapers, 212–13; compared to Progressive Era news, 164, 168, 184; effectiveness of strategy, 185–90; ethical views of, 192–94; goals of, 159; prevalence among newspapers, 15; preventing negative articles from appearing, 176–78; relation to ads, 15, 157–58, 167
Spargo, John, 147
speeches. *See* lectures
spirit of service. *See* ideology
spokesmen, 39, 214

state information committees (bureaus). *See* information committees
Steffens, Lincoln, 6, 20
Stimson, Henry L., 146
stock market crash of 1929. *See* Depression
streetcar lines, 1, 8, 19, 27, 39, 75, 80–81, 138, 159, 163–64, 232; and corruption, 20; and customer stock ownership, 126, 137, 147; omnibuses, 24–25; and poor service, 20–21; and rates, 186; and textbooks, 199, 204
students. *See* education
superpower grids, 150–51
supervision/surveillance, 9, 14, 103; continuous, 8; internal, 9; with microphones in desks, 55; percentage of interactions surveilled, 56; in relation to clerks' behavior, 57
surveys, 56, 57, 58–59, 175; extent of, 59; of newspaper content, 177, 187
switchboards, 105

Tarbell, Ida, 36
Taylorizing, 116
telephone nationalization, 83–86
telephone operators: work experience of, 105, 116–17. *See also* clerks
textbooks: content of, 201–2, 203–5; determining content of, 195–96, 198; effectiveness of, 205, 239; by numbers of students using, 199–201; placing in schools, 197–99; reception of, 202–3; subsequent history, 305n47
Thompson, Carl D., 177, 190, 218–19, 221–22, 239
tours of utility buildings, 115–18
two-step flow of communication theory, 16, 213

unions, 68–69, 86, 171
United Press (UP), 170
unit plan, 97–98
utilities, 1; critiques of, 60; government operation of, 29; Insull utilities, 222–23, 229; in Los Angeles, 1; and negative public opinion, 2, 6, 19, 20, 21, 25, 88, 127; Pacific Gas & Electric (PG&E), 125, 220, 237; physical service, percentage of Americans with, 28, 89; rates, 29, 130–31, 226, 235;

utilities (*continued*)
  Southern California Edison (SCE), 1, 2, 23, 26, 37, 57, 71, 89, 98, 127, 130, 184, 244; Southern Pacific Railroad, 2; Stone and Webster, 1

Vail, Theodore, 152, 166
Vanderbilt, William H., 21; "the public be damned" and, 21, 22, 214, 253n17
Victorians, 11–12; declining cultural hegemony, 77; delayed gratification and self-control, 77; and sincerity, 34

Walsh, Thomas J., 160
Wanamaker, John, 37, 241

Weber, Max, 51, 96
welfare capitalism, 71–73, 118
Western Electric Company, 72
White, William Allen, 184
Whitney, William C., 20
Wilke, Wendell, 166
Wilson, Woodrow, 6, 19, 83
window displays, 139, 232
World War I, 61, 130–31, 191; and government public relations, 161–63; and telephone nationalization, 83–86

Yerkes, Charles, 20